Systemic Cycle and Institutional Change

Josip Lučev

Systemic Cycle and Institutional Change

Labor Markets in the USA, Germany and China

palgrave
macmillan

Josip Lučev
Faculty of Political Science
University of Zagreb
Zagreb, Croatia

ISBN 978-3-030-66052-9 ISBN 978-3-030-66053-6 (eBook)
https://doi.org/10.1007/978-3-030-66053-6

This Palgrave Macmillan imprint is published by the registered company Springer Nature Switzerland AG
The registered company address is: Gewerbestrasse 11, 6330 Cham, Switzerland

Preface

The motivation for this study has been primarily to open a dialogue between the mutually relatively isolated genres of institutional change and the long waves of capitalism. Their isolation has perhaps led to unresolved issues in both. In particular, endogenous institutional change has proven to be a long-standing open question in new institutionalism and the systemic cycle theory has left the issue of institutions largely unresolved. The intuition of a mutually beneficial intertwining of these genres and their theories is tested through a new metatheoretical framework. Their interactions are followed through separate drivers and channels of change, with the central issue being the inclusion of cyclical power relations in a functional framework of institutional change. This framework is then applied to three illustrative empirical chapters showing the change of labor institutions since 1980 in the USA, Germany, and PR China. In the USA, the lack of path-deviating tendencies (through a power resources reshuffling or radical political reforms) led to the most prominent role for path dependence, securing the continuation of labor market deregulation. Germany started the observed period with relatively well-protected labor institutions, but has since increased the dualization of labor markets, which is interpreted as a shift toward an extensive developmental strategy. In China, a distinct context of a one-party rule permeates politics, but decades of low-wage regime and low labor protection have given way to an increase in labor protection and coordination, which is interpreted as a shift toward an intensive developmental strategy.

This study could have gone a different route. The original intention was also to analyze financial regulation and macroeconomic policy in a much broader framework and apply it to four cases which would also include UK. If this remained the idea, this book would likely remain unfinished. As it is, the result is a study focused on the central position of labor in capitalism and the crucial role that the interactions of power and the systemic cycle play in the change of labor institutions. Any broadening of the scope will have to be done in further studies. Likewise, the future application of this framework to more cases may be useful, particularly the smaller and more peripheral ones.

This study has developed from my PhD dissertation, and as such, it benefitted from the support and advice of a number of people. First and foremost, if the late professor Dag Strpić from the University of Zagreb had not convinced me to study Political Economy and enroll in doctoral studies, I would likely not be in the position to write this book. He was the first supervisor of my dissertation and he passed away while it was still in the very early planning stages. After this, the late professor Uwe Becker from the University of Amsterdam agreed to become my supervisor, started me thinking in terms of time-frames and cases, and passed away while I was working on the first chapter and synopsis. After this second tragedy, professor Bogomir Kovač from the University of Ljubljana accepted to supervise me and forced re-write after re-write of crucial parts of this text. Without his dedication and guidance as a supervisor, this study would be far less than it is. There were other influences as well. In particular, I owe a debt of gratitude to the advisors: professors Hrvoje Šimović, Zdravko Petak (who in particular has convinced me to narrow the scope—which resulted in the focus on labor institutions), and Kristijan Kotarski, as well as the anonymous reviewers of this book for all of their suggestions. I have also immensely benefited from advice from professor Andreas Nölke, as well as professors Luka Brkić, Zoran Kurelić, Dragan Lalović, Nebojša Blanuša, and others too numerous to recount here. I was fortunate enough to be able to design and teach the course Institutional Change at UCIRD Dag Hammarskjöld in academic years 2017/2018 and 2018/2019. I would like to thank the students that attended this course as they helped me hone and test many of the ideas present in this book. Finally, I would like to thank my friends and family (they know who they are) for all the love, support, and patience in the years in which this study was created.

Zagreb, Croatia
November 2020

Josip Lučev

Contents

List of Figures

List of Tables

CHAPTER 1

Introduction

Capitalism is a global phenomenon which transforms entire societies after its own image. Capitalism is regulated, mediated, and modified on a local and national level. Both statements hold equally true. Therefore, it is an equally large mistake to either assume that global economic phenomena like globalization and financialization impact every location in the same way or to assume that "national" capitalism types are completely distinct and immutable. However, both mistakes are often implicitly made in literature which tends to focus either on the global process or on the national institutional stability. This book will deal with two types of research genres which have historically tended to exhibit such mistakes—with the goal of locating the compatible synergetic elements to formulating a new framework of institutional change. Ultimately, this framework will be used to offer an analysis of labor markets in the USA, Germany, and China.

More specifically, endogenous institutional change has proven to be a long-standing open question in new institutionalism. This book will strive to provide another answer through explicit inclusion of overlapping global processes with variegated effects as drivers of institutional change. There are several theories available that could be used to this effect and they range from the French school of regulation, through the systemic cycle to new economic geography. However, these theories have always had severe issues in penetrating into the mainstream of social sciences, which tends to prefer theories that do not try to do too

J. Lučev, *Systemic Cycle and Institutional Change*,
https://doi.org/10.1007/978-3-030-66053-6_1

much at once but focus on the visible, the incremental, and often on the local/national. It seems plausible that the limits of new institutionalism in explaining endogenous institutional change are at least partially caused by this desirable restriction. Specifically, the game-theoretical/rational choice branch of new institutionalism traditionally focuses on strategic interactions and treats the rules that govern these interactions as external with the change of these rules necessarily being exogenous. The sociological branch most often deals with the interpretation, spreading, and internalization of meanings attached to institutions rather than their origins or change. Finally, the historical institutionalism branch is concerned with predictable and stable change through path dependence, while the unpredictable change of critical junctures is treated as exogenous. This book will elaborate on these, as well as some useful attempts to overcome the broadly recognized issue of insufficiently explained institutional change.

To attempt to move beyond this problem and add to the attempts of explaining endogenous institutional change, the theoretical strategy of this book revolves around the inclusion of relevant drivers of institutional change in the analysis. To do so, it is necessary to use a theory which has a broader unit of analysis than is usually the case in new institutionalism—specifically one that can handle transnational or global processes but still distinguish their national manifestations. This distinction is necessary considering that most political-economic institutions, including labor institutions are still formed, interpreted and subverted or upheld on the national level, but the economic processes that influence them or even drive the need for their change are often global. Arrighi's systemic cycle theory is chosen rather than new economic geography or regulationist school because it enables an explanation and prediction of global processes and their effects on national settings through a long-term historical lens within the world-system, and even more importantly theorizes cyclical power shifts. The world-system itself implies a complex unit of analysis which will enable the observance of national processes in their interactions with global processes. However, Arrighi's theory itself is not sufficient for the analysis of national institutional change as it lacks an understanding of national institutions as well as institutional variety. We therefore engage in a dialogue with theories of institutional stability and change in new institutionalism and the systemic cycle theory.

The method of this dialogue is the construction of a new framework, in which we take our cue from Elinor Ostrom who distinguishes between frameworks, theories, and models. Frameworks utilize a metatheoretical language and a wide set of variables. They can be compatible with many theories. In other words, theories can be grouped into a framework. Models are at the lowest level, as many models may be grouped into theories, and models offer very specific sets of causal relationships (Ostrom 2005: 27–29). In constructing a new framework, this book seeks to group the systemic theory with several specific theories within new institutionalism (which itself is a collection of research genres rather than a single theory), including power resource theory, Varieties of Capitalism, Keynesian macroeconomics, and Northian institutionalism. However, these theories do not yet share a metatheoretical language necessary for a single framework. This is why another prerequisite is an adequate reinterpretation of the systemic cycle through the prisms of demand-side issues, power, and institutionalism. After this reinterpretation, we can construct the framework which utilizes these theories as well as a number of drivers of institutional change (or models, in keeping with Ostrom's terminology). Within this framework, we will identify three interacting channels of institutional change: path dependence, systemic cycle driven power relations, and institutional design via formal politics. This book is theoretical in nature, but it will use three illustrative empirical chapters showing the change of labor institutions since 1980 in the United States of America, Germany, and the People's Republic of China. In the USA, the lack of path deviating tendencies (through a power resources reshuffling or radical political reforms) led to the most prominent role for path dependence. In Germany and China, the situation is substantially more complex, but dominated by shifts in developmental strategies within the logic of the systemic cycle.

Labor institutions were chosen for several reasons. Firstly, labor is crucial to capitalism as such as the logical tension between capitalism as a global/local process could be conceptually simplified to a tension between global capital and local labor. In the simplest sense, we can observe the systemic cycle as a process dealing with profitability and investments (i.e. the global capital part of the equation), while labor is less mobile and therefore more based in the national level (i.e. the national/local part of the equation). Logically, both must come together to manufacture products. But if capital should move toward speculative activities, labor becomes increasingly superfluous to the achievement of profit. Also, the increasing mobility of capital suggests its possibility of fleeing the labor-friendly locations and looking to capital-friendly locations for the organization of manufacturing. Such a low-resolution diagnosis has prompted some overly simplistic conclusions concerning the destructive effects of globalization on labor-rights. Nevertheless, while the effects were not as stark as initially imagined, the dual global/local nature of capitalism has in recent decades certainly shown an underlying disbalance of power between the interests representing capital and interests representing labor in a large part of the developed world. Secondly, labor also stands at a crucial point of national-level political-economic systems. Labor rights have a substantial effect on the distribution of income, which makes them an important part of aggregate demand management (i.e. macroeconomics). Therefore, they influence both distributional inequality and the ability to manage economic crises. Thirdly, labor rights were traditionally under the influence of worker self-organization via trade-unions, which could give a direct political voice to a concerned party in any change, and this also allows the relative power of the unions to be clearly tracked. While this labor-party identification was clearly subverted by the changing nature of employment structure and the focus of political elites, recent years have also brought an "electoral turn" of institutional literature, arguing for a certain measure of reconnecting of class interests and electoral politics. Finally, growth models (i.e. developmental strategies) are interconnected with labor institutions—with an export-led model more compatible with flexible employment and a domestic demand-led model more compatible with protected labor institutions. A combination of these factors means that labor institutions are particularly well suited to show the feasibility of the new framework. The inverse is also correct, as the framework is constructed particularly with labor in mind, considering the specific position of labor institutions in modern capitalism.

Chapter 2 will portray Arrighi's strand of world-systemic research culminating in his systemic cycle theory and offer a criticism of Arrighi's approach as insufficiently sensitive to demand-side factors and as essentially under-equipped to deal with specific national institutional iterations of capitalism. While offering a useful predictive tool, superior to the economic mainstream in some respects, Arrighi is nevertheless perhaps overly focused on capitalism as a global phenomenon with the institutions supporting it locally assumed to be closely associated to the paradigmatic case in the center of the world-system. However, the interpretation of the systemic cycle by Beverly Silver offers crucial insights into the power-related effects of the systemic cycle. Chapter 2 will use them in order to outline the systemic cycle through three overlapping aspects of systemic cycle phases, trade relations, and developmental strategies. The first two aspects can be used to predict shifts in labor power, while a demand-side interpretation of the third element is necessary to complete the triangle and eventually apply it to institutional change analysis. Chapter 3 will cover the contemporary approaches to institutions and institutional change (historical institutionalism, sociological institutionalism, rational-choice institutionalism and its definitive form in comparative capitalisms research) in order to identify the elements useful in constructing a new framework of change—and one useful to deciphering the change of national institutions. It will also offer a critique of a large part of new institutionalism as still dependent on exogenous shocks to deal with issues of institutional change—enabling it to stick to implicit institutional stability and typologies of national capitalisms as the prevalent research agenda. Chapter 3 will finish by defining three channels of institutional change: path dependence, deliberate institutional design via formal political channels, and the less codified political interactions underscored by power resources. This approach to institutional change will require a theory of change in power relations to function and the following chapters will attempt to integrate the systemic cycle theory with concepts of institutional change. Chapter 4 will explore the compatibility of respective strengths and weaknesses of the systemic cycle theory (often focusing on the global and ignoring the institutional) and institutional approaches (often focusing on the national and stable and ignoring the global processes). Particularly useful is the world-systemic unit of analysis which transcends the local and national and finds its contemporary unit in the global division of labor among the developed and the underdeveloped. Analyzing institutional change on this basis enables us to interpret global processes as endogenous and therefore to increase our understanding of interactions of transnational economic processes and national institutions. This is the reason for starting with the world-systemic theory and the systemic cycle and then entering into the institutional debate rather than the other way around. Chapter 4 will also develop the Keynesian demand-side elements necessary to meaningfully interpret and utilize Arrighi's categories in the metatheoretical language needed for the interaction with institutional theories. This chapter also offers a conceptualization of institutions, their relationship to change and the logic of institutional drivers needed for this metatheoretical interaction.

Chapter 5 will operationalize the central hypothesis of this book through a new framework of institutional change, which utilizes the elements developed in the previous chapter. The central hypothesis of this book states that the changes in labor institutions are influenced by the systemic cycle. The systemic cycle is operationalized as three interconnected drivers of institutional change: phase of the systemic cycle (real or financial expansion), trade relations, and developmental strategies. These drivers of change will be grouped with technological advances and power positions as a channel of institutional change producing cyclical power shifts and contextualized through the two additional channels of path dependence and institutional design (via formal politics or transnational conditionality). While some of these seven drivers are traditionally well understood, we will argue for the inclusion of systemic cycle drivers—trade relations (a proxy for positions in the world-system), developmental strategies, and the systemic cycle phase. They are Arrighian rather than Arrighi's as they are all operationalized via demand-side considerations—i.e. with the necessary metatheoretical reinterpretation. It is the inclusion of these drivers into a new framework of institutional change that represents the central conceptual novum of this book.

Chapters 6, 7, and 8 are illustrative chapters which use the framework from Chapter 5 on the changes in labor institutions in the USA, Germany, and China since 1980. Chapter 6 will examine the US labor market in which all the drivers point in the direction of labor market deregulation. In this sense, US labor institutions started relatively deregulated and continued on the same path. The next two cases are more challenging. Chapter 7 will analyze labor institutions in Germany which started from a relatively well-protected position, but have increased the dualization of German labor markets with a well-protected manufacturing core and a deregulated service sector and in the legal sense—a well-protected permanent employment laws and an increasingly liberalized fixed term employment laws. This is primarily the result of a history of coordinated market economy, moderately high union density rates in manufacturing, the systemic cycle which has enabled the formation and strengthening of new global production centers and an increase in trade surplus as a result of a move from an intensive to an extensive developmental strategy coinciding with the introduction of the euro and the intensifying of the eurozone economy interaction with Germany.

Finally, Chapter 8 will explore the increase in labor protection and coordination in China as a result of a recent history of catch-up favoring a continued increase of labor use, a history of a planned economy not geared toward labor protection since the 1980s, very little independent power of labor, the systemic cycle which has enabled the formation and strengthening of new global production centers and increase in trade surplus due to supply-side competitiveness until the global crisis of 2009 after which the surplus has significantly declined prompting an ongoing move to a wage-led developmental strategy.

The final chapter, Chapter 9 will summarize the illustrative Chapters 6, 7, and 8 and interpret their findings in light of the theoretical part of the book. The period of interest has been marked by financial expansion in the USA as the center of the world-system and the growth of manufacture elsewhere. In the USA, we can observe the labor institutions changing as a consequence of a diminishing significance and power of organized labor. Germany and China are, on the other hand, two of the possible contenders for future central positions—or in other words, alternative developmental strategies, both of which hinge on the role of labor. In Germany, we can see institutional change from a well-protected labor market with a wage-led (intensive) strategy toward a dualistic labor market and an export-led (extensive) strategy. The Chinese shift in labor institutions is showing some signs of movement opposite to the German one creating a very interesting global asymmetry. China has had to realign its strategy as the possibilities of its catch-up on the labor-intensive path became exhausted, and this process was exacerbated by losses caused by the collapse of its export markets in the 2009 crisis. The result is an incremental shift into some of the labor regulation and organization institutions taken for granted in the western developed world. However, in a one-party setting, these institutions often take a vastly different meaning, particularly as the capacity for worker self-organization is fairly low.

Ultimately, the goal of this theoretical book is to meaningfully add to the many voices attempting to explain endogenous institutional change. It does so by analyzing Arrighi's and Silver's theory of the systemic cycle in order to reconcile a global (process-based) and national (institutions-based) conception of capitalism. It will attempt to benefit from a sufficiently broad unit of analysis and identify and analyze the global and national institutional drivers which interact to produce variegated national institutional effects.

Literature

Ostrom, E. (2005). *Understanding Institutional Diversity*. Princeton, NJ: Princeton University Press.

CHAPTER 2

World-Systems Analysis and the Systemic Cycle

2.1 Introduction

This book seeks to contribute to the theory of institutional change by analyzing changes to national institutions under the influence of global processes. To do so we must first develop a theory of global capitalist processes which can be used to research institutional change. The purpose of this chapter is to explore the theory of the systemic cycle with the purpose of developing a useful interpretation (Chapter 4) necessary to identify Arrighian institutional drivers (Chapter 5), and to establish its advantages and failings when compared to mainstream social sciences. These further chapters will utilize the critical confrontation of the systemic cycle theory in this chapter and the analysis of institutional change in Chapter 3 in order to enable its inclusion with elements of institutional theory into a new framework of institutional change.

To enable this, the first section of this chapter looks at the process of capitalism, a subject often absent in comparative political economy. We will firstly outline the specific unit of analysis at the foundations of world-systemic analysis, as exemplified by Immanuel Wallerstein. This will provide us with a basic reading of the relationship of the world-system and the national level. Secondly, we will describe the assumptions, models, and conclusions of the systemic cycle theory, as developed by Giovanni Arrighi. This will provide us with a comprehensive model of economic change which focuses on historical (and predictive) processes

J. Lučev, *Systemic Cycle and Institutional Change*,
https://doi.org/10.1007/978-3-030-66053-6_2

of global capitalism. Although Wallerstein also conducted a historical analysis, Arrighi's reading of the systemic cycle in many ways provides a temporal dimension to Wallerstein's spatial/geographical playing field. Finally, we turn to Arrighi's frequent co-author Beverly Silver, who offers an interpretation of the systemic cycle which puts power and cycles of labor commodification and decommodification into focus. This will provide us with a subtler re-reading of the systemic cycle which accentuates agency on the national level alongside the global processes. The result of this section will be a theory of the systemic cycle with three defining aspects: the world-system as the spatial unit of analysis and the position of national capitalisms within it; the systemic cycle as the theory of global processes and an understanding of the role of power and agency in constructing the results of these processes on the national level.

The second section of this chapter argues for the continued usefulness of the systemic cycle theory with noting a number of specific improvements on mainstream social sciences and criticizing Arrighi's approach for several important failings. This critical confrontation of Arrighi's theory in the context of its mainstream alternatives is necessary as we will depend on Arrighi to deal with two types of a damaging dual focus of the mainstream on the national and the static. Firstly, even when considering this initial step of describing the global process of capitalism, mainstream approaches tend to implicitly ignore time and focus on the atemporal concept of equilibrium instead—itself often conceptualized in single markets. Secondly, we will eventually turn to the analysis of the variegated national-level institutional outcomes of this global process. This is another area in which static models prevail, which is the reason why change in new institutionalism tends to be understood as exogenously induced. As we develop a turn toward an Arrighian approach to endogenous change we must first ascertain what it is that the models of systemic cycles have to offer us. This section will also utilize Silver's analysis to further outline the effects of the systemic cycle on labor power, pointing to separate, but intertwined effects of (a) phases of the systemic cycle, (b) trade positions, and (c) arguing for a need to conceptually develop the effects of developmental strategies (which will be undertaken in Chapter 4). These three elements give us the contours of the systemic cycle theory and clear the way for its uses as a predictor of institutional change.

2.2 The Process of Capitalism: World-Systems Analysis and the Systemic Cycle

Firstly, we will define the unit of analysis in the definition of which Arrighi built on the earlier contributions of the world-systemic theory, as exemplified by Wallerstein. This very first building block of this thesis is crucial in understanding the relationship between the global processes and national institutions. Secondly, we will analyze Arrighi's approach to changes within the world-system dealing with various aspects of the systemic cycle.

2.2.1 *Defining the Unit of Analysis: Immanuel Wallerstein*

The most influential version of the world-systems analysis surely belongs to Immanuel Wallerstein.[1] It was developed in the 1970s, most obviously through Volume I of *The Modern World-System* (Wallerstein 1974a) and an essay titled *The Rise and Future Demise of the World Capitalist System: Concepts for Comparative Analysis* (Wallerstein 1974b). The Modern World-System project has produced three further volumes[2] and at the time of the publication of the last volume, the late author planned to write one or two additional ones (Wallerstein 2011: xvii).

Wallerstein created an epistemological alternative to mainstream science (as he saw it). He insists it is a separate perspective, rather than a theory within mainstream social sciences. It was created "as a moral, and in its broadest sense, political, protest" (Wallerstein 2000: 129). The prevailing social science, grounded as it is within the nineteenth-century limits, provides us with a limited outlook of which questions to ask and have solved. It is therefore necessary to "unthink" these constricting

[1] As of September 2020 and according to Google Scholar, Wallerstein's *The Modern World-System I* was cited 17,568 times in academic research, compared favorably to other important titles: e.g. Andre Gunder Frank's seminal *Capitalism and Underdevelopment in Latin America* (1967) at 6994, Arrighi's *The Long Twentieth Century* (1994) at 5962, Fernand Braudel's *The Mediterranean and the Mediterranean World in the Age of Philip II* at 4860, and Samir Amin's *Unequal Development; An Essay on the Social Formations of Peripheral Capitalism* (1976) at 3185.

[2] The first volume dealt with Europe in the sixteenth century, the second volume first published in 1980 dealt with the 1600–1750 period (Wallerstein 1980), the third volume was originally published in 1989 and covered the 1730s–1840s (Wallerstein 1989), while the fourth was published relatively recently in 2011 and covers 1789–1914 (Wallerstein 2011).

assumptions (Wallerstein 2001: 2), including the false dichotomy between nomothetic and idiographic (Wallerstein 2000: 149–159). In particular, Wallerstein's world-systemic analysis is an attempt to cut through "the intellectual morass" of claiming there are four social sciences: anthropology, economics, political science, and sociology (ibid.: 134), and in response, world-systems analysis encompasses them all through a radical opening of a quest for the appropriate unit of analysis of modern social activities (see also Wallerstein 1974a: 8–10; 2000: 129–148). This resulted in world-systems analysis consciously removing the state as a unit of analysis in favor of the world-system itself[3] (Wallerstein 1974a: 3–11; 2000: xviii).

In order to explain capitalism/modernity, Wallerstein contrasts two predominant historical types of world-systems[4]: empires and world-economies. Empires are a staple of world history and have been occurring for the past 5000 years. They are extractive social systems characterized by centralization and political unification of the area controlled. "The political centralization [...] guaranteed economic flows from the periphery to the center by force (tribute and taxation) and by monopolistic advantages in trade [, however, its] weakness lay in the fact that the bureaucracy made necessary by the political structure tended to absorb too much of the profit" (Wallerstein 1974a: 15). World-economy is a description of modern Europe, characterized by the participation of many political units (states) and therefore a decentralized nature. This type of a social system has developed in the past (China, Persia, Rome), but has invariably transformed into an empire (ibid.: 16). The sustainability of a world-economy is the great European innovation synonymous with both capitalism and modernity. While empires are a primitive mechanism of extracting tribute, capitalism enables a more lucrative alternative of vying for monopolistic positions. Political activity is directed at achieving this and a state becomes decreasingly an enterprise in its own right and increasingly a mechanism of "assuring certain terms of trade" (ibid.).

[3] This is a conscious move by Wallerstein in the attempt of finding an adequate methodology which would allow him to "unthink" traditional social sciences and bypass their inherent obstacles (Wallerstein 2001: vii).

[4] Some authors prefer to write it as world system rather than world-system. For the sake of simplicity, we always include the Wallersteinian hyphen.

World-economies have three logical structural positions: core, periphery, and semi-periphery.[5] Core areas have a strong state apparatus and peripheral areas have weak states. This enables the core to enforce unequal exchange to the periphery. And therefore, "capitalism involves not only appropriation of the surplus-value by an owner from a laborer, but an appropriation of surplus of the whole world-economy by core areas" (Wallerstein 1974b: 401). These three positions provide a general outline of the modern geographic division of labor between the developed and the underdeveloped in the world-systemic approach.

In this sense, Wallerstein's *Modern World-System* was an enquiry into the fundamentals of our modernity: which elements combined into the capitalist system which emerged in Europe and spilled over to colonize, permeate, and eventually encompass the entire planet. There were three prerequisites for the success of the capitalist world-economy: "an expansion of the geographical size of the world in question, the development of variegated methods of labor control for different products and different zones of the world-economy, and the creation of relatively strong state machineries in what would become the core-states of this capitalist world-economy" (Wallerstein 1974a: 38).

The second prerequisite essentially means that the same world-system supports feudalism, slavery, sharecropping, wage-labor, and self-employment at the same time. It does so because each method of control is best suited for a certain type of production. Feudalism and slavery are concentrated in the periphery, sharecropping in the semi-periphery and wage-labor and self-employment in the core (ibid.: 87). The variegated modes of control of labor tie into different types of political organization, with the modes in the core requiring strong states (ibid.), which was Wallerstein's third prerequisite of modernity. These strong states are a function of a coalition of two types of power players: capitalist landowners and merchants (Wallerstein 1974b: 402). The distinction also concerns the skill levels, with lower skill levels being compatible with slavery/feudalism and the less complicated economic activities in the periphery, and higher skill levels being compatible with wage-labor grounded in the market of the more complex core. In fact, this combination is "the essence of capitalism" (Wallerstein 1974a: 127).

[5] In 1974, Wallerstein already considers core and periphery "widely used concepts" (Wallerstein 1974b: 402), and has attributed them to Raul Prebisch (Wallerstein 2011: xiii). He did, however, add a category of semi-periphery to the two earlier concepts.

Another essential element of the world-systemic analysis is the immanent possibility of only a single state in the center of the core of the world-system. Only one state occupies the most competitive position and benefits the most from world trade. This means that that state accrues the most trade surplus, and benefits from a larger GDP growth. Those conditions may be conveyed into a larger fiscal maneuvering space, and larger military budgets. In this nexus of economic and military (and thus political) power lies what is usually understood as a *hegemony* in the world-system.

According to Wallerstein, hegemony is a situation in which "products of a given core state are produced so efficiently that they are by and large competitive even in other core states, and therefore the given core state will be the primary beneficiary of a maximally free world market. Obviously, to take advantage of this productive superiority, such a state must be strong enough to prevent or minimize the erection of [...] political barriers to the free flow of the factors of production; and to preserve their advantage, [...] the dominant economic forces find it helpful to encourage certain intellectual and cultural thrusts, movements, and ideologies" (Wallerstein 1980: 38). Here, we can see that Wallerstein provides a materialist logic in which the free trade policies depend on the clearly historically positioned hegemonic moment.

Wallerstein identified only three historical hegemonies: "only Holland, Great Britain, and the United States have been hegemonic powers [...], and each held the position for a relatively brief period, Holland least plausibly because it was least of all the military giant of its era" (Wallerstein 1980: 38). In other words, the materialistically determined free trade policies could be found during the British and American hegemonies with the free market ideas of the first globalization (late nineteenth, early twentieth century) being the result of the British supremacy and the Bretton-Woods and Washington consensus eras of trade liberalization (or second globalization) being the result of the American supremacy.

The mechanism of hegemony is a succession of superiorities: superiority in agro-industrial productive efficiency is followed by superiorities in commercial distribution of world trade, financial sectors of banking and investment (ibid.). There is only a short moment in time when "a given core power can manifest simultaneously productive, commercial, and financial superiority over all other core powers. This momentary summit is what we call hegemony" (ibid.: 39).

Wallerstein's analysis shows an understanding not only of static elements suggested by the relations of the developed and the underdeveloped, but also a certain logic of change in these hegemonic shifts. Building on these concepts, Arrighi developed a more advanced and comprehensive model of capitalist change in his systemic cycle. But where Wallerstein saw momentary summits of hegemony, Arrighi identified much longer processes hinging on a number of elements and describing capitalist change.

2.2.2 *Explaining the Process of Capitalism: Giovanni Arrighi and the Systemic Cycle*

Building his contribution within the logic of the world-system, Arrighi insists that even as there can exist national dynamics of development, the proper unit of analysis is not the individual state or the sum of individual states, but a "*system* of states in which world capitalism has been embedded" (Arrighi and Moore 2001: 56). It is within such a system that an economic development of long duration takes place. In other words, the conceptual tension between capitalism as a universal, global process and the national state as its specifically transforming locus is resolved through the categories described by Wallerstein.

Within this system, Arrighi has isolated several crucial changes which define the long-term functioning of capitalism. Specifically, Giovanni Arrighi brought the process of financialization[6] into the foreground

[6] Financialization is an increasingly popular term firmly embedded in several schools of thought. Broadly defined, financialization is "the increasing role of financial motives, financial markets, financial actors and financial institutions in the operation of the domestic and international economies" (Epstein 2005). In *Financialization and the US Economy*, Ozgur Orhangazi (2008) offers an overview of approaches to financialization. He suggests that there are three relevant veins of research: firstly, the Arrighian perspective shown here, which he calls Long Waves of Capitalism (Orhangazi 2008: 42). Secondly, the perspective on neoliberalism (Harvey, Crotty, Dumenil and Levy) emphasizing the deregulations since the 1970s as a result of falling demand. Thirdly, a perspective on the impact of financial markets on corporate governance including that of the French regulation school (see Orhangazi 2008: 41–71). This third strand of literature focuses on changes toward a greater emphasis of shareholder value in corporations, with the profit for shareholders becoming the primary motive. The third group of financialization theories uses the concept of a "finance-led capitalism" as a new growth regime within regulation theory (see Aglietta and Rebérioux 2005: 1). In this vein, a corollary of financialization is an increase of debt among wage earners. Similar to regulation theory, Colin Crouch deals with financialization without using the term. He identifies two policy regimes, i.e.

of world-systems analysis. In the context of Marxian economics, the pronounced tendency toward financial expansion was recognized time and again, most famously by Hilferding (1910/1981), Bukharin (1917/1972), and Lenin (1917/1999). Arrighi's approach, however, is quite different from these three authors. While they explain the financial expansion as the latest or highest stage of capitalism, Arrighi places it into the world-systemic and diachronic framework in which financializations are no more than a repetitive phase in global economic development. For this insight, Arrighi was indebted to the vastly influential French historian Fernand Braudel, and particularly volumes two and three of his *Civilisation Matérielle, Économie et Capitalisme, XVe–XVIIIe* trilogy (Arrighi 1994/2010: ix–x), originally published in the 1967–1979 period (see Braudel 1992a, b, c). Braudel's description of the world-economy in the fifteenth-eighteenth century described successive phases of capital accumulation which historically tended to finalize through notable expansions of financial markets. Arrighi developed this theme primarily through his books *The Long Twentieth Century: Money, Power, and the Origins of Our Times*, originally published in 1994 and *Adam Smith in Beijing: Lineages of the Twenty-First Century*, published in 2007, but also several chapters in edited books (Arrighi and Silver, eds. 1999; Arrighi and Moore 2001; Arrighi et al., eds. 2003).

Arrighi's key contribution is the concept of the systemic cycle, which has two phases with material expansion being followed by financial expansion (Arrighi 1994/2010: 88; Arrighi and Moore 2001: 56). In material expansions, "money capital sets in motion an increasing mass of commodities" (Arrighi 1994/2010: 6). In this phase, production and trade expand through a regime of capital accumulation on a single developmental path (ibid.: 9) which causes rapid growth (ibid.: 170). Such an expansion only takes place through a concentration of power in an agency or a coalition of agencies which is able to control the world-economy as a new dominant block (ibid.: 12–13). However, the specific organizational structure that each regime of capital accumulation establishes is

Keynesianism and Privatised Keynesianism, with the distinguishing characteristic of the latter being the consumer demand management through greater debt (Crouch 2009: 12 and passim). Coming to a similar conclusion, but thinking more aggregately, Thomas Piketty mentions financialization once in his seminal *Capital in the Twenty-First Century* as a process which changed the global "structure of wealth in the sense that the total amount of financial assets and liabilities held by various sectors (households, corporations, government agencies) increased more rapidly than net wealth" (Piketty 2017: 139).

progressively undermined by its own expansion (ibid.: 226). The more production expands, the more it enters into a process of vicious competition. Diminishing returns in a given production are countered through strategies of diversification, but this brings entrepreneurs into a closer proximity to their competitors, contributing to the fall of average profit rates (ibid.: 222–226). This process suggests a necessary exhaustion of material expansion in some point. As "capitalist agencies" (entrepreneurs) are by definition profit maximizers, they will attempt to find the most profitable venues for their capital (ibid.: 228–229). Historically, this exhaustion of profit rates in production and trade caused systemic turns toward greater investments in financial markets.

In symbolically explaining the systemic cycle, Arrighi uses Marxian concepts: "Marx's general formula of capital (M-C-M') can [...] be interpreted as depicting not just the logic of individual capitalist investments, but also a recurrent pattern of historical capitalism as world-system. The central aspect of this pattern is the alternation of epochs of material expansion (MC phases of capital accumulation) with phases of financial rebirth and expansion (CM' phases). [...] Together, the two epochs or phases constitute a full systemic cycle of accumulation (M-C-M')" (Arrighi 1994/2010: 6). Through a financial expansion, "an increasing mass of money capital 'sets itself free' from its commodity form" (ibid.: 6). Financial expansion is "a system-wide tendency, centered on the leading capitalist economy of the epoch, towards the 'financialization' of processes of capital accumulation. Integral to the transformation of inter-capitalist competition from a positive into a negative-sum game, this tendency has also acted as a key mechanism of the restoration of profitability, at least temporarily, in the declining but still hegemonic centers of world capitalism" (Arrighi 2007: 118).

Arrighi recognizes Braudel's economic history as the starting point for his analysis (Arrighi 2010: 6–7), but his explanation conceptually and theoretically hinges on Adam Smith and Karl Marx. Arrighi's theory of the systemic cycle in its process of material expansion and its shift into financial expansion explicitly follows these authors (ibid.: 228). While Adam Smith did not develop a theory of crises, he did utilize an important concept at the center of Arrighi's systemic cycle. As he put it, "when the stocks of many rich merchants are turned into the same trade, their mutual competition naturally tends to lower its profit; and when there is a like increase of stock in all the different trades carried on in the same society, the same competition must produce the same effect in them all"

(Smith 1776/2003: 122). As this tendency is a function of development and competition, the lower profit rates are to be expected in richer countries and in towns rather than in the countryside (ibid.: 122–137, 451). This gives us an understanding of the tendency of the profit rate to fall which is dependent on increasing competition, which is itself a function of increasing development.

Karl Marx certainly built upon this concept and involved it in a much broader perspective. The economic movements observed by Marx are very historical and therefore time-sensitive, but in taking the long view to the classical labor theory of value, Marx foreshadows the future long run equilibrium tendencies of the neoclassical school. For him, the fluctuating market relations obscure the over-riding law of the socially necessary labor-time which truly determines value. It is comparable to "a natural law" like gravity which inescapably asserts itself, even as it remains overshadowed by exchange relations (Marx 1867/1979: 77). Therefore, the value of commodities is determined by labor in the long run, even if other elements seem to determine it in the apparent fluctuations of the short run.

The crucial element in Marx's approach to crises, important to this chapter and the understanding of Arrighi is the tendency of the profit rate to fall. In Marx, the profit itself is derived from surplus value. In this chapter of Capital Vol. 3, he explains surplus value as the labor embodied in a commodity in excess of its cost. Of course, this is precisely where we see the labor value theory at work—with the value extractable through production and circulation necessarily being derived from labor (i.e. variable capital). The profit rate itself differs from the rate of surplus value in that it is a ratio of surplus value to total capital while the rate of surplus value is a ratio of surplus value to variable capital. Therefore, the root of profit is always in unpaid labor and surplus value and profit are "two different measurements of the same entity" (this chapter). However, the distinction between surplus value and profit is also in the crux of the much-vaunted transformation problem (i.e. transformation of value into market prices), as the profit rate is discernible on the market surface (ratio of various prices and costs), while surplus value is invisible (see also Strpić 2010: 13–69). Marx interprets the gradual and inevitable fall in the profit rate as a result of a reducing variable capital in the organic capital composition as a result of capital accumulation (Marx 1894/1979: 1311–1329).

Accordingly, while both authors subscribe to the idea that continued economic development leads to a fall in the rate of profit, Smith views it as a result of increased competition, while Marx explains it as a result of capital accumulation. Arrighi needs this notion to explain the shift between material and financial expansion as well as a shift toward new centers (into a new material expansion). He uses both Smith and Marx's mechanisms and claims the former is "more useful in explaining the inner dynamic of systemic cycle" (Arrighi 1994/2010: 228), while the latter "is more useful in explaining the transition from one cycle to another" (ibid.). In other words, Arrighi sees the Smithian dynamics of increasing competition as the primary reason for the flight of capital from manufacture into finance and the Marxian dynamics of accumulating capital as the primary reason for a shift toward a new geographic center of manufacturing. Therefore, Arrighi essentially based the systemic cycle on a tacit composite theory of investment according to which increased competition gradually depresses profits through the material expansion phase and the crisis of this material expansion result due to overaccumulation. The first is a result of a competition between many entrepreneurs, whereas the second is a structural tendency of capital as a whole.

Using this conceptual basis, Arrighi described four distinct (if overlapping) historical phases of capital accumulation encompassing our modernity. The four such cycles identified by Arrighi are the Genoese cycle, fifteenth-early seventeenth centuries; the Dutch cycle, late sixteenth-most of eighteenth; the British cycle, last half of eighteenth century-early twentieth century; and the US cycle, beginning in the late nineteenth century and continuing into the phase of financial expansion Arrighi was witnessing in 1994 when he wrote *The Long Twentieth Century*.

This suggests another important Arrighian element in the continuous geographic dislocation of the primary capital accumulation location (i.e. the center of the world-system). Each successive center is necessarily the outgrowth of the old, as it is a by-product of increased quest for profit in the financial expansion phase (ibid.: 347). The headquarters of the world-economy is not only the location of "capitalist agency" (ibid.: 88) but also the hegemon of the international order, which enabled the necessary degree of both political and economic control.

Even though Arrighi uses the categorical apparatus of the world-systemic analysis, his approach is somewhat more subtle. In order to underline his unit of analysis Arrighi distinguishes a space-of-places and a space-of-flows.[7] This dichotomy is used to point out the already mentioned inconflatable nature of the system of states (world-system) and specific locations within it. Even though it is easier to notice the territorially fixed states (places) than it is to take stock of the ever-flowing capital, both elements are unavoidable in explaining economic development in its time and space. In Arrighi's analysis, space-of-places corresponds to the sequence of hegemonies through modernity and space-of-flows corresponds to the regime of accumulation (Arrighi 1994/2010: 23, 80–84, 212). Here we have a fundamental conceptual issue of capitalism, which develops through both tendencies at the same time (ibid.: 85): the processes that can be discerned on the national unit of analysis are located in a space-of-places, while the world-systemic processes are located in a space-of-flows. These can never be completely mutually exclusive as even a fully global process must have some fixed points (accounts, stock-markets, loci of production, regulation and distribution…)—they are necessarily two coexisting aspects of capitalism. However, as these are distinct tendencies, we may benefit from understanding some processes as more dependent on the space-of-flows and others as more dependent on the space-of-places. In the example above, hegemony is a trait of a given state (space-of-places), but historical hegemonies have always included a fundamental transformative action (ibid.: 28), which re-created the world-system after its own image (space-of-flows).

The regimes of accumulation in question are strategies and structures employed by a complex of governmental and business agencies that lead the world-system through material and financial expansions. The strategies and structures are ways of promoting, organizing, and regulating "the expansion or the restructuring of the capitalist world-economy" (Arrighi and Moore 2001: 60). Therefore, a particular systemic cycle is simultaneous with a particular accumulation regime for Arrighi. In order to lead the world-system into material expansion, a wider or a deeper division of labor is necessary (ibid.; Arrighi 2007: 231). The Genoese and British systemic cycles are examples of a wider division of labor (an extensive accumulation regime type) while the Dutch and American systemic

[7] Arrighi adopted these two concepts from John Gerard Ruggie (1993: 172). However, both before and after Ruggie, these concepts were used by Manuel Castells in a more general sense of a contrast between a space of places which describes social activity with meaningful physical proximity and a space of flows which describes networked interactive communication (Castells 1989: 126–171, 348–353; 2000: 696).

cycles are examples of a deeper division of labor (an intensive accumulation regime type; Arrighi and Moore 2001: 73). This historical pendulum between extensive regimes focused on cosmopolitan capital widening the reach of the world-system and intensive regimes focused on the development of domestic productive capabilities obscures the cumulative increase of complexity and size of the world-system itself.

Each of the last three systemic cycles increased the complexity by internalizing a further type of cost in the context of the world-system and the role its center plays with respect to the periphery. The starting Genoese cycle was a project of a cosmopolitan capital not bound directly to a military power (as the political and military power of Genoa had already faded) but seeking an alliance with the Iberic states and funding their global expansion through the sixteenth century (Arrighi 1994/2010: 111–129). Compared to this, the Dutch cycle was the first to provide an intimate link between the governmental (state) and the business (capital) agencies as both were located in the Netherlands and the military power of the first protected and was funded by the second (Arrighi 1994/2010: 130–162). This means that the radically new innovation that propelled the Netherlands into the center of the world-system was in fact the internalization of protection costs (ibid.: 148). In effect, this particular Dutch organizational innovation was a precursor to what will become known as the nation-state (Strpić 2010: 111–143). The British cycle internalized production costs by focusing and intensifying manufacture through the industrial revolution (Arrighi 1994/2010: 179–218; Arrighi and Moore 2001: 73). Finally, the American cycle internalized transaction costs by enveloping the entire world in a nexus of corporations as a new and modern form of organizing capital and military power able to intervene globally (ibid.; Arrighi 1994/2010: 247–276).

These organizational innovations occur in the globally divergent economic context and stable strategic responses to this context. Arrighi emphasizes this by paralleling the Western capital-intensive industrial revolution with the East Asian labor-intensive industrious revolution (Arrighi 2007: 32–34). This is a very old East Asian tendency of organizing production by utilizing a combination of labor-intensive and capital saving methods. Arrighi follows Kaoru Sugihara (2003) in this parallel. Sugihara traces this development to a sixteenth-eighteenth-century population growth in East Asia enabled by a technological adaptation to the natural resource constraints, particularly a scarcity of land compared to the available workforce (ibid.: 82).

We can discern a harmonious aspect of the systemic cycle via organizational innovations and the interconnectedness of capital flight from the old center into the fledgling future center. However, we can certainly also expect a contentious element as well—with the old center using its military might to compensate for the loss of the economic central position, or perhaps with the new pretenders for the central position determining the future hegemon through military conflict. Therefore, the hegemonic cycle intertwines with the described systemic cycle. It describes the periods of relative peace that accompany the trade expansion. The financializations are periods of economic instability that necessitate a competition of pretenders on the central world-systemic position. In time, a global conflict may develop to resolve the underlying economic competition. However, Arrighi identified the current situation as unprecedented. While a financialization historically also meant a race in military power, with the new center overtaking the old, we are witnessing "a bifurcation of global military and financial resources that has no precedent in earlier transitions" (Arrighi and Moore 2001: 74), which precludes a great power war which would resemble the two world wars, Napoleonic Wars or the Thirty Year War. Current trends confirm this bifurcation as stable, as the US military still dwarfs the rest of the world in most important naval assets necessary for global power projection, and trends in both shipbuilding and fiscal capability show that this balance of power is not likely to change in the next 15 years (Lučev 2014a: 131–145).

World-systemic analysis is not alone in predicting cyclical wars. A number of authors have researched the cyclical nature of large wars starting with the pioneering work of Quincy Wright (1942), and continuing with Toynbee (1954), Modelski (1978), Goldstein (1985, 1988, 2006), Chase-Dunn and Podobnik (1999), Tausch (2006), etc. While this crucial type of analysis is often overlooked, this thesis does not use the war cycle as a predictor of institutional change, and the analysis of these theories fall beyond its scope.

2.2.3 Understanding the Effects of the Process of Capitalism on Labor Power: Beverly Silver

Arrighi's narrative did not specifically focus on labor when he wrote as a sole author. However, he has co-authored several important works with Beverly Silver (Arrighi and Silver 1984, 1999, 2001; Silver and Arrighi 2003) who did so, and she masterfully continued her own approach to the systemic cycle (Silver 2003, 2014, 2019). Her approach emphasizes the cyclical nature of labor power and militancy in describing the global process of capitalism. In doing so, Silver created a broad perspective explaining labor movement oscillations, and within it she considers Arrighi's approach to financial expansions to be critical as an explanatory factor (Silver 2003: 176). Therefore, she continues the work on the systemic cycle (or the long waves of capitalism) with a more nuanced approach. She has taken issue with a simplistic reading of a world-system according to which social relations on the local or national level are deterministically and completely transformed from the level of the world-system, excluding the possibility of local action significantly impacting local or global outcomes (ibid.: 29–30). She prefers an approach which would be aware of the real restricting nature of the world-system, but still accepts that the system is created through the activities of various sub-units of the system (ibid.: 30).

The process of global capitalism as described by Silver is an oscillation between two contradictory crisis tendencies (profitability and legitimacy crises) which delimit the process of commodification and decommodification of labor. An expansion of production tends to create stronger labor movements which are well positioned to force the creation of labor friendly social compacts (i.e. a tendency toward de-commodified labor), but these contribute to a crisis of profitability. Resolutions of profitability crises tend to break the labor friendly social compacts and commodify the labor, leading to a legitimacy crisis which causes backlash resistance (Silver 2003: 20, 178).

These restorations of profitability consist of four possible "fixes"[8] (Silver 2003: 39–40). These are essentially recurrent methods for countering the crises of profitability which plague the process of capital accumulation. The first is the spatial fix (which Silver adopts directly from David Harvey), which is a geographic solution to a profitability

[8] The term "spatial fix" is taken from the works of David Harvey (1989, 1999), and the three additional processes Silver describes are analogous to his original concept. According to Harvey (2001) the term itself has been often misunderstood as the word fix has several possible meanings in the English language. Harvey did not wish to suggest the meaning of a fix as a permanent solution to a problem or as a fixated position in space, but rather as an addict's use of drugs which offers only a short-term relief of a pervasive and recurrent need (ibid.: 24). This was suggestive of the need of capitalism to resolve its internal contradictions by geographically relocating the profit creation to an untapped area. Such a fix will always be eventually followed by another.

crisis. In terms of labor militancy, a strong organization of labor could provide a profit crunch in a developed country, and capital could migrate to a new location (e.g. shifting production to a less developed country). After a necessary period of organization, the new location will also be able to organize its labor and provide a profit crunch necessitating a new relocation. Such a view has prompted one of Silver's central claims, according to which: "where capital goes, conflict follows" (Silver 2014: 50). The second fix is technological and describes the post-Fordist cost-cutting movements toward greater control of labor (*lean* manufacturing). The third process is the product fix, describing the quest for enlarged profits through expansion into new industries and products. Silver uses the Vernon (1966) model of a product life-cycle to show that the innovations tend to cluster in the capitalist core and the production of new products only shift to less developed countries (or rather, their companies) once the profit bearing monopoly phase of the product life-cycle has been exhausted. Finally, there is the financial fix, which is explicitly adopted from Arrighi and his concept of financial expansions.

The basic idea of a pendulum between the two tendencies of commodification and decommodification of labor is taken from Karl Polanyi, who interpreted labor markets as subjected to a double movement—where the extension of the free market role is continuously met by efforts to protect labor via mechanisms like legislation, unions, and unemployment insurance (Polanyi 1957/1999; Silver 2003: 17–18). This view of labor markets is supported by Polanyi's idea of labor, money, and land as three fictitious commodities, which was a point not lost on Silver or Arrighi.[9] These three must be treated as commodities in order to organize large-scale industrial production, but none of these are produced for sale on the market, with labor being human activity, produced only inasmuch life itself is produced, money is produced only metaphorically as it represents only tokens of payment and land is inherited rather than produced. This makes them fictitious as commodities and opens the possibility for disaster if these should be subjected to self-regulating markets (Arrighi 1994/2010: 263–265). This underlying logic helps us locate labor in the

[9] Polanyi is often referred to throughout *Chaos and Governance in the World System* (Arrighi and Silver 1999) and *Adam Smith in Beijing* (Arrighi 2007), as well as Arrighi's crucial book *The Long Twentieth Century* (1994/2010), which bore the subtitle *Money, Power and the Origins of Our Times* which was a nod to Polanyi's seminal book *The Great Transformation* and its subtitle of *The Political and Economic Origins of Our Time.*

basic concepts of capitalism, where it stands both in markets and societies. Labor is necessary for production, and therefore subjected to markets with workers driven to extremes of toil when this market is not regulated. Simultaneously, labor refers to an activity of human beings, who will try to protect themselves from abuse in a way no other commodity ever could. Therefore, labor uniquely stands on the crossroads of markets and political power.

In her conceptualization of labor power itself, Silver follows Erik Olin Wright (2000) and his distinction of associational and structural power. Associational power refers to the ability of labor to collectively organize through unions and parties. Structural power refers to the bargaining power of labor, which is a result of the position in the economic system. Structural power is further divided on *marketplace bargaining power*, which is a consequence of the position of workers on the labor markets as a whole, and *workplace bargaining power* which is a result of a strategic location of a specific group in a key industrial sector (Silver 2003: 13).

The four fixes have specific effects on these types of labor power. Spatial fixes diffuse structural power, reducing it in the old center of production (i.e. its material expansion has ended) but eventually increasing it in the new center of production (ibid.: 169). Technological fixes do not have clear-cut results in terms of power, but the historical late twentieth-century trend toward lean manufacturing and *just-in-time* systems of production has contributed to greater workplace structural power (making the system vulnerable to a limited obstruction). Product fixes tend to reproduce the divide between the core and the periphery, with the monopoly phases clustering in the core and the diminished profit phases of the product life-cycle clustering in the periphery. This creates a potentially explosive situation created by a combination of spatial fixes—which increase labor power—and product fixes—which decrease the possibilities of labor friendly outcomes due to lower wealth creation to be distributed between capital and labor (ibid.: 170). Finally, the financial fix creates structural unemployment and reduces marketplace labor power (ibid.: 176). In all of these cases, the lack of structural power can be offset by associational power, suggesting a need to observe specific national context in which labor is organized (i.e. unions and labor-oriented political parties).

Silver provides us with a somewhat subtler reading of the systemic cycle, focused on several explanatory factors and describing the pendulum of labor power as shifting in terms of workplace and marketplace bargaining and associational capacity power. These forms of power shift as a result of the dynamics between profitability and legitimacy crises which also underscore the creation and dissolution of labor friendly social compacts (commodification-decommodification). Within these shifts, there is also a Polanyiesque logic in which a greater power of labor suggests the ability of the society to protect itself from the disruptive capacity of free markets. Within the systemic cycle, this gives us an image of two interlocking processes: the dominantly global process of capital and investment and the dominantly local or national process of labor. While the interests of groups representing either capital or labor could conceivably be very complex, this subtle reading of the systemic cycle by Silver already gives us a historically influenced image of a modern world. It assumes the accumulation of capital which is sufficient both for the global mobility in very large patterns and for the wage-workers to become a very strong social force. This makes labor the crucial societal element which is, however, already on the defensive from the free market forces embodied by the mobile capital. In other words, labor power and labor institutions tend to be the societal bulwark against free market tendencies and therefore stand at the decisive juncture of the divide of national and global levels of capitalism. Labor can be therefore understood as supremely political and its link to profitability makes it a crucial element in growth models as well. However, the notions of social compacts and commodification/decommodification of labor are insufficiently developed and could benefit from a far more explicit treatment in order to be able to better outline the effects of labor mobilization.

2.3 The Uses of the Systemic Cycle

Arrighi has developed an advanced version of the world-systemic analysis, primarily through his appreciation of the role played by the global interplay of material and financial expansions and the intensive and extensive strategies that underline them. Silver added a logic of labor power to the systemic cycle predicting pendulum swings between crises of legitimacy and crises of profitability. The central contention of this thesis is that the conceptualization of the systemic cycle as capitalist development is useful to understanding institutional change. Segment 2.3.1 will deal with elementary methodological issues with temporality at stake to show the differences between the systemic cycle and equilibrium inspired social sciences. These advantages of the systemic cycle are crucial as the equilibrium atemporality tends to create significant obstacles in conceptualizing endogenous institutional change, as we will see in the next chapter. Segment 2.3.2 will show the importance of the systemic cycle process for the interpretation of financialization, trade, and crises. It will also outline domestic labor power effects of trade and finance expansions. Finally, segment 2.3.3 will outline the issues with organizations and institutions in systemic cycle theory—outlining labor power changes in response to the organizational strategic shifts.

2.3.1 Historical Grounding Versus Equilibrium Atemporality

World-systemic analysis has the potential to be historical in a meaningful sense. Braudel, Wallerstein and Arrighi have all undertaken to write dense historical studies of early capitalism while Arrighi and Silver have strived to offer a theory of future movements. If successful, such theories may provide us with useful predictive capabilities. The predominant mainstream alternative to this potential is the equilibrium analysis, with all its predictor failings. Historically grounded analysis offers a great improvement over such sterile and abstracted (essentially nomothetic) type of analysis in much of social science. This static tendency is well exemplified by the widely implied notion of equilibrium in economics (Blyth et al. 2011: 2), from where it proliferated into political science and elsewhere.[10] As explored in the next chapter, the notion of equilibrium is one of the

[10]The mainstream of economics is known as the neoclassical school of economics and it owes its existence to the marginal revolution in the second half of the nineteenth century (Leon Walras, Carl Menger and William Stanley Jevons). This generation of scientists brought concepts of marginal utility and partial equilibrium into the foreground analysis and set categorical foundations for the economic science as it exists today (see Schumpeter 1954). Neoclassical economics is sometimes known as Marshallian economics due to its synthesizer Alfred Marshall and his ubiquitous textbook *Principles of Economics* (1890). This was the mainstream economics before the Keynesian revolution and is the basis for the new classical economics (sometimes indiscriminatingly also known as neoclassical economics and sometimes pejoratively as neoliberal economics) which proved to be the mainstream position after the 1970s (see also Strpić 1998: 7–19). Neoclassical economics is based on the mathematical abstraction of marginal utility, which simplifies the economy in several important ways. Methodological individualism focuses on individual activity, while presumption of rationality subsumes also the full information these individuals ostensibly possess. It focuses on equilibrium (e.g. supply and demand) as the default position, and tacitly assumes that the equilibrium position free markets tend to automatically move toward is that of full employment. This creates substantial challenges for neoclassical economics in explaining the business cycle (Lučev 2014b).

most limiting factors in approaching endogenous institutional change. This is the case as the very analogy of equilibrium, borrowed as it is from physics, forms an important part of the cognitive map of various epistemic communities related to social sciences (and creates significant obstacles in conceptualizing institutional change, crises, trade policies, market failures etc.).

The devastating critique along similar lines of what is today known as neoclassical economics is what propelled the thought of John Maynard Keynes into the fore after *The General Theory of Employment, Interest, and Money* (Keynes 1936/2013). The principal authors of the marginal revolution mostly explored the partial rather than the general equilibrium,[11] which is suitable for assessing the growth of the economy as a whole. Nevertheless, the equilibrium as a conceptual tool has informed the subsequent work on economic growth. The very concept of equilibrium was introduced into economics after its apparent success in Newtonian physics. But while it may successfully explain the statics and dynamics of objects, its use in social sciences suggests the expectancy of a simplified world with immutable laws and predictable behavior of all agents. There are obvious and often reiterated issues that may arise in conjecture with such concepts—including the fact that humans are, unlike stones or apples, often unpredictable, irrational, and reflexive agents. Apart from these, the equilibrium as a central concept has the implied flaw of being a static state. To theorize change using equilibriums may result in describing the starting and final position of agents and not explaining the movement between the two. While neoclassical economists were and are aware of time as a concept, they tend to circumvent the issue by discerning merely the short and long run scenarios of two equilibrium points. To describe the microeconomic functioning of markets, the earlier forms of neoclassical economics focused on the *perfect competition* model, with a multitude of unrealistic assumptions (perfect rationality, perfect knowledge, absence of the ability to set prices, very large number of very small suppliers, homogeneous products, no barriers to market entry, no transaction costs, no super-profits, etc.). This model of a market structure is very optimistic in its predictions as the outcomes are best from the point of view of both the consumer and the as it predicts the largest output for

[11] With the notable exception of Leon Walras.

the lowest price. While modern approaches to markets are increasingly subtle, they often bear the markings of the original simplification.[12]

All of this helped create an overly market-optimistic mainstream of economic science, but it also helped economics become a mathematically rigorous science reminiscent of natural sciences. This made it attractive as a model for other social sciences (and as we will see in Chapter 3, the notion of equilibrium informs much of modern institutional thought). However, what it gained in rigor, it lost in the need to abstract and assume—i.e. in foregoing the messy and fully detailed historical world for one of perfect rationality, perfect competition, and efficient markets. Social sciences in general have, in taking after economics, started to favor research-in-small-chunks preferring micro- or perhaps meso-approaches and viewing the macro- only with suspicion. It was against such a view of social sciences that Braudel, Wallerstein, and Arrighi have argued and their alternatives came in forms of dense historical descriptions. In Arrighi's version we also see some ability to predict future economic movements. The very long period of European and then global capitalism is divided in consecutive periods of material and financial expansions led by the geographically shifting core of the world-system.

Crucially, what enables this maneuver is the unit of analysis which is simultaneously national and transnational (world-systemic). The first belongs to the space-of-places in that the space in which a process takes place is fixed. The second belongs to the space-of-flows in that the process is unlimited by fixed places. Wallerstein opted to focus on the world-systemic and see states as mere sub-units. While this is a possible conceptualization, it seems to point toward a static structure of core/periphery/semi-periphery and itself represent a form of self-replicating equilibrium. Silver successfully challenged this view as simplistic and argued that while there are world-systemic constrictions on the national level, it is equally true that agency on the national level

[12] Most obviously, the perfect competition model was augmented in the early 1930s with the more realistic model of monopolistic competition (Robinson 1933/1969; Chamberlin 1933/1962), which modeled markets with diversified products (brands), and recognized the possibility of large, profit generating suppliers which by itself meant lower quantities produced and higher prices achieved as a result of market forces when compared to perfect competition. However, the long and short-run in monopolistic competition to indicate that in the long period monopolistic competition will generate more competitors and therefore gradually move toward the perfect outcomes of the optimistic equilibrium of perfect competitions.

constructs, replicates, or changes the world-system itself. To follow the logic of the systemic cycle theory, we must concede that capitalism is simultaneously both national and world-systemic. The result is a unit of analysis which recognizes both the structure of the world-system (and the unequal positions of states within it) and the ability of states to influence their positions and the world-system itself. This enables the systemic cycle theory to potentially move beyond determinism and focus on the various national-level effects of global processes which were themselves the result of processes which are best discernable on national levels. Our aspiration is to discern the national-level institutional processes in such an interaction. In order to eventually do so, we will first use the next two segments to develop the specific effects of the systemic cycle on social power underlying changes in institutions.

2.3.2 *The Capitalist Structure, Process, and Crisis*

The systemic cycle is a theory of a capitalist process based in the logic of sequential material and financial expansions. These are bracketed by signal and terminal crises which are explained through an overlapping Smithian and Marxian theory of investment. A significant corollary is the effect on marketplace power, with the financial expansion bringing lower levels of labor power, and material expansions bringing higher levels of labor power. In both cases, the shift is a result of a different role that the workforce (particularly the industrial workforce) has to play in the economy as a whole. In material expansions, industrial labor is crucial to the growth of the economy, and a general strike could conceivably largely stop the economic life in a given location. In financial expansions, industrial labor is not as important as the financial sector increases in importance. Likewise, large trade deficits suggest a diminishing role of domestic labor, as a large part of domestic demand is met by foreign production. Both financial expansion and adverse trade relations diminish the structural power of domestic labor, which makes them relevant to projecting the bargaining power of labor in national level processes.

Both instances (crises defining the material/financial phases and adverse trade relations) are examples of disharmonious market relations. To have a theory which entertains and explains both is itself an advantage over the mainstream social sciences. Crises are particularly difficult to foresee from the efficient market-driven models in the mainstream economic thought. As we have seen, mainstream economics expects efficient markets and rational actors.[13] While Arrighi is certainly at an advantage when compared to the neoclassical school as he provides endogenous mechanisms of crises, his approach leaves much to be desired. Arrighi's strengths and weaknesses stem from assumptions and categorical apparatus of classical political economy,[14] particularly from Adam Smith and Karl Marx. In either case, Arrighi stays largely limited to supply-side phenomena: in the Smithian sense to the number and size of competing players in each market and in the Marxian sense to the overinvestment in production. This is somewhat in conflict with monopolistic tendencies of developed capitalism. Although the monopoly capitalism[15] does not suggest literal monopolies and large multinationals must still compete, their development suggests a tendency of diminishing rather than increasing competition (and therefore increasing and not diminishing profits). This suggests that profit crunches need to be explained as results of at least partially demand related issues which exert pressures toward lower profits. While various developments of Marxist thought through the twentieth century have increasingly advocated the interpretation of overaccumulation crises as a demand-side phenomenon (as the diminishing share of variable capital may translate into diminishing total labor income), Arrighi does not stress this issue. In fact, it seems that his overreliance on Smith and Marx creates an approach which does not sufficiently take into account the various possibilities of aggregate demand

[13] Not surprisingly, one of the most serious failures of mainstream economics was the seeming inability to predict the financial and real economic crisis of 2007–2009. At the same time, many authors of the world-systemic approach including Arrighi have predicted the proximate start of a systemic crisis even though they could not pinpoint its beginning.

[14] Before the late nineteenth century and the slow development of separate social sciences of sociology, political science and economics the idiom "political economy" was the preferred term that cut across these categories we take for granted today. Adam Smith spoke of political economy, which he defined as "a branch of the science of a statesman or legislator" (Smith 1776/2003: 537). David Ricardo, Thomas Malthus, James Mill, and John Stuart Mill titled their ubiquitous books after political economy (Ricardo's *On the Principles of Political Economy and Taxation* from 1817, Malthus's *Elements of Political Economy* from 1820, James Mill's *Elements of Political Economy* from 1821, John Stuart Mill's *Principles of Political Economy* from 1848). It was not until Alfred Marshall that a central text was to mention economics as the new term (*Principles of Economics* from 1890). The new term, and its success, is therefore a function of the success of neoclassical economics which made its first appearance in the writings of Alfred Marshall as well.

[15] In the sense used by Baran and Sweezy or Cowling and Sugden (see Ietto-Gillies 2005).

management. The risk in not taking demand seriously enough is therefore present in both neoclassical economics and Arrighi. The great, but unrecognized, theoretical interlocutor should be John Maynard Keynes, who put precisely aggregate demand at the center of his theory. When applied to the real world in the form of *Keynesian welfare state* these policies were directed at a more active fiscal policy and some vastly more redistributive taxation systems, which were aimed at achieving economic growth through increasing domestic demand. Chapter 4 will develop the Keynesian interpretation of Arrighi in an attempt to remedy the supply-side limitations in the systemic cycle. What can be gained is a more precise approach to growth models and their effects.

Apart from crises as processes bracketing material and financial expansions, world-systemic analysis incorporates expected structural trade instabilities, a possibility which also eludes the tradition of mainstream neoclassical thought. A significant advantage is the understanding of free trade preferences as structurally biased. We can also connect these to labor power by analogy to the theses of Beverly Silver. In countries with growing manufactured goods deficits, the marketplace structural power of industrial labor is diminishing as its importance to the economy is reduced. Likewise, in countries with growing surpluses, the marketplace structural power (and the political influence) is increasing. When discussing trade relations, the mainstream of modern economic science tends to consider the effects of the free market beneficial to all parties. This tradition is often connected to Ricardian economics of comparative advantage.[16] The point of comparative advantage is that even the country with higher comparative costs of production of all goods benefits from free trade. Even though it is least competitive in terms of labor needed to produce, it will be able to export its goods. This is because the country with lower costs will import the more expensive goods in order to reorient its resources into those areas in which it is the most productive. Free trade will therefore always be beneficial to all countries involved.[17]

[16] The origins of the concept of comparative advantage should be traced at least to Adam Smith's analysis of absolute (or natural) advantage in *Wealth of Nations*, first published in 1776. The development of the more complicated concept of comparative advantage is attributed to Ricardo (for a debate on the authorship of comparative advantage see Aldrich 2004; Ruffin 2003).

[17] For this point see Torrens (1815: 262–265), Ricardo (1817/2016: 77–93), and Mill (1844: 53–55). A more recent variant of comparative advantage position is the Heckscher-Ohlin theorem (Ohlin 1933/1935), also known as the neoclassical theory of trade, which

An alternative to the mainstream and liberal side of the debate are theories that stress the fact that free trade does not benefit all of the participants, but rather produces relatively fixed positions, primarily benefiting specific sets of actors. Some of these directly inform world-systemic analysis and Arrighi's research. An important genre of literature in this vein was the dependency theory,[18] postulating that in the long run the prices of primary products will tend to fall compared to prices of manufactured products. Therefore, the export of industrialized countries will *ceteris paribus* increase in value compared to the export of countries which are not industrialized and produce only primary products. In other words, the developed, industrialized parts of the world will in the long run have a considerable advantage in terms of economic growth over the underdeveloped, agrarian parts of the world.[19] World-systems analysis postulates a division of labor in the global economy between the countries/areas of

introduced capital to the Ricardian scheme and predicted capital abundant countries will specialize in exporting capital-intensive goods and labor abundant countries will specialize in exporting labor-intensive goods. The free trade optimum predicted by this theory was a result of problematic assumptions which included perfect competition.

[18] Dependency theory originated in the 1949–1950 works of Raul Prebisch and Hans Singer (hence the Prebisch-Singer thesis—or PST).

[19] See Raffer and Singer (2001: 16–31), Toye and Toye (2003), Sapsford et al. (1992), Harvey et al. (2010). Apart from the world-systems analysis, another path to addressing the insufficiencies of neoclassical trade models emerged in the 1970s through the new trade theory, which built on neoclassical foundations in order to model situations in which non-free-trade policies were. As neoclassical trade models assume perfect competition, there was ample room in acknowledging the developments in monopolistic competition from the early 1930s and using them as a part of trade theory. An influential foundation for this inclusion was created through the Dixit-Stiglitz macroeconomic model (Dixit and Stiglitz 1977) which acknowledged monopolistic competition and was used by a number of sub-fields including new trade theory. Further corrections in new trade include the acknowledgment of other market distortions and the economies of scale (Helpman and Krugman 1985, 1989). The two main points (monopolistic competition and economies of scale) suggest that agglomeration of industry is possible (as the largest players may have the lowest costs of production). Therefore, free trade can lead not to mutually beneficial specialization as postulated by classical and neoclassical trade theory, but rather to further clusters of production located perhaps partially according to factor endowments, but also according to existing agglomerations. In other words, production may shift to where labor is abundant, but it may also shift to the already more developed parts of the world. These questions were further developed through new economic geography, which is a "new genre of research" starting around 1990 (Krugman 1998: 7) and building on the mathematical modeling strategies that made new trade theory so successful including the tendencies toward general equilibrium set ups.

the core (centers of global industrial production and finance) and countries/areas of the periphery (locations with primary products) mediated through the countries/areas of semi-periphery. Compared to mainstream trade theories, this approach is decided in claiming the benefits of global free trade are largely concentrated in the core of the system. The advantage of such an approach is the ability to survey international trade as benefiting some economies in particular, even though it cannot be construed as a zero-sum game. The world-system is a complex level of analysis, enabling a very broad view, but great care must be awarded in avoiding determinism.

In moving beyond the equilibria-inspired views of markets, the systemic cycle theory surpasses not only the efficient free market views, but also the more naïve versions of the world-system. At the center of world-systemic analysis we find a geographic division of labor which spells out differences in economic development. In Wallerstein's version of world-systemic analysis there was a tendency to predict relatively static positions of this division of labor (i.e. core and periphery), while the subtler Arrighi/Silver reading of the systemic cycle presented here gives us a dynamic of development though which strategies on the national level create the world-systemic dynamic while at the same time being shaped by it. This version is much less dependent on deterministic views of market processes and capable to validate successful national-level growth models. This is relevant not only in the sense of world-systemic analysis being more useful to analyze the real world, but also by virtue of the possibility of including the market instabilities (crises and trade relations) into a functional cyclical view of labor power, which can be used to predict institutional changes.

2.3.3 Institutions, Organizations, and Agency

Following Smith, Marx, Braudel, and Wallerstein, Arrighi created an intriguing explanatory and predictive scheme on the behavior of world capitalism in broad strokes. He tracked the changing of capital accumulation regimes and complementary transformations of capitalist organization which formed the competitive edge of various economic centers vying for the hegemonic position during financial expansions. This organization is increasingly complex and increasingly comprehensive even as the patterns Arrighi recognizes shift from a wider division of labor (extensive and financially influenced capitalism during the Genoese and British regimes) to a deeper division of labor (intensive and monopoly influenced capitalism during the Dutch and US regimes). However, Arrighi does not go into the minutiae of what such organizational swings might precisely entail (e.g. what kind of laws, norms, transnational forms, etc.). While such broad strokes are necessary for the kind of grand historical project found in Arrighi's writing, they do not necessarily provide a scheme precise enough to gauge the contemporary world[20] and its organizational and institutional alternatives. Likewise, Arrighi does not need to identify precise drivers of institutional change to fulfill his purpose of describing the organizational innovations and providing a model and theory of their movements. He merely points to the fact that the leading agencies are generally an effective mix of business and state actors. If he were more precise and offered clear distinctions, he could have convincingly been considered an author in historical institutionalism.

As it is, we have an entangled notion of institutional and organizational change with an essentially Darwinistic mechanism underlying hegemonic shifts. A successful organizational innovation propels an aspirant center into the hegemony position, establishing an organizational example to follow for other countries. The two general strategies are identified as extensive and intensive, but we know little of how they interact and how the developed countries chose the strategies to model. This distinction is obviously not sufficient to compare various types of capitalisms in the core or explain institutional change in its details. In focusing on the global process of capitalism, he was less interested in analyzing its relative fixtures. Silver fared somewhat better, recognizing the importance of the institutional context (e.g. Silver 2014: 55–58), plotting the pendulum between the breaking and making of social compacts, which are themselves in part the labor-friendly or labor-unfriendly institutional arrangements. This provides a vital element in predicting institutional change—i.e. the crises of profitability and legitimacy. However, like Arrighi, Silver was not interested in minutiae of institutional solutions, preferring broad strokes necessary for the analysis of the labor militancy aspect of the systemic cycle. The result is the finished form of

[20] As mentioned before, his similar shyness in providing empirical data or measurements to support his thesis on financialization in the USA prompted Greta Krippner (2005) to fill this gap, which he would duly note in a later work (Arrighi 2007).

the systemic cycle, which is able to predict a low-resolution image of economic and political shifts but retaining somewhat of a blind spot for institutional diversity and change. It is therefore a vastly important tool, left insufficiently used in this vital area.

Crucially, the systemic cycle theory draws our attention to labor as the key subject of the global/national tension of capitalism and its dynamics. Properly understood, labor stands at the pivot of growth models, defining both international competitiveness and aggregate demand management. However, the conceptual apparatus of the systemic cycle is insufficient to describe such a position and role of labor markets. The power resources of labor in terms of its capacity to organize and its structural leverage on the economy are vastly important but are only an isolated part of the equation. It is the institutions that provide both the context in which power resources materialize and are often the result of their use. They provide the context for labor power as the regulations and practices determine the very existence of unions, as well as the rules according to which they function, collectively bargain and achieve both membership and financial resources with which they can exact pressure. Institutions are also the result of labor power, as labor can mobilize political resources to influence regulation and standard practices that surround them. Without a clear understanding of labor market institutions, national level changes to labor remain tied to economic and power shifts. Therefore, to fulfill its potential, systemic cycle theory must be taken a step further.

To do so, we must also disentangle organizations and institutions in the systemic cycle. This is particularly important as the shifts between strategic intensiveness and extensiveness of capitalism also bring transformative organizational innovations (e.g. internalizations of protection through the nation-state in the Dutch cycle or the internalization of transaction costs through the modern corporation in the American cycle), and the agents of these shifts are at the same time states and business organizations. This aspect of the systemic cycle theory is conceptually underdeveloped. The intensive and extensive developmental strategies can be a third labor power predicting element (alongside the phase of the systemic cycle and trade positions), but we must clearly interpret it in this sense (which we do in Chapter 4) and clearly distinguish the organizational from institutional elements (Chapter 5).

2.4 Conclusion

This chapter sets out to explain the approach to the global process of capitalism within the world-systemic unit of analysis and through the theory of the systemic cycle, which itself builds on alternating material and financial expansions. While numerous authors explain financial expansions, the concept of the systemic cycle provides a deep historical context for financializations (Arrighi 1994/2010; Arrighi and Silver 1999; Arrighi 2007). Following Braudel (1992a, b, c), Arrighi explains a logic of economic development in which real and financial phases succeed one another. An expansion of real economy in the center of the world-system is followed by an expansion of the financial economy and vice versa. The mechanism behind Arrighi's concept of financialization is essentially the Smithian and Marxist notion of the profit rate tendency to fall. The conflict that drives the prices down can be horizontal (inter-capitalist competition), but also vertical and therefore pertaining to the relationship between capital and labor (Arrighi 2007: 130). The capitalist process of accumulation necessitates a point at which there is a vicious competition driving the average profit rate down. The profit rates in manufacture and trade will fall, and as Braudel and Arrighi note, capital will turn to finance in search of higher profit rates.

The point in economic development at which growth slows in any given sector (and this is what should interest us) was noted repeatedly through the history of economic thought. Such notions exist in Marxist economics, classical economics (both the tendency of the profit rate to fall in Adam Smith and the law of diminishing returns), and neoclassical/new classical economics (e.g. the Solow-Swan model). The specific explanations of these approaches may differ, but the salient point is the same: in a developed economy, the growth will eventually slow down in the absence of large and continuous technological developments, and the prevalent profit rates will fall. Therefore, it would surely not be implausible to claim that in the described case, corporations in a developed country try to find more lucrative investment opportunities abroad. Under favorable conditions the amassed investments in a specific less developed country might be sufficient to turn it into a very large net exporter. These favorable conditions in the country targeted for investment may include a functional judicial system, sufficient infrastructure, a relatively stable political situation, high quality of labor expressed in high levels of self-management, literacy and education and low real costs of labor and other inputs. When these conditions are met, the growth of the less developed country may be spurred in a way that may change its position in the world-system dramatically.

To summarize, Arrighi has substantial advantages over the economic mainstream in the apparent ability to explain structured and unequal trade positions and crises and explain both through historically grounded research. However, serious flaws in Arrighi stem from his Smithian and Marxian limits, focusing on the supply-side developmental mechanisms. A demand-side oriented theory could help transcend these difficulties, particularly in explaining the extensive and intensive strategies of organizational innovation. These should, in the contemporary world, be observed through the easily measurable prism of the foreign or domestic orientation of the economy in question. Arrighi's lack of interest in particular institutions and institutional change can be compensated by the available categories, models, and theories in institutional thought (Chapter 3).

Power is the element which will enable us to connect them. We have identified three aspects of the systemic cycle theory which can help us decode power: phase of the systemic cycle (using Silver's thesis), trade positions (by analogy with Silver) and, if properly interpreted, the extensive/intensive developmental strategy. To offer such an interpretation, we will develop the concepts of intensive and extensive capitalism with macroeconomic demand-side implications in Chapter 4.

Literature

Aglietta, M., & Rebérioux, A. (2005). *Corporate Governance Adrift: A Critique of Shareholder Value*. Cheltenham, UK: Edward Elgar Publishing.

Aldrich, J. (2004). The Discovery of Comparative Advantage. *Journal of the History of Economic Thought, 26*(3), 379–399.

Arrighi, G. (1994/2010). *The Long Twentieth Century: Money, Power, and the Origins of Our Times*. London and New York: Verso Books.

Arrighi, G. (2007). *Adam Smith in Beijing*. London: Verso.

Arrighi, G., Hamashita, T., & Selden, M. (Eds.). (2003). *The Resurgence of East Asia: 500, 150 and 50 Year Perspectives*. New York: Routledge.

Arrighi, G., & Moore, J. W. (2001). Capitalist Development in World Historical Perspective. In R. Albritton, M. Itoh, R. Westra, & A. Zuege (Eds.), *Phases of Capitalist Development* (pp. 56–75). London: Palgrave.

Arrighi, G., & Silver, B. J. (1984). Labor Movements and Capital Migration: The United States and Western Europe in World-Historical Perspective. In C. Bergquist (Ed.), *Labor in the Capitalist World-Economy* (pp. 183–216). Beverly Hills: Sage.

Arrighi, G., & Silver, B. (Eds.). (1999). *Chaos and Governance in the Modern World System*. Minneapolis, MN: University of Minnesota Press.

Arrighi, G., & Silver, B. J. (2001). Capitalism and World (Dis)order. *Review of International Studies, 27*(5), 257–279.

Blyth, M., Hodgson, G. M., Lewis, O., & Steinmo, S. (2011). Introduction to the Special Issue on the Evolution of Institutions. *Journal of Institutional Economics, 7*(3), 299–315.

Braudel, F. (1992a). *Strukture svakidašnjice*. Zagreb: August Cesarec.

Braudel, F. (1992b). *Igra razmjene*. Zagreb: August Cesarec.

Braudel, F. (1992c). *Vrijeme svijeta*. Zagreb: August Cesarec.

Bukharin, N. (1917/1972). *Imperialism and World Economy*. London: Martin Lawrence.

Castells, M. (1989). *The Informational City: Information Technology, Economic Restructuring, and the Urban-Regional Process* (pp. 234–235). Oxford: Blackwell.

Castells, M. (2000). Toward a Sociology of the Network Society. *Contemporary Sociology, 29*(5), 693–699.

Chamberlin, E. (1933/1962). *Theory of Monopolistic Competition*. New York: Oxford University Press.

Chase-Dunn, C., & Podobnik, B. (1999). The Next World War: World-System Cycles and Trends. In V. Bornschier & C. Chase-Dunn (Eds.), *The Future of Global Conflict*. London: Sage.

Crouch, C. (2009). Privatised Keynesianism: An Unacknowledged Policy Regime. *The British Journal of Politics & International Relations, 11*(3), 382–399.

Dixit, A. K., & Stiglitz, J. E. (1977). Monopolistic Competition and Optimum Product Diversity. *The American Economic Review, 67*(3), 297–308.

Epstein, G. A. (Ed.). (2005). *Financialization and the World Economy*. Cheltenham, UK and Northampton, MA: Edward Elgar Publishing.

Goldstein, J. S. (1985). Kondratieff Waves as War Cycles. *International Studies Quarterly, 29*(4), 411–444.

Goldstein, J. S. (1988). *Long Cycles: Prosperity and War in the Modern Age*. New Haven: Yale University Press.

Goldstein, J. S. (2006). The Predictive Power of Long Wave Theory, 1989–2004. In T. C. Devezas (Eds.), *Kondratieff Waves, Warfare and World Security*. Amsterdam: IOS Press.

Harvey, D. (1989). *The Condition of Postmodernity: An Enquiry into the Origins of Cultural Change*. Oxford: Blackwell.

Harvey, D. (1999). *The Limits to Capital*. London: Verso.

Harvey, D. (2001). Globalization and the "Spatial Fix". *Geographische Revue, 3*(2), 23–30.

Harvey, D. I., Kellard, N. M., Madsen, J. B., & Wohar, M. E. (2010). The Prebisch-Singer Hypothesis: Four Centuries of Evidence. *The Review of Economics and Statistics, 92*(2), 367–377.

Helpman, E., & Krugman, P. R. (1985). *Market Structure and Foreign Trade: Increasing Returns, Imperfect Competition, and the International Economy*. Cambridge, MA: MIT Press.

Helpman, E., & Krugman, P. R. (1989). *Trade Policy and Market Structure*. Cambridge, MA: MIT Press.

Hilferding, R. (1910/1981). *Finance Capital: A Study of the Latest Phase of Capitalist Development*. London: Routledge.

Ietto-Gillies, G. (2005). *Transnational Corporations and International Production: Concepts, Theories and Effects*. Cheltenham, UK: Edward Elgar Publishing.

Keynes, J. M. (1936/2013). *General Theory of Employment, Interest and Money*. Cambridge University Press.

Krippner, G. R. (2005). The Financialization of the American Economy. *Socio-Economic Review, 3*(2), 173–208.

Krugman, P. (1998). What's New About the New Economic Geography? *Oxford Review of Economic Policy, 14*(2), 7–17.

Lenin, V. I. (1917/1999). *Imperialism: The Highest Stage of Capitalism*. Online Version: Lenin Internet Archive (marxists.org).

Lučev, J. (2014a). How Long Before NATO Aircraft Carrier Force Projection Capabilities are Successfully Countered? Some Effects of the Fiscal Crises. *Croatian International Relations Review, 20*(71), 121–151.

Lučev, J. (2014b). Duhovi kapitalizma i mjere štednje. *Politička misao, 51*(04), 26–40.

Marx, K. (1867/1894/1979). *Kapital: Kritika političke ekonomije I-III*. Beograd: Prosveta.

Mill, J. (1844). *Elements of Political Economy* (3rd ed.). London: Henry Bohn.

Modelski, G. (1978). The Long Cycle of Global Politics and the Nation-State. *Comparative Studies in Society and History, 20*(02), 214–235.

Ohlin, B. (1933/1935). *Interregional and International Trade*. Cambridge, MA: Harvard University Press.

Orhangazi, Ö. (2008). *Financialization and the US Economy*. Cheltenham, UK: Edward Elgar Publishing.

Piketty, T. (2017). *Capital in the Twenty-First Century*. Harvard University Press.

Polanyi, K. (1957/1999). *Velika preobrazba: Politički i ekonomski izvori našeg vremena*. Zagreb: Jesenski i Turk.

Raffer, K., & Singer, H. W. (2001). *The Economic North-South Divide: Six Decades of Unequal Development*. Cheltenham and Northampton, MA: Edward Elgar Publishing.

Ricardo, D. (1817/2016). *Principles of Political Economy and Taxation*. London: Dover Publications.

Robinson, J. (1933/1969). *The Economics of Imperfect Competition*. London: Macmillan.

Ruffin, R. (2003). David Ricardo's Discovery of Comparative Advantage. *History of Political Economy, 34*(4), 727–748.

Ruggie, J. G. (1993). Territoriality and Beyond: Problematizing Modernity in International Relations. *International Organization, 47*(1), 139–174.

Sapsford, D., Sarkar, P., & Singer, H. W. (1992). The Prebisch-Singer Terms of Trade Controversy Revisited. *Journal of International Development, 4*(3), 315–332.

Schumpeter, J. A. (1954). *History of Economic Analysis*. New York: Oxford University Press.

Silver, B. (2003). *Forces of Labor: Workers' Movements and Globalization Since 1870*. New York: Cambridge University Press.

Silver, B. (2014). Theorising the Working Class in Twenty-First-Century Global Capitalism. In M. Atzeni (Eds.), *Workers and Labour in a Globalised Capitalism* (pp. 46–69). New York: Palgrave Macmillan.

Silver, B. (2019). "Plunges into Utter Destruction" and the Limits of Historical Capitalism. In R. Atzmüller, B. Aulenbacher, U. Brand, F. Décieux, K. Fischer, & B. Sauer (Eds.), *Capitalism in Transformation*. Cheltenham, UK and Northampton, MA: Edward Elgar Publishing.

Silver, B. J., & Arrighi, G. (2003). Polanyi's "Double Movement": The Belle Époque of British and US Hegemony Compared. *Politics & Society, 31*(2), 325–355.

Smith, A. (1776/2003). *The Wealth of Nations*. New York: Bantam Dell.

Strpić, D. (1998). *Promjena*. Zagreb: Politička Misao.

Strpić, D. (2010). *Karl Marx i politička ekonomija moderne*. Zagreb: Nacionalna zajednica Crnogoraca Hrvatske.

Sugihara, K. (2003). The East Asian Path of Economic Development. In A. Arrighi, H. Takeshi, & M. Seldon (Eds.), *The Resurgence of East Asia* (pp. 78–123). London: Routledge.

Tausch, A. (2006). From the "Washington" Towards a "Vienna Consensus"? A Quantitative Analysis on Globalization, Development and Global Governance. In *Centro Argentino de Estudios Internacionales, EU-Latin America and Caribbean Summit 2006*. Vienna, 11 May–12 May [Online]. Available at: http://www.forschungsnetzwerk.at/downloadpub/CAEI_Buenos_Aires_Vienna_Summit_arno_tausch.pdf.

Torrens, R. (1815). *An Essay on the External Corn Trade: With an Appendix on the Means of Improving the Condition of the Labouring Classes*. London: J. Hatchard.

Toye, R., & Toye, J. F. (2003). The Origins and Interpretation of the Prebisch-Singer Thesis. *History of Political Economy, 35*(3), 437–467.

Toynbee, A. J. (1954). *A Study of History, Volume 9*. London: Oxford University Press.

Vernon, R. (1966). International Investment and International Trade in the Product Cycle. *The Quarterly Journal of Economics, 80*, 190–207.

Wallerstein, I. (1974a). *The Modern World-System I: Capitalist Agriculture and the Origins of the European World-Economy in the Sixteenth Century*. New York: Academic Press.

Wallerstein, I. (1974b). The Rise and Future Demise of the World Capitalist System: Concepts for Comparative Analysis. *Comparative Studies in Society and History, 16*(4), 387–415.

Wallerstein, I. (1980). *The Modern World-System II: Mercantilism and the Consolidation of the European World-Economy, 1600–1750*. New York: Academic Press.

Wallerstein, I. (1989). *The Modern World-System III: The Second Era of Great Expansion of the Capitalist World-Economy (1730–1840s)*. San Diego: Academic Press.

Wallerstein, I. (2011). *The Modern World-System IV: Centrist Liberalism Triumphant, 1789–1914*. Berkeley: University of California Press.

Wallerstein, I. M. (2000). *The Essential Wallerstein*. New York: New Press.

Wallerstein, I. M. (2001). *Unthinking Social Science: The Limits of Nineteenth-Century Paradigms*. Philadelphia, PA: Temple University Press.

Wright, E. O. (2000). Working-Class Power, Capitalist-Class Interests, and Class Compromise. *American Journal of Sociology, 105*(4), 957–1002.

Wright, Q. (1942). *A Study of War*. Chicago: University of Chicago Press.

CHAPTER 3

Institutions and Institutional Change

3.1 Introduction

The second chapter has analyzed Arrighi's concept of the systemic cycle in the context of its assumptions inherited from Smith, Marx, and Wallerstein and criticized it in comparison with its significant alternatives. One of the significant advantages of the systemic cycle over the categorical apparatus of mainstream economics is the implicit tendency of the latter to model in terms of atemporal equilibria. This chapter will deal with the concepts of institutions[1] and institutional change in order to show the state of the art, but it also serves a practical purpose, as it will expose the building blocks of the approach used in this book. Chapters 4 and 5 will develop a new account of endogenous institutional change, while many existing institutional approaches tend to relegate the role of institutional change to exogenous factors (Mahoney and Thelen 2010: 2–7). With the developing economic environment always providing its own incentive-disincentive set, it is surely crucial to endogenize it in accounting for institutional change.

[1] It is quite difficult to segregate institution-pertinent literature from economic literature as such, even when the original authors do not explicitly focus on institutions. Therefore, even when neoclassical economists operate in complete abstractions of subjects and their surroundings, they operate with a specific ideal type institution of a perfectly informed, perfectly rational, fixed preferences motivated free market.

J. Lučev, *Systemic Cycle and Institutional Change*,
https://doi.org/10.1007/978-3-030-66053-6_3

This chapter explores possible contemporary theoretical venues and the models they employ. There is a number of alternative approaches to exploring the diversity in institutionalism: one could find an overview in Crawford and Ostrom (1995) discerning approaches focusing on *institutions-as-equilibria, institutions-as-norms*, or *institutions-as-rules*, while Tang (2011) discerns the *harmony paradigm* and *conflict paradigm* of approaches to institutions. This chapter will first focus on the various approaches in new institutionalism[2] in political science (historical institutionalism, rational choice institutionalism, sociological institutionalism) and on their methodological strengths and limitations—most notably the wide-spread blindness to endogenous institutional change.

Typologies of capitalism and/or of welfare regimes have proven to be a crucial genre in new institutionalism in political science. They employ an ideal-type-based research agenda which attempts to group different national institutional frameworks according to their similarities and at the

[2] The "newness" of new institutionalism and new institutional economics is in reference to older classical theory which did not sharply delineate institutional from political or economic thought and "old institutionalism" which found its focus in institutions, but was far less rigorous in its approach compared to the "new" options. Classical theory preceded the marginalist revolution and its conceptual implications. After the 1860s, and particularly after the neoclassical Marshallian synthesis of the 1890s, the mainstream was under the influence of the specific type of disembedded methodological individualism which relegated the micro-foundations of the economy onto a rational, perfectly informed individual, motivated by simple utility. However, preceding this development, it would have been difficult to delineate structure and agency in the sense it is done today. E.g. the writings of Adam Smith, simplified and caricaturized though they may be in the origin stories of modern liberalism, belonged to the old, embedded thought. His individual would not be solely under the influence of utility (or rapacity) but also under the influence of pre-existing social institutions (see Elsner 1989; Arrighi 2007: 40–68). Karl Marx (1979) is also a good example of embedded thought in that the economic analysis is contextualized in the social, historical, and institutional (see also Strpić 1998: 7–19; 2010: 13–37; 2015: 29–42). Following the marginalist revolution, the "old institutionalism" developed, epitomized by the writings of Max Weber, Thorstein Veblen, John Commons, and Karl Polanyi. Unlike the disembedded mainstream of social science, institutionalism emphasized the specific legal norms and cultural background to the subject of economic analysis. Parallel to this, the Austrian school developed its own views on what we would today consider institutions, focusing on the communication mechanisms implicit in the market and in the legal frameworks (Hayek 1945, 1990; see also Mises 1949; Schumpeter 2013). In political science, the study of formal institutions was a matter of course until the 1950s. As Lowndes laconically put it, before the behavioral revolution, "institutionalism was political science" (Lowndes 2005: 86). Supplanted by the new foci of behavioralism and rational choice it was not until the 1980s that institutionalism found its new voice in new institutionalism (ibid.: 86–87).

same type construct representative theoretical models of economies which supposedly describe the economies so grouped. This type of research sacrifices empirical exactness but enables an abstracted view of interconnectedness of various institutions as well as a focus on the differences in national approaches to markets and capitalism. This makes the typological approaches relevant and has contributed to their ubiquity. Arguably the most important and certainly very influential point of departure in comparative-static research is a *Varieties of Capitalism*-based view of two complementary institutional sets: the Liberal Market Economy (LME) and the Coordinated Market Economy (CME). This chapter will show that this approach was the pinnacle of new institutionalism in terms of our present needs. It has admirably created a logic of mutual interactions and complementarities between national-level institutions, which was a step in the right direction, as institutions were not limited to isolated analysis.

However, this approach has continued the new institutional difficulties with interpreting endogenous institutional change due precisely to its national-level unit of analysis, ideal-type-based research and the very logic of complementarity that made it successful. This chapter will also show the generations of research within the *Varieties of Capitalism* which recognized the flaws of the original formulation and worked to remedy them. Finally, the models and theories described here are utilized to identify three channels of institutional change: path dependence, intentional institutional design through formal political channels, and less formal political interactions leveraged by power relations. The first two channels are clearly researched, but the latter one will require developing, which this book will undertake using the systemic cycle theory on the transnational level in Chapters 4 and 5. Ultimately, the goal is to transcend the limitations of institutional change approaches which have hitherto functioned best as instruments of comparative statics, and formulating a new framework of comparative dynamics enabling the observing of endogenous institutional change. Finally, this framework will be applied to labor market institutions in the later chapters.

3.2 The Emergence of New Institutionalism in Political Science: Arguing Endogenous Stability

Political science has largely oriented itself toward functionalism and instrumental rationality in the first decades after World War II. These were the years of the behavioral revolution with the domination of rational choice approaches. A conceptual response to the reductivist limitations could be felt since the late 1970s and was succinctly and explicitly postulated by an influential article by March and Olsen (1983). This signaled a new movement toward the institutional context of political outcomes. While new institutionalism was developed on the basis of existing contributions in various social sciences it was also to manifest as a notable shift in political science, developing through several distinct approaches. The usual typology of new institutionalism mentions three approaches: historical, sociological, and rational choice institutionalism (Hall and Taylor 1996). Some authors tried to improve upon this three-pronged systematization of new institutionalism. Schmidt (2010) argued for a fourth, discursive new institutionalism, and Peters (1999) added four streams of thought to the original three (normative, empirical, interest representation, and international branches). This chapter will, however, follow the original triple division. This segment will survey these original branches of new institutionalism in order to critically confront their inability to deal with endogenous institutional change, but also to isolate useful elements of their respective theories.

3.2.1 *Rational Choice Institutionalism*

Rational choice institutionalism is linked to the neoclassical disembedded type of methodological individualism, in that the actors are generally assumed to have fixed preferences and behave instrumentally. In other words, this approach hinges on the earlier developments in social sciences, primarily economics. These are essentially assumptions and methods of dealing with the selected issues, as well as the framing of these issues. They enable rational choice institutionalism to delimit the scope and nature of its analysis, but also constrict importantly constrict its ability to deal with endogenous change. To frame it in briefest terms, modern rational institutionalism in political science is intertwined with new institutional economics (NIE). Both are crucially defined by game theory and transaction costs economics. These developments trace their heritage to the 1930s, which were a general period of breakthroughs for economics (Keynesian macroeconomics, neoclassical trade theory, monopolistic competition). In 1937, Ronald Coase created the theory of the firm which could be used by the mainstream economics. The reason why we have firms rather than mere individuals operating on the free market is the costs connected with using the price mechanism. Examples of such costs are the costs of information and negotiating contracts and they are largely diminished when long-term contracts can be in place (Coase 1937: 390–391), implying the existence of companies.

Eventually, the costs of using the price mechanisms became referred to as transaction costs. These could be internalized by including the client or supplier who hitherto existed as another agent on the market into the organizational structure of the company (e.g. purchasing another company). The internalization of transaction costs (or their diminishing through long-term contracts) is the *raison d'etre* of firms, so it is worthwhile to note that these costs do not exist in the simple neoclassical market structure models that informed the neoclassical trade theory. Specifically, the neoclassical perfect competition market structure describes efficient markets with perfectly informed rational agents which establish situations with maximum quantities consumed at lowest prices and no superprofit being possible. In these circumstances, producers are assumed to be small and extremely plentiful. The functioning of perfect competition (assumed by numerous neoclassical models including the Heckscher-Ohlin) would preclude bounded rationality, market failure, and the existence of companies of any significant size (as there would be no need for companies on perfect markets and also limited possibilities of capital accumulation). In describing transaction costs, Coase framed an important discussion on market failure and organizational and institutional emergence.

Building on Coase (1937, 1960) and his conceptualization of transaction costs as the basis of organizational emergence, effective institutions were defined as uncertainty and transaction cost reducing mechanisms (Wallis and North 1986; North 1990, 1991, 1994; see also Williamson 2000). Another development which greatly informed NIE has been the game theory (Neumann and Morgenstern 1944; Nash 1950), which has, for decades, focused on formal analysis of player strategies and resulting equilibriums. Such a focus on actors, their choices, and possible payoffs to their strategies in cooperative and non-cooperative games can be invaluable in understanding the evolution of institutions as such and their role in structuring agency. However, this approach is less useful in explaining how these institutions change as they are usually taken for granted in a scenario.

A far more nuanced and encompassing approach can be found with Douglass North. For North, institutions are essentially rules in a society, or humanly devised constraints that shape human interaction (North 1990: 3–4).[3] Institutions can be formal (laws and statutes) or informal (norms and customs, ways of doing business). In terms of development and change, some of them are created deliberately in order to create an incentive structure which can then guide behavior, while others evolve through behavior patterns (ibid.: 4). It is important to note that some subjects are effectively constrained by formal and informal institutions, and others are not (ibid.)—some organizations and individuals therefore develop strategies which revolve around the avoidance or circumvention of laws and norms. Actual institutions which structure agency should therefore in the Northian sense be conceptualized in the triangle of formal, informal, and inactive institutions. Or in other words, institutions do not necessarily apply universally in any given spatial unit, as some institutions do not constrict all players equally. In terms of institutional change, North describes the constriction of agency by institutional structures, which means that the best players will be the ones who invest in necessary skills and knowledge and can subsequently use these in order to change the institutional structure (North 1991: 108–109). This process is then a matter of constraining pressures that the structure exacts on the agents and pressures toward change that the most powerful agents can exact on the institutional structure. After such a change, the institutions exhibit tendencies of path dependence—i.e. a pronounced tendency to continue developing in the same direction as they have started to

[3] In this approach to institutions as rules, North mirrors other authors, most notably John Commons (1934/1959) who defined institutions as "Collective Action in Control of Individual Action" (ibid.: 69). Commons did not sharply distinguish organizations and institutions, but he did focus on incentives and disincentives as the "cause, effect, or purpose common to all collective action" which are understood as working rules enforced by collective sanctions (moral sanctions, gain/loss or physical force) which then determine what individuals "can, must, or may, do or do not do" (ibid.: 71). These individual actions which concern institutional economics as it is defined by Commons transcend the focus of "classical and hedonic" economics as they no longer concern themselves with "commodities, individuals and exchanges" but shift the unit of analysis to transactions between individuals and working rules which govern them (ibid.: 73).

develop in (North 1990: 103–104). This process is construed as historically contingent; "[i]f economies realize the gains from trade by creating relatively efficient institutions, it is because under certain circumstances the private objectives of those with the bargaining strength to alter institutions produce institutional solutions that turn out to be or evolve into socially efficient ones" (ibid.: 16).

Elinor Ostrom was another important researcher in this vein although her name is connected to both NIE and political science. Her definition of institutions is similar to North's: "institutions are the prescriptions that humans use to organize all forms of repetitive and structured interactions including those within families, neighborhoods, markets, firms, sports leagues, churches, private associations, and governments at all scales" (Ostrom 2005: 3). Institutional change is viewed as a problem of higher order rules, as any set of rules is "nested in another set of rules that define how the first set of rules can be changed" (Ostrom 2005: 58). *Operational rules* guide daily decisions, while *collective-choice rules* determine who the subjects of operational rules are, and these rules can change and *constitutional choice rules* do the same for collective-choice rules. Finally, there could also be a fourth, metaconstitutional level determining constitutional choice rules[4] (ibid.). In terms of labor institutions, the operational rules could be construed to mean a daily job description or task, the collective-choice rules are on the policy level arena which is what will interest this thesis (e.g. a law on labor), and the constitutional choice arena is a matter of rules that govern the policymaking (constitution, electoral law).

While her IAD (Institutional Analysis and Development) framework[5] was not intended to track institutional change, Ostrom's later work suggested guidelines for this following Donald Campbell. In order to

[4] Oliver Williamson (2000) also identifies four levels of institutions: L1 are norms, customs, and religion which change with a frequency of 100–1000 years, L2 are the formal rules of the institutional environment like polity and judiciary (it seems these represent aspects of Ostrom's collective choice and constitutional choice rules) and they change at the frequency of 10–100 years, L3 are contracts changing at the frequency of 1–10 years, and L4 are resource allocation and employment which change continuously (ibid.: 597).

[5] Ostrom distinguishes frameworks from theories and models and this distinction is crucial to the new framework of institutional change in Chapter 5 and its illustrations in Chapters 6, 7, and 8, but it is worth noting that this book also uses the term institutional framework, i.e. an interlocking set of institutions.

describe the evolutive process of institutional change Ostrom and Basurto explain that a variety of rules must first be generated. After this, the selection of rules based on performance and the retention of rules that perform better can take place (Ostrom and Basurto 2011: 333). Chapter 2 described the Arrighian perspective of systemic cycles and the organizational changes they engender. In doing so, Arrighi described a specific model of evolutive institutional change which is fully compatible with Ostrom's description. The generated varieties of rules are different organizational strategies (e.g. intensive and extensive), the selection based on performance is a matter of achieved trade positions (competitiveness) and higher growth rates. This evolution may, however, become stalled on the macro-level (or the constitutional choice arena). To fully drive the Darwinian metaphor home, this evolutionary process would require the retention process, implying the possibility of the eradication of institutions. On the macro-level, however, it is possible to encounter inefficient institutions which are very slow to change (corruption, authoritarian regimes).

Rational choice institutionalism describes institutions as solutions to collective action dilemmas mapped often after models like the *prisoner's dilemma* and focusing on strategic coordination calculus (Hall and Taylor 1996: 12–13, see also Shepsle 2006). Underlying the rational choice institutionalism is both game theory and New Institutional Economics, and the result can be a focus on stable equilibria rather than dynamic change which is not induced by an exogenous shock (Mahoney and Thelen 2010: 6). This is potentially a great handicap in viewing institutions as the equilibrium can be linked to the same neoclassical assumptions of market efficiency and actor rationality explored in Chapter 2. In the sense of rational choice institutionalism, the danger is viewing institutions as at least locally optimal (or at least optimal concerning local parameters) and therefore static in absence of exogenous change (i.e. change in these parameters). Examples of such works are Kandori (1992) and Hardin (1982) which are game-theoretical explanations of assuring cooperation (see also Greif and Kingston 2011).

Avner Greif and David Laitin are often pointed to as authors of a worthwhile attempt at bridging this gap. Greif and Laitin (2004) start with the traditional game-theoretical view of institutions-as-equilibria which explains institutions as results of strategies under external parameters. Strategies cannot change the parameters into which they are embedded[6] which can make game-theoretical endogenous institutional change a contradiction in terms (ibid.: 633). The institutions in traditional game theory could change only if the external parameters changed—as institutions are by definition optimal strategies to external parameters (ibid.). In response, they formulate a model of endogenous change within the game-theoretical view of institutions. Some endogenous aspects should be considered quasi-parameters which can be changed from within the game and can influence either the self-reinforcing (leading to stability) or self-undermining (leading to a break-down) nature of institutions[7] (ibid.: 636–640). Their contribution is a way of transcending the constricting assumptions of game theory in enabling games with parametric change—i.e. with endogenous institutional change even though it escaped the focus of earlier theory. It is worth noting that they could only do so by re-writing the traditional concepts of game-theory and enabling the bottom-up channel (i.e. the structuring elements of the game being influenced from within the game) apart from the usually exclusive top-down channel.

[6] Note the mentioned notions of rule embeddedness in Ostrom (2005) and Williamson (2000).

[7] A historical example used by Greif and Laitin to illustrate their theory is the comparison of the evolution of political institutions in medieval Venice and Genoa (as two of the most successful Italian maritime city-states). Both states were based on the power of clans (extended families)—and the initial political structure was similar (oligarchies electing magisters or podesta). However, in Genoa, the relationship between clans was substantially more competitive and the endogenous changes to quasi-parameters contributed to a worsening of outcomes. The first such change was the increase of economic prosperity (as a result of a solid political structure)—which increased inter-clan competition. The second such change was a result of greater competition which manifested in an arms race including the solidification of social networks and socialization of clan members into the loyalty to the clan (causing greater societal rifts). The political system was therefore self-enforcing, but for an ever-smaller number of possible situation (e.g. external threats). On the other hand, Venice has had the same problems with interclan rivalry, but as cooperation became necessary, clans became motivated to contain any clan which wanted to dominate, rather than to try to dominate themselves. The formal political institutions in Venice became oriented toward the weakening of the clans, which meant that this system was self-enforcing for an ever-increasing number of situations. In other words, it became self-reinforcing (Greif and Laitin 2004: 640–644).

3.2.2 *Sociological Institutionalism*

Sociological institutionalism focuses on culture as institutions, and serves as a worthwhile reminder that value and role systems structure agency as much as formal rules do (Hall and Taylor 1996: 14–17). Focusing on "noncodified, informal conventions and collective scripts that regulate human behavior" (Mahoney and Thelen 2010: 5), it explains the spread and resilience of norms rather than their change (ibid.). Like rational institutionalism, the limits of this approach are also the result of its conceptual foundations and intellectual history. Sociological institutionalism originated primarily in organizational theory in 1970s.

The strength of this approach lies in its avoidance of functionalism as institutional forms and procedures are understood not necessarily as results of attempts at rationality, but cultural practices like myths and ceremonies (Peters 1999: 25), where rationality is merely one of the possible goals or strategies. The emergence and stability of such practices is therefore similar to the transmission of cultural practices in general. Sociological institutionalism tends to focus on the self-replicating nature of social institutions. Either through socialization (where norms, values and patterns of behavior are passed down to younger generations only for them to pass them on further) or the unconscious acceptance of cognitive institutions (so taken for granted that the patterns are beyond scrutiny)—the patterns of behavior are stable and replicate themselves. The institution itself is largely indistinguishable from the meaning ascribed to it (Beckert 2010: 607) and therefore becomes stronger by the greater importance and more capacity being ascribed to it by its members through a greater sense of belonging to its cognitive frame. This suggests that sociological institutionalism is not well suited to explain institutional change inasmuch as it is concerned with cultural norms.

3.2.3 *Historical Institutionalism*

Finally, historical institutionalism originated as a departure from functional structuralism in the past decades. It elucidates power asymmetry and path dependence with broad historical strokes dependent on both the notions of utility and culture (see Hall 2010; Thelen and Steinmo 1992; Acemoglu and Robinson 2005, 2013). As Hall and Taylor summarize it, historical institutionalism is defined by four distinct traits: the tendency to conceptualize the relationship between institutions and individuals in terms of both rationality and socialization, the emphasis on political power, focus on path dependence and the integration of factors like socioeconomic development and ideas with institutional analysis (Hall and Taylor 1996: 7). Historical institutionalism was one of the voices in political science which contributed to the "temporal revolution" (Thelen and Mahoney 2015: 25) beginning in the 1990s which brought time once more into the mainstream. It seems to be best honed to issues of institutional change, and it has produced several structured attempts at tackling the issues of persistence and evolution. The emphasized eclectic conceptual nature of historical institutionalism is also a significant advantage. Regarding the distinction of institutions-as-rules, institutions-as-norms, and institutions-as-equilibria, Steinmo (2008: 125–126) argued that the first is an all-encompassing tendency of all three types of new institutionalism. The third view is clearly connected with rational choice institutionalism, and the second with sociological institutionalism. This leaves the concept of institutions in historical institutionalism as both norms and equilibria. This view can also be found in Hall and Taylor (1996: 8). Steinmo (2008) argues for historical institutionalism as an eclectic perspective where individuals should not be assumed to be merely rational calculating and strategic utility maximizers, not the blind followers of norms. All three approaches to institutions are needed to be able to respond to the historical record rather that to observe data through any specific conceptual lens. This argument is a consequence of the broad (almost synthetizing) conceptualization of institutions.

In terms of its analysis of institutional change, it tends to predict only very stable and monotonous change in absence of exogenous shocks, which means that it is difficult to expect solutions in endogenous institutional change. Historical institutionalism accentuates an interplay of path dependence and critical junctures. Path dependence conceptualizes the process of institutional change as highly predictable: "preceding steps in a particular direction induce further movement in the same direction" (Pierson 2000: 252). Pierson links this with the principle of "increasing returns," according to which "the relative benefits of the current activity compared with other possible options increase over time" (ibid.). In other words, the more a set of institutional arrangements develops, the better it can influence the economy but even more importantly, the costlier it becomes to switch to a different development path. Such a transition will also become costlier as the institutional development progresses along a certain path for political reasons. Institutions have winners and losers, and capturing the benefits of specific institutions can mean that a specific group has increased its resource stocks and flows and can now more effectively argue for the development along the same lines and prevent a switch to a different institutional strategy (Pierson 2015: 133–137).

A compatible concept is that on a *critical juncture*, which helps explain how an institution may change despite path dependence. Critical junctures are "major exogenous shocks and crises that disrupt the status quo and trigger fundamental institutional changes" (Campbell 2010: 92). A shock such as a crisis or a war shakes the foundation upon which the existing institutions are founded and may start off a movement in a different direction, starting to exploit increasing returns to a set of completely new set of institutions. This view is known also as a *punctuated equilibrium*—in which critical junctures create conditions for path-dependent movements toward new equilibriums. Punctuated equilibrium is originally a concept from biology (where it described the evolution of species) from where it was adapted into the described institutional concept by Krasner in the mid-1980s (see Streeck 2010: 663).

These developments spelt out a return of social science to institutional research. All of the three classical research venues of new institutionalism were valid in that they provided useful abstractions and categories for surveying the role of institutions. Therefore, none of the three may be ignored even today. However, all of them encountered substantial challenges in dealing with institutional change and as new institutionalism moved toward comparative capitalisms, these challenges carried over into this new agenda. This makes the successes and failures of new institutionalism important to bear in mind as we discuss the institutional side of national capitalisms.

3.3 Varieties of Capitalism: Systemic Institutional Thought

Institutional thought is indeed still "a boiling cauldron of ideas" (Williamson 2000: 610). However, the froth on the top of this boiling cauldron today belongs to typological research, which in the context of comparing capitalisms tends to build on Hall and Soskice (2001) and their Varieties of Capitalism (VofC).[8] Even those authors who contest the premises or conclusions of VofC have often found it necessary to start their own approaches with references to Hall and Soskice in the years since it was published (see Nölke 2016: 145). This approach is an influential hybrid of new institutionalisms which takes an ideal-typical research agenda to comparative political economy.

As a hybrid approach, Hall and Soskice recognize the conceptualizations of institutions in the three approaches to new institutionalism discussed above: the socializing function of institutions from sociological institutionalism (Hall and Soskice 2001: 13), the power-based view of institutions from historical institutionalism (ibid.) and institutions as formal and informal incentives and sanctions explicitly following Douglass North (ibid.: 9). To this they add the growing need to recognize institutions as strategic interactions from rational choice institutionalism (ibid.: 12–13). In other words, Hall and Soskice conceptualized institutions in accordance with preceding developments in new institutionalism—all of which had substantial problems with tracing institutional change. An unsurprising consequence is that VofC was itself to display the very same issue.

Hall and Soskice used these institutionalist conceptual insights in order to produce a framework of comparative capitalisms,[9] which was to become contested, but nevertheless by far the most important one in new institutionalism. In doing so, they explicitly attempted to move beyond the existing (in some cases far earlier) comparative approaches and argued against some of the tenets of existing theories that they found to be dominant and problematic: they attempt to move beyond the focus on the strength of states in modernization theory of Andrew Shonfield (1965), and wish to focus on the private sector; move beyond the exclusive focus on trade unions in neocorporatist literature of the 1970s and

[8] Hall and Soskice (2001) were not the only attempt to classify contemporary national economies or capitalisms—although they were in general most successful by far. A notable exception was the somewhat earlier classical contribution of Gosta Esping-Andersen (1990) which has had a somewhat narrower focus of welfare regimes. According to Google Scholar data, Esping-Andersen (1990) was cited 35,524 times and Hall and Soskice (2001) were cited by 14,984 scientific texts as of September 2020. Projects of comparable period and purpose have substantially fewer citations: Crouch and Streeck (1997) at 1230, Kitschelt et al. (1999) at 872, Wilensky (2002) at 896, and Amable (2003) at 3286.

[9] It is worth noting that many of the basic elements of this approach seem to be attributable to writings of David Soskice in the 1990s (see Hall 1999).

1980s and attempt to also take firms and employer organizations into account and finally, move beyond the social systems of production (innovation systems, production regimes, sectoral governance) from the 1980s and 1990s which focus on many levels of the political economy, while VofC considers only a strong orientation on national political economies appropriate (ibid.: 3–5). This last point is crucial, as it delimited the unit of analysis in what was to become the most important contemporary approach to comparative capitalisms.

The national level of economy is the appropriate level of analysis for VofC as Hall and Soskice argue that the most important institutions—labor market regulation, education and training, corporate governance are all "the preserve of the nation-state" (ibid.: 4). Clearly and explicitly, this approach finds capitalism in its institutions on the national level. This was a significant step in the right direction, as it enabled observing the systemic interactions of various institutions on the national level, replacing the limited focus on isolated institutions and economic areas. However, we will argue that the lack of a global perspective in the unit of analysis is one of the three principal reasons of the lack of an endogenous theory of change in VofC.

Nevertheless, the state-level focus combined with a subtle and encompassing theory of institutions made this approach useful for the comparative research of national institutions. The ideal types like those employed by VofC can in general be a useful tool in comparative statics as they abstract the simple form from the complex reality and therefore enable a sharp relief between similarities and differences in national institutional forms. However, the complex empirical reality is not only more diverse than the ideal types would lead one to believe, it is also constantly changing. In other words: "ideal types are fixed, empirical cases are moving" (Becker 2009: 12). The reliance on ideal types is the second principal reason for VofC having issues with the research of institutional dynamics.

The third principal reason stems from the elementary logic behind it. The key concept here is the complementarity of institutional arrangements in which "two institutions can be said to be complementary if the presence (or efficiency) of one increases the returns from (or efficiency of) the other" (Hall and Soskice 2001: 17). Therefore, the precondition for economic success of any given country is not any single institutional solution, but rather a consistent approach throughout the political economy.

There are five important political-economic areas that were initially identified as significantly affecting the overall complementarity. *Industrial relations* describes institutional arrangements which resolve bargaining over wages and working conditions between the firm and its labor. This process has a profound effect on the wage levels and productivity levels for the firm. *Vocational training and education* is the institutional sphere in which firms need to achieve a suitable skill level of its workforce, and workers need to decide the skills in which they will invest in and the level of this investment. *Corporate governance* describes institutional arrangement in which firms secure financing while investors seek returns on investment. *Inter-firm relations* are types of relationships formed between enterprises (suppliers, clients), encompassing issues of securing appropriate technology, demand for products and supplies for inputs. Finally, *employees* describe institutional arrangements which ensure the cooperation of employees with each other in the best interests of the firm while using their specific knowledge of the functioning of the enterprise itself (ibid.: 7).

The number of these areas has varied in accordance with the intent of specific research. Even the original contribution used schemes which removed employees as a special institutional sphere (ibid.: 28, 32), while later contributions introduced various other spheres (e.g. social protection and product market regulation in Hall and Gingerich 2009; and aggregate demand management systems in Carlin and Soskice 2009). The concept of complementarity hinges on the three institutional areas that the original authors emphasized in their insistence on the nation-state unit of analysis, i.e. corporate governance, industrial relations and education and training systems.

VofC produced a narrative according to which the crucial predictor of national competitiveness[10] and high rates of growth is the mutually complementary institutional alignment of the relevant areas. In other words, the more complementary the national regulatory framework is, the higher sustained growth rates we can expect from the economy it steers. The analysis of developed countries by Hall and Soskice revealed

[10] The full title *Varieties of Capitalism: The Institutional Foundations of Comparative Advantage* is a clear nod to Ricardo, whose concept of comparative advantage dominated mainstream ideas on trade throughout most of the nineteenth and twentieth centuries. Hall and Soskice were suggesting that national competitiveness has a strong foundation in institutions.

two principal types of such institutional consistency—the coordinated market economy (CME) as a more restrictively regulated and strategically oriented variety of capitalism and the liberal market economy (LME) as a more flexible variety oriented in the direction of free markets. CME path to efficiency and growth is based on specific skills formation, protected and organized labor markets and long-term bank-centric corporate governance systems. This was considered an adequate representation of Scandinavian countries, Germany, Austria, Switzerland, Belgium, the Netherlands, and Japan. On the other hand, LME countries base their institutional comparative advantage on general skill formation, flexible labor markets with low unionization, and short-term-oriented corporate governance with predominant stock-market financing. These were identified as USA, Canada, Ireland, UK, Australia, and New Zealand[11] (Hall and Soskice 2001: 19–21).

In general, these are ideal-typical institutional architectures which are themselves results of different political-economic organizations (long running corporatist tendencies in Europe, and a dismantling of an initially comparatively weak labor structures in the USA). The different economic results can most succinctly be postulated for a marginal case of a crisis, which inevitably brings severe pressures for a company. An LME will have corporate governance favoring profitability and the price of stocks, suggesting a need to keep the company "lean and mean." If demand should drop, the tendency will be to reduce the workforce, and the flexible labor market in combination with low labor organization will allow this to happen. As the workers have non-specific skill sets and do not typically represent irreplaceable assets for the company, which will therefore be prepared to lay them off. If a CME should experience a crisis, markets will react in the opposite way. The patient bank capital will not necessarily push for lay-offs, the companies see their employees as irreplaceable assets due to the educational investment they represent, the workers may easily be formally represented in the decision-making bodies of the company (e.g. through the German principle of codetermination) and are protected

[11] VofC has served as a worthy reminder of complexity with which social sciences are faced and served to revitalize this field in the context of simplistic free market policy recommendations, informed by either race-to-the-bottom globalism or one-size-fits-all type of free market ideal. The message was clear: even in the post-cold-war era of increasing trade and capital mobility there can be such a thing as effective strategic coordination (CME). In fact, more efficient developed countries follow this route than that of market coordination (LME).

by strong labor unions and a relatively rigid employment law. However, all of this suggests that workers cannot be easily laid off even in times of reduced demand. This suggests that profits and stock prices will be vulnerable.

The organizational premise and the result in terms of distribution can be vastly different in these two models. However, the central message of VofC is that both models work, and both can be used to produce high levels of growth. Corporate governance systems dictate the pressures toward investment returns, with the prevalent stock markets in LMEs dictating a fast tempo of returns with hostile takeovers as a constant threat and large banks with strategic stocks in CME allowing for a slower and less profit-oriented tempo of decision making. Consequently, an LME company faces short time-horizons caused by impatient stock-market investments and it pushes it in the direction of ensuring greatest possible profits/stock prices. Labor is weak and unprotected and cannot push back when the profit priority threatens it. At the same time, the education and training system suggests little sunk costs into the employee skill set—meaning that from the point of view of the company in an LME, labor can be easily disposed of in a crisis because there are pressures toward it, no protection or intrinsic motive to keep it. The opposite holds true for a CME company. Longer time horizons are made possible by the patient strategic investments, and the labor is not only well protected but also embodies sunk costs through the training system. Both LME and CME models offer viable survival strategies for companies, as they are complementary systems (all arrangements point in the same direction). The problem occurs when the institutional arrangements are not complementary. E.g. if the pressures from impatient capital should manifest, but the employment law is prohibitive, the unions are strong and/or the workers have specific skill sets useful to the company. In this case, the company would have to either suffer the consequences of diminished financing or incur various labor-related costs.

The framework offered by Hall and Soskice was both vastly successful and severely flawed. It offered concepts that were in line with the best new institutionalism had to offer and created an encompassing framework in which various institutional arrangements interact with each other. This enabled a national unit of analysis which used the point of view of a private sector company to identify the relevant institutional spheres in which it encounters coordination issues. The result was an institutional framework which could be portrayed in terms of prevalent strategies which are a result of formal and informal restrictions/rules (which is a complex consequence of the rational choice institutionalist concepts). But it also created an understanding of a very deep path dependence (an application of historical institutionalism restrictions), because the successful states were already reaping the benefits of institutional complementarity and therefore had no incentives to change. This section has argued that there are three methodological strategies of VofC which limit its possibility to explain endogenous change: apart from the logic of complementarity, there are the equally significant restriction connected to ideal-typical comparative-static research and the definition of capitalism as a phenomenon on the national level.

3.4 Beyond Varieties of Capitalism: Issues with Dynamics and Types

The limitations of VofC became apparent in the years following its publication, not least because national economies began to change in unpredicted ways, while the original framework offered limited possibilities in institutional change analysis. Andreas Nölke (2016) points out that the VofC agenda represented ground zero for contemporary comparative capitalism research (he treats the original VofC as the first generation of such research) and offers a survey of attempts to correct the original flaws which he sees as "binary orientation, exclusive focus on the supply side and neglect of common tendencies within contemporary capitalism" (Nölke 2016: 145). The second generation of research (post-VofC) focused on expanding the binary orientation by exploring new geographic areas not covered by the CME-LME binome and the third-generation critical comparative capitalism attempted to incorporate the demand side, and interaction of national capitalisms with each other (ibid.: 145–146). The aspirations of this thesis put it in the context of this, third generation of comparative capitalism research.

The authors understood by Nölke to belong in the second generation focused on type expansion and historical interpretation of these groups. Their research agenda started with the obvious recognition that not all developed economies correspond to the LME and CME descriptions. One type of attempt to address this problem has been to hypothesize new ideal types. The original contribution referred to a possibility of a Mediterranean group combining large agrarian sectors with liberal labor markets but non-market capacities in corporate governance (Hall and Soskice 2001: 21), while Schmidt (2003) has similarly argued for a third, French variety of capitalism.

The relatively recent EU members (since the 2004 expansion) in Central and Eastern Europe have proven to be another promising field of VofC research. These post-socialistic political-economies enjoyed in relatively steep growth rates before the 2009 contractions and attempts were made to link some of these with institutional-complementarities. Estonia, Latvia, and Lithuania were sometimes viewed as LME-type economies (Feldmann 2006; Buchen 2007; Bohle and Greskovits 2007, Lučev and Babić 2013), Slovenia was often, and Croatia sometimes, classified as kindred to the CME type (Feldmann 2006; Buchen 2007; Knell and Srholec 2007; Bohle and Greskovits 2007; Adams 2011; Lučev and Babić 2013). Also, Nölke and Vliegenthart (2009) called for an enlargement of VofC literature to encompass the Dependent Market Economy (DME) variety in Hungary, Poland, Czech, and Slovak Republics (mirrored also in Bohle and Greskovits 2007).

Another early criticism of VofC was directed at the discrepancies between the ideal-typical models and empirical situation, as the actual levels of complementarity differ even inside the CME and LME groups, and may change over time.[12] This was a clear effect of the conceptual limitations of ideal types as not all developed economies were identical with the VofC categorical apparatus used to group them, particularly as they changed over the course of time. The contention of this thesis is, however, that some developed countries do display certain important complementary institutional solutions. The focus of Chapters 6–8 will be on labor policy which was originally assumed to be oriented toward labor protection in well-defined CME cases and oriented toward labor flexibility in well-defined LME cases (Hall and Soskice 2001; Hall and Gingerich 2004). In such a research agenda, the idea of complementarity and the interlocking logic of institutional spheres still represents the best starting position for research.

In fact, the central idea of VofC remains the capability of a simultaneous existence of divergent national capitalist models which center of the USA and Germany as typical cases. In this, there is a striking similarity between VofC and alternative typologies of advanced capitalisms and

[12] For criticisms of the VofC framework along these lines see Becker (2007) and Blyth (2003) and Hancké et al. (2007) and for an explicit response to Blyth see Hall and Soskice (2003).

welfare regimes. The two genres of welfare regime and capitalism research are usually considered compatible due to both the notion of complementarity which underlies the logic of VofC and a certain overlap to groups of states that are grouped into types. Table 3.1 shows the groupings postulated by selected typologies, focusing on the position of Germany and the USA as the two cases of interest to this thesis which are easily typified.

Wilensky (2002) analyzed 19 developed countries and created a typology according to "national bargaining arrangements among major interest groups and government" (Wilensky 2002: 83). His typology bears a great resemblance to the VofC: the democratic corporatist group of cases encompasses Sweden, Norway, Austria, the Netherlands, Belgium, Finland, Denmark, Italy, Israel, and West Germany, meaning it excludes only Japan and Switzerland (and adds Israel and Italy) to the CME variety of capitalism in VofC, while 8 out of 10 cases remain the same. Japan, France, and Switzerland form Wilensky's Corporatism-without-Labor category, and his Least-corporatist category is a perfect overlap of the VofC LME group (US, UK, Canada, Australia, New Zealand, and Ireland).

On the other hand, Esping-Andersen (1990) created a seminal distinction of three welfare state regimes: Liberal, Corporatist-statist, and Social-democratic. His typology is not as explicit as the others discussed here as the analysis is more complex and encompasses several separate elements. Esping-Andersen preferred to use examples of "direct representatives" of these regimes: e.g. Germany for the Corporatist regime, the USA for the Liberal regime, and Sweden for the Social-Democratic regime (Esping-Andersen 1990: 192). It is important to note that Esping-Andersen argued that "welfare-state structures are systematically related to labor-market outcomes" (ibid.: 159), and that Social-Democratic countries are devoted to maximizing labor supply through promoting both female labor participation and low labor exit rates, while Corporatist states maintain lower labor supply through incentivizing exit rates and Liberal states promote neither female participation nor exit rates (ibid.).

These influential typologies do not have significant problems with discussing the similarities and differences of the USA and Germany. All of them place them in different categories emphasizing the relative orientation to free markets (e.g. commodification/decommodification) with the USA always fitting into the free market-oriented type and Germany fitting into the decommodified/coordinated type. In fact, while these typologies construe their types around different policies and arrangements, they

Table 3.1 Typologies of capitalism in institutional literature

Typology (original number of types)	*Type including the USA*	*Type including Germany*	*Other types*
Esping-Andersen, 1990 (3)	Liberal	Corporatist-statist	Social-democratic (Scandinavian)
Hall and Soskice, 2001 (2)	Liberal Market Economy	Coordinated Market Economy	Various expansions as discussed above
Wilensky, 2002 (3)	Least-corporatist	Democratic Corporatism	Corporatism-without-Labor
Amable, 2003 (5)	Market-based capitalism	Continental-European capitalism	Asian capitalism, Social-democratic capitalism, Mediterranean capitalism
Becker, 2009 (5)	Liberal	Corporatist	Statist, Meso-communitarian, Patrimonial
Beramendi et al. 2015 (4)	Competitiveness-Oriented Capitalism	Status-Oriented Capitalism	Capture-Oriented Capitalism, Equality-Oriented Capitalism

mostly accept the USA and Germany as representative cases. However, these typologies are mostly focused on the developed world with long corporatist and/or democratic traditions (e.g. old OECD members). The categorical apparatus they develop is therefore challenging for adaptation to very specific cases like the People's Republic of China, which is neither democratic nor corporatist in the western sense of these words and which combines an ideologically charged one-party system with many free market institutional solutions. The easier option is to discard any attempt of meaningful comparison of Germany, USA, and China along the lines of VofC. But this option would rob us of a better understanding of the similarities and differences of the old developed world and one of the most important and largest political economy of the world. Chapter 8 will go the harder route and strive to analyze China with the VofC matrix in mind in order to better outline its specificity.

Finally, the years since the global recession of 2009 have brought forth various research that focuses on the role of the global economy (therefore transcending the national unit of analysis) and demand-side issues (Nölke's third generation of comparative capitalist researchers). An important expansion of the VofC research agenda has been the incremental addition of various institutional arrangements into the original framework. These have already included social protection, product market regulation, and electoral systems, but this wave of research also included aggregate demand management regimes, which are particularly important during economic downturns. As Soskice (2007: 89–90) and Carlin and Soskice (2009: 21) pointed out, there are substantial institution-based differences among countries in the aggregate demand management during crises. LME countries are supposed to be inclined toward fiscal expansion and other forms of anti-cyclical economic policy. CME, on the other hand, are supposed to be inclined toward conservative, pro-cyclical policies. In other words, CME countries would naturally enact fiscal consolidations in face of falling GDP. There are significant aberrations, as Scandinavian countries and Japan tend to act fiscally expansionary (Carlin and Soskice 2009: 21–22). This agenda became significant in the specific transnational context of EMU as new VofC research suggested the frictions between EMU level prescriptions and national trade unions or fiscal and monetary preferences (Hancké 2013; Iversen et al. 2016; Hall 2017). Other authors have expanded the ideal type structure in order to include the states more heavily dependent on the international economy (Nölke and Vliegenthart 2009; Nölke et al. 2015). Still others have connected comparative political economy and international political economy to note that the absence of a stronger international financial regime may well be a consequence of different preferences based in domestic institutional frameworks (Kalinowski 2013). What all of these have in common is the attention given to the transnational/international arena and a greater understanding of demand-side issues. This latter issue was most significantly opened by a recent debate sparked by the critique of comparative political economy as insensitive to growth models. Baccaro and Pontusson (2016) have interpreted the comparative literature of the 1980s and 1990s as heavily influenced by the anti-Keynesian, pro-market shift in economics (ibid.: 4). The result was that most of the VofC literature did not account for demand factors, choosing instead to focus on supply-side elements as necessitated by its general firm-centric approach. This approach may do very well in discovering and describing institutional restraints and incentives as experienced by a firm, in other words an individual actor that is in the micro-economic focus. This is fully compatible with the economic mainstream since the 1970s, which accentuates micro-founded, supply-side phenomena. However, it is not always well suited to uncover the demand-side issues accentuated by macroeconomics. In an attempt to further the comparative political-economic agenda, Baccaro and Pontusson identify (primarily) export and consumption-led growth patterns in developed countries. These are essentially paths of institutional change following the crisis of the Fordist wage-led growth pattern prevalent in the Western world until the 1970s (ibid.: 24). This article prompted two very different types of responses. Wolfgang Streeck (2016) pointed out that VofC types have always been a kind of historical snapshot (Streeck 2016: 244), rather than a valid description of economic functioning of developed countries. Streeck interprets Baccaro and Pontusson (2016) as "dealing a death blow to the so-called firm-centered [...] concept of 'capitalist' diversity" (Streeck 2016: 244)—in other words to VofC literature. In this interpretation, Streeck continues his own criticism of VofC as overly focused on the differences, rather than convergences of modern capitalism (Streeck 2010, 2011). On the other hand, David Soskice (one of the original editors of the Varieties of Capitalism project) was involved in a rather different response, claiming that Baccaro and Pontusson are "wholly consistent with and ultimately dependent upon varieties of capitalism" (Hope and Soskice 2016: 3), as a broadening to a wider set of advanced economies shows the significance of VofC with the export-led economies proving to be CME economies, and consumption-led economies being LME economies (ibid.: 4). Lucio Baccaro has since continued his promising project of integrating growth models and institutional analysis, most notably with his coauthored book (Baccaro and Howell 2017), which analyzes the institutions of industrial relations since the late 1970s focusing on Britain, France, Germany, Italy, and Sweden, arguing for a common neoliberal trajectory involving an increase of employer discretion in all of these countries (ibid.: 197).

The previous section has argued that the original VofC framework was ill-equipped to deal with issues of institutional change due to three methodological factors: the ideal-type research strategy, the national unit of analysis, and the logic of complementarity. This section has shown that the years of research following the original publication have relaxed the crucial obstacles: various authors have begun approaching the VofC scheme by exploring new varieties of capitalism and questioning the monolith and unchanging nature of the old, by acknowledging the shortcomings of the merely national level. This suggests that the time is ripe for theories of institutional change which can use the complementarity without understanding it as contributing to only two local optimums of CME and LME and without understanding it as immutable. Such theories are crucial to us, as they create the ability to observe national level institutions of capitalism and are sensitive to their changes or even able to predict the course of change. The following section will survey the existing approaches to institutional change in new institutionalism, both within and outside the logic of VofC.

3.5 Toward a New Framework: Comparative Dynamics in New Institutionalism

This section will survey the several promising ways of thinking about institutional change in new institutionalism. Firstly, there is the sometimes overly simplistic, but otherwise sound logic of path dependence. As we have seen in the first two sections, the study of institutions tends to emphasize their enduring and unchanging nature, and they can conceivably do so for good reasons (Djelic 2010: 27). Path dependence is a useful concept in terms of explaining institutional stability even in the presence of external pressures. It can help explain why different systems tend to move in the direction in which they have started. However, institutions operate in a system of varied trade, technology, and politics-related pressures which influence the returns on specific paths. This suggests that in a simplified sense, one could foresee the imperviousness of current institutional arrangements as they are influenced by path dependence and supported by norms which are slow to change. One could expect a system which has begun to invest in CME-type institutions to remain on this path and continue to invest as the system would start facing increasing returns as the institutional framework sufficiently develops. To switch to an LME-type path would mean a costly dismantling of many CME elements before new regulations could be put into place and much time lost before growth rates respond to the new LME-type economy. However, it should be noted that CME and LME arrangements as documented by Hall and Soskice (2001) reflect particular power relations and a particular sectoral employment stratification which in turn reflects a specific historical technological situation. Any of these can change and therefore influence the strength with which path dependence asserts itself on the process of institutional development.

These concepts are certainly not without value and can help explain many cases of institutional change. Chapters 4 and 5 will develop these elements in the sense useful for the analysis of change in labor institutions in the three chapters that follow. E.g. in the case of labor institutions in Germany, the critical junctures were at least the reunification of 1990, which brought a different and challenging structure of labor, the adoption of euro in the 1999, which started an era of sustained trade surpluses for Germany and ushered in further deepening of the European project. However, it would be dangerously misleading to stop at the punctuated equilibrium as a model of change, as it hinges on internal stability in absence of exogenous shocks that actually propel change. Such a description bears a semblance to the neoclassical approach to growth. The neoclassical approach is curiously atemporal as it focuses on long-term timeframes with assumptions of efficient markets and rational individuals. In doing so, the mainstream of economics tends to take the static equilibrium as the conceptual fundament of its analysis and transplant it into the concept of growth which necessitates some concept of time. Likewise, the described simplistic account of institutions could take the static institution as the conceptual fundament and transplant it into the concept of institutional change as endogenously predictable.

Both approaches would then need exogenous shocks to account for fluctuations—in growth because crises are neither theoretically covered nor visible in the long run and in institutional analysis due to path-dependent scenarios. This description also bears a resemblance to rational-choice institutionalism, which assumes that strategies in iterated games reach an optimal point of equilibrium which represents institutions themselves. In absence of an exogenous change in parameters, the strategies do not change as they are already optimal. As noted above, Greif and Laitin (2004) make an interesting conceptual foray into endogenous change that is compatible with the idea of institutions-as-equilibria. However, while intriguing, it remains a descriptive rather than predictive tool.

The second way of thinking about institutional change is modes of change—also mostly centering on descriptions. Particularly of interest to this thesis is the work of Kathleen Thelen on varieties of liberalization, where various pressures connected with movements toward the deregulation of labor markets are aggregated into very different reforms in different institutional settings. This research has started in co-authorship with Wolfgang Streeck, one of the staunch critics of VofC, but has eventually been used to explicitly explain the different patterns of change in VofC terms. Kathleen Thelen and her co-authors (2014; Streeck and Thelen 2005; Mahoney and Thelen 2010) define five modes of institutional change. These are *displacement*, *layering*, *conversion*, *drift*, and *exhaustion*. The size of that list and focus of these categories has changed over the years. Table 3.2 summarizes the definitions tracks the differing focus.

Displacement is a model of institutional change in which new institutions form and replace the old ones (Streeck and Thelen 2005: 19–22; Mahoney and Thelen 2010: 16). In her 2014 volume on varieties of liberalization, Thelen compared the USA, Germany, and Denmark across three comparative dimensions: Industrial relations, Vocational Education and Training (VET), and Labor market policy. She argues that displacement is largely applicable to institutional change in US institutions. It is a typical process of pure deregulation, or a direct attack on the existing institutional arrangements. The USA always lacked strong coordinating capacities in industrial relations, but the trajectory of liberalization in recent decades saw a collapse of extant unions and collective bargaining and an erosion of real values of statutory minimum wages and benefits. Other institutional domains seem to carry traits of risk individualization and recent developments in education are focused on increasing college enrollment, but without care for successful completion. Education system therefore goes a long way in preserving the socio-economic *status quo* and

Table 3.2 The evolution of models of change in Kathleen Thelen

	Streeck and Thelen (2005)	*Mahoney and Thelen (2010)*	*Thelen (2014)*
Displacement	In sociology, "new models emerge and diffuse which call into question existing, previously taken-for-granted organizational forms and practices" and in political science "the emphasis is typically more on political than on cognitive or normative factors, with change emanating mostly from shifts in the societal balance of power" (p. 19) Mechanism: **defection**	Change is led by insurrectionaries (enabled by weak veto power of defenders of *status quo*, low levels of discretion in interpretation of institutional rules)	direct attack on the existing institutional arrangements, largely descriptive of US liberalization
Drift	"institutions require active maintenance; to remain what they are they need to be reset and refocused, or sometimes more fundamentally recalibrated and renegotiated, in response to changes in the political and economic environment in which they are embedded." Without it they may experience erosion or atrophy through drift (p. 24) Mechanism: **deliberate neglect**	Change is led by parasitic symbionts (enabled by strong veto power of defenders of *status quo*, high levels of discretion in interpretation of institutional rules)	dualization processes typical of Germany—a tendency to continued protection of insiders, coupled with a disregard for new social risks on the periphery

(continued)

Table 3.2 (continued)

	Streeck and Thelen (2005)	*Mahoney and Thelen (2010)*	*Thelen (2014)*
Conversion	"institutions are not so much amended or allowed to decay as they are *redirected to new goals, functions, or purposes*" (p. 26) It is a result of new environmental challenges or changes in power relations. Mechanism: **redirection, reinterpretation**	Change is led by opportunists (enabled by weak veto power of defenders of *status quo*, high levels of discretion in interpretation of institutional rules)	*conversion* describes institutional changes toward embedded flexibilization typical of Denmark, which reorient institutions in order to collectivize risks in accordance with shifting social coalitions
Layering	Vested interests behind existing old institutions are circumvented by adding another layer of institutions. "The actual mechanism for change is **differential growth**; the introduction of new elements setting in motion dynamics through which they, over time, actively crowd out or supplant by default the old system as the domain of the latter progressively shrinks relative to that of the former" (p. 24)	Change is led by subversives (enabled by strong veto power of defenders of *status quo*, low levels of discretion in interpretation of institutional rules)	
Exhaustion	"institutional exhaustion is a process in which behaviors invoked or allowed under existing rules operate to undermine these." Mechanism: **depletion**		

similarly, the diminutive active labor measures are limited to a short-term perspective and aimed at securing any form of jobs (see Chapter 6).

Drift as a type of institutional change occurs when the existing institutions remain stable, but exogenous events change their context and outcomes (Streeck and Thelen 2005: 24–26; Mahoney and Thelen 2010: 17).[13] This mode of change occurs when the existing institutions remain stable, but exogenous events change their context and outcomes. She argues that it describes dualization processes typical of Germany—a tendency to continued protection of insiders, coupled with a disregard for new social risks on the periphery (Thelen 2014: 47–58). While German industrial relations appear to remain typical of a CME invested in high skills, a strong social partnership in the manufacturing core of the economy with high unionization rates conceals low union coverage for the emergent service sector. Changes in the education system complement these developments. The high-quality apprenticeship model is today challenged by the growth of the service sector (not based in specific skills required in manufacturing) and a drop in apprenticeship slots available. Regardless of a continued need for institutional reform to remedy this, the traditional institutions were generally defended resulting in poor distributive effects with the winners and losers distinguished early in their careers. Germany also witnessed a substantial growth of a low-wage sector (after Hartz reforms 2002–2005) with substantial deregulation of agency work, fixed-term and "mini jobs" even as the well-protected blue-collar core was preserved (see Chapter 7).

Layering is a form of change in which new rules and arrangements are instituted alongside old ones (Streeck and Thelen 2005: 22–24; Mahoney and Thelen 2010: 16–17). Layering essentially involves "amendments, additions, or revisions to an existing set of institutions" (Streeck and Thelen 2005: 22) which may suggest an active competition between two sets if institutions, with the new sometimes able to "crowd out or supplant by default the old system as the domain of the latter progressively shrinks relative to that of the former" (ibid.).[14] *Conversion* is a mode describing

[13] It should be noted that the concept of institutional drift appears in different form elsewhere. Acemoglu and Robinson (2013) discuss institutional drift as a process of gradual institutional divergence between various localities (ibid.: 108–109).

[14] Chapter 8 shows that institutional change in China exhibits some signs of layering at the macro-level with the "old" Party goals sometimes clashing with "new" elements of the capitalist system.

the type of change in which the old institutions remain in place but begin serving new purposes (Streeck and Thelen 2005: 26–29; Mahoney and Thelen 2010: 17–18). It may be a result of exogenous change "to which policymakers respond by deploying existing institutional resources to new ends" (Streeck and Thelen 2005: 26), or a result of changes in power relations implying that new actors may take the institution "over and turn it to new ends" (ibid.). This mode of change is said to typify the evolution of labor institutions in Nordic countries, which Thelen showed on the example of Denmark (Thelen 2014). Finally, *exhaustion* describes the gradual breakdown of existing institutions (Streeck and Thelen 2005: 26–29).

Mahoney and Thelen (2010) go a step further and connect the modes of change with the political context, institutional characteristics (particularly the level of discretion in interpretation and enforcement), and the likely type of agents of change. Specifically, displacement typically occurs where the defenders of old institutional arrangements have weak veto possibilities (cannot prevent change), and the levels of discretion in institutional interpretation are low (existing institutions cannot be reinterpreted). In this context, insurrectionaries can deregulate existing arrangements and possibly institute their new versions. They do so as defenders of old institutions have strong veto power (and institutions cannot be changed outright), but there are high levels of discretion in interpretation of institutions, meaning the institutions can be reinterpreted rather than changed. Parasitic symbionts are the actors that typically guide drift, as they require the formal status quo to continue but wish to alter the spirit of the institution.

Conversion typically occurs where the defenders of existing institutions have weak veto power (institutions can be changed), high levels of discretion in interpretation (institutions can also be reinterpreted). The actors that thrive in such an environment may be described as opportunists as they are able to recycle the prevailing rules in order to suit their own purposes. Finally, layering occurs as the defenders of existing institutions have strong veto power (cannot be directly attacked) and in the context of low levels of discretion in interpretation (cannot easily be reinterpreted)—this requires both the form and content of old institutions to remain unchanged, but an alternative may be set up alongside it. The typical agents of change are subversives, who operate within the system and set up rules on the margins of old arrangements, which may then proliferate and coexist as an alternative to the older arrangement (ibid.: 14–29). Thelen's research was groundbreaking in that it connected types of agents, patterns of change, and varieties of capitalism in order to explain the changing national-level capitalisms beyond what was possible in the original VofC framework. However, her work has remained locked in the national unit of analysis and is largely descriptive, mostly dealing with how changes take place rather than explaining why institutions change.

The third common way of thinking about institutional change is evolutionary analogies. We have seen that they were a staple of institutional thought (Commons and Ostrom), but recent authors feel Darwinism has not yet been sufficiently conceptually tapped. The described tendency of social sciences toward equilibriums was particularly worrying for Sven Steinmo who saw it as an application of a static physical concept to a very dynamic social reality. Steinmo acknowledges the relatively recent tendencies in evolutionary narratives in historical institutionalism including the work of Streeck, Thelen, and Pierson. However, he argues for a better inclusion of biological evolutionary concepts as more applicable to complex adaptive systems with complex causation (Steinmo 2010: 7–10), as institutions could essentially be thought of as "genes of society" (ibid.: 219), which can be subject to evolution. In doing so, he utilizes explicit analogies from evolutionary science. The spread of US institutions through Northern America is likened to allopatry, which is an evolution of a splintered species in a new environment, sometimes in conditions of explosive and unchallenged growth (ibid.: 25). Another example is exaptation, which is a type of evolution where old features adopt new roles (e.g. feathers first serving for thermoregulation and then for flight). Steinmo suggests that exaptation can be used to illustrate institutional change as layering (where new and old institutions can coexist) as described in Streeck and Thelen (2005) and described below. As related in Table 3.2, exaptation would more easily be compared to change as conversion where an institution transforms to take new forms. Perhaps Steinmo sees exaptation as layering because he uses it to illustrate the evolution of Japanese institutions as a hybrid mix of old and new and imposed American type institutions after World War II (Steinmo 2010: 110–111, 151).

Tang also explains institutional change as an evolutionary process consisting of five phases: generation of ideas, political mobilization, struggle for power, setting the rules, and legitimatization/stabilization/reproduction. These phases represent the biological evolution elements of variation (mutation), selection (variation reduction), and inheritance: with phase 1 corresponding to mutation, phases 2 and 3 to selection, and phases 4 and 5 to inheritance (Tang 2011: 34).[15] This generalized Darwinistic insight mirrors other applications of evolutionary narrative onto institutional change and is a welcome insight into how institutional change may take place. Nevertheless, it is necessary to identify specific phases of selection, and some institutional processes may have few of them. A socially suboptimal institution like corruption, clientelism or the governance patterns focused on the rent-extraction of predatory elites may be preserved indefinitely. They may cause great harm

[15] There are obviously a number of approaches focusing on Darwinistic evolutions as an analogy of institutional change. This type of analogy has a very long history—at least since John Commons (1934/1959), who did not necessarily focus on change, but did explain it in passing as an evolutionary process: "custom is the mere repetition, duplication and variability of practices and transactions" (ibid.: 44–45), this variability produces both alternative customs and the elimination of some customs, which suggest a "survival of customs fitted to the changing economic conditions and the changing political and economic dominance" (ibid.). This process is in fact, explicitly "much like the artificial selection of Darwin's evolution" (ibid.). Why should evolutionary analogies then be construed as essentially new and under-used? The answer may lie in the assumptions of neoclassical economics that Chapter 2 has already described. In the context of business cycles and development, this approach can either be focused on the atemporal micro-perspective (supply and demand equilibrium where all bargaining has already taken place in an undefined time-period) or on the atemporal long-term perspective (long-term growth where crises can be averaged out and assumed away as statistical aberrancies). Likewise, in the institutional analysis, one can focus on the essentially atemporal micro-perspective (institutions-as-equilibria, where bargaining has already taken place, and parameters are exogenous) or on the essentially atemporal long-term perspective focusing on stability through notions of critical junctures and path dependence. The result of the first set of somewhat simplified views is that markets are inherently efficient, and the result of the second set is that institutions are inherently stable. Both would then explain any empirical inconsistency as a consequence of an external shock and remain blind to endogenous change. These tendencies are also often implicit in the game-theoretical institutionalism hinging on New Institutional Economics and VofC as the developed genre in new institutionalism in political science. In game theory this is due to reliance on institutions-as-equilibria changing as a result of higher order rules/parameters suggest the elementary inability to process endogenous change—as it must come from beyond the game itself. The exception presented by Greif and Laitin (2004) was possible only through a successful redefining of core concepts. On the other hand, VofC is over-reliant on static ideal types and defines successful institutions as parts of an institutional complementary framework. This suggests mutual reinforcement of institutions and their probably static nature in absence of exogenous shocks. While evolutionary narratives have been present as an alternative, institutional theory always seems to revert to the static due to its methodological constraints.

to the well-being of citizens or growth and development of the economy. However, that does not suggest that there are mechanisms in place that can select an alternative. If these mechanisms can be identified, then the evolutionary perspective can be used to describe change. However, it can scarcely be used to predict change. The clue is in Steinmo's research strategy which focuses on societies and defines them as complex adaptive systems. These are, by definition, unpredictable.

The fourth way to think about change is to connect it with power. Power in a social/political sense is in social sciences often reduced to its sterilized and visible version of electoral politics. However, we must also recognize the power element at play in the typologies of national capitalism varieties. Colin Crouch sees capitalism typologies as implicitly following a logic of compromises between opposing political forces (Crouch 2010: 133). What he is referring to is the power resource theory well represented by the works of Walter Korpi. Power resource theory sees institutions "largely as the residues of previous activations of power resources, often in the context of manifest conflicts which for the time being have been settled through various types of compromises" (Korpi 1985: 38). These institutions do not change when there is a pronounced asymmetry of power favoring their current form, but when this asymmetry weakens there can be another conflict between various groups with various powers eventually solidifying in another compromise, i.e. in institutional change (see Korpi 2001, 2006; Pierson 2015: 127–128). This basic insight is not contrary to either rational choice analysis or Varieties of Capitalism, and Korpi has entered into a dialogue with both approaches (Korpi 2001, 2006). Nevertheless, there is a tendency to overlook power vested in groups whenever we focus on the top-down models of policy reform or on the simplistic models of social cooperation via game equilibria, or the inherent stability of institutions. Pierson explains this blindness to power as a result of the preferred "atomized and micro orientations of contemporary research" in social sciences which prevents the systematic research of influence (Pierson 2015: 128). This presents us with a significant issue, as power resources certainly must be taken very seriously by any theory that wishes to understand the dynamics of institutional change. The power resources must therefore be studied in order to predict their fluctuation and the end result of their activation.

Finally, the fifth way of thinking of institutional change is the change by deliberate design via formal political channels. Here, we need a theory connecting electoral politics (for democracies) with institutional change. The last few years have brought a renewed interest in electoral politics in new institutionalism (including Hall 2018; Iversen and Soskice 2015; Rovny and Rovny 2017; Lefkofridi and Michel 2017). Within this context, an intriguing new approach has been suggested by Beramendi et al. (2015) who link the political party systems and electoral constraints with the general logic of VofC.[16] They point out that parties increasingly move away from old ideological models and construct their policies in line with particular constituencies they represent. The authors limit themselves to four key class groups in the developed world: low-skilled wage earners, socio-cultural professionals (employed in public or nonprofit organizations, typically with high education), business-finance professionals (typically with high education, high earnings, and finance assets), and petty bourgeoisie (self-employed, owners of small enterprises, typically with low education and relatively high income) (ibid.: 21–22). Firstly, the specific sets of institutions are a function of historical power resource distribution and the class structure is a function of institutions (ibid.: 24). Secondly, various reform projects that could be undertaken in these arenas reflect the possible coalitions between the four classes and their interests. Coalitions of either low skilled labor and business-finance professionals or petty bourgeoisie and socio-cultural professionals are considered impossible as they have interests which are too divergent to be able to find common ground in any given reform (ibid.: 55–57). This model has some obvious failings based in its ideal-typical nature. However, it admirably copes with the limitations of the VofC framework in that it includes both politics (agency) and reform (institutional change) which are significant steps in the right direction.

[16]As we have seen, referring to VofC has become inevitable, as it represents the most successful venue of modern comparative research. However, Beramendi et al. (2015) also build upon Kitschelt et al. (1999), an edited volume which anticipated Hall and Soskice (2001) in some respects and included chapters by David Soskice and Peter Hall, both of which discussed what was to become the VofC agenda. The volume was more in tune with issues of change and even ended with a *croquis* of a model of institutional change which even included internationalization of finance and trade patterns. Had this volume been more successful, we might not have had to wait for a decade and a half to further the agenda on institutional change. As it were, this model remained merely an afterthought, while the dominant VofC agenda used complementarity and ideal types to steer research in a static direction.

As we have seen, all these models leave something to be desired in view of developing a theory of endogenous institutional change with predictive capabilities. However, these five models can each explain a facet in a larger picture embedded in a higher-level unit of analysis. Evolutionary narratives and modes of change both explain how institutions change rather than why they change. This suggests that they may be useful as tools of analysis, but they do not offer any predictive capabilities. Path dependence (particularly through the notions of institutional complementarity) and deliberate institutional design via formal political channels are both clearly elements of institutional stability and change. Power relations are an important, but underdeveloped predictor of change which can benefit from a theory predicting the fluctuations of power. We have outlined such a theory in the systemic cycle in Chapter 2 and will further develop it in Chapter 4 in order to make it compatible with a framework of institutional change.

3.6 Conclusion

This chapter has outlined the central issues of institutional change in new institutionalism. It has first shown the foundations of new institutionalism through rational choice, sociological and historical institutionalism and their respective issues with explaining institutional change—with rational choice institutionalism focusing on optimization problems, sociological institutionalism on the spread and resilience of norms and historical institutionalism on path dependence. These three approaches do deal with change, but it must mostly be understood as exogenous. In other words, these approaches could mostly explain the effects of change, but not when and why the institutional change occurs. Then, this chapter dealt with the literature on comparative capitalisms, focusing on varieties of capitalism and the generations of research it engendered. The endogenous change issue persisted through the crucial logic of institutional complementarity within VofC. However, developments in recent years brought some novel solutions. The last section of this chapter identified five common or promising ways to conceive institutional change: evolutionary approaches, electoral approaches, power resource approaches, path dependence approaches, and mode of change approaches.

Even in most recent literature, many authors have attempted to approach the issue of institutional change in order to offer models of change—although successful descriptions of endogenous change remain scarce. Chapters 4 and 5 will interpret and use the models explained in this chapter to construct a new framework of institutional change utilizing Arrighian concepts in the hope of adding to these voices. This maneuver will enable the explicit inclusion of global processes in institutional change by broadening the unit of analysis beyond the restrictive national setting. The endogeneity of change will therefore be conceptualized in a much wider system than that presented by most games or institutional models. After all, the institutional changes we hope to explain are often also results of processes internal only to the world-system and not to national or local levels. To do so, we will utilize the channels of institutional change identified in this chapter. Path dependence and political/electoral outcomes will be used alongside an interpretation of power relations that utilizes the insights from Chapter 2. This will, after conceptual clarifications of the next chapter, be used in the new framework of institutional change in Chapter 5. Thelen's modes of change and evolutionary analogies will be revisited in Chapter 9 in order to observe the patterns from Chapters 6–8.

Literature

Acemoglu, D., & Robinson, J. A. (2005). *Economic Origins of Dictatorship and Democracy*. New York: Cambridge University Press.

Acemoglu, D., & Robinson, J. A. (2013). *Why Nations Fail: The Origins of Power, Prosperity and Poverty*. New York: Crown Business.

Adams, J. (2011). *The Political Economies of Slovenia and Croatia: Does EU and Eurozone Membership Play a Role at All?*. EUSA 2011 conference: Boston.

Amable, B. (2003). *The Diversity of Modern Capitalism*. Oxford University Press.

Arrighi, G. (2007). *Adam Smith in Beijing*. London: Verso.

Baccaro, L., & Howell, C. (2017). *Trajectories of Neoliberal Transformation: European Industrial Relations Since the 1970s*. Cambridge: Cambridge University Press.

Baccaro, L., & Pontusson, J. (2016). Rethinking Comparative Political Economy: The Growth Model Perspective. *Politics & Society, 44*(2), 175–207.

Becker, U. (2007). Open Systemness and Contested Reference Frames and Change: A Reformulation of the Varieties of Capitalism Theory. *Socio-Economic Review, 5*(2), 261–286.

Becker, U. (2009). *Open Varieties of Capitalism: Continuity, Change and Performances*. Basingstoke: Palgrave Macmillan.

Beckert, J. (2010). How Do Fields Change? The Interrelations of Institutions, Networks, and Cognition in the Dynamics of Markets. *Organization Studies, 31*(5), 605–627.

Beramendi, P., Häusermann, S., Kitschelt, H., & Kriesi, H. (Eds.). (2015). *The Politics of Advanced Capitalism*. Cambridge: Cambridge University Press.

Blyth, M. (2003). Same as It Never Was: Temporality and Typology in the Varieties of Capitalism. *Comparative European Politics, 1*(2), 215.

Bohle, D., & Greskovits, B. (2007). Neoliberalism, Embedded Neoliberalism and Neocorporatism: Towards Transnational Capitalism in Central-Eastern Europe. *West European Politics, 30*(3), 443–466.

Buchen, C. (2007). Estonia and Slovenia as Antipodes. In D. Lane & M. Myant (Eds.), *Varieties of Capitalism in Post-Communist Countries* (pp. 65–89). Basingstoke: Palgrave Macmillan.

Campbell, J. L. (2010). Institutional Reproduction and Change. In G. Morgan, J. Campbell, C. Crouch, O. K. Pedersen, & R. Whitley (Eds.), *The Oxford Handbook of Comparative Institutional Analysis* (pp. 87–116). Oxford: Oxford University Press.

Carlin, W., & Soskice, D. (2009). German Economic Performance: Disentangling the Role of Supply-side Reforms, Macroeconomic Policy and Coordinated Economy Institutions. *Socio-Economic Review, 7*(1), 67–99.

Coase, R. H. (1937). The Nature of the Firm. *Economica, 4*(16), 386–405.

Coase, R. H. (1960). The Problem of Social Cost. *Journal of Law and Economics, 3*(1), 1–44.

Commons, J. (1934/1959). *Institutional Economics: Its Place in Political Economy*. Madison: University of Wisconsin Press.

Crawford, S. E., & Ostrom, E. (1995). A Grammar of Institutions. *American Political Science Review, 89*(3), 582–600.

Crouch, C. (2010). Complementarity. In G. Morgan, J. Campbell, C. Crouch, O. K. Pedersen, & R. Whitley (Eds.), *The Oxford Handbook of Comparative Institutional Analysis* (pp. 117–137). Oxford: Oxford University Press.

Crouch, C., & Streeck, W. (Eds.). (1997). *Political economy of modern capitalism: Mapping convergence and diversity*. Sage.

Djelic, M. L. (2010). Institutional Perspectives—Working Towards Coherence or Irreconcilable Diversity? In G. Morgan, J. Campbell, C. Crouch, O. K. Pedersen, & R. Whitley (Eds.), *The Oxford Handbook of Comparative Institutional Analysis* (pp. 15–40). Oxford: Oxford University Press.

Elsner, W. (1989). Adam Smith's Model of the Origins and Emergence of Institutions: The Modern Findings of the Classical Approach. *Journal of Economic Issues, 23*(1), 189–213.

Esping-Andersen, G. (1990). *The Three Worlds of Welfare Capitalism*. Cambridge: Polity Press.

Feldmann, M. (2006). Emerging Varieties of Capitalism in Transition Countries: Industrial Relations and Wage Bargaining in Estonia and Slovenia. *Comparative Political Studies, 39*(7), 829–854.

Greif, A., & Kingston, C. (2011). Institutions: Rules or Equilibria? In N. Schofield & G. Caballero (Eds.), *Political Economy of Institutions, Democracy and Voting* (pp. 13–43). Berlin: Springer.

Greif, A., & Laitin, D. D. (2004). A Theory of Endogenous Institutional Change. *American Political Science Review, 98*(4), 633–652.

Hall, P. (1999). The Political Economy of Europe in an Era of Interdependence. In H. Kitchelt, P. Lange, G. Marks, & J. Stephens (Eds.), *Continuity and Change in Contemporary Capitalism* (pp. 135–163). Cambridge, MA: Cambridge University Press.

Hall, P. (2010). Historical Institutionalism in Rationalist and Sociological Perspective. In J. Mahoney & K. Thelen (Eds.), *Explaining Institutional Change: Ambiguity, Agency, and Power*. Cambridge : Cambridge University Press.

Hall, P. (2017). Varieties of Capitalism in Light of the Euro Crisis. *Journal of European Public Policy, 25*(1), 7–30.

Hall, P. (2018). *The Electoral Politics of Growth Regimes* (Working Paper). Available at https://scholar.harvard.edu/files/hall/files/hall2018_growth_regimes.pdf.

Hall, P., & Gingerich, D. (2004). Varieties of Capitalism and Institutional Complementarities in the Macroeconomy: An Empirical Analysis. *Max-Planck-Institut für Gesellschaftsforschung Discussion paper*, 4/5. http://www.mpi-fg-koeln.mpg.de/pu/mpifg_dp/dp04-5.pdf.

Hall, P., & Gingerich, D. (2009). Varieties of Capitalism and Institutional Complementarities in the Political Economy: An Empirical Analysis. *British Journal of Political Science, 39*(3), 449–482.

Hall, P., & Soskice, D. (Eds.). (2001). *Varieties of Capitalism: The Institutional Foundations of Comparative Advantage*. Oxford: Oxford University Press.

Hall, P., & Soskice, D. (2003). Varieties of Capitalism and Institutional Change: A Response to Three Critics. *Comparative European Politics, 1*(2), 241–250.

Hall, P., & Taylor, R. C. (1996). Political Science and the Three New Institutionalisms. *Political Studies, 44*(5), 936–957.

Hancké, B. (2013). *Unions, Central Banks, and EMU: Labour Market Institutions and Monetary Integration in Europe*. Oxford: Oxford University Press.

Hancké, B., Rhodes, M., & Thatcher, M. (2007). *Beyond Varieties of Capitalism: Conflict, Contradictions, and Complementarities in the European Economy*. Oxford: Oxford University Press.

Hardin, R. (1982). *Collective Action*. London/Baltimore: John Hopkins University Press.

Hayek, F. A. (1945). The Use of Knowledge in Society. *American Economic Review, 35*(4), 519–530.

Hayek, F. A. (1990). The Fatal Conceit. *University of Chicago Press Economics Books*.

Hope, D., & Soskice, D. (2016). Growth Models, Varieties of Capitalism, and Macroeconomics. *Politics & Society, 44*(2), 209–226.

Iversen, T., & Soskice, D. (2015). Democratic Limits to Redistribution: Inclusionary Versus Exclusionary Coalitions in the Knowledge Economy. *World Politics, 67*(2), 185–225.

Iversen, T., Soskice, D., & Hope, D. (2016). The Eurozone and Political Economic Institutions. *Annual Review of Political Science, 19*, 163–185.

Kalinowski, T. (2013). Regulating International Finance and the Diversity of Capitalism. *Socio-Economic Review, 11*(3), 471–496.

Kandori, M. (1992). Social Norms and Community Enforcement. *The Review of Economic Studies, 59*(1), 63–80.

Kitschelt, H., Lange, P., Marks, G., & Stephens, J. D. (Eds.). (1999). *Continuity and Change in Contemporary Capitalism*. Cambridge: Cambridge University Press.

Knell, M., & Srholec, M. (2007). Diverging Pathways in Central and Eastern Europe. In D. Lane & M. Myant (Eds.), *Varieties of Capitalism in Post-Communist Countries*. Basingstoke: Palgrave Macmillan.

Korpi, W. (1985). Power Resources Approach vs. Action and Conflict: On Causal and Intentional Explanations in the Study of Power. *Sociological Theory, 3*(2), 31–45.

Korpi, W. (2001). Contentious Institutions: An Augmented Rational-Action Analysis of the Origins and Path Dependency of Welfare State Institutions in Western Countries. *Rationality and Society, 13*(2), 235–283.

Korpi, W. (2006). Power Resources and Employer-Centered Approaches in Explanations of Welfare States and Varieties of Capitalism: Protagonists, Consenters, and Antagonists. *World Politics, 58*(2), 167–206.

Lefkofridi, Z., & Michel, E. (2017). The Electoral Politics of Solidarity. In K. Banting & W. Kymlicka (Eds.), *The Strains of Commitment: The Political Sources of Solidarity in Diverse Societies* (pp. 233–267). Oxford: Oxford University Press.

Lowndes, V. (2005). Institucionalizam. In D. Marsh & G. Stoker (Eds.), *Teorije i metode političke znanosti* (pp. 86–104). Zagreb: Politička misao.

Lučev, J., & Babić, Z. (2013). Tipovi kapitalizma, ekspanzija neoliberalizma i socijalni učinci u baltičkim zemljama, Sloveniji i Hrvatskoj: komparativni pristup. *Revija za socijalnu politiku, 20*(1), 1–19.

Mahoney, J., & Thelen, K. (Eds.). (2010). *Explaining Institutional Change: Ambiguity, Agency, and Power*. Cambridge: Cambridge University Press.

March, J. G., & Olsen, J. P. (1983). The New Institutionalism: Organizational Factors in Political Life. *American Political Science Review, 78*(3), 734–749.

Marx, K. (1867/1894/1979). *Kapital: Kritika političke ekonomije I-III*. Beograd: Prosveta.

Mises, L. V. (1949). *Human Action*. Ludwig von Mises Institute.

Nash, J. F. (1950). Equilibrium Points in N-Person Games. *Proceedings of the National Academy of Sciences of the United States of America, 36*(1), 48.

Neumann, J., & Morgenstern, O. (1944). *Theory of Games and Economic Behavior*. Princeton, NJ: Princeton University Press.

Nölke, A. (2016). Economic Causes of the Eurozone Crisis: The Analytical Contribution of Comparative Capitalism. *Socio-Economic Review, 14*(1), 141–161.

Nölke, A., & Vliegenthart, A. (2009). Enlarging the Varieties of Capitalism: The Emergence of Dependent Market Economies in East Central Europe. *World Politics, 61*(4), 670–702.

Nölke, A., ten Brink, T., Claar, S., & May, C. (2015). Domestic Structures, Foreign Economic Policies and Global Economic Order: Implications from the Rise of Large Emerging Economies. *European Journal of International Relations, 21*(3), 538–567.

North, D. C. (1990). *Institutions, Institutional Change and Economic Performance*. Cambridge: Cambridge University Press.

North, D. C. (1991). Institutions. *Journal of Economic Perspectives., 5*(1), 97–112.

North, D. C. (1994). Economic Performance Through Time. *The American Economic Review, 84*(3), 359–368.

Ostrom, E. (2005). *Understanding Institutional Diversity*. Princeton, NJ: Princeton University Press.

Ostrom, E., & Basurto, X. (2011). Crafting Analytical Tools to Study Institutional Change. *Journal of Institutional Economics, 7*(3), 317–343.

Peters, B. G. (1999). *Institutional Theory in Political Science: The New Institutionalism*. London: Pinter.

Pierson, P. (2000). Increasing Returns, Path Dependence, and the Study of Politics. *American Political Science Review, 94*(2), 251–267.

Pierson, P. (2015). Power and Path Dependence. In J. Mahoney & K. Thelen (Eds.), *Advances in Comparative-Historical Analysis* (pp. 123–147). Cambridge: Cambridge University Press.

Rovny, A. E., & Rovny, J. (2017). Outsiders at The Ballot Box: Operationalizations and Political Consequences of the Insider-Outsider Dualism. *Socio-Economic Review, 15*(1), 161–185.

Schmidt, V. (2003). French Capitalism Transformed, Yet Still a Third Variety of Capitalism. *Economy and Society, 32*(4), 526–554.

Schmidt, V. (2010). Taking Ideas and Discourse Seriously: Explaining Change Through Discursive Institutionalism as the Fourth 'New Institutionalism'. *European Political Science Review, 2*(1), 1–25.

Schumpeter, J. A. (2013). *Capitalism, Socialism and Democracy*. London: Routledge.

Shepsle, K. A. (2006). Rational Choice Institutionalism. In R. A. W. Rhodes, S. A. Binder, & B. A. Rockman (Eds.), *Oxford Handbook of Political Institutions* (pp. 23–38). Oxford: Oxford University Press.

Shonfield, A. (1965). *Modern Capitalism*. Oxford: Oxford University Press.

Soskice, D. (2007). Macroeconomics and Varieties of Capitalism. In B. Hancké, M. Rhodes, & M. Thatcher (Eds.), *Beyond Varieties of Capitalism: Conflict, Contradictions, and Complementarities in the European Economy* (pp. 89–121). Oxford: Oxford University Press.

Steinmo, S. (2008). Historical institutionalism. In D. Della Porta & M. Keating (Eds.), *Approaches and Methodologies in the Social Sciences: A Pluralist Perspective* (pp. 118–138). Cambridge: Cambridge University Press.

Steinmo, S. (2010). *The Evolution of Modern States: Sweden, Japan, and the United States*. Cambridge: Cambridge University Press.

Streeck, W. (2010). Institutions in History: Bringing Capitalism Back in. In G. Morgan, J. Campbell, C. Crouch, O. K. Pedersen, & R. Whitley (Eds.), *The Oxford Handbook of Comparative Institutional Analysis* (pp. 659–686). Oxford: Oxford University Press.

Streeck, W. (2011). E pluribus unum? Varieties and commonalities of capitalism. In M. Granovetter & R. Swedberg (Eds.), *The Sociology of Economic Life* (pp. 419–455). Boulder: Westview Press.

Streeck, W. (2016). Varieties of Varieties: "VoC" and the Growth Models. *Politics & Society, 44*(2), 243–247.

Streeck, W., & Thelen, K. A. (Eds.). (2005). *Beyond Continuity: Institutional Change in Advanced Political Economies*. Oxford: Oxford University Press.

Strpić, D. (1998). *Promjena*. Zagreb: Politička Misao.

Strpić, D. (2010). *Karl Marx i politička ekonomija moderne*. Zagreb: Nacionalna zajednica Crnogoraca Hrvatske.

Strpić, D. (2015). *Prema novoj političkoj ekonomiji*. Zagreb: Disput.

Tang, S. (2011). *A General Theory of Institutional Change*. London: Routledge.

Thelen, K. (2014). *Varieties of Liberalization and the New Politics of Social Solidarity*. Cambridge: Cambridge University Press.

Thelen, K., & Mahoney, J. (2015). Comparative-Historical Analysis in Contemporary Political Science. In J. Mahoney & K. Thelen (Eds.), *Advances in Comparative-Historical Analysis* (pp. 3–36). Cambridge: Cambridge University Press.

Thelen, K., & Steinmo, S. (1992). Historical institutionalism in comparative politics. In S. Steinmo, K. Thelen, & F. Longstreth (Eds.), *Structuring Politics: Historical Institutionalism in Comparative Analysis* (pp. 1–32). Cambridge: Cambridge University Press.

Wallis, J. J., & North, D. (1986). Measuring the Transaction Sector in the American Economy, 1870–1970. In *Long-Term Factors in American Economic Growth* (pp. 95–162). University of Chicago Press. Available at http://www.nber.org/chapters/c9679.pdf.

Wilensky, H. L. (2002). *Rich Democracies: Political Economy, Public Policy, and Performance*. Berkeley, CA: University of California Press.

Williamson, O. E. (2000). The new Institutional Economics: Taking Stock, Looking Ahead. *Journal of Economic Literature, 38*(3), 595–613.

CHAPTER 4

Framework-Oriented Interpretations of the Systemic Cycle and Institutional Theory

The purpose of this chapter is to enable a framework which utilizes both institutional approaches and the systemic cycle theory. The first section will revisit the problematic issues in the systemic cycle theory, notably the lack of institutional and macroeconomic insights. It will also attempt to overcome the supply-side focus of this theory by offering a Keynesian/demand-side reinterpretation of Arrighian concepts of extensive and intensive capitalism strategies. The second section will survey the open issues of institutional analysis, notably the problem of endogenous institutional change. It will also offer a conceptual synthesis intended to overcome this issue by defining institutions and institutional change in a manner consistent with a global-level theory of endogenous institutional change. The third section will argue there are asymmetrical similarities in these faults. In other words, the two research agendas could substantially benefit from searching for their mutually complementing elements.

The interpretations offered in this chapter are an attempt to bridge the gap between these two theoretical approaches and enable the explicit framework using these theories in Chapter 5. In particular, Chapter 2 has identified the power resources effects of two elements of the systemic cycle: trade relations and the phase of the systemic cycle. It has also argued that the third element—extensive and intensive developmental strategies—should be better developed in order to build the links with

J. Lučev, *Systemic Cycle and Institutional Change*,
https://doi.org/10.1007/978-3-030-66053-6_4

power relations and offer institutional change predictions. Chapter 3 identified two adequate channels of institutional change: path dependence and deliberate institutional design. It has also argued that the third channel of power resources should be better developed for their fluctuations to become predictable, and in turn to be used to explain endogenous changes in institutions. This chapter will present two crucial elements: the demand-side interpretation of intensive and extensive developmental strategies, and the conceptual interpretations of institutions and institutional change. If successful, this chapter will develop crucial links between the two theories and enable a metatheoretical language that the framework of the next chapter can utilize in order to push the institutional change agenda onto the transnational level.

4.1 Demand- and Supply-Side Interpretations of the Systemic Cycle Theory

Chapter 2 explored the systemic cycle and its effects on power distribution in the context of world-systemic dynamics. The point of departure for world-systems analysis was the world-system as *the* appropriate unit of analysis of social systems. Among other abstractions, this also necessitated the removal of the state from analysis (Wallerstein 1974: 3–11; 2000: xviii). The inherent disadvantage of world-systems analysis is directly connected to this simplification: the scheme of center/semi-periphery/periphery does not in principle allow for a plethora of functional institutional arrangements. It is also possible that some world-system theoreticians did not see this as a significant disadvantage due to their Marxist theoretical origins and accompanying difficulties in theorizing the state. This does not suggest that Marxist theory is an obstacle for such research, as the Regulation Theory clearly shows (e.g. Jessop 1990; Boyer 2005; Aglietta 1979/2015), but it does present a critical issue for any Marxian-based analysis including that of Giovanni Arrighi.

Building on Wallerstein and Braudel, Arrighi made some progress in explaining "organizational structures," but he did so constrained by his theoretical foundations. Arrighi describes regimes prevalent in the core, but he does not explain the institutional heterogeneity of the core (Arrighi 1994/2010; Arrighi and Moore 2001). In other words, while presenting a functional theory of change, Arrighi does not create a corresponding theory of institutions (Robinson 2011). He did, however, provide some important and valid conceptual innovations. Particularly striking is the notion of alternating extensive and intensive strategies employed by the competing governmental and business agencies (countries competing for the central position) in financial expansions. This insight could be used to provide elements of a theory of institutional change, provided it could be interpreted in the context of institutions. However, in order to understand these strategies not merely as preferences of capital, but also as developmental processes which involve various groups with various interests and political power, we must turn to a reconstruction of a national-level process of capitalism. In other words, we must turn to macroeconomics. As argued in Chapter 2, Arrighi focuses on supply-side phenomena, due to his theoretical background. This somewhat counter-intuitively makes his historical structuralist and global approach resemble neoclassical microeconomic or micro-founded approaches, which also overly focus on the supply-side. This is fundamentally dangerous as a research strategy, as it creates difficulties in conceptualizing crises, growth models, or the effects of labor markets. In order to remedy this and make the systemic cycle theory adaptable to the research of institutions on the national level, we must first interpret the crucial categories through the lens of demand and macroeconomics. To do so, we will first turn to an overview of Keynesian ideas on the importance of demand-side thinking. Then, we will offer a demand-side interpretation of intensive and extensive developmental strategies.

In terms of research strategy, Keynes did not agree with the atemporal equilibrium/long-termism of the neoclassical school (which we can argue is implicitly present in Marx as well). As he colorfully argued in connection with the quantity theory of money: "long run is a misleading guide to current affairs. In the long run we are all dead. Economists set themselves too easy, too useless a task if in tempestuous seasons they can only tell us that when the storm is long past the ocean will be flat again" (Keynes 1924: 80). In focusing on the short run, Keynes could zoom into actual causes and effects, rather than averaging data out into optimistic determinism of self-sustaining free markets.

Keynes summarized the inability to fathom crises in mainstream thought preceding him[1] through the idea that "supply creates its own demand" which he called "Say's law" (Keynes 1936/2013: 18). As no

[1] Unlike the more usual distinction between classical and neoclassical thought used here, Keynes invariably referred to the mainstream thought which preceded him as classical (Keynes 1936/2013: passim).

level of production can be too much for the market to clear, any and all unemployment must be voluntary. Labor is after all, but another marketable commodity, and the equilibrium it forms means that the real wage must be equal to the disutility of labor that the worker incurs (ibid.: 21–22). What Keynes developed to replace such an inadequate understanding was a logic of the interaction of maximum GDP (i.e. potential output or potential supply) and effective aggregate demand (i.e. actual current GDP). It was the responsibility of government to spend away in order to raise the aggregate demand in a depression, provided loose monetary policy failed to resuscitate the investment demand (known as a liquidity trap).[2]

Keynes suggested large deficit spending was a necessary solution to recessions. Even though Keynes added numerous new elements (including the psychologically tinted *animal spirits*, the focus on the short run and aggregates, crisis resolution policies, etc.), his analysis was based on the categories of contemporary economics including equilibrium analysis. His name is synonymous with mainstream policy prescriptions in the post-war *trente glorieuses* (1945–1975) and cotemporaneous ever-increasing role of state. *Big Government*, *Great Society*, and the continental European social state can all be viewed as essentially Keynesian, essentially demand-side (i.e. spending) based. This was

[2] There are two argumentations upon which Say's law could be easily critiqued. The first is time based: one man's spending is another's earnings, but for supply to create its demand the earnings must perpetually be spent instantaneously, thus instantly becoming the first man's earnings. In practice, a portion of new income is always saved (Keynes called the ratios of spent and saved new income the Marginal Propensity to Consume and the Marginal Propensity to Save), which means that this transfer is not instantaneous. Under numerous assumptions, savings would become investments, contributing to aggregate demand and boosting GDP, but in crises they do not get utilized, as investment would entail too much risk. Thus, new income will be fully spent only with the passing of time, which was ignored before Keynes. I owe this point to the late professor Dag Strpić. The second is a matter of unit of analysis. Even new consumed income is often expended onto imported goods and services, thus failing to boost domestic GDP (which may be a problem in countries suffering from dramatic trade deficits). Viewed in a simple, closed model, the trade issue is abstracted from, but it often presents a significant challenge in practice (except perhaps in a complete autarchy). Likewise, if we were to observe the aggregate demand in the whole world at the same time, trade imbalance could not be a problem as one country's trade deficit is another country's trade surplus. If the first issue was timelessness (or atemporality), the second issue is spacelessness—as soon as we acknowledge the existence of time and significant trade with other countries, Say's law cannot be true.

an era of the *neoclassical synthesis* in which neoclassical microeconomics adopted elements of Keynesian macroeconomics and began stressing market failure and the desirability of aggregate demand management. As mentioned before, the 1970s saw a return back to the traditional neoclassical staples of long run and supply-side-oriented research through the Chicago counter-revolution also critically known as neoliberal economics. The concept of macroeconomics was also transformed through the prevalence of general equilibrium analysis (DSGE—Dynamic Stochastic General Equilibrium) which has greatly supplanted the Keynesian logic of aggregates through microfoundations which are a calculation of an economy-wide result through the modeling of individual agents. In practice, DSGE models tend to reflect the neoclassical tendencies to the static and efficient equilibrium and have the same old problems in predicting crises (Orrell and Chlupatý 2016: 153, 165). This presents significant challenges to the economic profession as these DSGE models have permeated not only the neoclassical mainstream, but also the post-Keynesian and New Keynesian circles (see Krugman 2012). Nevertheless, while neoclassical long-termism, micro-founded research, and assumptions of actor rationality and market efficiency seem to have dominated over the Keynesian challenge to the mainstream, classical Keynesian thought provides Arrighi with an explanation he lacks in the far greater ability to utilize aggregate demand in modeling crises and intensive and extensive national strategies of global economic domination.

We can now recognize the intensive capitalism strategy as the strengthening of the middle class through Keynesian policies aimed at greater regulation, income redistribution, and wage-led growth. These were in vogue in the USA and Western Europe from the end of World War II and the 1970s. In this, they coincide with Arrighi's material expansion phase of the US capital accumulation regime. A Keynesian spin on the two strategies explained by Arrighi gives us an interpretation which overcomes his simplification of the business cycle. Table 4.1 offers a scheme of such a Keynesian demand-side spin of extensive and intensive capitalism.

Extensive capitalism could in the modern context be taken to mean a supply-side orientation, which logically deals with a given (i.e. external or export) demand structure and limits itself to the management of production costs (as it cannot influence quantities demanded). With cost reduction in mind, labor is viewed merely as one of those costs. A primary competitive strategy would be concerned with a reduction

Table 4.1 Arrighian categories with a demand-side interpretation

	Extensive capitalism	*Intensive capitalism*
Primary orientation	Supply side (production wages must be low as they are primarily considered as input costs)	Demand side (production wages must be sufficiently high as they are considered as demand inducing)
Alternative interpretations	Neoliberalism, Washington consensus, finance-led capitalism, race to the bottom, globalization, the third way, Liberal Market Economy, export-led growth, monetarist policy regime	Keynesian welfare state, industrial society, import substitution, traditional Coordinated market economy, development state
Expected outcomes	High income inequality, disorganized labor, labor market deregulation	Lower income inequality, more ability of labor to organize and higher levels of labor market regulation

of costs including labor. In contrast, the orientation of intensive capitalism is to the demand-side, where labor costs eventually translate into disposable income of the workers and therefore effective domestic demand. Therefore, high labor costs mean higher product prices, but also a strong domestic demand, while lower labor costs suggest lower product prices, but also a weaker domestic demand. Logically, the extensive capitalism strategy is export oriented (with competitive prices but insufficient domestic demand) and the intensive capitalism is domestic market oriented (with less than competitive prices, but a strong domestic demand). A successful intensive capitalism may therefore also be somewhat protectionist, as high product prices in an open economy would translate into a large trade deficit.[3] In ideal-typical terms, we could construe intensive capitalism as a development strategy hinging on high levels of trade protectionism and labor market protection essentially pointing to import substitution. The extensive capitalism strategy would then be understood as an export-oriented strategy of both trade and labor market liberalization.

[3]This connection between trade openness and labor protection has also been proven empirically (see Rueda et al. 2015).

We can now integrate these insights with the world-systemic outlook. We need to interpret the ideal-type systemic cycle as encompassing the world-systemic unit of analysis (in focusing specifically on cores and centers—Wallerstein via Silver), the capital-led processes of material and financial expansions as the basis of the systemic cycle (Arrighi), the power dynamics under the influence of the systemic cycle (Arrighi and Silver) and the macroeconomically interpreted developmental strategies (Arrighi via Keynes).

The systemic cycle influences the various sub-units of the world-system in a variegated way—an insight, which is one of the predominant strengths of this approach. Starting with the three phases of the systemic cycle (Financial I, Material, Financial II) we can track the cycle through sub-units. Figure 4.1 shows the dynamics between new and old centers schematically. During the Financial I phase, movement away from production and trade in the old center brings investments looking for profitable opportunities to possible future global centers of production; several

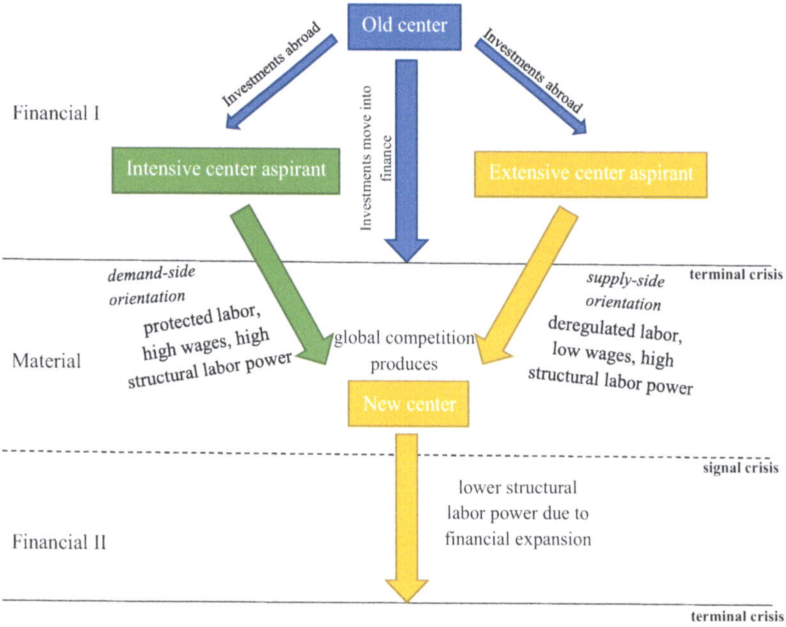

Fig. 4.1 Ideal-typical systemic cycle

such possible new centers compete and political/organizational innovations abound attempting to formulate the winning growth model; trade position of possible future centers is improved, with a falling unemployment as a result, and the marketplace structural power of labor in the aspirant center increasing. These experimental political/economic innovations may be very complex, but their growth model aspect can be reduced to two developmental strategies: intensive (own market) and extensive (global market oriented)—in the highly complex modern stage of world capitalism, they can therefore be a result of social compromises directed either at strengthening of the middle class (intensive) or at reducing production costs in order to produce competitive exports (extensive). As a terminal crisis weakens the old center, these new strategies become more important on the world stage. This is a period of systemic chaos in which the economic and political hegemony of the old center has weakened and the world-system grows increasingly multi-polar.

During the Material phase, the divergent effects of the two development strategies intensify, with the intensive strategy increasing the marketplace structural labor power, incentivizing relatively well-protected labor markets, and rising living standards (real wages). On the other hand, the extensive strategy banks on the relatively low real protection of labor markets and moves toward greater income inequality. Either successful strategy will result in an expansion of production (sustained output and GDP growth) and rising development indicators (GDP/capita). One strategy will prevail by profiting most and becoming the global center politically and economically dominating the club of the developed countries (core). Such a domination will ideal-typically produce a hegemony, in which the economic, political and military capacity comes together to advance the interests of the new center, and international organizations are aligned to support the general hegemonic arrangement. This moment of hegemonic realignment can be extremely prolonged in the modern world, and its results are not immediately observable. We will eventually analyze the limits of hegemonic transitions as darwinistic moments rewarding the successful strategy. The Material phase is drawn to an end as the investment cycle will eventually result in a profit crunch in manufacture and trade and a signal crisis.

The Financial II phase commences with the signal crisis questioning the efficiency of the existing regime of capital accumulation based on the real economy, and capital, hitherto employed in production, finds higher yields in the financial sector and in the real sector abroad. The result is a relative deindustrialization of the old center with the structural labor power decreasing. The trade position of the center is exacerbated, and the result is a jobless recovery (stagnating unemployment) from the signal crisis, with structural labor power further decreasing. The financial sector becomes dominant in the economy and monopolistic tendencies become increasingly apparent. Income inequality increases in an increasingly deregulated economy. Ultimately, another terminal crisis creates a sufficient downturn in the center to incentivize the development of political/economic innovations in new aspirant centers as they vie for hegemonic dominance in a new period of systemic chaos.

We can observe the interplay of power, the investment finance cycle, and the two mentioned strategies during material expansions. This distinction seems to point to the crucial strategic moment of choosing alternative paths to developing own internal markets through new social compacts (even though a resulting higher leverage in the hands of the labor may contribute to the profit crunch following the material expansion) or developing production runs for external markets (an export-led strategy). They describe vastly different growth models, with the intensive strategy hinging on domestic demand and extensive strategy depending on foreign demand. These strategies are a result of the changing dynamics of power in the national context, most importantly the power of interests contrary to the dynamics of capital/entrepreneurship driving the systemic cycle. The power of these contrary interests, largely represented by the marketplace structural power of labor, is itself influenced by the systemic cycle. Structural labor power in the marketplace is reduced whenever the importance of manufacturing labor in the economy is reduced. These are circumstances in which the hypothetical influence of strikes as the final measure of union power is diminishing for a number of possible reasons: the diminishing relative importance of manufacture (e.g. due to a financial expansion), trade deficits, or growing unemployment. Therefore, we can discern the basic elements of interactions between power and developmental strategies which underscore the elementary economic processes. An extensive strategy focuses on improving aggregate supply—as demand is in great part foreign, while an intensive strategy focuses on issues of aggregate demand—which has repercussions on the connectedness with the interests of labor. This leads us to a contentious issue: while material expansions can occur in both types of strategies (suggesting high structural labor power), only one of these strategies (i.e. intensive) is fully labor-friendly. To understand what factors outside the systemic cycle lead to a choice of developmental strategy, we will turn to institutional analysis.

4.2 Addressing the Issue of Endogenous Change in Institutional Analysis

Chapter 3 has analyzed the general tendencies in institutional approaches and identified endogenous institutional change as the crucial open issue. It is argued that the insufficiently explored status of endogenous institutional change is a result of the conceptual basis of research. It also identified several approaches which offered conceptual answers to the issue of institutional change.

In terms of definitions, a common type of understanding of institutions is the institutions-as-rules approach most influentially expounded by Douglass North. A welcome implication here is the need to seek any type of rule which structures activity. An alternative is the institutions-as-equilibria approach which sees institutions as repeating strategies in response to exogenous parameters. This approach has significant issues with explaining institutional change as the rules of the game are understood as exogenous to strategies which can only be modified as a result of exogenous change (itself strategies subject to some higher order parameters). In order to endogenize these changes, it was necessary to start thinking in terms of quasi-parameters which are simultaneously rules and changeable within the game (Greif and Laitin 2004). In general, new institutionalism has shared these difficulties with conceptualizing endogenous change and has stressed mechanisms like path dependency which also logically stress endogenous stability or stable development with discontinuities brought about only by exogenous critical junctures.

These approaches have a number of interesting qualities: the game-theoretical approach of institutions-as-equilibria focuses on the incentives and disincentives (i.e. structure) formulated by both external parameters and expectations of the activity of other players. In other words, it tells us something about the importance of rule embeddedness (higher order parameters) and also the importance of trust and defection as elements of game strategies. New institutionalism approaches, which focus on path dependency and critical junctures, remind us of the inherent stability of institutions and the many conditions under which institutions either remain unchanged or change slowly and predictably. A large change under these conditions is conceivable only as exogenous. However, in the case of both game-theoretical approaches and general tendencies in new institutionalism, it seems that any theory of change which hinges on external (and therefore unexplained) drivers may have only a limited appeal.

The most important version of new institutionalism in political science is the *Varieties of Capitalism* approach (Hall and Soskice 2001), which has developed a useful and empirically substantiated typological framework. However, while it has presented a theory of institutional differences, it struggled from the very beginning to provide a temporal dimension. There were several attempts to remedy this notable shortfall. Beramendi et al. (2015) continue the older Kitschelt et al. (1999) project to provide an electoral politics dimension, while Kathleen Thelen has devoted a number of works to the analysis of specific modes and actors in institutional change (Thelen 2004; Streeck and Thelen 2005; Hall and Thelen 2009; Thelen 2014), notably following and arguing against the faults of both the VofC project and the power resource theory. None of these has, however, outlined an endogenous change approach which could predict and explain the nature of institutional change. The previous chapter has suggested that the difficulties in approaches building on game theory (NIE, rational choice institutionalism) may be a result of its very conceptualization of game-parameters creating structured responses amounting to institutions-as-equilibria. These institutions can only be changed according to rules specified in higher order institutions and those rules can only be changed in higher orders still, which essentially gives us an explanation of change devoid of endogeneity. In fact, the success of Greif and Laitin (2004) in offering a game-theoretical endogenous change explanation was possible only through the subversion of rules other authors often take for granted. Likewise, the difficulties in VofC can be attributed not only to the ideal-type method which inherently focuses on stability, but also to the central concept of complementarity according to which the gains from a proper institutional alignment can be preserved only through the stability of individual institutions.

Institutional approaches in general have long been aware of the underdeveloped analysis of issues of change (as seen in Chapter 3) and have found various explanations of how change happens (mostly dependent on evolutionary narratives). Nevertheless, the issue of endogenous change (i.e. the explanation of why change happens) remains underexplained. A specific traditionally missing component was the explanation of international mechanisms such as the effects of trade positions on institutions. As explained above, a 2016 article by Baccaro and Pontusson which included growth models in VofC prompted formal responses from one of the originators of VofC and one of its most important critics. In order to attempt to help solve the open question of endogenous change, a good theory of change would need to take into account all the significant drivers of institutional change and, when possible, to endogenize them. To endogenize these drivers is to explain them with the same framework used to explain changes in institutions. In other words, we must strive to expand the number of explained drivers of change. Chapter 5 will attempt to include the predictable effects of trade relations into the list of endogenized and explained drivers of institutional change. However, we must first offer conceptual clarifications which will enable such an endogenous theory of change.

4.2.1 Conceptualizing Institutions Between Power Resources and Externalities

As shown in Chapter 3, North defines actually active institutions as dependent upon three important aspects: formal institutions (codified laws and statutes), informal institutions (uncodified "ways of doing business" and norms), and partially avoidable institutions (actors' ability to avoid them—this is particularly important in gauging the actual impact of formal policy). This approach is useful as it enables us to focus on manifest institutions (i.e. those that actually function as rules and structure activity) rather than ideas, policy prescriptions, or unimplemented laws. In terms of labor institutions, this distinction covers laws regulating labor contracts and organization via unions and collective bargaining (i.e. formal institutions—these can be studied by comparing written documents), uncodified practices in collective bargaining and trade union organization (i.e. informal institutions—these can be studied inferentially by observing power relations embodied in union density and bargaining centralization), and loosely implemented labor regulations observable in wage theft and poor working conditions (avoidable institutions—these can be studied by analyzing existing research).

Another important aspect of institutions is their connection with power. Firstly, institutions tend to favor or target specific actors which incentivize the favored actors to strive for institutional stability and preservation. If the resources accrued by the functioning of these institutions are sufficient, this fact itself may be enough to exert substantial pressures toward path dependence (as explained by Pierson). Secondly, institutions themselves can be thought of as results of compromise between various actors according to the power they had to influence the process of institutional emergence (as explained by Korpi). Once the relative power available to these actors changes, the change in institutions becomes possible. If a research strategy focused only on institutions, it may be tempting to focus on power as something which stems only from institutions—and therefore to proclaim institutional stability in the absence of exogenous shocks. Realistically, however, power resources are a result of a myriad of factors, both national and global in nature. This suggests that a power-based concept of institutional change must take the nationally and globally induced complex changes of power into account. The most visible and the most formal manifestations of political power are those pertaining to the election (or selection) and actions of those who govern. In democracies, the focus would naturally fall to electoral politics, the ways in which the expectations of the electoral body change, and the reactions of the parties which attempt to mold their electoral programs to best capture the votes. Chapter 3 has shown a modern institutional version of such a focus in the Beramendi project. However, the past few decades have seen political science focus on the less formal and less visible channels of policymaking in the various approaches to structured policy interactions starting from corporatism and more recently expanding to epistemic communities, policy communities, and policy networks. The predictors of the power of the interested groups in the first type of research (more visible and formal) are the changes in voter preference and the composition of the electorate (which would favor a certain type of party), while the predictors in the second type of research (less visible and formal) are the ability of the interested groups to organize and the strength of their bargaining position. Both types of research are relevant in conceptualizing power in institutional change and should be taken into account wherever possible.

Finally, institutions interact with other institutions—and the conceptualization of these interactions has had two effects: firstly, the development of an influential genre of institutionalism as a form of typological thought (seeking to explain and classify different institutional frameworks) and substantial theoretical problems for approaches to endogenous institutional change. As already shown, game theory has severe problems in explaining endogenous change stemming from the conceptual barrier between parameters and strategies, with the former structuring the latter (while the endogenous change would require that this relationship could move in the other direction). Nevertheless, the nested rules approach offers an important insight in that the institutions are dependent on higher order institutions for change (Ostrom, Williamson). Much like the parameter-strategy relationship, this view of change only takes one possible direction. The notable difference between two versions is that while Ostrom created a legal-hierarchical version of nested rules, Williamson argued primarily for a hierarchy according to time needed for change. The primary difficulty in describing endogenous change is the ever-expanding nature of the unit of analysis—the rules are changed according to rules *of* change inscribed in higher order institutions—and it is very difficult to see how the actors which are only active at lower levels could enact change at higher levels (as imagined by game theory). But crucially, we are reminded that there are many arenas in which these actors can function and enact change, and in actuality, the same actors may be activated across a number of possible levels (e.g. by a union being consulted during a labor law reform).

In contrast to these rational choice and NIE issues of endogenous change, VofC provides a logic not of hierarchical nested rules/institutions, but rather of a circular complementarity of rules/institutions. Those systems/institutional frameworks which are properly aligned (LME, CME) have substantial advantages in terms of growth. The primary issue is that endogenous change is difficult to project, as partial change is costly in the long term due to the lost advantages of the initial structure, and a comprehensive change is a rare and even more costly in the short term. The principal advantage of this approach is the specific logic of complementarity according to institutional externalities—according to which many institutions have unintended impact upon others by providing them with a state of affairs which can be usefully exploited by a specific alignment of an institutional arrangement. In other words, when properly aligned, institutions provide functional incentives for other institutions to remain unchanged.

We would like to conceptually further this approach by two suggestions. Firstly, it is not merely the institutions that can provide externalities affecting institutional change/stability. The state of affairs affecting the advantages of a specific institution may come from a number of political and economic factors including technological shifts, global processes, and growth models—and not only from other rules. Secondly, if we accept that externalities come from economic processes, then the incentives may actively change through time. In other words, the complementarities and externalities become incentives for institutional change rather than merely incentives for institutional stability. The implicit danger in these suggestions is slipping into functionalism by claiming that institutions change merely because they have a possible better form. Any change is mediated by power relations, specific interests, and the mobilization of political power or lack thereof.

Therefore, we can define institutions as active formal and informal rules which structure social activity. Their functioning is influenced by other rules and other economic, technological, and political factors—and their creation and maintenance are underwritten by the power of interested actors, with changes of this power (itself a result of overlapping global and national processes) enabling the change in institutions. All of these factors and processes can therefore be understood as mutually nested, or potentially complementary. Shifts in any of these may provide the needed drive for institutional change, which is why all of these can be referred to as drivers of institutional change. A non-deterministic hierarchy may be discerned between these change drivers according to the time interval needed for change in a specific process—and these timeframes will provide us with a logic of embeddedness of institutional drivers.

4.2.2 *Similarities and Synergies of the Systemic Cycle and Institutional Analysis*

The previous two segments have outlined the crucial issues of systemic cycle theory and institutional analysis. The first segment answered the demand-side underdevelopment of the systemic cycle, but delayed the issue of the lacking institutional theory. The second segment conceptually addressed the issue of a lacking endogenous change in institutional analysis, but delayed the application of these concepts. This suggests that the two theories have now been brought to an intersection at which they may benefit from each other. Institutional theories can help the systemic cycle achieve insights into the national functioning of capitalism via its institutions. More importantly from the standing point of this thesis, the systemic cycle as a theory of global change may help institutional analysis endogenize drivers of institutional change which cannot be found on the mere national level. To do so, we must first outline the compatible and contradictory elements of these theories.

The crucial point of difference between comparative institutional thought (and therefore VofC) and world-systemic literature (and therefore Arrighi) is the research strategy pertaining to capitalism—and particularly the unit of analysis at which capitalism is to be researched. For the *Varieties of Capitalism*, capitalism is about the functioning of national markets. The obvious assumption is that regulation is formed on the national level, and the appropriate unit of analysis is therefore the state. In the systemic cycle, the unit of analysis is the world-system, and the various states are interconnected through the logic of core/semi-periphery/periphery. The crucial point was made by Beverly Silver who rejected the determinism of a simplistic reading of the world-system. She explicitly asserts the bottom-up processes which determine the position of the specific state in the world-system. National movements continuously construct and reconstruct, hinder or replicate the relations within the world-system. Developmental strategies, as we have defined them in this chapter, are processes which influence the composition of the world-system by allowing peripheral or semi-peripheral economies to climb into the core and even become the new center of the world-system. These strategies are also embedded in the power relations which occur on the national level, but often have global causes.

This interpretation enables us to view the global system of trade as the relevant playing field and to comprehend the global mechanisms which have vastly diverse effects on different states—i.e. mechanisms such as the systemic cycle. And vice versa, it enables us to view the strategies of specific states as influences on the composition of the world-systems. In both cases, nation-states are sub-units of the world-systemic unit of analysis of capitalism—global interactions are therefore far more than just the sum of all exports and imports. This is not merely a conceptual difference and if approached carefully could offer a possible solution to the central issue of endogenous change. Namely, if we accept that global phenomena provide significant incentives for national institutional change, then we must accept either the need for exogenous change or the need for a unit of analysis broader than the nation-state. Here, the endogeneity and exogeneity are essentially functions of the appropriateness of the unit of analysis, which must be large enough to encompass the relevant mechanisms of change if it is to strive for endogenous change.

For example, if we were observing the social life of a child instead of institutional change in capitalism, we would have to adjust the unit of analysis to the nature of child's behavior. If we were analyzing a one-year-old, the nuclear family may provide us with the necessary unit of analysis as the small child's interactions remain restricted to the family. If we were observing a 10-year-old, we would face an important choice. We could either preserve the old and restrictive unit of analysis and be unable to explain the child's social life without resorting to elusive exogenous factors. Or we could broaden the unit of analysis to encompass the relevant organizations (school, sports clubs, social networks...), which would keep all relevant mechanisms endogenous. Institutional thought has a tendency to choose the first strategy by insisting on the national level of analysis and comparing only internal tenets of institutions. This thesis suggests that the second strategy is a viable alternative and consists of recognizing that the relevant unit of analysis has long outgrown the size of a nation-state.

In other words, we need a framework which takes the state and its regulatory apparatus seriously, but at the same time acknowledges their immersion into the global system of trade.[4] Only then can trade positions be thought of as more than a matter for individual countries to resolve for themselves.[5] More importantly, the choice of the appropriate unit of analysis allows us to move to an endogenous theory of institutional change.

This expansion has not already occurred as it requires a theory ambitious enough to simultaneously explain global distributions of growth, trade, income, production, and possibly even power. The two obvious candidates are new economic geography and Arrighi's systemic cycle, and as explained in Chapter 2, Arrighi's theory has several advantages going

[4] An application of dependency/world-systemic theory to a comparative analysis of capitalism varieties has been undertaken before. Senghaas and Menzel applied the world-system analysis of Samir Amin to several projects involved with mapping the global versions of capitalism starting as soon as the 1970s (Mjøset 2007). Also, there were several attempts which aimed at the integration of Arrighi-inspired financialization perspective and VofC literature. For example, Jessop (2012) dubbed his combination variegated capitalisms, while Van Treeck (2009) attempts to include the macroeconomic perspective into the financialization and VofC fields which he sees as basically microeconomic. Lapavitsas and Powell (2013) relatively recently published an attempt at quantifying some data on financialization across the capitalisms, and Nölke and May (2013) open some broad questions including the possibility of including Arrighi in the study of institutions.

[5] E.g. one could be puzzled that vast national reforms related to greater competitiveness (supply side measures like cost-cutting through reducing labor cost) does not improve the trade position of a given country. "Zooming out" to a broader geographic area may reveal that the most important trade partners have been conducting similar reforms which means that the specific national competitiveness remained unchanged.

for it including a long-term historical perspective. Here, we can use it to recognize that the CME and LME institutional positions are ideal-typical descriptions of national markets in the 1980s and 1990s (as recognized by Streeck 2016) and that these descriptions lose their attractiveness in the empirical sense as soon as we recognize the capacity of institutions for change. However, VofC has provided a vastly useful template for institutional analysis and it would be dangerous to throw the baby out with the bathwater. The concepts of institutional complementarity which underline it can be used alongside path dependency and institutional embeddedness to explain change instead of stability, provided we can make sense of it through an appropriate theory of global economic change.

Arrighi has provided such a theory, predicting trade relations and the shifts from global material to global financial expansions. This suggests that a successful inclusion of Arrighi's theory (with the mediations via Silver and Keynes) into institutional thought could provide a useful tool which would expand the theory of institutional change into a significant and currently unincluded area. A significantly important similarity of Arrighi and the *Varieties of Capitalism* strand of institutional thought is the firm-centric nature of their explanation. *Varieties of Capitalism* identified the five institutional arrangements by explicitly positioning the firm at "the center of analysis" (Hall and Soskice 2001: 5) and elucidating the restraints and incentives it faces and coordination mechanisms it uses. Arrighi speaks of business and governmental agencies and capital, often seemingly presuming the monolith nature of these. However, when one wishes to research the mechanisms he identified (e.g. the flight of capital into finance in the USA), one must necessarily take a look at firm-level data as pointed out by Krippner (2005) and accepted by Arrighi (2007: 140–141). The business decisions entailed in the flight of capital are made on the level of firms/corporations (at least in the USA), and the data through which such a flight may be measured is reported at firm level (tax reports).

Ultimately, there is a somewhat natural compatibility between Arrighi's theory which does not really extend to institutions but explains predictable economic and developmental change and institutional approaches like the Varieties of Capitalism which explain institutional typologies but struggle with endogenous change. Their issues can be transcended by constructing a framework which utilizes a world-systemic unit of analysis and systemic cycle theory together with an institutional categorical apparatus.

4.2.3 *Delimiting the Two Groups of Theories via Drivers*

As discussed in the introduction, the basic methodology follows Ostrom in constructing a framework from different theories, which themselves support various models. We construct a framework of labor-institutional change by utilizing systemic cycle theory and institutional analysis (itself a spawning ground for numerous theories), which support various drivers of institutional change (or models in Ostrom's parlance). The systemic cycle theory provides us with three drivers: systemic cycle phases (material or financial expansions), within which the developmental strategies (extensive or intensive) can develop and then manifest as trade relations. The institutional theories provide us with further three drivers of path dependence, power relations, and formal politics. Power relations are the element in which these two strands most clearly overlap as institutional analysis can make strong predictions concerning institutional effects of labor power, while systemic cycle theory makes strong predictions concerning its causes. However, there is also a seventh driver we will take into consideration—that of technological shifts. It is implied by both theoretical strands, but hardly presents a central point of either, which is the reason for its avoidance in the previous two chapters. This driver takes a long timeframe to develop but may have enormous bearing on the structural and associational power of labor. This makes it a crucial contextual element, which must nonetheless remain exogenous. Its effects have hitherto been avoided but merit a theoretical discussion before we proceed with the framework in the next chapter.

Technological change has at least two aspects of use to our scheme: the cumulative and the developmental aspect. The cumulative is a matter of best available technology or the global sum of useful innovations. This changes through the long run as various innovations propel growth and social development. The developmental aspect of technology is a matter of capital deepening or the availability of useful technology in a specific location. As far as the cumulative aspect goes, innovations shape the models of growth and the modes of production and trade. The steam engine and the telegraph shaped the late nineteenth and early twentieth centuries as much as the computer, robotics, and satellite communications have shaped the late twentieth and early twenty-first centuries. Consequently, they provide the impetus for institutional change as well. On the lowest level of technological and (therefore) social development, all individual members must take part in the production of food. As the availability of farming equipment and organization increases, societies may urbanize. With the advent of industrial development, societies move toward greater preponderance of secondary sector employment with industrial workers gaining in relative importance (for the USA, the plurality of primary sector employment was lost around 1905 in favor of a rise of both secondary and tertiary employments). In the thirty years, following World War 2, the developed Western countries met the conditions for a growing divergence between industrial (secondary sector) and service (tertiary sector) employment. The technological development and continued capital deepening process meant that a diminishing portion of all employed needed to work in either agriculture or industry in order to supply the quantities sufficient for global demand. This provides the true postindustrial society.[6] This development also has profound effects on the functionality of labor organization. In general, union power is linked to skill-set specificity, with bargaining leverage being more acute when a strike of a worker would incur a large price for the employer in replacing the worker (as his/her skill is specific and therefore more difficult to replace). Again, in general, skill sets are more specific in industry than in service employment (waiters are easier to train and therefore to replace than automobile plant workers). This is a possible cause of union density generally being lower in service employment.[7] As the service employment in the developed world continued to rise in the past few decades, this created incentives for liberalizations of labor markets as labor organization lost the leverage it once enjoyed.

The developmental aspect is something useful to consider when discussing China, which underwent a significant developmental leap in recent decades. Firstly, technology tends to migrate from the most developed toward the least developed in patterns, with the peripheral areas organizing production at lower technological levels than those found in the core.[8] In Chapter 2, we saw that labor-intensive industrialization was the traditional East Asian approach. This long-standing developmental strategy was made possible in recent decades through a constant inflow

[6] For classical treatments, see Illich (1973) and Bell (1976/1999).

[7] For example, in 2008, the union density rates for manufacture and services were 17 and 7% in Germany, 48 and 34% in Belgium, 45 and 30% in Norway, 61 and 43% in Sweden, etc. (Hassel 2015: 256).

[8] For classical contributions, see Vernon (1966) and Akamatsu (1962).

of migrant workers from rural and comparatively underdeveloped areas (e.g. Szechuan Province) towards the increasingly complex production on the coast (e.g. the Guangdong Province). These workers were abundant and cheap, and it seems their incessant flow has very recently subsided (Chapter 8), resulting in their scarcity, and therefore greater labor power by definition. Capital deepening and cutting-edge technology will now have a different functionality, replacing the labor made troublesome by its sudden scarcity.

Technology is also important as it causes different employment profiles. In turn, specific employment structures create specific incentives and disincentives for regulation and/or institutional change. The manufacture labor-dominated post-World War 2 continental European economies (or CMEs) had strong incentives to develop the systems associated with the quasi-corporatist structure that dominated Europe. The vast number of workers was a potential threat to the continued functioning of the economy as a whole (had they decided to strike), and the corporatist tripartite structures helped defuse this threat through co-opting. High levels of unionization helped organize one of the sides in the negotiations. A predictable result was a well-protected labor market focused on labor rather than capital. Such an arrangement did not go to waste as the German-led CME model included well-developed VET (Vocational Education and Training) focused on manufacture, which developed a fresh employee into a valuable resource based on very specific skills. Such a specific skill set benefited from well-protected, unionized labor market as it made job-mobility scarce. The investment into worker education and into specific skill set was therefore well protected.

All of this suggests that there are good reasons to distinguish between cumulative (the innovative aspect) and developmental (strategies of capital deepening) aspects of technology. The former suggests links between innovations, their gradual application, and resultant employment compositions. This driver is a long-term process and most closely associated with the general meaning of technology. While this driver is very important and technology is included in the framework in this sense of the word, it must be clear that the long-term nature of the driver makes it exogenous to the theory of change presented here. All other drivers can be explained by their interactions and theories of their development, but we treat technology as external. The latter meaning most probably entails a change of a mid-term proportion and directly interacts with the systemic cycle. It interacts with the systemic cycle as one of the possible outcomes of developmental technological progress is the accumulation of capital, which under the conditions of stiff competition causes the shift from the material expansion phase to the financial expansion phase.

In this, we can see the composite Arrighian dynamics of investment (referred to here as the developmental aspect of technology) as driving the systemic cycle through an increase of individual production in competitors (accepting a resulting drop in profits) followed by a crisis showing the structural issues of capital as a whole which resulted from this gradual individual increase of capacity. We could add that the development of markets increases monopolistic tendencies which are a result of expected means to increase profits (there is always an option of mergers and acquisitions to neutralize irritating competitors). Also, the Marxian dynamics of capital overaccumulation has an inherent tendency to overlook demand management (as argued in the previous chapter)—as it is generally a supply-side argument. Therefore, what could be operationalized as a developmental aspect of technology, we will cover through the notions of the systemic cycle and the developmental strategies, while the technological factor we focus on remains the exogenous driver of cumulative technology.

4.3 Conclusions

This chapter needed to interpret the two theoretical strands from the previous chapters in a way consistent with an idea of a meta-theoretical framework that is to be developed in the next chapter. It has first outlined two major issues in the systemic cycle theory as the underdevelopment of demand-side arguments and the underdevelopment of institutional analysis. It addressed the first issue by offering a macroeconomic or demand-side interpretation of Arrighi's categories of intensive and extensive strategies as models of growth. It suggested combination with institutional analysis as the appropriate solution to the second issue. It also outlined the major issue of endogenous institutional change in institutional approaches as the second theoretical strand. The solution offered here was a conceptual interpretation utilizing Northian insights alongside the concepts of power resources, institutional embeddedness (NIE), and institutional complementarity (VofC). Institutions have their formal, informal, and avoidable aspects, and they are intimately connected with power. This chapter suggested that the logic of embeddedness and complementarity can be used to model institutional change as path deviation occurs when such change is complementary to the various drivers of change.

The goal has been to show that some of the most notable shortfalls of both systemic cycle and institutional analysis are mutually compatible and to offer a reinterpretation of Arrighi's categories of intensive and extensive capitalism which may make his theory more useful for a research into the modern world and more useful from the point of view of institutional thought. Specifically, a significant and as of yet insufficiently recognized issue in institutional change is the effect of trade positions, growth, and system development on the institutions. The inclusion of the systemic cycle in the quest for various drivers of institutional change is an attempt to overcome this issue. Chapter 5 will offer a framework which includes both theories, and the subsequent three chapters will apply it to the three selected labor market cases.

Literature

Aglietta, M. (1979/2015). *A Theory of Capitalist Regulation: The US Experience*. London: Verso Books.

Akamatsu, K. (1962). A Historical Pattern of Economic Growth in Developing Countries. *The Developing Economies, 1*(s1), 3–25.

Arrighi, G. (1994/2010). *The Long Twentieth Century: Money, Power, and the Origins of Our Times*. London: Verso Books.

Arrighi, G. (2007). *Adam Smith in Beijing*. London: Verso.

Arrighi, G., & Moore, J. W. (2001). Capitalist Development in World Historical Perspective. In R. Albritton, M. Itoh, R. Westra, & A. Zuege (Eds.), *Phases of Capitalist Development* (pp. 56–75). Basingstoke: Palgrave.

Bell, D. (1976/1999). *The Coming of Post-Industrial Society: A Venture in Social Forecasting*. New York: Basic Books.

Beramendi, P., Häusermann, S., Kitschelt, H., & Kriesi, H. (Eds.). (2015). *The Politics of Advanced Capitalism*. New York: Cambridge University Press.

Boyer, R. (2005). How and Why Capitalisms Differ. *Economy and Society, 34*(4), 509–557.

Greif, A., & Laitin, D. D. (2004). A Theory of Endogenous Institutional Change. *American Political Science Review, 98*(4), 633–652.

Hall, P., & Soskice, D. (Eds.). (2001). *Varieties of Capitalism: The Institutional Foundations of Comparative Advantage*. Oxford: Oxford University Press.

Hall, P., & Thelen, K. (2009). Institutional Change in Varieties of Capitalism. *Socio-Economic Review, 7*(1), 7–34.

Hassel, A. (2015). Trade Unions and the Future of Democratic Capitalism. In P. Beramendi, S. Häusermann, H. Kitschelt, & H. Kriesi (Eds.), *The Politics of Advanced Capitalism* (pp. 231–258). New York: Cambridge University Press.

Illich, I. (1973). *Tools for Conviviality*. New York: Harper & Row.

Jessop, B. (1990). *State Theory: Putting the Capitalist State in Its Place*. University Park: Penn State Press.

Jessop, B. (2012). The World Market, Variegated Capitalism, and the Crisis of European Integration. *Globalisation and European Integration: Critical Approaches to Regional Order and International Relations, 25*, 91.

Keynes, J. M. (1924). *A Tract on Monetary Reform*. London: Macmillan. http://delong.typepad.com/keynes-1923-a-tract-on-monetary-reform.pdf.

Keynes, J. M. (1936/2013). *General Theory of Employment, Interest and Money*. Cambridge: Cambridge University Press.

Kitschelt, H., Lange, P., Marks, G., & Stephens J. D. (Eds.). (1999). *Continuity and Change in Contemporary Capitalism*. Cambridge: Cambridge University Press.

Krippner, G. R. (2005). The Financialization of the American Economy. *Socio-Economic Review, 3*(2), 173–208.

Krugman, P. (2012). *End This Depression Now!* New York: W. W. Norton.

Lapavitsas, C., & Powell, J. (2013). Financialisation Varied: A Comparative Analysis of Advanced Economies. *Cambridge Journal of Regions, Economy and Society, 6*(3), 359–379.

Mjøset, L. (2007). An Early Approach to the Varieties of World Capitalism: Methodological and Substantive Lessons from the Senghaas/Menzel-Project. In L. Mjøset & T. H. Clausen (Eds.), *Capitalisms Compared* (pp. 123–176). Amsterdam: Elsevier.

Nölke, A., & May, C. (2013). Vergleichende Kapitalismusforschung im Zeitalter der Krise der Finanzialisierung: Vom inter-nationalen zum inter-temporalen Studium ökonomischer Institutionen. *Zeitschrift Für Außen-Und Sicherheitspolitik, 6*(1), 51–70.

Orrell, D., & Chlupatý, R. (2016). *The Evolution of Money*. New York: Columbia University Press.

Robinson, W. I. (2011). Giovanni Arrighi: Systemic Cycles of Accumulation, Hegemonic Transitions, and the Rise of China. *New Political Economy, 16*(2), 267–280.

Rueda, D., Wibbels, E., & Altamirano, M. (2015). The Origins of Dualism. In P. Beramendi, S. Häusermann, H. Kitschelt, & H. Kriesi (Eds.), *The Politics of Advanced Capitalism* (pp. 89–111). New York: Cambridge University Press.

Streeck, W. (2016). Varieties of Varieties: "VoC" and the Growth Models. *Politics and Society, 44*(2), 243–247.

Streeck, W., & Thelen, K. A. (Eds.). (2005). *Beyond Continuity: Institutional Change in Advanced Political Economies*. Oxford: Oxford University Press.

Thelen, K. (2004). *How Institutions Evolve: The Political Economy of Skills in Germany, Britain, the United States, and Japan*. Cambridge: Cambridge University Press.

Thelen, K. (2014). *Varieties of Liberalization and the New Politics of Social Solidarity*. New York: Cambridge University Press.

Van Treeck, T. (2009). The Political Economy Debate on 'Financialization'—A Macroeconomic Perspective. *Review of International Political Economy, 16*(5), 907–944.

Vernon, R. (1966). International Investment and International Trade in the Product Cycle. *The Quarterly Journal of Economics, 80*, 190–207.

Wallerstein, I. (1974). *The Modern World-System I: Capitalist Agriculture and the Origins of the European World-Economy in the Sixteenth Century*. New York: Academic Press.

Wallerstein, I. M. (2000). *The Essential Wallerstein*. New York: New Press.

CHAPTER 5

A Systemic Cycle-Oriented Framework of Institutional Change

5.1 Introduction

As Chapter 3 has shown, the number of authors arguing for the better development of endogenous theories of institutional change has grown in previous years, and there are attempts to include new drivers of institutional change such as economic growth models. To this end, Chapter 2 has argued for the usefulness of Arrighi's thought which enables perceiving the global picture as more than just the sum of its national parts and supplies a theory of change in a unit of analysis broad enough to capture the relevant processes. Arrighi explains both national and global developments cyclically through his concept of the systemic cycle, which makes them well suited to be explained as endogenous elements in a framework of institutional change. Furthermore, trade positions are often a result of development strategies which Arrighi has called extensive and intensive and interpreted them as successive deeper and wider elaborations of the division of labor through the centuries since the late middle ages. The previous chapter has developed these strategies further in explaining them as supply- and demand-driven growth strategies with the former one being more compatible with general free market policies sometimes critically known as "neoliberalism." This chapter will offer a new framework of institutional change which takes development strategies, trade, and global economic development explained by the systemic cycle into account. Alongside these elements, it will also

J. Lučev, *Systemic Cycle and Institutional Change*,
https://doi.org/10.1007/978-3-030-66053-6_5

contextualize them through the inclusion of others, more familiar drivers of change: technology, power relations, transnational conditionality, and institutional starting positions. Finally, as this framework is to be illustrated in Chapters 6, 7, and 8 by changes in labor institutions in the USA, Germany, and P.R. China, this chapter will explain the selection of these three cases and the selection of the post-1980 timeframe.

5.2 Drivers of Institutional Change: Building the New Framework

As stated in the previous chapter, a good theory of endogenous institutional change must strive to include all significant drivers of change that it logically can. A particular issue of institutional change theory is the insufficient inclusion of drivers of institutional change stemming from the economic environment. Both global economic development and trade positions create specific opportunities which institutional changes may capture, and the Arrighian conceptualization of the systemic cycle provides us with a theory which may predict them. On this basis, a dynamic of specific developmental strategies may develop, for which Arrighi has offered a simple framework of intensive and extensive strategies developed further in the last chapter. This section will explain the three channels of institutional change—path dependence, systemic cycle-driven power relations, and institutional design. Through these three channels, we can observe an interaction of several significant drivers of change: technology, transnational conditionality, starting institutional positions, trade relations, the systemic cycle, developmental strategies, and power resources/political struggle. The section will close with connecting these elements in a framework of institutional change suited to the purpose of identifying drivers of change in labor institutions in the USA, Germany, and China since 1980.

There are three channels of institutional change emphasized in Fig. 5.1—these will be narratively explored in the rest of this section and connected graphically at its end. Firstly, there are the path-dependent effects of the existing institutional structure. The institutional frameworks often tend to change in predictable and stable ways because of the efficiency/successfulness of their growth model (where changes need to be comprehensive due to the complementarity of successful institutional frameworks, are therefore expensive, and have unpredictable effects). Also, the path dependence is caused by the relationship of power

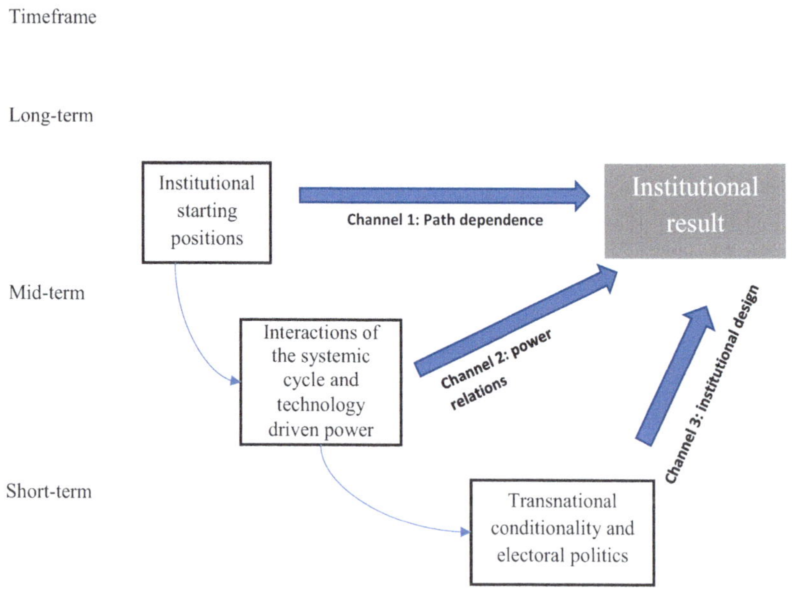

Fig. 5.1 Three channels of institutional change

resources and institutions where the power resources of those favored by the institutions can be used to maintain their stability. Therefore, path-dependent effects are the first possible channel of institutional change taken into account by Fig. 5.1. However, the pressures toward institutional stability or stable change stemming from such path dependence are confronted with other types of pressures which may be directed toward change. They may be a result of a changing economic environment or changes in power relations, both of which are precisely what this framework seeks to endogenize. In any event, the result of institutional change will be the balance between several types of pressures of which path dependence is merely one.

The second channel of institutional change is a complex interaction of technological change, power resources, and the systemic cycle including phases of the systemic cycle, developmental strategies, and trade relations. Considering the timeframe of this analysis, technology in its cumulative aspect represents the most long-term process which could be considered a driver of institutional change. This makes it a context for all other processes, but that should not suggest technological determinism. Technology plays a part in economic development only through a necessary interaction with mid-term processes including the developmental aspect of technology, i.e. with the technology actually in place in production (and it could go in the labor-saving or the labor-intensive direction). The effects could therefore be either greater or smaller capacity of labor to exert political pressure and influence institutional change. Specifically, the USA was already a capital-intensive market in the timeframe considered here. The capital deepening should be considered a driver of the systemic cycle (as it suggests greater capital accumulation), but it has already taken place in this case. Since 1980, the manufacture jobs have been replaced by service jobs, and the trend was exacerbated by growing net imports (i.e. by the trade positions driven in turn by the systemic cycle). In Germany, the trend was similar as the markets already underwent capital deepening, but the systemic cycle playing out in the USA as the center of the world-system caused an improving trade position in Germany (increasing the importance of manufacture in the economy) although service sector employment was taking over (decreasing it). The result was a dualistic labor market with well-protected manufacturing core and a liberalization of the most others. The mentioned timeframes mean that the cumulative aspect of technology is exogenous to our analysis which does not predict great shifts in innovations. In China, the trend was entirely different with a development and capital deepening taking place in the past decades (and in the context of the US systemic cycle with an influx of manufacturing jobs) with the effect that employment in manufacturing sector was rising together with the service sector subsuming technologically outdated agricultural employment. This enabled the vast influx of low-cost labor into manufacturing sector enabling labor-intensive techniques to dominate the developmental aspect of technology in China. The developmental aspect of technology is therefore important, but it significantly overlaps with our understanding of the systemic cycle, and we have subsumed this type of process under the developmental strategy as a part of the systemic cycle.

It follows that the interplay of technological factors, the overlapping global process of the phases of the systemic cycle, and developments in trade relations all help determine the sectoral composition of employment. This suggests something of the developing power relations—i.e. the significance of manufacturing for the economy as a whole (manufacturing jobs being important as they are most easily organized due to the skill specificity they entail). These economic factors then come into interaction with the more overtly political ones which codetermine the decision-making playing field. The changing sectoral composition is only significant in the context of the initial institutional structure (protecting some actors and not others and suggesting an initial and somewhat path-dependent power resource composition) and the newly developing power relations (union density, bargaining coverage) which is an indirect result of both the initial institutional structure and the sectoral compositions changes. All of this influences the developmental strategy (intensive, extensive) which is crucial in determining the institutional change in labor markets. Factors favoring an intensive strategy are the scarcity of labor (and a developing capital-intensive developmental technological aspect), a CME-like composition of initial institutions, an increasing role of manufacturing labor (itself a function of the systemic cycle and trade positions), and the increasing ability of labor to organize. Inverse also holds true: an extensive strategy is favored by the overabundance of labor, an LME-like composition of initial institutions, a decreasing role of manufacturing labor (itself a function of the systemic cycle and trade positions), and the decreasing ability of labor to organize.

Finally, there is the third channel, focusing on visible formal power in transnational conditionality and electoral politics. These two short-term drivers can only become intelligible within the presented complex nexus. The first is included here for the sake of completeness and is endogenous in the sense of the world-system. The issue there is the relative power of states and transnational organizations, and current or aspiring centers of the world-economy are not likely to be significantly affected. The second is the most visible level of formal politics with parties vying for political power by ostensibly offering policy programs to the voting public. However, it is clear that more than mere informed interest is at play in voting behavior and that a range of issues can be operationalized politically including the cultural, the symbolic, and the ideological. It would therefore be naïve to claim that the power relations directly translate into electoral coalitions. However, it is possible that sometimes electoral coalitions do in fact form with the goal and ability to influence institutional change. In other cases, it is worth reminding that formal institutions (i.e. those likely to be influenced via elections) are merely one of the three relevant aspects, while the informal and avoidable aspects are equally likely to be influenced by power relations as the formal ones.

5.2.1 Channel 1: Path Dependence—The Importance of Institutional Starting Positions

Institutional starting positions are central to the study of institutional change, as no change occurs without the significant context of what it is that changes. The same liberalizing tendencies can exert pressure in many developed countries, and yet they will manifest in drastically different ways. Part of the reason for this lies in the substantial starting differences in these countries. By its very definition, the "starting" position is an imagined static context preceding institutional change. However, an implication of stasis is not always a realistic one, even if it is necessary in the sense of an analysis always having to start at some point in time (in our case 1980) and gauge change against this benchmark. Institutions are not static, but evolve over time, and if the institutional frameworks of the VofC are what we are observing, it would take a mid- to long-term perspective to delineate.

Chapter 3 developed the fundamental elements of institutional economics and static comparative research of institutions. Some of the most promising research in this vein was conducted through or explicitly against the Varieties of Capitalism approach—and it can serve us here to very briefly show the importance of starting positions. This approach postulated that developed capitalisms are grouped into two general varieties: liberal market economies (LME) and coordinated market economies (CME). Even though both are market oriented, these two types organize economic activities through very different mechanisms. The former functionally couple the impatient capital of the stock markets with flexible labor laws and low capacity for labor organization and non-specific skill sets in workers while the latter (also) functionally couple the patient capital of large banks with more rigid labor laws, larger union presence, and specific skill sets managed by well-developed vocational training systems. The first (LME) type was modeled after the economic, legal, and political structure of the USA (Chapter 6), while the second (CME) type was modeled after the economic, legal, and political structure of Germany (Chapter 7). However, China (Chapter 8) is one of the countries which do not easily fall into either category. Varieties of Capitalism (alongside much institutional thought) more often than not look for elements of stability in institutions. According to VofC, if the existence of specific institutional arrangements in a well-developed system is preconditioned by the complementarity within the institutional framework, then an institution will tend to remain in place regardless of power relations underlying it.

This approach is a specific example of the path dependence principle suggesting that developments in critical junctures tend to significantly influence further reform choices. New institutionalism traditionally placed too much emphasis on the combination of path dependence and critical junctures. The result was sometimes a stationary view of institutions, all but blind to issues of endogenous change (much like the original VofC views), and this is precisely the limitation that this thesis is attempting to help transcend. Nevertheless, it would be misleading to suggest that path dependence was not an important element in play. Even though institutional thought must no longer be satisfied with merely explaining stability, it is clear that previous choices and structures restrict the plausible choices today and therefore contribute to the shape and direction of institutional change.

The present scheme will explain the varied influences behind Chinese development as well as the dynamics of German and US development. These starting positions suggest a different path of institutional change in these countries. The global incentives for policy reform were universally geared toward free markets in the 1990s and early 2000s, the various countries responded to these liberalization pressures differently.

Interactions with other drivers and the result

(a) Power resources: initial structure has a path-dependent effect via power relations. A structure which has very low labor organization capacities but is oriented toward profit maximization (e.g. LME) will exhibit pressures to further flexibilization as it will have no power structures capable and willing to prevent it. A structure with high labor organization (e.g. CME) may exhibit pressures toward lesser flexibilization as there are power structures which may undermine such a project. In both cases, institutional structure presents itself as a historical compromise between societal powers and its functioning is dependent on the balance of these powers (most notably employees and employers).

(b) Phase of the systemic cycle: financial expansion will progress more quickly with financial deregulation or without formal institutions which would prevent rapid capital accumulation. Historically, an initial corporatist CME-like structure may have delayed a move from material to financial expansion in the 1970s, while the market-oriented LME structure in the USA accelerated it.

(c) Developmental strategy: on the most elementary level, one could be tempted to argue along the lines of path dependence: a coordinated market structure allows a strong institutional channel for labor organizing power to act through and be active in attempting to achieve labor-friendly results. This would suggest that path-dependent effects push toward an intensive developmental strategy and path-dependent effects of a market-oriented initial structure push toward an extensive developmental strategy. However, social reality is far more complex. Developmental strategies need to shift in response to the changing political-economic environment if they are to be successful, and this suggests a different line of reasoning. The point in time in which the circumstances and power compromises embodied in the initial institutional structure have changed is the point in time which is ripe for an alternative developmental strategy which will, if successful, be institutionalized as a part of the new institutional structure. If we opted for a narrower unit of analysis, this institutionalization could be interpreted as a critical juncture. Critical junctures (as we have seen in Chapter 3) are periods of large decisions with long-term path-dependent results. However, they are by definition exogenous. If we were willing to redefine critical junctures to be endogenous, then the initial steps of developmental strategies would certainly provide the critical junctures crucial to this framework. If successful, these strategies could ex-post be defined as critical junctures, would provide elements of the institutional result, which in turn provides us with a path-dependent channel of the next institutional change iteration.

(d) The result of institutional change: path dependence of initial structures tends to produce stable change in the direction of initial institutions. This framework suggests that while this is one of the tendencies, there are several other influences connected with economic development, global processes, and power that are endogenous to our analysis and compete with path dependence, diminishing its effects.

5.2.2 *Channel 2: Complex Interaction of Power Relations and the Systemic Cycle*

The second channel of institutional change is more complex than the first one. It hinges on an interplay of five drivers, including the predictable fluctuations of structural power as a result of technological and systemic cycle shifts. Figure 5.2 shows the interactions within this channel.

Phase of the systemic cycle, developmental strategies, and trade relations constitutes the three systemic cycle drivers, organized here according to the timeframe necessary for their development. Figure 5.2 also shows their interactions with the long-term driver of technology shifts and the power relations. The rest of this segment will elaborate these interactions, and a simplified version of Fig. 5.2 will be included in the comprehensive Fig. 5.3 at the end of this section.

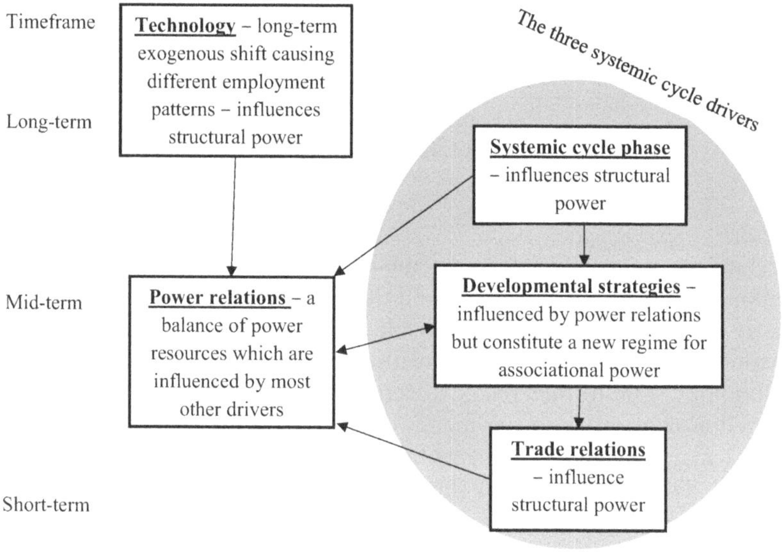

Fig. 5.2 Channel 2—power relations and systemic cycle

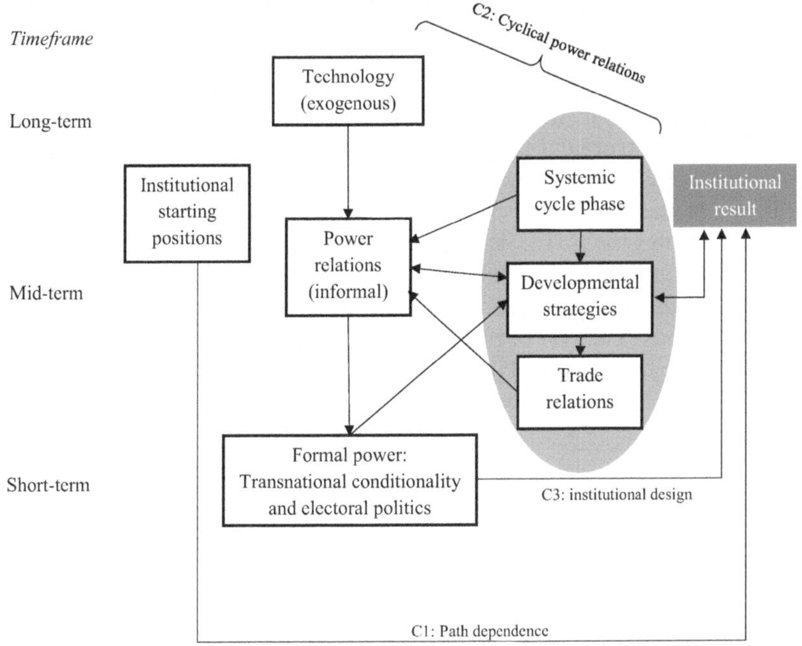

Fig. 5.3 A general framework of institutional change

5.2.2.1 *Technology*

Technology is an important element in growth and development—although the selected timeframe and the complexity of the subject require us to use it as an exogenous variable. As we have seen in the previous chapter, we can discern the cumulative and the developmental aspect of technology. The former refers to actual innovations, which can only be treated as exogenous to the framework as they not predictable and their effects may take a long time to manifest in terms of productivity and growth. The latter refers to the application of technology (e.g. capital deepening) and could be understood as endogenous as underdeveloped (lower tier in the world-system) countries can experience a growth-boost by enjoying the possibilities of technological catch-up, while the developed world experiences such boosts only in periods of great technological transformation. By treating these two aspects as a single driver, we avoid unnecessary complexity of the framework, but more importantly, also conform to the selected timeframe, which is relatively brief from the point of view of technological shifts. In any event, the crucial point is the changes in employment compositions and the role of labor in the economy. Owing to the long-term technological tendencies of the twentieth century, a developed, post-industrial economy hinges on the service sector, which largely employees easily replaceable personnel operating in a decentralized context. This influences both the structural and associational labor power, as labor has severe issues in organizing (lower associational power), and the workers have a diminishing role in the economy (lower structural power). The inverse also holds true, as an agricultural country experiencing an industrial shift may find the power of its labor increasing in both elements.

Interactions with other drivers and the result

a) Power resources: as technology changes, it creates different methods of production, which may substantially change the power resources. Historically, it reduced the number of workers needed in manufacturing. This changed the elementary power resources and diminished the bargaining position of labor.
b) Developmental strategy: a technological shift may create new investment possibilities making the old growth models obsolete and trigger a choice of new developmental strategy.

5.2.2.2 *Phase of the Systemic Cycle*

Dynamics of phases of the systemic cycle may greatly influence the distribution of power resources. The periodization of these dynamics is dependent on large crises which can be indicators of shifts in accumulation regimes. The process of economic development in the developed world (core) tends to fluctuate between periods of material and financial expansion. The mechanism of this shift is a wide profit crunch occurring in the real sector and the capital fleeing into the more short-term-oriented financial activities and triggering the financialization (financial expansion). This suggests different prospects for labor as the inability of generating large profits in manufacture also means that a traditionally unionized labor has become unattractive for use in production (i.e. capital will move into a less labor-intensive use of speculative finance).

The systemic cycle is best described as a sum of interacting and overlapping global processes with specific geographic origins (cores or centers). It consists of two distinct general types of processes: material and financial expansion. Both together may take more than a century to develop (i.e. Arrighian long centuries), but their duration has increasingly diminished historically and our chosen timeframe suggests that these processes cannot be analyzed in terms of entire financial-material-financial scope. We are interested in the period after 1980, and the US financial expansion has taken 35 years from the signal crisis of 1973 to the terminal crisis of 2008. We are now arguably observing the initial period of the new material expansion which may take even less. In other words, the systemic cycle processes that we are interested in are mid- to long-term duration processes.

Interactions with other drivers and the result

(a) Trade relations: material expansion (particularly in the context of the extensive developmental strategy) suggests a substantial trade surplus, while a financial expansion of the old center suggests a widening trade deficit.
(b) Power resources: material expansion creates more manufacturing employment, creating a bigger role for manufacturing labor in the economy, suggesting more bargaining and organizational power. A shift from material to financial expansion suggests lower manufacturing employment levels and lower labor power.
(c) Developmental strategies: financial expansion signals the waning of power in the old center and its finishing phases provide a context for the choice of the developmental strategy in prospective new centers. The successful developmental strategy becomes the new global center and leads the new material expansion.

5.2.2.3 Trade Relations—Current and Changing Positions in the World-System

The systemic cycle suggests that employment shifts away from areas in which manufacture-related activities are facing a profit crunch (core areas during financial expansions) and into semi-peripheral and currently underdeveloped areas which can hold promises of larger profits in manufacture (e.g. China since the 1980s). Such a shift holds specific incentives for institutional change with workers in deindustrializing countries becoming increasingly superfluous and therefore decreasingly powerful. Liberalizations of labor markets may, then, proceed with greater intensity. An employment importing country on the semi-periphery does not, however, automatically move toward greater coordination of labor as a prerequisite for this is twofold. Firstly, the workers must become scarce and therefore gain functional bargaining power, which can then manifest in formalized power relations (greater union density, higher-level collective bargaining, and more bargaining coverage). Secondly, the institutional framework must be able to orient toward such a move, according to issues of institutional complementarity.

In this view, the trade relations are a somewhat delayed effect of the systemic cycle, but they are certainly influenced by a vast number of other factors as well (global prices of goods, resources and transport, exchange rate changes, etc.). A significant and durable change in trade relations could be observed in the short- or mid-term.

Interactions with other drivers and the result

(a) Power resources: an increase in trade surplus suggests an increasing role of manufacturing in the economy and a greater bargaining power of the workers. An increase in the trade deficit suggests a diminishing role of manufacturing in the economy and a lower bargaining power of the workers.

(b) Transnational conditionality: a large trade surplus is a conceivable way to development and growth. It can therefore contribute to the countries' power substantial enough to avoid transnational conditionality.

(c) Systemic cycle phase: a shift from trade surplus to a trade deficit is compatible with a shift from material expansion to a finance expansion.

(d) Developmental strategies: an extensive strategy is oriented to the export markets in its growth model, while an intensive strategy is oriented toward domestic markets. This duality was logically developed in the previous chapter (as high wages of the intensive strategy contribute to domestic demand but reduce external competitiveness and low wages of the extensive strategy reduce domestic demand but increase external competitiveness). However, this is a matter of strong tendency rather than mutual exclusiveness as an intensive strategy could still attempt to formulate a strong export niche—what defines it as intensive is the relatively larger importance of the domestic markets rather than the absence of export markets.

5.2.2.4 Developmental Strategies

We can state this in another and less general way by utilizing Arrighi's dichotomy of intensive/extensive accumulation regimes. If we interpret the modern iterations of intensive and extensive accumulation regimes as those seeking the demand for their output increase at home (intensive) or abroad (extensive), we can again see that specific institutional change incentives attach. A country with an intensive accumulation regime looks for domestic demand for its output and enters into a specific dialectic between real wages as the source of a demand increase and real wages as a source of rising costs of production. The latter can either drive the aggregate prices upward (triggering wage-pull inflation and/or reducing the quantity demanded) or drive profits downward. This suggests a domestic equilibrium like the ones found in the Keynesian era of the first three decades after World War II in the developed world (Chapter 6). If such a regime is undergoing a material expansion, this expansion is fully compatible with rising labor coordination tendencies, as each job is important not only because the skill set of the worker employed is scarce, but also because it carries in it the vital element of aggregate demand. China may be currently turning toward such a regime (Chapter 8).

On the other hand, in an extensive accumulation regime, material expansion is intended for consumption abroad. Real wages primarily factor in as production costs to be frozen or eliminated in order to manifest as international competitiveness. Therefore, it may become necessary to move toward greater liberalization of labor institutions. This is indicative of Germany since the adoption of the euro (Chapter 7).

Developmental strategies are, in this context, a mid-term phenomenon, plausibly taking a longer time to develop than issues of transnational conditionality or electoral policies, but a shorter time than issues of substantial technological change.

Interaction with other drivers and the result

(a) Power resources: intensive strategies increase the resources of workers which can increase their capacity to organize and vice versa. However, the long-term effects of intensive strategies could be the diminished bargaining position of workers (as they have a diminishing role in the economy) and vice versa.

(b) Trade relations: extensive strategy focuses by definition on external markets suggesting an increase in exports, while intensive strategy focuses on domestic markets (see above).
(c) The result of institutional change: developmental strategies have clear short-term societal winners (labor in intensive strategy) and losers (labor in extensive strategy). As the intensive strategy is a likely effect of high power resources of labor and as these are likely increased in the short run by the intensive strategy, this strategy is essentially the moment in which the compromises of power relations are institutionalized. In other words, the changing power relations overcome path dependence of the initial structure and help formulate a new strategy and a successful developmental strategy becomes a part of the result of institutional change. Once more, if the strategy is successful, and if we are willing to redefine critical junctures as endogenous events, this institutionalization can *ex-post* be interpreted as a critical juncture.

5.2.2.5 *Power Relations*

Power is crucial to this framework and its functioning, and it is also the node in which the first two chapters can come together most fruitfully. Chapter 2 has outlined the approach to labor power in the context of the world-system (via Silver and Wright). Associational power refers to the ability to organize, whereas structural power refers to the bargaining position of labor which stems from its location on the labor markets and the workplace. Chapter 3 showed the dynamic relationship between institutions and power (via North, Korpi, and Thelen). Institutions can be thought of as results of power relations and compromises between the interests of various groups endowed with power resources. Likewise, a change in institutions can be thought of as induced by a change in the power relations. Power resource theory tells us that institutions are a function of political power held by various organized groups. An institution is a compromise between various powers (e.g. organized labor and organized employers) and institutional change is a result of a change in power relations underlying the institution.

In this context, the relevant position of labor is underlined by the capacity of labor to organize and influence decision making. The relevant data according to the power resource theory would therefore consist primarily of union density and collective agreement coverage. Together, these figures testify to the power of organized labor in terms of the labor they represent (and could mobilize in strikes or otherwise) and the scope of its actions (bargaining coverage figures can be much higher than density figures). If unions have a high membership rate (i.e. density) and conduct bargaining which applies to majority of workers, then its power position is certainly strong and vice versa. Such power relations are results of at least mid-term processes as densities dissolve in terms of decades rather than years.

The most visible institutional change is one that occurs through formal political channels (next driver). But, as explained in the previous chapter, the Northian conceptualization of institutions accepted here sees institutions as far wider reaching than the legislative power could provide by itself. In terms of labor market reforms, the actual protection of labor is a result of not only the laws regulating labor, but also the practices of collective bargaining and the leverage represented by the unions. Therefore, the most essential element of power relations is the irreplaceable nature of the workers these organized labor structures represent. A worker in a setting which promotes high skill-set specificity (manufacturing workers in the CME context in the *Varieties of Capitalism* approach) is difficult to replace as he represents an investment in the specific skill set needed for his job description. A worker with a low skill-set specificity (a tertiary sector worker or a worker specific for the LME economy) represents an easily replaceable asset. In the first case, a representing union may wield substantial power, while in the second case it most likely does not. We must, therefore, distinguish between at least mid-term power relations, which are a matter of the ability of labor and/or capital to organize and protect its interests through all institutions, and short-term electoral coalitions, which build upon these power relations (but also the cultural, symbolical, personal, unconscious, etc.) in order to produce change in formal institutions. The relationship between these two levels is not one sided: it is not a matter of power relations stemming from production determining the electoral coalitions and results. Rather, these processes are parallel: the power relations are a matter of the bargaining position and organizational capacities and the electoral politics leading to the control of formal political institutions may mobilize these or other capacities.

Interactions with other drivers and the result

(a) Phase of the systemic cycle: organized investor interests and the absence of opposition may accelerate the shift from material to finance expansion via quicker financial deregulation and vice versa.
(b) Developmental strategy: as explained above, a dynamic between path dependence via power relations and a shift to a new growth model.
(c) Result of institutional change: power relations in many ways determine the effectiveness of formal reforms (as the mobilization of relevant power resources enables the reflection of the intent of formal institutions in informal institutions and prevents their avoidance).

5.2.3 *Channel 3: Institutional Design—Domestic Politics and Transnational Conditionality*

The last driver and one with the shortest timeframe is the formal political channel, which describes the institutional change that is induced either through domestic politics (e.g. electoral, legislative, executive) or the transnational conditionality of various transnational organizations. As explained above, these attempts at reforms are the most visible and provide for one of the three channels of institutional change identified here. However, their effectiveness is dependent on power resources and path dependence (including issues of institutional complementarity). Specifically, Chapter 3 has explored the Beramendi project which hinges on the democratic process and the role that these groups play in terms of enticing electoral coalitions designed to capture their votes. While such a focus is interesting and significant, the substitutions of the more invisible mid-term power relations and mid- to long-term path dependence for the highly visible and short-term electoral and coalitional policies do not seem advisable. However, if its limitations are properly understood, the formal political relations can be an informative driver of change.

Not all power-driven institutional change has its origins within states. Institutions may be influenced by various transnational organizations either by offering advice or by exerting pressure. The latter mechanism becomes important if the organization in question holds a resource needed by the state (e.g. funds needed to stabilize a crisis or fund developmental projects) and is in the position to condition its use with the enacting of institutional reforms. This suggests that the prevailing intellectual ambience in these transnational organizations is relevant, but not as relevant as the external power position of the state. A large, developed, and economically stable state is far less likely to be in the position to be transnationally conditioned than a small, underdeveloped, and economically destabilized state. As an additional note, this driver would be considered exogenous if the unit of analysis remained the isolated national state. However, the world-systemic lens allows us to view individual states in the context of the global world-system in which the power relations between states and between transnational organizations and states become endogenous issues—as they are covered by the used theory and its models. Conditionality as conceived here is most often a short-term horizon driver of change. It is a visible form of power in which a transnational organization influences a state by applying pressure and attempting to achieve reforms in accordance with its own economic agenda.

Benefiting from a world-systemic lens, we can see that the transnational conditionality is dependent on existing power relations between individual states and transnational organizations. Firstly, the most powerful states most strongly influence the rules and decision making in large transnational organizations. Secondly, the most powerful states are least likely to be put in the position of being dependent on the conditionality.[1] The two possible types of formal political power are grouped into a single driver as they (a) share a timeframe and (b) transnational conditionality may or may not be present (it is not in our three cases). However, even when it manifests itself, the ultimate influence will have to be exerted via the domestic formal political channels (the executive power entering into international agreements and/or legislative power passing of formal institutions).

Interactions with other drivers and the result

(a) Developmental strategy: transnational conditionality can influence large parts of the developmental strategy by requiring changes in labor laws or even specific macroeconomic (investment, fiscal, monetary...) targets.

[1] The only exception for this timeframe may be the Chinese accession to the WTO in 2001, although it had little bearing on labor institutions.

(b) Result of institutional change: formal domestic politics play a crucial part in formal reforms (as the control of formal political institutions enables an explicit attempt at reform). Transnational conditionality can also influence the final institutional framework, but the focus on visible results suggests a focus on a change of formal institutions rather than a change in the underlying power resources which will tend to determine the informal and avoidable aspects of institutions.

5.3 The Framework of Change in Labor Institutions

Complex institutional systems are outcomes of many necessary and sufficient causes, making them difficult to analyze in terms of causality. Our strategy consists instead of expanding the notions of embeddedness and complementarity via externalities in order to accommodate the elusive endogenous change in a sufficiently broad (global, world-systemic) unit of analysis. The rest of this section will explain the time-based logic of embeddedness, according to which institutions are embedded not only in other institutions (as explained by Ostrom, Williamson, and others) but also in contextual factors which provide externalities conducive to change or stability. In this sense, we can conceive of a hierarchy of institutional drivers which is based on time—with long-term (40+ years), mid-term (10–40 years drivers), and short-term drivers (–10 years drivers).

A process taking a longer time to develop provides a context for the development of a process with a shorter period of development. In this sense, these drivers of institutional change (themselves institutions or economic and political processes) are embedded in higher order processes (i.e. those of longer duration). Long-term technological change provides a context for institutional frameworks and systemic cycles which in turn provide a context for the development of power resource relations and the implementation of development strategies, which are themselves a context for the development of trade relations which finally support the short-term processes of electoral coalitions and transnational conditional pressures. This hierarchy of embeddedness does not, however, necessarily imply one-way causality (as New Institutional Economics/NIE authors might well assume according to their conceptualizations of embeddedness). Even though (e.g.) development strategies and power relations provide the crucial context for the electoral politics, they can certainly stand to be modified by the outcomes of elections. Therefore, while this NIE-influenced hierarchy provides crucial insight into the relationship of institutional drivers, it does not help us to decode their effects. To do so, we must turn to VofC notions of institutional externalities. Through the prism of this analogy, it becomes apparent that institutional drivers reinforce or undermine each other's effects and that the role that they play can only be made apparent in context with other drivers.

It is also worth noting that institutions in this framework are effectively evoked in several positions which are a consequence of their definition. The definition of institutions-as-rules structuring activity suggests that there are active institutions governing each of the institutional drivers (e.g. tariffs and international agreements governing trade and financial and corporate regulation governing the systemic cycle). However, this is another factual, but ultimately irrelevant and tautological position where institutions exist by definition and therefore must be functional. This framework suggests that specific labor institutions are most clearly discerned on the level of starting institutional frameworks (where we can observe the complementarity with other institutions) and on the level of the development strategies which suggest either strong or flexible regulation of labor, provided we observe development strategies through the lens of demand management (as we did in Chapter 4). In other words, we have institutions explicitly evoked in the initial institutional structure and the result of institutional change, but the third institutional element is the developmental strategy which may, in the case of its success, become a part of the long-term institutional result (hence the double-arrow in the representation in Fig. 5.3).

Focusing on the temporal embeddedness could favor observing top-down mechanisms, which would suggest a form of determinism. However, there are feedback loops which exist on every level, with the most significant ones shown in the figure. Starting from the bottom, the two short-term drivers can influence almost every other level described. The outcomes of elections and transnational conditionality can influence the mid-term processes: power relations (e.g. by the passing of laws and regulations inhibiting or promoting labor organization or its functioning in bargaining practices), trade positions (e.g. by changes in trade policy), systemic cycle (e.g. by tax incentives or stimulus packages temporarily increasing profits and staving off the shift from material to financial), and developmental strategies (e.g. by the expansion of the household demand via tax reforms). By doing so, they influence the long-term processes in adding to a new institutional framework which then provides the context for a new iteration of institutional change, promoting a new type of developmental aspect technology (e.g. encouraging a specific type of investment) or even the cumulative aspect (promotion of R&D).

Same holds true for the possibilities of feedback in processes of longer duration. Changing power relations in favor of labor can be a powerful deterrent and/or a generator of informal political pressure which may be exerted in the direction of a more progressive taxation (i.e. a changing developmental strategy) and may lead to higher wages which can contribute to a profit crunch (leading to the financial stage of the systemic cycle) or a deteriorating trade position (if felt in price levels). On the other hand, a change in developmental strategy has effects on trade relations and the systemic cycle (same reasons reinforced in both counts). Finally, the systemic cycle in its shift from material to financial phase starts a form of deindustrialization even though production may remain capital-intensive (USA since 1980). Or, a material expansion of aspiring centers (Germany, China since 1980) causes an increase in capital deepening. In either case, it is a change in the developmental aspect of technology effected by a lower order process.

The obvious existence of these feedback loops suggests that neither determinism nor functionalism are prudent assumptions in institutional research. Determinism would suggest one category shaping all others, while the modern structures of capitalism seem to be composed of numerous local (i.e. national) and global, economic and political, dynamic, overlapping, and mutually interacting complex processes. Functionalism would suggest the existence of institutions is merited on their functionality, instead of the power alliances and specific processes which underlie them (something that the VofC agenda is often accused of). This framework is built on the premise of continuous and power-laden mutual interaction of both institutions and economic and political processes. The selection of successful cases prohibits us to explore the decidedly dysfunctional combinations of institutions and their drivers, however. Nevertheless, it remains clear that institutions can be contended or stabilized by those with power, and that institutional frameworks which are dysfunctional in terms of growth and development can be maintained by vested interests of powerful minorities. The numerous examples of underdeveloped countries with corrupt elites should point to the desirability of avoiding functionalism as an assumption in institutional analysis.

This suggests an interpretation of difficulties in deliberate and successful reform initiation. For a government (which is a short-term, 4-year formal political process in most Western democracies) to initiate a labor market reform, it must first recognize the prevalent power-positions (which are results of mid-term processes) and which may work to informally subvert the new formal institutions and render them inactive. It must then successfully manage to build this reform into a successful growth model, or it will be self-defeating (it must be aligned with another mid-term process of 10–15 years). Finally, for the institutional reform to give positive results in terms of growth or unemployment, it must be aligned (complementary) with a mid- to long-term process of institutional frameworks (particularly with financial market regulations and educational systems, but also macroeconomic management) which we treated as initial structures. A successful reform of the formal (regulatory) aspect of the labor market must either identify and align with processes already underway or initiate a very broad reform covering diverse areas (i.e. labor, education, finance, and macroeconomic management) and negotiate this broad reform against the vested interest in all of these areas.

This framework has suggested a logical alternative where the temporal hierarchy of institutional drivers may even render the formal political process irrelevant, as the results of uncodified practices may provide a stronger effective institutional protection than the formal system or undermine the formal system and result in effectively more flexible institutions. An example of a stronger effective network was Germany where the wide-spread protection awarded by collective bargaining was sufficiently strong that a minimum wage law was passed only in 2015. Such regulation was not deemed necessary before due to the strong effective institutions on the level of informal uncodified bargaining processes. An example of an undermined formal system is the Chinese labor regulation which is formally among the strongest in the world but has been largely unenforced for decades as the power relations and informal practices do not support it. Either way, neither a purely top-down nor a purely bottom-up mechanism is something to be expected in institutional change. This framework used a temporal embeddedness of drivers in an attempt to clarify their mutual interactions and feedback loops in the interactions of three recognized channels of institutional change.

In the event of successful developmental strategy change, the elements of the strategy become the new rules of the game (i.e. the strategy becomes institutionalized). Figure 5.4 shows a simplified model of such successfulness.

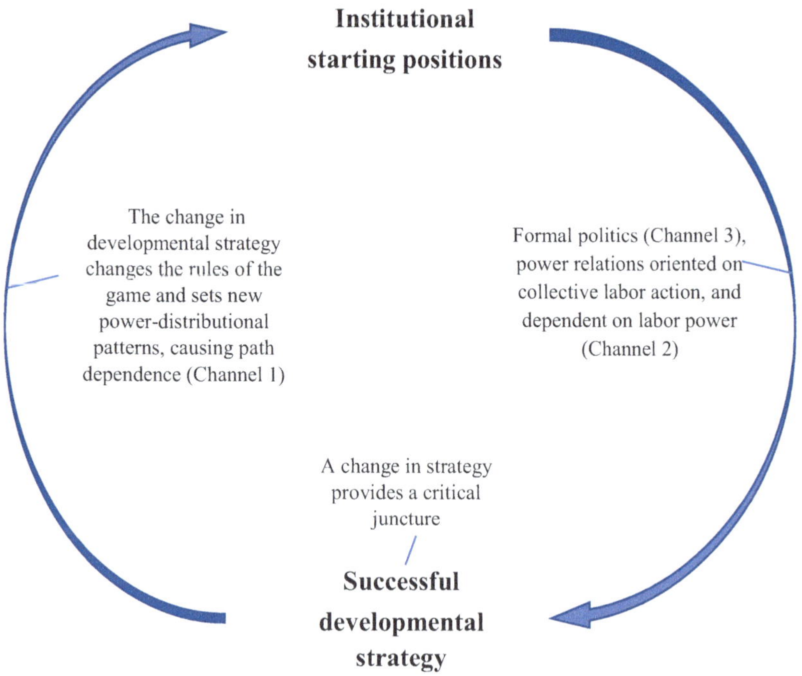

Fig. 5.4 Success of developmental strategies in labor institutions

If the strategy were unsuccessful (perhaps due to the lack of complementarity with existing active arrangements), it could merely signify a failed reform. However, a successful change in developmental strategy (e.g. shift from extensive to intensive) institutionalizes new rules of the game. This shift may *ex-post* be identified as a critical juncture, but Fig. 5.4 shows such path deviation (i.e. a shift in strategy) as a result of formal political processes (which we identified as channel 3) or shifts in labor power resources effecting a change in its ability to influence the more informal aspects of institutions (channel 2). Once institutionalized, the developmental strategy sets the tone for further development, setting in a path dependence of its own (channel 1). However, once we acknowledge the full macroeconomic effects of such shifts, we must also notice that the long-term effects may run counter to the initial intentions. If a labor-friendly high-wage intensive strategy is institutionalized, it will reduce the international competitiveness by raising the costs of production. The new intensive strategy will provide an internal market for higher price goods, but in an open economy, cheaper foreign goods will eventually crowd out some domestic manufacturing. In this event, a successful shift to intensive strategy (originally enabled by high structural labor power) eventually reduces the structural power of labor, enabling an eventual shift back into an extensive strategy.

5.4 Illustrating the Framework of Labor-Institutional Changes

The next three chapters will illustrate the central claims of this chapter by applying this framework on the labor institutions in China, Germany, and the USA since 1980. This section explains this selection by focusing on the choices of institutions, cases, and intervals in turn.

5.4.1 The Importance of Labor Institutions

It seems almost redundant to point out that class-based politics has largely lost its thrust in recent decades. This made labor power a somewhat unattractive area of research. However, while this old reason for studying labor is perhaps gone, there are a number of crucial reasons to focus on labor institutions. Firstly, demand management is greatly influenced by income distribution, which makes labor institutions a prime (and under-recognized) subject for macroeconomics-inspired research. It also makes labor institutions intertwined with growth models. Secondly, labor can be, and historically often was, mobilized to achieve political goals. This makes the presence or absence of manifestation of political labor power a relevant political science issue. Thirdly, the combination of visible power foundations and economic effects of labor institutions makes them a relevant issue in the study of institutional change as labor institutions include the predictors of institutional change that can be found in existing literature.

5.4.2 Case Selection: USA, Germany, PR China

The three cases could be interpreted as a most different case study design. As shown in Chapter 3, the USA and Germany are consistently discerned in typologies as typifying different varieties of advanced capitalism. China, on the other hand, represents a third distinct option where the rule of law and organized labor are yet to fully develop. However, these cases were selected according to the findings of the systemic cycle approach described in Chapter 2. The USA was clearly the center of world production in the latter half of the twentieth century, as well as the center of global finance, political and military power. In using Arrighian systemic cycle theory, one would expect to see a waning hegemony/center of the world-system in the years following the crisis of 1973 which would also suggest a financialization in this aging economic center. When we observe the macroeconomic data on the USA in this period, we therefore expect to see signs of reduced production and increased financial activity. The selection of the two remaining cases reflected the need to locate competitor-states for the new hegemony or rather the competitors for the new world-systemic center of production as the first step toward such a hegemony.

Looking at data on net trade in goods in billions USD (OECD 2020), three large economies dominate. USA has sported the largest trade deficit since mid-1970s (at yearly record level in 2018 at $872 billion and at $854.4 billion in 2019), while China and Germany have enjoyed the largest trade surplusses in the past 15 years (at $417.7 billion and $256.7 billion in 2019, respectively). They were only surpassed in specific years by Russia and Saudi Arabia (which are energy-dependent exporters whose exports are far more volatile in value). This data shows the value of trade in produced, physical items and it is particularly relevant as it represents the first element in Wallerstein's discussion of hegemony. As we will observe in following chapters, manufacturing labor tends to be most productive and most protected by regulation and prevalent practice.

Table 5.1 shows the cumulative net goods exports of the three selected cases in the 1992–2016 period as reported by OECD in current USD billions.

Table 5.1 Cumulative net goods exports

Time	*Cumulative net goods exports (1992–2001)*	*Average year (1992–2001)*	*Cumulative pre-global recession (2002–2008)*	*Average year (2002–2008)*	*Cumulative (2009–2016)*	*Average year (2009–2016)*
Germany	492.6	54.7	1488.6	186.1	1985.3	248.2
USA	−1855.9	−206.2	−5273.2	−659.2	−5503.8	−688
China	169.4	18.8	932.4	116.6	2517.3	314.7

Source of data OECD 2017; own calculation

Table 5.1 shows the evolution in these three states. It is clear that the combined global effect of German and Chinese trade (both consistently in surplus) has grown increasingly comparable to the global effect of US trade (consistently in deficit). In the 1990s, the combined cumulative surplus of China and Germany was approximately at 1/3 of the US trade deficit in goods; in the years preceding the global recession of 2009 (2001–2008), the Chinese and German surpluses stand at almost 1/2 of US deficits; and in the post-recession years; they climb to over 4/5. Table 5.1 omits the post-2016 era, which was marked by protectionist inclinations of the Trump administration in USA and the COVID-19 pandemic. The former resulted in significant trade confrontations in 2018 and 2019, and the responses to the latter produced a sharp and wide-spread economic downturn in 2020. The results of these events may not be fully understood for some time. However, such data as is currently available does not suggest that the trends described here will be substantially affected.

All of this suggests that China and Germany are the two suitable candidates for the next center of the world-system in a Wallersteinian/Arrighian sense. These are the two countries with the largest global export of goods which together make up most of the net deficits of the old center which has turned to a financial expansion in the past 40 years and has become the importer of goods. According to Arrighi, these two countries should be expected to compete with alternative organizational innovations which could cement their material expansions eventually translating in a massive financial expansion of their own following a period of global dominance of one of them and a signal crisis eventually serving as a harbinger of the shift from material to financial expansion.

5.4.3 *Interval Selection: 1980s to Today*

The period since 1980 has been momentous for labor institutions as it brought wide sweeps of liberalizations in very specific national contexts. These were also accompanied by large-scale historical shifts toward free markets and geopolitical oscillations from bipolarity via unipolarity to multipolarity and with the rise of China as a global superpower. The general idea is to make sense of these shifts via the systemic cycle theory, and in this context, organizational innovations in the systemic chaos periods may result in a central position in the world-system. Therefore, they represent new ways of being more productive and more competitive as an exporting center. They also represent ways of economic growth beyond demographic growth, by which national economies become richer. World-systems analysis assumes the unity of these two world center characteristics, and Arrighi's analysis of the systemic cycle shows us how these two are diachronically connected. A geographic location will start to assume the role of the most competitive part of the world during the inevitable downturn in competitiveness of a far richer world-systemic center now turning to financial activity. With time, this most competitive location will become the new world-systemic center: it will grow richer and expand its production and trade for decades. However, the initial competitiveness increase is owed to a specific political-economic innovation—i.e. a specific set of policy reforms best suited to economic expansion. Within the systemic cycle logic, the relevant dates for such an innovation are 1973 at the earliest and 2008 at the latest (i.e. the period between the signal and the terminal crisis roughly delimiting the period of financialization in the old center or the USA).

This interpretation is crucial to the idea of the systemic cycle, but also unintelligible outside the actual historical context. Arrighi interprets the 1973 crisis as a signal crisis, which caused a shift into the hard financial expansion. This crisis was accompanied by several shocks. The Nixon shock was the 1971–1973 breakdown of the Bretton-Woods system of currency stabilization with the USD no longer serving as the anchor of currencies, ushering a new period of uncertainty in international trade. The OPEC shock (1973–1974) was intended as an economic punishment of the Western world for its support of Israel in the context of the 1973 Yom Kippur War. It introduced a period of higher oil prices which presented substantial challenges for the trade balances of the underdeveloped world and other oil importers. The Volcker shock sharply increased key interest rates in the 1980–1981 period in the USA in an effort to curb inflation. The repercussion was a different financial atmosphere with more abundant capital (due to the Nixon shock) but temporarily more difficult to procure by regular crediting channels (due to the Volcker shock)—spelling out some difficulties for the increasingly externally indebted developing world as well. All these developments provided a context for the Reagan era deregulations and liberalizations that would produce what David Harvey has called a neoliberal state (Harvey 2005). Other statewide free market experiments could be found from Chile and UK in the 1970s to the transition in Central and Eastern Europe in the early 1990s.

The pressures toward the free markets were strengthened through the conditioned loan activities of international organizations like the IMF and the IBRD, spreading what has become the free market policy-prescription mainstream known as the Washington consensus (Stiglitz 2002). It was in this context that a general pressure toward liberalization could be felt. We can interpret this as a pressure toward the extensive capitalism strategy which is deregulationist and attempts to reduce production costs in order to produce competitive exports. Again, from the Western point of view, the first strategy could describe the first decades after World War II with various types of protection combining into a Keynesian welfare state. The second strategy may sound like the prescriptions of the Washington consensus that strived to formulate policy advice in the 1980s, 1990s, and early 1990s through the free market orientation of mainstream economic science. However, actual economic development strategies do not necessarily change though a change of atmosphere in the economic science, or a change in prevalent opinions in international organizations. After all, many voices predicted a regulatory *race-to-the-bottom* as a result of increasing trade openness and the liberalization of capital flows in the 1990s. As capital became migratory and labor remained stationary (Tilly 1995), it stood to reason that a new globalized world would suggest that foreign investment would flow toward countries which had least regulation and therefore enabled the most profit. This would trigger competitive deregulation and supposedly destroy the welfare state. While such pressures certainly materialized, the results fell far short of expectations (Weiss 1998). Certainly, the institutional changes were mostly neither instantaneous nor enormous. Various countries dealt with pressures toward liberalization in various ways as shown in Chapter 3. Arrighi can help us understand such changes in a broader historical context. A general free market-oriented shift in the last few decades from the Western perspective (i.e. toward extensive capitalism) does not mean that trade-related pressures will not incentivize a shift toward more regulation and higher worker incomes in China. In fact, in order to interpret the modern institutional shift, we must first understand the role that these shifts play when embedded in broader strategies interacting with trade positions and the systemic cycle itself.

However, practical considerations have pushed the present research agenda somewhat, as the macroeconomic data is sometimes unavailable for the period before 1980 and it is more prudent to start the analysis later, when more details may be observed. Also, this year is consistent with the initial Chinese moves toward liberalization which have started through the 1980s. The following three chapters will therefore focus on events occurring post-1980 and analyze latest available data, which in practice puts the end-date in 2018 or 2019.

5.5 Conclusions

The goal of this chapter has been to use the elements explained and interpreted in the first three chapters in order to develop the approach to institutional change of this thesis. The primary method was the construction of an overarching framework of institutional change which encompasses several institutional approaches and an Arrighian approach to global capitalism and its iterations. The approach hinges on the idea that modern global capitalism has variegated national effects which have specific institutional repercussions. These effects can be thought of as endogenous due to the world-systemic unit of analysis which allows us to treat national institutions as sub-units of a far larger system. In order to analyze the effects of global capitalism on national systems, we must first understand the many levels which shape the national institutional outcome.

To do so, the chapter has used the conceptualization of institutions from Chapter 4, which draws on North, power resource theory, and new institutionalism to provide a concept of power-based and temporally grounded institutions which are capable of path dependence *and* path deviation according to the complex interplay of various political and economic factors which we have identified here as institutional change drivers. Their mutual interaction was depended on externalities and embeddedness. Using a logic of complementarity (VofC), this chapter suggested that there are institutional externalia (effects which a specific institution may exploit) not only in other institutions, but also in various political and economic processes which therefore contribute not only to institutional stability as assumed by VofC but, in their changing nature, to institutional change. Using a logic of embeddedness (NIE), this chapter further suggested that these drivers are mutually contextualized according to the timeframes necessary for each driver to develop. The long-term processes of technological change and institutional frameworks (considered here as institutional starting points) provide the context for mid-term processes of developmental strategy, trade relations, the systemic cycle, and changing power relations which in turn provide the context for the short-term processes of formal electoral politics and transnational conditionality.

All of these together provide three distinct but overlapping channels of institutional change. Firstly, the institutional starting position provides path dependence, influencing the process of change in the direction of existing institutional arrangements. This is the channel emphasized by historical institutionalism and VofC. We have argued that it can only explain exogenous institutional change and is therefore insufficient in and of itself. Secondly, the formal political power channel (provided by national electoral politics and transnational conditionality) attempts to enact reforms to directly change institutions. This channel has been traditionally emphasized by political science (rational choice, public choice, international relations and foreign policy, Europeanization, coercive isomorphism…). We have developed a logic of temporal embeddedness of institutional change drivers to show the problems which this channel would face in providing efficient change if it existed in isolation. The third channel is the complex interaction of various institutional drivers putting the power relations and the systemic cycle in its center. We have suggested that the inclusion of systemic cycle theory allows us to predict the changes in political power of labor through several processes. The phase of the systemic cycle influences power resources as material expansion creates a greater structural power as it tends to increase the structural importance to the manufactured goods producers and financial expansion tends to reduce structural power as it decreases the structural importance of these workers. Developmental strategies are attempts at maneuvering the phases of the systemic cycles by specific aggregate demand management regimes which may initially reflect the high (intensive strategy) or low (extensive strategies) resources of labor but also influence trade. Finally, trade relations contribute in a similar way, as export increases tend to favor the structural power of manufacturing labor and vice versa. The power resources of labor can in turn influence either the formal legislative politics or more likely use the less formal structured interactions (e.g. collective bargaining) to influence the developmental strategies. Developmental strategies are themselves attempts at institutionalizing labor-friendly and domestic market-oriented intensive regimes or alternatively export market-oriented extensive regimes. If successful, the developmental strategies provide the third channel of institutional change.

Finally, the chapter explained the choice of observed institutions, cases, and the timeframe for the use of the three following chapters. Labor institutions are important because of their interactions with labor power, income distribution, and trade relations. This makes them an adequate subject for the illustration of the systemic cycle led framework of institutional change. The choice of cases of the USA, Germany, and PR China reflects their positions in the world-system. The three cases are major economies with dramatically different institutional arrangements, power relations, and positions within the systemic cycle, which makes them adequate for the illustration of a labor-oriented framework. Finally, the post-1980 period was chosen due to data availability and the fact that this is the timeframe in which the last financial expansion occurred enabling the observance of the effects of a global process on three divergent national institutional settings.

Literature

Harvey, D. (2005). *A Brief History of Neoliberalism.* Oxford: Oxford University Press.

OECD. (2017). *OECD Data [online].* Available at. <https://data.oecd.org/>.

OECD. (2020). *OECD Data [online].* Available at. <https://data.oecd.org/>.

Stiglitz, J. (2002). *Globalization and Its Discontents.* London: Penguin Books.

Tilly, C. (1995). Globalization Threatens Labor's Rights. *International Labor and Working-Class History, 47,* 1–23.

Weiss, L. (1998). *The Myth of the Powerless State.* Ithaca: Cornell University Press.

CHAPTER 6

Labor Market in United States of America

6.1 Introduction

This chapter will use the framework of institutional change outlined in the previous chapter and apply it to a case study of US labor institutions. Firstly, we will research the institutions in their formal, informal, and avoidable iterations. In short, the USA is a political-economic system which traditionally hinges on market-based institutional solutions to social and economic issues. As shown in Chapter 3, this is a trait it shares with other developed countries with a Common Law tradition (i.e. Canada, Ireland, UK, Australia, and New Zealand). In terms of labor institutions this suggests the absence of strong unions, low peak levels of collective bargaining, flexible labor laws, etc. In terms of formal institutions, this traditional orientation of the USA was softened in the 1930s through the labor components of the New Deal (Wagner Act and FLSA) which guaranteed some federal level labor rights including the right to collective bargaining and strike unfettered by federal courts. Many of these rights have been reduced in subsequent decades, and the USA is today the developed country with the least protected labor markets. In terms of informal institutions, the collective bargaining structure is decentralized and both bargaining coverage and union density, never high to begin with, are consistently dropping. In terms of avoidable institutions, it seems that many employers are able to habitually ignore even the modest regulation in place. Also, a potential result is a very high-income inequality, with no

J. Lučev, *Systemic Cycle and Institutional Change*,
https://doi.org/10.1007/978-3-030-66053-6_6

strong union presence to cause similar wages. Secondly, this chapter will examine the possible drivers of change. Institutional change in the case of the US labor institutions 1980–2019 seems to point to a continued deregulation of an already relatively deregulated system. Most importantly, this chapter will argue for the role that the systemic cycle and the extensive developmental strategy played in causing this type of stable change.

6.2 Labor Institutions in USA

Douglass North offered a very useful definition of institutions, according to which institutions should be understood through three key aspects: formal, informal, and avoidable. In the context of the labor market, these correspond to: formal institutions (Labor Law and other laws governing labor organization and collective bargaining), informal institutions (uncodified practices in collective bargaining which may be under strong influence of power relations, and the degree of centralization of negotiations) and avoidable institutions (selectively applied regulation or practice that does not follow the law). We will survey these in turn.

6.2.1 Formal Labor Institutions

Formal institutions are codified and enforceable materials like laws and, in precedent-based legal systems, court decisions as well. Table 6.1 brings the formal landmark events which have contributed to the modern labor institutions. Some of them fall far beyond our timeframe, but they are either still in force, or contribute to the context of change of labor institutions in the USA.

As we can see from Table 6.1, the drama of formal institutional change has largely played out by the post-1980 timeframe that interests us. The crucial period of labor organization was the New Deal which brought American labor the Wagner Act which institutionalized collective bargaining and strikes. Already in 1947, many formal stipulations of the Wagner Act were repudiated by the Taft-Hartley Act, banning strikes for federal employees and closed shops (plants/factory floors which only employ union members) and closely regulating union shops (shops which accept non-members provided they become members

Table 6.1 Landmark reforms of federal level US labor regulation

Year	*Decision/Law*	*Explanation*
1842	*Commonwealth v Hunt*	A court decision legalizing trade unions—before they would have been seen as a conspiracy to raise wages
1890	*Sherman Antitrust Act*	Unions in consequence understood as trusts (monopolies)
1926	*Railway Labor Act*	First collective bargaining in federal legislation. It still covers railway workers (expanded to airlines in 1936). These were seen as important to the economy as a whole and substantial efforts were made to prevent strikes through a complex system of bargaining
1932	*Norris La-Guardia*	Banned yellow-dog contracts (which would prevent an employee to enter a union) and prevented the courts to intervene against nonviolent labor disputes
1935	*National Labor Relations Act (Wagner Act)*	Guaranteed the right of private sector employees to trade unions which could engage in collective bargaining and conduct strikes
1938	*FLSA (Fair Labor Standards Act)*	Prevention of oppressive child labor and the establishment of the right to a federal minimum wage (with several decisions to increase to 75 cents in 1950, 1$ in 1955, 1.25$ in 1961, 1.60$ in 1966, 2.30$ in 1974, 3.35$ in 1977, 4.25$ in 1989, 7.25$ in 2007) and an overtime pay of 1.5x hourly wage
1947	*Labor Management Relations Act (Taft-Hartley Act)*	Closed shops (prevention of non-union employment) were banned, union shops (obligation to join unions after employment) were strictly regulated, and strikes were restricted (banned for federal employees)—an effective reversal of some stipulations of the Wagner Act

(continued)

Table 6.1 (continued)

Year	*Decision/Law*	*Explanation*
1959	*Labor Management Reporting and Disclosure Act (Landrum-Griffin Act)*	Established a framework for internal affairs of unions including the right to secret elections and the obligation to submit to financial oversight
1965	*Civil Rights Act*	All employees must be treated equally by employers and unions
1970	*OSHA (Occupational Safety and Health Act)*	First effective occupational safety regulation in the USA
1974	*ERISA (Employee Retirement Income Security Act)*	Pension plan minimums for private industry
1978	*FLRA (Federal Labor Relations Act)*	Most public sector workers guaranteed the right to collective bargaining which existed for private sector since 1935
1993	*FMLA (Family and Medical Leave Act)*	Guarantees the right to paid leave for family-related illnesses or health issues to eligible employees
1996	*Small Business Job Protection Act*	A federal freeze on tipped employee minimum wage at 2.13$
2010	*Patient Protection and Affordable Care Act (Obamacare)*	While this is not a labor regulation law, it did potentially significantly alter the disposable income of workers by creating a modern health system
2018	*Janus v. AFSCME*	A Supreme Court decision preventing agency shops (fees of non-union members for collective bargaining) in the public sector

Sources Doyle (2017), Compa (2014), Godard (2009), Thelen (2014), Tang (2019)

after employment). This was clearly a set of anti-labor-oriented regulations in the sense of curbing associational power of labor (i.e. the power of unions). However, the following decades brought numerous improvements to labor standards and worker rights (Civil Rights Act in 1965 for anti-discrimination, OSHA in 1970 for workplace safety, ERISA in 1974 for the pensions system, FMLA in 1993 for family leave, and Affordable Care Act in 2010 for the health system). These improvements did not change the general framework for labor organizing, apart from the FLRA in 1978 which guaranteed collective bargaining rights to federal employees.[1] In this sense, there were no substantial changes to report in the post-1980 period. In fact, what is conspicuous is the absence of a labor re-regulation. In 1978, the Carter administration narrowly failed to enact legislation intended to promote labor organization as the business community successfully outspent and out-lobbied organized labor in influencing the US Congress. The effort passed the House of Representatives but was successfully filibustered in the Senate (Hacker and Pierson 2010: 127–132). The Clinton administration failed to pass its Worker Fairness Acts in 1993. It would have protected the striking workers from being permanently replaced but was likewise defeated by a Republican filibuster (Early 2013: 82). Finally, another hypothetical pro-labor piece of legislation was the Employee Free Choice Act, which could have enabled easier organization of Unions by supplanting the restricting secret ballot in place since 1959 with a simpler card check. The possible effort to pass EFCA was essentially avoided during the Obama administration.

We can also benefit by observing comparative instruments which can help us compare the US system to those found elsewhere. Consistently with our analysis, such data shows that the USA has had a consistently deregulated labor market, without any substantial change in the observed period. OECD publishes the EPL index for regular and temporary employment. The index for regular employment weighs items like the difficulty of dismissal, length of mandatory notice period, and size of severance pay to gauge the levels of legal protection of the labor market. In the USA, these index for individual dismissal of individual workers is the lowest measured by the OECD at the index value of 0.09 (possible values are 0–6). This is due to the fact that workers (excepting public sector or union members) are employed according to the at-will principle, which does not foresee the possibility of an unfair dismissal, barring discrimination according to creed, sex, race, impairments, etc. There are

[1] A smaller shift occurred in June 2018, as an important income source of public sector unions was cut off. Somewhat unusually from a European standpoint, US labor laws recognize the right of unions to gather dues from non-members as compensation from benefits derived from collective bargaining (agency shop). States may circumvent agency shops by passing right-to-work laws prohibiting this practice (at the time of writing, 27 states have opted to enact them). The recent Supreme Court ruling in *Janus v. AFSCME* essentially elevated the right-to-work principle to the federal public sector level by prohibiting the application of agency-shop principle to public workers. This will diminish the income of public sector unions, which is relevant as the public sector is currently a rare bastion of union activity in the USA.

no federally mandated notification procedures[2] (with some state jurisdictions requiring service letters be issued explaining the reasons for the dismissal) and no legal regulations covering the right to a notice period at dismissal (OECD 2020).

The temporary employment EPL index weighs items like the restrictions of fixed-term and temporary work to types of work, restrictions on maximum duration of fixed-term work and the maximum number of such contracts it is legal to sign. In this index, the USA is also at the bottom of comparative rankings of protection. Among stable results, it is tied for the least protected market with Canada, UK, and Ireland at the index value of 0.25 (with possible values also at 0–6) as there are no limits to duration or successive numbers of contracts. Both of these indices remain unchanged during the entire duration of the OECD time series in the 1985–2019 period (OECD 2020). Another index is published by the Heritage Foundation yearly as the *labor freedom* index. Heritage is a free-market-oriented policy-advocacy group, and its conception of free labor is essentially oriented toward labor flexibility, i.e. the absence of labor protection. The items weighed to construct the labor freedom index are "Ratio of minimum wage to the average value-added per worker, Hindrance to hiring additional workers, Rigidity of hours, Difficulty of firing redundant employees, Legally mandated notice period, and Mandatory severance pay" (Heritage 2020a). According to this index, the USA has one of the most *free* labor markets in 2020 (87.9/100 with the global average at 59.6), trailing only Singapore, Brunei, and Hong Kong (Heritage 2020b). This is in itself a slight drop since 2015—the index was first calculated in 2005, with values in most years of its first decade fluctuating around 95% (Heritage 2020c). Such fluctuations are possible as the index includes legal categories (slow to change, and as seen by the EPL index unchanged since 1985) as well as economic ones (average value-added per worker, which may change rapidly).

To summarize, formal labor institutions in the USA did not significantly change in the selected period. They were not and are not well

[2]This chapter focuses on the national level of labor US institutions. The institutional diversity among states is however worthwhile noticing. Bjorklund (2019) analyzes fiscal constraint, tax progressivity, family and social welfare and employment policy to derive five clusters of federal states in USA (progressive, contested progressive, boilerplate, frontier conservative, and southern conservative).

suited for labor organization, and labor legal protection remains extremely flexible[3] when compared to the rest of the world.

6.2.2 *Informal Labor Institutions*

Informal labor institutions are unwritten, but relatively stable ways of doing things. Uncodified norms, values, and expected practices are all examples of informal institutions. As shown in Table 6.1, the conduct of collective bargaining has been legal and encouraged in the private sector since 1935 and in the public sector since 1978—although such encouragement was less enthusiastic than in Europe. In theory, the 1930s changes in formal institutions created a framework of "soft corporatism" for informal institutions, but it turned to be "largely a mirage" (Godard 2009: 92), as union density increased only from 13% in 1936 to 36% in 1945 which was to prove to be the historical peak (ibid.: 91).

The level at which collective bargaining takes place is also indicative of the coordination in the institutional system. As we will see in the next chapter, CME countries tend to have more centralized levels of collective bargaining, which is conducted at the cross-industry level or more commonly in recent years on the level of the entire sector or industry. The cause may be a high union density (or share of the workforce represented by unions) which lends necessary legitimacy to unions, and the effect is a high bargaining coverage for both members and non-members of unions. In the USA, the appropriate level of collective bargaining is determined by the National Labor Relations Board (NLRB), which seems to favor a very decentralized structure with bargaining most often taking place at the level of the enterprise. In fact, the ICTWSS database invariably classifies the predominant level of collective bargaining in the USA as the enterprise level through the entire duration of the series 1960–2018 (Visser 2019).

[3] The scope of active labor market policies which contributes to the overall institutional effects in labor has also become increasingly diminutive. These policies have undergone an evolution from being centered on job-creation (as late as 1960s and 1970s) through allowing for some support for training programs (1980s and early 1990s) to their present minimalist state. ALMPs are now comparatively small and limited to a short-term perspective aimed at securing any form of jobs (Thelen 2014: 120–130). Indeed, at 0.1% GDP in 2018 the public expenditure on active labor market policies is one of the lowest among OECD members with only Mexico at a lower level (OECD 2020).

Another type of developing practice was the openly anti-union strategies that many employers began to adopt in the 1970s, with delaying union certifications, calling for union decertification elections, moving production to the less unionized American South, and hiring of professional anti-union management consultants (Thelen 2014: 40–42). The result is that a typical NLRB union election (determining the union which is to conduct bargaining) will take place in the context of employer intimidation and various delays caused by expensive litigation (Brudney 2005: 108). This could essentially be described as class warfare directed at diminishing the associational power of labor. If the unions are present, they may well be seen merely as drags on profitability by the employers, and obstacles to overall market efficiency of the firm. This view is in stark contrast to those found in CMEs as we will see in the next chapter.

The failing strength of unions is visible in the lack of open struggle in terms of successful strikes. However, it is also visible in the inability of unions to postpone or prevent adverse change in institutionalized practices like the shift from temporary to permanent layoff as prevalent policy in the 1980s (Jung 2017). This system of low-strength unions combined with the militant anti-union stance of the employers to produce a large low-wage sector. OECD defines low wages as a proportion of workers earning less than two-thirds of median earnings. In the observed post-1980 period, the lowest proportion of low-wage work was in 1983 when it stood at an already high 20.4% and it gradually grew to 25.2% in 2012 after which it fell to 24.1% in 2018 and 23.4% in 2019 (OECD 2020). This is a very high percentage compared to the latest available OECD average of 15.3% for 2018.

6.2.3 Avoidable Labor Institutions

The third Northian aspect of institutions are the avoidable ones. This is a particularly important element to bear in mind in the context of the US system. Elsewhere, strong unions, present work councils, and rigid laws offer various types of protection of workers who have been treated unfairly. In the USA, the mistreated worker (i.e. a worker whose employer has avoided a labor regulation) often has the expensive court system as the only recourse. This means that a low-wage earner will not be able to react if labor rights or contractual obligations are not honored by the employer. It should therefore not be surprising that many low-wage workers report violations of their labor rights. A fairly large 2008 study surveyed 4387 workers in Chicago, Los Angeles, and New York on conditions in the week prior to questioning and found that 26% report minimum wage violations, 76% of overtime workers report overtime violations, and 70% report meal break violations. A substantial 68% of all workers have reported at least one pay-related violation in the past week. This study suggests that even the low level of labor regulation in the USA is easily avoided among the low-wage earners. In fact, workers often did not even attempt to fight for their rights: 50% of those who informed their employers of a workplace injury suffered an illegal reaction (the employer fired the worker for filing the claim or instructed the worker not to file it). As a result, only 8% of the injured workers filed a compensation claim. When the workers attempted to form a union or made complaints to their employer or a governmental body, 43% of them experienced an illegal reaction with employer firing, suspending, reducing worker hours or pay (Bernhardt et al. 2009; see also Thelen 2014: 45). The worker groups most likely to experience the pay-related violations were women and foreign-born workers, and the authors estimate the average loss at 15% of earnings (Bernhardt et al. 2009: 5).

Another important area is the absence of discrimination, and the discrimination against women is a very visible and easily verifiable area. While there are many legal protections of pay equality, these are obviously avoidable to some extent. The World Economic Forum attempts to measure the gender wage gaps comparatively with its "The Global Gender Gap Index." This index examines the gender gap in several areas: "Economic Participation and Opportunity, Educational Attainment, Health and Survival and Political Empowerment" (WEF 2016a). This index ranked the USA 45th in its 2016 index (compared to German 13th and Chinese 99th rank), fairing particularly poorly in political empowerment. In the survey rate of wage equality for similar work in which the USA ranked 66th globally with index score of 0.653 (WEF 2016b).

To summarize, the ability of employers in the USA to avoid institutions when facing vulnerable groups seems to be quite high. This is a side-effect of low union strength, lack of firm-level employee organizations intended to protect them and the prohibitively expensive nature of the court system—in other words a side-effect of the formal and informal institutional framework of the USA as a whole.

6.3 Changes in Labor Institutions in USA

The previous section has described the general state of labor institutions in the USA and the tendencies of change since 1980. This section will apply the framework developed in the previous chapter on these changes. We will focus on the operation of the three identified channels of path dependence, cyclical power relations, and institutional design. Figure 6.1 lays out the framework for US labor institutions, and the rest of the section describes the channels, drivers, and their interactions.

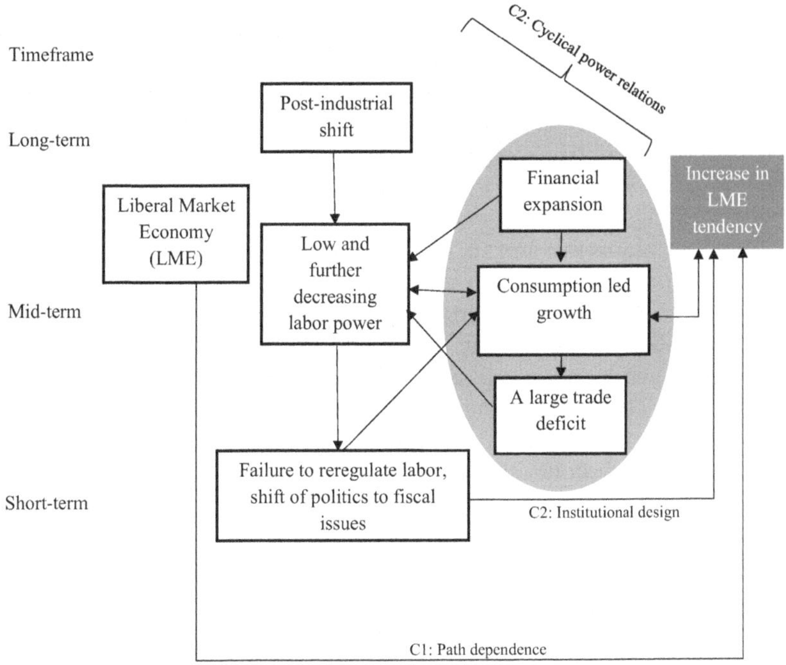

Fig. 6.1 A framework of labor institutional change in USA since 1980

6.3.1 *Channel 1: Path Dependence—Institutional Starting Positions of USA*

The first channel of institutional change identified in Chapter 3 is path dependence as determined by institutional starting positions. Most of the definitions of institutions covered by Chapter 3 stress the stability of institutions. In other words, the best indicator of the future state of institutions would be the previous state of institutions. One of the channels of institutional stability is the power-based path dependence stressed by Pierson (2015). According to this perspective, power tends to accumulate as those with power have the resources to influence policy outcomes which allow them to accrue more power. In this sense, the USA always had relatively low union power and lacked strong coordinating capacities in industrial relations. The trajectory of liberalization in recent decades saw a collapse of existing unions and collective bargaining and erosion of real values of statutory minimum wages and benefits (Thelen 2014: 37–47). This is precisely why it was repeatedly classified as a liberal market in various typologies (LME, Atlantic capitalism, liberal welfare state). This institutional starting position was the prerequisite of a pronounced and continued deregulation. Had the unions been stronger, they could strive to prevent this departure from an organized labor market. As they were already weak, the various drivers of economic change which pointed to a decrease in coordination could not be prevented. This interpretation suggests that a strong path-dependent element is at play with LME structures pronouncedly vulnerable to direct deregulatory and/or decoordinatory tendencies. This is the reason why Thelen considers *displacement* as a typical process conveying pure deregulation or a direct attack on the existing institutional arrangements, largely descriptive of US liberalization (Thelen 2014: 13). Considering this finding in the light of relative power of interested parties, it becomes clear that institutions are displaced if the defenders of status quo are considerably weaker than its attackers. Labor organization in the USA was already weak and this enabled the swift disassembly of labor institutions once it was triggered (see drivers below).

It is this dual determination that creates a conceptual confusion: starting institutions have their winners in those actors that accrue power through the institutional solutions. In order to enact pressure toward change or preservation of these institutions, policy advocates must have power. This point would drive us toward the conclusion that institutions are inherently stable—as those who are benefited by the present institutions are abler to drive change that those who are not. This point has been well taken by both old and new institutionalism, and the essential result is the dependence on exogenous change (i.e. critical junctures creating punctuated equilibria as shown in Chapter 3). We must move beyond this view and recognize path dependence in its proper context. The next segment broadens the lens in order to notice and endogenize further, Arrighian drivers of change.

Interactions with other drivers and the result

(a) Power relations: initial structures have a strong effect on power relations, as the initial institutional framework enables or restricts the functioning and the accrual of resources of actors. The USA is a paradigmatic LME structure, which has very low labor resources and a history of decentralized bargaining. Such a system accrues political power of the employers rather than trade unions and the ability to influence institutional change is therefore concentrated beyond the reach of organized labor to begin with.
(b) Phase of the systemic cycle: the lack of focus on labor protection and the importance of industry have enabled a shift into finance expansion to take place without much resilience from the productive/manufacturing sector of the economy, which was neglected in terms of power which organized labor could muster, embedded as it was within it.
(c) Developmental strategy: the USA did not have a notable shift in its developmental strategy since 1980. The growth model was always consumption driven and labor has always been relatively deregulated, and the systemic cycle has already shifted to a finance expansion. The result is a severe drag on GDP growth, as production was in the aggregate kept neither for domestic nor for foreign markets and trade deficits soared.
(d) The result of institutional change: path dependence tends to produce institutional end-results similar to starting positions. This was the case in the USA as the deregulating path was undertaken in an already relatively deregulated context, essentially continuing and exacerbating the free market LME tendencies in labor markets.

6.3.2 Channel 2: Cyclical Power Relations in USA

Figure 6.2 outlines the second channel of institutional change. The five drivers it incorporates are technological change (an exogenous factor providing a long-term context), three drivers constituting the systemic cycle—the phase of the systemic cycle, developmental strategies and trade relations—and the power relations as the balance of power resources.

These interactions are explored in greater detail through the rest of this segment, organized by specific discussions of the five drivers in this channel.

6.3.2.1 Technology and Sectoral Labor Market Structure in USA

The second channel of institutional change is a nexus of drivers influencing labor power and linking it to developmental strategies and the result of institutional change. The first such driver is technological change. Chapter 5 explained the distinction between the cumulative and development aspects of technology. The cumulative aspects are a matter of

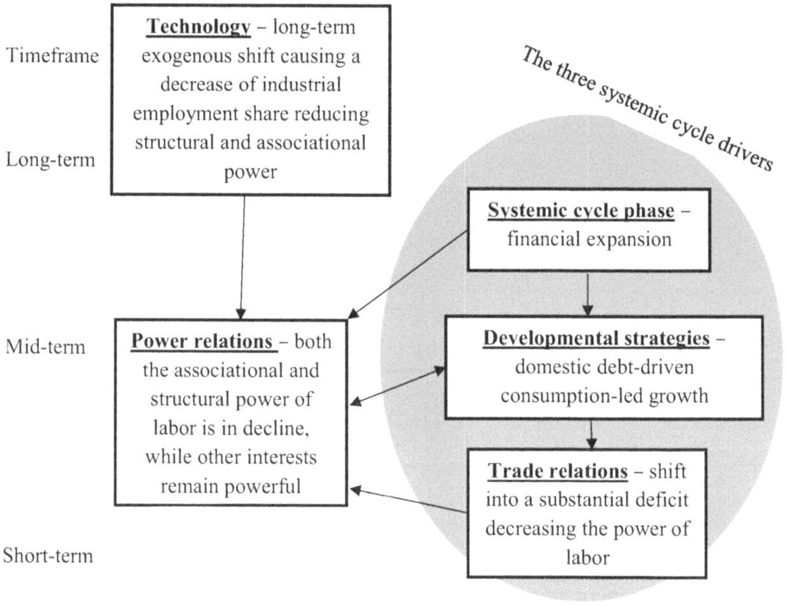

Fig. 6.2 Cyclical power relations in the USA

technological innovations which enable a more efficient production and in effect, less labor used per same output. The developmental aspect is a matter of choosing the appropriate technology and implementing it. From the western perspective, the developmental aspect was a matter of continuous capital deepening which enabled shifts in sectoral composition of employment as shown in Fig. 6.3. The US strategy of Taylorization (which Silver would treat as a technological fix) could be interpreted as one of the building blocks of the LME alternative (Thelen 2014: 38). With a greater shop-floor division of labor, skill sets could be non-specific. This rationalization of space and movement created productivity gains which were not dependent on high union density, corporatist structures, or protective labor market regulation in order to function.

Taking a look at ILO estimates (reported in the World Bank database) for USA in Fig. 6.3, we observe trends that can be expected bearing in mind the development-sectoral employment connection. The 1991–2020 interval shows an incremental and consistent increase in the share of service and decrease in industry. In the USA, the most recent data shows 79% of employed work in services (compared to 72% in 1991),

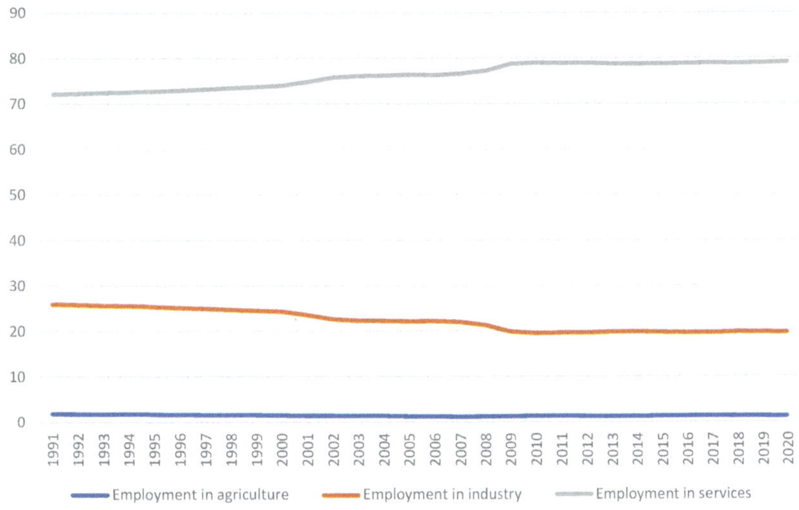

Fig. 6.3 Employment structure in USA (*Source of data* World Bank 2020)

19.7% in industry (compared to 26% in 1991), and a very small share of 1.3% is employed in agriculture (compared to 1.9% in 1991).

Here we can see that the interaction of the short-run Luddite anxiety of losing jobs due to technology and the long-run re-shuffling of the occupational structure. Acemoglu and Restrepo (2017) model the effect of robots on employment and claim there are "large and robust negative effects of robots on employment and wages" (ibid.: 36). We could claim the same for the effects of introduction of tractors on agricultural employment or the effects of the introduction of the *Spinning Jenny* machine on outdated weaving jobs.

Frey and Osborne (2013) estimate that 47% of all occupations are at a high risk of replacement through computerization. These losses are dominated by administrative support, sale, and service jobs (ibid.: 37). If these jobs were not replaced by others, we may have a significant issue with what Keynes called "technological unemployment" (Keynes 1930/2009: 196), which we know today under the more familiar term of structural unemployment. But, in spite of his usual far-sightedness, he did not foresee large shifts in sectoral employment as his classical essay Economic Possibilities of our Grandchildren (ibid.) was notoriously wrong on this point. The current short-term anxiety may also be at fault. More relevant for our purpose, these sectoral shifts have a power-related issue of attached union density which is related to skill specificity, and in this sense, we must turn to plotting the relationships of technology and labor power.

Interactions with other drivers and the result

(a) Power relations: the ability to organize labor (associational power) and bargain (structural power) is far higher in industry than in the service sector. As technology enabled a smaller proportion of labor to work in the secondary sector, labor power diminished overall in the USA.

(b) Developmental strategy: technological process innovations may create incentives for new development models, but this did not happen in the USA. The new labor-saving production methods including robotics and IT can be seen as a continuation of skilled-labor avoiding Taylorism which was omnipresent as a production strategy. The growth model was consumption-led at least since the end of World War II, but the shifts in productivity eventually made it uncompetitive in foreign markets causing a greater role for imports in satisfying this demand. This does not yet amount to a change in the developmental strategy (as that was necessitated by the systemic cycle), but merely a change in its successfulness in terms of growth.

6.3.2.2 *Phase of the Systemic Cycle*

From the viewpoint of the USA, the systemic cycle describes its establishment as a mature economy in late nineteenth century and early twentieth century, the significant material expansion in middle twentieth century and its financial expansion between the signal crisis in 1973 and the terminal crisis in 2008 and even beyond. It would also describe the increasingly intricate behavior of global supply chains with the center of the world-economy moving elsewhere through globalization in the long-term aftermath of the signal crisis. This gives us an appreciation of the assumptions of the systemic cycle theory in that the manufacturing labor was not as necessary for the core reproduction processes of the US economy after 1973 (although the reduction of manufacture logically went hand in hand with the rising trade deficits and the rise of new global production centers). In being increasingly superfluous, the power of manufacturing labor to theoretically strike or organize became less of a threat, adding therefore to the decreasing power of labor visible in the declining union density rates.

To establish the extent of financial expansion (or financialization) in the USA, we can observe several types of measurement, depending on the aspect we would wish to focus on (Table 6.2). It will perhaps suffice to show one type of measurement for every unit of analysis.

Table 6.2 Financial expansion/financialization conceptualizations

Unit of analysis	*Financialization conceptualization*
Individual/household	Increase of indebtedness, credit cards, and mortgages
State/Country	Second pillar pension systems, increased dependence on financial markets or organizations (ratings agencies, IMF, ECB...), increase of overall importance of stock markets (market capitalization as % of GDP)
Company	Generates profit in various situations (shift from real to financial activities), shifts in corporate governance regimes (shareholder value)

Firstly, the household indebtedness has grown substantially in the financial expansion period as the liabilities of households and non-profit organizations were at 1.3 trillion dollars in 1980 or 41% GDP and reached a peak in 2008 at 14.3 trillion or 97% GDP to nominally deflate and recover at a lower ratio to GDP at 14.7 trillion by 2016 or 79% GDP (FRED 2017). In other words, we can use this type of data to observe the effect on households and, according to the FRED data, confirm the Arrighian systemic cycle theory.

Secondly, within VofC, a great deal of importance is awarded to the way in which corporate finance is arranged. The firms in some economies (CME) rely on long run financing by the mother-banks with a stake in the firms themselves. The firms in other economies (LME) are more reliant on financial market financing and more vulnerable to fluctuation of the stock market. Attempts have been made from the beginning to show the difference by comparing market capitalization[4] to GDP ratios (Hall and Soskice 2001: 19). Figure 6.4 shows the developments of bank credit to private sector and market capitalization.

In the USA, the bank credit to private sector is a relatively steady indicator with the minimum at 44.2% of GDP in 1993 (an all-time low in the time series was in the starting 40.7% in 1961) the maximum at 59.8% in 2008, and a decrease as a consequence of the intervening credit crunch/recession. The latest data is for 2019 when this indicator was at 52.1% GDP. The market capitalization ratio is much higher and much more volatile with the last 20 years mostly staying in the 80–160% GDP range (with a pronounced growth since 1994, a marked yearly peak in 1999 at 153.4% and strong recoveries with yearly peaks in 2006 at 141.7%, 2014 at 150.3%, and 2017 at 164.8%). These volatilities also correspond to the intensity of trading, the value of shares traded as a percentage of GDP tends to be highest during market capitalization peaks or their immediate aftermath (as crises by definition may also be periods of large-volume trading). Trading reached a high point of 290.5% GDP in 2000, dropped to 140% in 2003, rose again to an incredible 321.1% in 2008, and discontinuously dropped to 108.5 by 2019 (World Bank 2020). These measures are in accordance with VofC theory, with the

[4] Market capitalization is the sum of all stock market listed shares prices. Ratio to GDP, even though very volatile, should show the comparative roles this type of financing has relative to the entire economy, particularly if specific market movements are averaged out and compared to other economies.

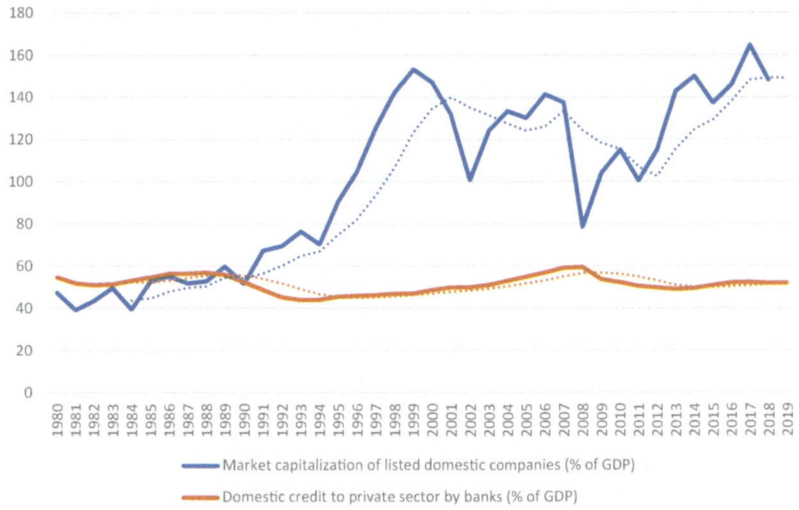

Fig. 6.4 Financing sources in USA (*Source of data* World Bank 2020 [trend-lines are 5-year moving averages])

USA being the paradigmatic LME case, and is theoretically expected to trade stocks in a relatively volatile fashion and also to have stock-market financing as the most relevant source of financing (i.e. pronouncedly higher ratio to GDP than the banking sector).

Thirdly, as already mentioned, the analysis of Greta Krippner (2005, 2011) was a direct attempt to follow Arrighi and complement his theory with an empirical measurement of corporate profits from National Income and Product Accounts. Her findings show that in the 1950–2001 period the share of manufacturing profits dropped from around 50% to around 10%, and that the share of Finance, Insurance and Real Estate (FIRE) profits climbed from about 10% in 1950 to about 45% in 2001 (Krippner 2005: 179). This shows empirically what Arrighi meant theoretically with the *flight of capital into finance*. The outcome is supposedly a deindustrialization (as financial resources are increasingly tied into non-productive investments). While deindustrialization is a result of numerous factors, the days of US material expansion are certainly long gone. Figures of manufacturing value-added as a percentage show a slow and steady drop from 16.1% in 1997 (time-series beginning) to 11.1% in 2017 (World Bank 2020). With market capitalization recovering since the drops of 2000–2002 and 2008 (and a far better performance of the stock markets compared to the real economy in 2020) and the deindustrialization continuing its slow pace, it seems that the US finance expansion is essentially continuing.

Interactions with other drivers and the result

(a) Trade relations: a financial expansion in the context of the systemic cycle suggests a decrease of material production translating into a widening trade deficit in the absence of a new growth model, which was the case in the USA.
(b) Developmental strategy: the financial expansion necessitated a new approach to investment compatible with a predominance of shareholder value—and therefore an extensive strategy. This nexus is essentially what the LME ideal-type is already attempting to describe. In the context of developmental strategies, the USA entered into an era of weak labor with weak wage growth, but high aggregate household consumption, plugging the difference with high-income inequality (enabling high aggregate demand alongside a low-wage sector) and increases in personal debt.
(c) Power relations: the USA underwent a shift from material to financial expansion which suggests lower structural labor power as the importance to the economy is reduced.

6.3.2.3 *Trade Relations of USA*

In the systemic cycle theory, the financial expansion is synonymous with a loss of global predominance in production, visible in a growing trade deficit. Chapter 5 has shown the empirical side of the US loss of a favorable trade position. Figure 6.5 shows current account balance as a rough measure of the trade balance in comparison with GDP growth rates.

We can observe that the current account balance in the USA was generally negative in the period of interest to us (the only exceptions are 1980, 1981, and 1991 with miniscule current account surpluses). Large deficits were mostly visible in the context of substantial real growth (mid-1980s and mid-2000s), the tendency to diminishing the deficit was visible in the context of real GDP contractions (1991 and 2009). Overall, the current

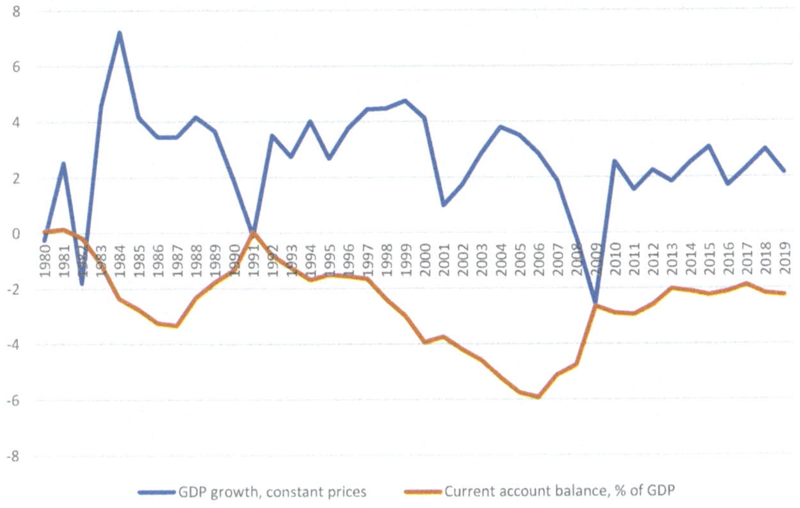

Fig. 6.5 Current accounts and real GDP growth in USA (*Source of data* IMF 2020)

account deficit expanded in the 1980s, briefly stabilized in 1991, and then substantially and consistently grew until 2006 (when it stood at −6% GDP) since when it readjusted to a lower level (mostly in the −2% to −3% range since 2009). To better grasp these trends, Fig. 6.6 disaggregates this data on absolute figures of imports and exports in goods and services in current USD.

This level of data shows the deficits of the mid-1980s and mid-2000s in absolute terms—and can also observe that the diminishing current account deficit was largely a matter of a growing GDP, as both imports and exports recovered very quickly after 2009.[5] The incentive structure for labor coordination and regulation under these conditions is the exacerbation of trends already described. In short, the fact that labor is not globally competitive leads to a trade deficit and a shift of domestic capital into finance. This means that a hypothetical strike of American manufacturing workers can no longer paralyze the economy. It can merely

[5] The effects of the 2018/2019 trade confrontations and the COVID-19 pandemic on trade patterns are not yet fully discernible.

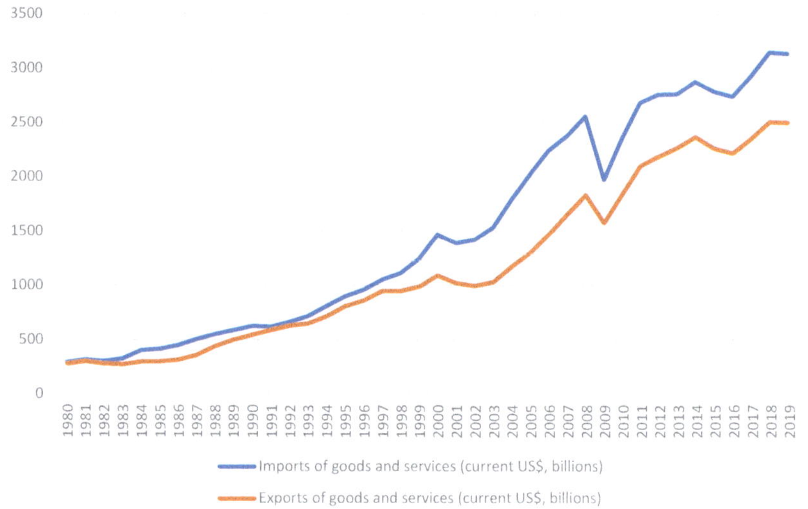

Fig. 6.6 US trade in goods and services (*Source of data* World Bank 2020)

incentivize the employers to shift the production into a different location. This was the logic of the now somewhat anachronistic *race-to-the-bottom* hypothesis. Nevertheless, the power of the unions to act must in general be lower in countries with large trade deficits as these countries already have domestic labor which is replaceable by imports. So, this shift into deficits joined the other five drivers, all of which pointed in the direction of further commodification of US labor.

Interactions with other drivers and the result

(a) Power relations: an increase in the trade deficit suggests a decrease of relative importance of domestic production for the economy as a whole and therefore reduces the structural power of labor.
(b) Systemic cycle phase: a shift from trade surplus to a trade deficit is a symptom of the financial expansion phase of the systemic cycle.
(c) Developmental strategies: the USA has kept the consumption-led model in the face of financial expansions. This would suggest a combination of an extensive strategy in the context of high household demand. Income derived from wages is gradually supplanted

by household debt and overall profits increasingly accrued in financial activities. Such an extensive strategy (one conducted through trade deficits) does not have the same effects as an extensive strategy in the context of material expansions as the financial expansion phase does not center on production and trade.

6.3.2.4 *Developmental Strategies of USA*

As explained in Chapter 4, we have taken the Arrighian category of extensive and intensive regimes and construed them as supply- and demand-side developmental strategies. A supply-side strategy hinges on low costs of labor and the export market, while a demand-side strategy hinges on the development of domestic markets and can therefore put a lower importance of low production costs. This shift from regimes to strategies allows us to move beyond simple determinism and see that the form in which the economic system reproduces itself, constricted by many drivers of change, but ultimately determined by none of them alone. The intensive strategy is synonymous with the Fordist regime of accumulation/Keynesian welfare state which typified the US economy until the 1970s, while the extensive strategy is the normative free market orientation since the 1970s, here explained as a consequence of the systemic cycle. Specifically, the development strategy takes place in the context of the phase of the systemic cycle: while the material expansion creates the dilemma between labor-compensation-as-cost and labor-compensation-as-demand (as we will see in the next two chapters), the financial expansion faced by the USA is oriented toward profitability. This creates a situation in which labor is in a similar position to an extensive strategy in a material expansion, but the consumption is in a similar position to an intensive strategy in a material expansion. This is essentially the face of an extensive strategy during financial expansions. Figure 6.7 shows the growing discrepancy between wage-related income and domestic consumption.

The graph shows two curves: the household consumption (i.e. the domestic market we could conflate with the position of the worker) and wages and salary accruals, both as a percentage of GDP. The difference in the two curves is logically made up of any domestic spending that is derived from non-wage-related earnings (rents, interest, debt). We can see that the trend of the two lines is essentially divergence since 1970. In 1970 their difference was 9.1%, and in 2018 it was at 25%. In our interpretation, this is due to the intensive (Fordist/Keynesian) strategy

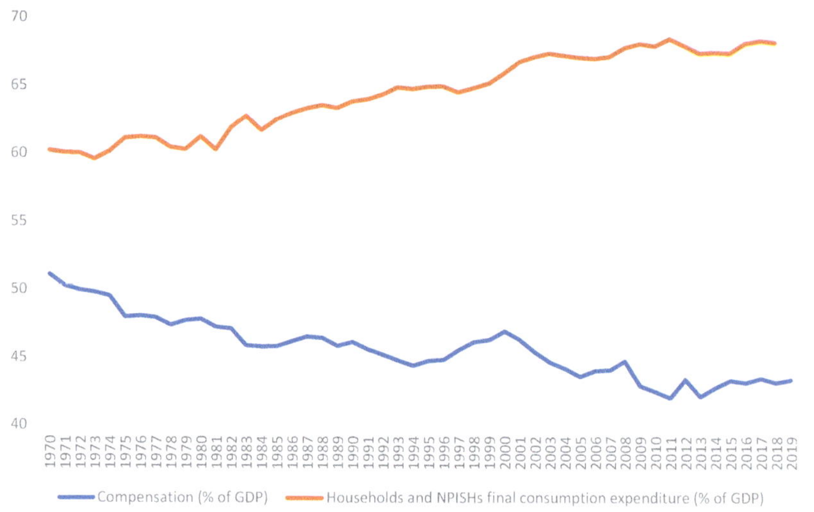

Fig. 6.7 Divergence between consumption and wages in USA (*Sources of data* FRED 2020; World Bank 2020)

favored the development of internal markets, while the extensive (Washington consensus) strategy favors the development of export capabilities at the detriment of labor costs and therefore of the domestic market. The discrepancy is made possible partially due to the explosion of household debt both in absolute terms and relative to GDP (as a GDP percentage, it more than doubled in the 1984–2008 period landing on 99% GDP in Q1 2008; Trading Economics 2018; FRED 2018).[6]

This comparison also hides the increasing divergence between the low wages of workers whom we could imagine seeking the protection of laws and unions and the increasingly high wages of top managers—with the aggregate consumption not necessarily reflecting the low-wage sector. We can confront issues of inequality in Sect. 6.4, but for now we are interested merely in the aggregates—i.e. in the relative motors of growth. Figure 6.8 tracks the demand composition in the USA as a manifestation of the developmental strategy.

[6] This is essentially a confirmation of the Privatised Keynesianism thesis of Colin Crouch (2009).

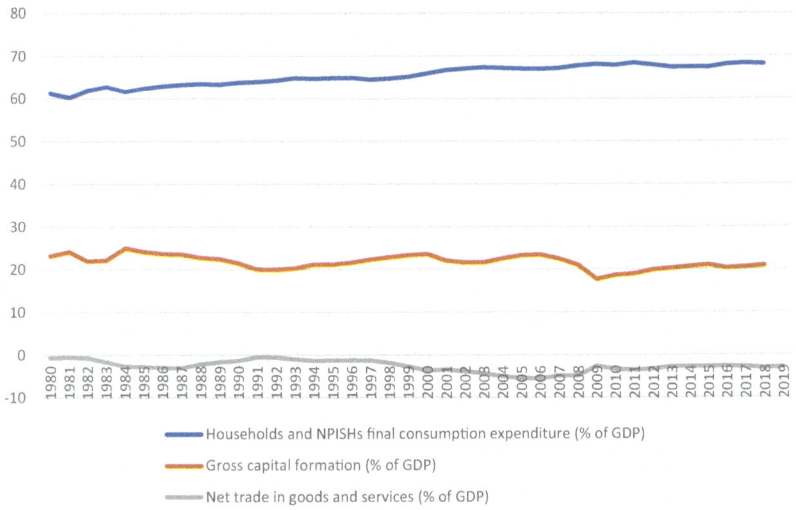

Fig. 6.8 Demand composition in USA (*Source of data* World Bank 2020 [Household final consumption, Gross capital formation], own calculation according to data for current US GDP and net trade in goods and services in World Bank 2020 [Net trade % GDP])

We can observe that household expenditure is by far the largest in terms of demand. Changes in the composition worked to accentuate this trend with household demand increased by 7.9% in the 1981–2018 period, investment demand decreased by 4.1% from the peak level of 1984 to 2018 and the effect of net trade was consistently negative, at a modest −0.6% in 1992, gradually reached a low-point of −5.5% in 2006 and somewhat corrected since to −2.9% GDP by 2019. The growth model has therefore been led by domestic consumption in the entirety of the timeframe and more so over time. However, this was largely funded by growing levels of debt and has resulted in a large trade deficit.

Interaction with other drivers and the result

(a) Power relations: consumption-led growth in financial expansion reduces the structural power of labor as the material needs of employees are large but the economy itself does not revolve around material labor. In other words, workers need to work more than their employers need them to work.

(b) Trade relations: a consumption-led growth in financial expansions certainly provides the major contours of a large trade deficit, as domestic demand is high, and competitiveness is low.
(c) The result of institutional change: the effects of developmental strategy on the institutional result in the USA is fairly low, as the continuing neglect of labor is more clearly a result of path dependence. This also suggests that critical junctures are difficult to find in the case of USA in the chosen period. However, low power of labor which is also an effect of developmental strategy helped steer the path-dependent outcome.

6.3.2.5 *Power Relations in USA*

In terms of informal institutions, we deal with stable and rule-like, but unwritten outcomes. These are under the influence of power relations as a relatively strong labor organization might produce labor-friendly institutional results and vice versa. We have followed Erik Ohlin Wright and Beverly Silver in focusing on the two types of labor power as structural (the role in the economy and the consequential bargaining power) and associational power (ability to organize). All of the previous drivers in this channel have had a negative effect on the structural labor power in the USA since 1980 and this is mirrored in the diminishing associational power as well. As shown in Fig. 6.9, the union density in the USA is at an all-time low—therefore showing very low associational power of US labor.

This suggests that the unions as the very organizations which should embody labor power and fight for its interests are severely diminishing in significance—and the bargaining coverage is very closely following this decline. Both were in the 30–35% range in the early 1960s but are in the 10–15% range today. According to the ICTWSS database, union density has dropped significantly in the traditionally relatively highly unionized transport workers (36.1% in early 1980s, 12.8 in 2018), and manufacturing workers (27.9% in early 1980s, 9% in 2018) and remained high in public sector (34.8–36.7% in early 1980s and 33.9–37% in 2010s up to 2018), with the overall union density dropping from 22.3% in 1980 to 10.1% in 2018 (Visser 2019). When we add to this the unchangeably decentralized structure of collective bargaining, we can see that the unions, although never overly powerful in the USA have come to a very low point in terms of power resources available to effect an institutional change.

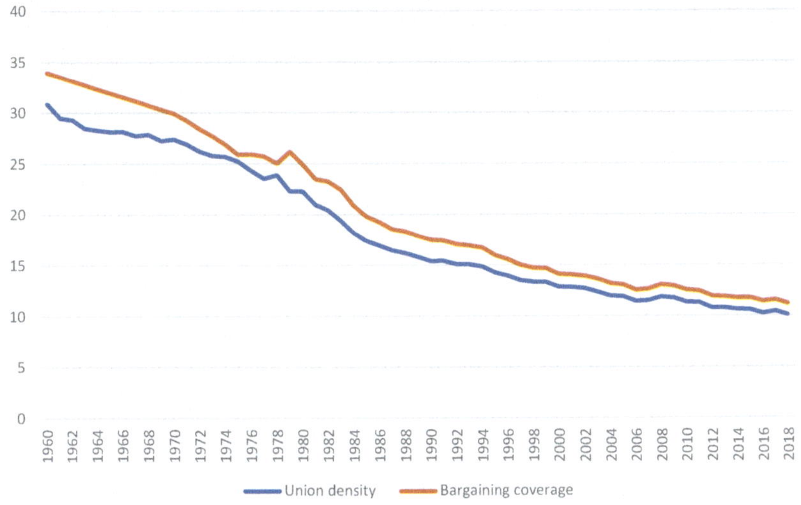

Fig. 6.9 Bargaining coverage and union density in USA (*Source of data* Jelle Visser ICTWSS database 6.0 [Visser 2019]—union density is composed of two metrics: 1960–1979 ud series, 1980–2018 ud_s series)

Interactions with other drivers and the result

(a) Phase of the systemic cycle: diminished power of labor—relative to the employers—would have been able to influence investment decisions in the USA. These are done according to the criteria of shareholder value and therefore have easily shifted toward financial expansion in the 1970s and 1980s.
(b) Developmental strategy: the development strategy did not change even in the face of a large trade deficit. The continued legitimacy of the American dream, such as it is, is premedicated on the seeming pro-labor quasi-intensive strategy. However, as we have seen, this is a matter of a continued consumption-led growth—supported increasingly by debt, rather than a successful development strategy.
(c) Result of institutional change: American power relations were not stacked in favor of labor influencing institutional change and the result seems to have been largely a result of path dependence, helped along by the decreasing power of labor to resist.

This channel has combined the drivers of technology (shifting the structure of the labor marker toward occupations with lower capacity to unionize), systemic cycle phase (shifting toward the superfluity of easily unionized manufacturing labor), trade relations (underlined by the export of easily unionized labor), developmental strategy (combining a high household demand growth model with an anti-labor extensive strategy) and power relations in which a diminishing labor power is interpreted as a consequence of the previous four elements (with primacy given to the systemic cycle encompassing the drivers of systemic cycle phase, trade relations, and developmental strategy). In terms of modes of change, this explanation of diminishing labor power as a mechanism of change in labor institutions is compatible with Thelen's idea of institutional change as displacement we accentuated in the context of the path-dependent channel of change. In the cyclical power relations channel we can achieve a slight zoom-in into the mechanics of the changing power relations beyond what interested Kathleen Thelen. However, the central point remains untouched—the institutions have a specific and unambiguous path of change provided there is a significant asymmetry of power. Her term of displacement may suggest an abrupt change, while our analysis shows a slow process, but the image is still precise enough.

6.3.3 Channel 3: Institutional Design—Domestic Politics and Transnational Conditionality in USA

The third channel of institutional reform identified by Chapter 5 is the deliberate institutional design, and the two obvious mechanisms in such formal politics are the domestic politics and transnational conditionality. The politics of USA are somewhat impervious to both transnational and unilateral domestic pressures, and this channel of institutional change is characterized by incremental reform. In terms of formal electoral and party politics, the USA are a democratic system with a *first-past-the-post* electoral system which favors a two-party system, as the smaller candidates (third parties) are mostly ruled out. The two modern parties are the Democratic Party which traditionally favored relatively more comprehensive regulation and social/labor rights and the Republican Party, which is relatively more free market oriented. On the federal level the formal US politics are conducted through the institutions of the President, the Senate, and the House of Representatives (which are the two Houses of the US Congress), with relatively high levels of political powers awarded to the President, making it a *presidential system.* In the Reagan Administration (1981–1989), the Republican president faced a democratic majority in the House of Representatives but had a Republican majority in Senate for the first six years. In the George H. W. Bush Republican administration (1989–1993) the Democratic Party had majorities in both Houses. In the Bill Clinton Democratic administration (1993–2001), there were Democratic majorities in both Houses for the first two years, but the tables were turned in 1995 with the Republican Party winning both majorities for the rest of Clinton's time in the White House. In the George W. Bush Republican administration, the Republican control of the Houses continued until 2007 (apart from a complex and shifting situation in the 2001–2003 Senate, i.e. the 107th Congress). The Democratic Party again dominated both houses for the 110th and 111th Congress (2007–2011), which was a problem for the last two years of the Bush presidency and a boon for the first two years of the Democratic Obama administration (2009–2017). In the 2011–2015 period Obama lost the control of Congress but kept Senate with a thin Democratic majority. In his last two years (2015–2017), Obama had to deal with a Republican Senate as well. The Republican Trump administration (2017–2021) presided over the 115th Congress with a double Republican majority. In the first approximation, one might expect to see real legislative-institutional change when these three institutions line up, neither restricting the others. Such windows of opportunity existed in the first two Clinton years (1993–1995—103rd Congress), the middle four Bush years (2003–2007—108th and 109th Congress), the first two Obama years (2009–2011—112th Congress), and during Trump's first two years (2017–2019—115th Congress). If we compare this expectation with landmark decisions and legislative action in Table 6.1, we can see that the Clinton and Obama double majority years brought two crucial reforms: the FMLA family leave of 1993 and a substantial reform of the health system in 2010—even as reforms of labor law were defeated (Worker Fairness Act in 1993) or not fully attempted (EFCA in 2009). These setbacks were made possible by the practice of filibustering, which is an obstruction mechanism, particularly effective in the US Senate where a minority can prevent legislation to be voted upon by exercising the unlimited right to hold the floor. To prevent the filibuster on legislation, the majority must have a supermajority of 60 out of 100 seats in the US Senate for a procedure known as cloture. This is not a typical situation and has not occurred in the Senate in the timeframe of interest to us here. This creates a situation in which even a party which dominates the legislative procedure often has to compromise and build a consensus over its proposals with at least some members of the opposite party. Large and controversial reforms are not a likely outcome in such a system, as they require substantial political resources even after a very successful election.

Additionally, recent scholarship (Gilens 2012; Gilens and Page 2014; Page and Gilens 2020) suggests that the expectations of direct connection between parties and their constituencies (e.g. the connection between the Democratic Party and organized labor) may be somewhat naïve in the US case. The authors analyze an impressively large database on policy preferences at different income groups and the policy outcomes and come to the conclusion that the political system is so much more responsive to the most wealthy group as to merit a description of economic elite domination rather than a majoritarian democracy (Gilens and Page 2014). Likewise, labor unions are far more likely to encounter resistance in areas of their preferences than other interest groups (Gilens 2012: 158), which certainly curbs their capabilities in lobbying. All of this helps us understand the lack of labor-friendly reforms in the period of interest.

The membership in WTO and FTA arrangements historically constricted the ability of the USA to act in the protectionist sense which, as we have seen in Chapter 4 correlates with labor regulation. However, the Trump administration strained these constrictions and brought active protectionism back to the agenda with a series of trade confrontations. In a more direct sense, the transnational organization which is charged with promoting labor standards is the ILO (International Labor Organization) by the UN. While the USA is the largest financial contributor to the ILO at 22% of its budget (ILO 2017a), the ILO conditionality could not have been very strong. Out of 189 conventions of the ILO (8 fundamental, 4 governance, and 177 technical), the USA has ratified only 14 (2 fundamental, 1 governance, and 11 technical), which testifies to its ability to ignore ILO[7] (ILO 2017b). The size and political power of the USA make it unlikely that a transnational organization could effect a substantial and

[7] To compare: Sweden has ratified 93, Russia 75, Japan 49, Slovenia 83, and Croatia 60 (ILO 2017b).

unwanted change in its institutions, and the relative powerlessness of the ILO should not be surprising.

Interactions with other drivers and the result

(a) Developmental strategy: neither formal political channel seems to have influenced the developmental strategy which is still focused on consumption in the face of a trade surplus.
(b) Result of institutional change: the specific political-institutional framework and the usual strategies in negotiating it have shaped the result, but only through inaction, as large-scale reforms of labor are difficult to imagine.

This channel brings us to an interesting dilemma in terms of modes of change. While we have accepted Thelen's view of labor institutional change in the USA as displacement in the first two channels, we must now take into account an alternative conceptualization. Hacker and Pierson (2010) forward the notion of institutional change in US labor as a form of drift. The key to their finding is the fact that the formal political process found itself in a gridlock after 1978 in matters concerning labor, which allowed for the economic processes to eat away at the power of the unions and no federal action to manifest itself to prevent it. The government has left the arena and the world changed around the old and increasingly ineffective institutions (ibid.: 56–61). The key level for Hacker and Pierson is therefore the formal political level, covered here as the third channel of institutional change. At that level, they are correct—the conspicuous inability of a redesign of formal institutions on the federal level covered in segment 6.3.1. is a logical prerequisite for the effectiveness of path dependence and power shifts. However, the absence of a redesign of institutions that seems crucial to Hacker and Pierson (named channel 3 here) did not happen in a vacuum—but was itself a result of power relations (channel 2) within the existing set of institutions (channel 1). Also, labor institutions on national levels of large countries are far too complex for their change to be governed by a single mode of change. Thelen is right to point to displacement in describing the long-term shifts, while Hacker and Pierson are right to point to drift while describing the effects of the political process taking a shorter term to develop. This chapter has taken both into account within the broader logic supplying also a cyclical notion of labor power shifts. Overall, the three channels in the US case of labor institutions provided a ripe terrain for the path dependence dominance, inasmuch as it defined the power to influence institutional design and the starting position of power shifts. Figure 6.10 summarizes these liberalizing tendencies.

The period since 1980 saw no path deviations, as formal institutions saw no crucial reforms via formal political system (channel 3) and informal institutions developed in the context of diminishing labor power (channel 2). This enabled the continued development of path dependence (channel 1), rather than a critical juncture scenario. The tendencies already active since the late 1940s simply continued and intensified. It produced what we cannot recognize as a successful developmental strategy as the financial expansion in progress accompanied a vast trade deficit. The next section surveys the social results of this process.

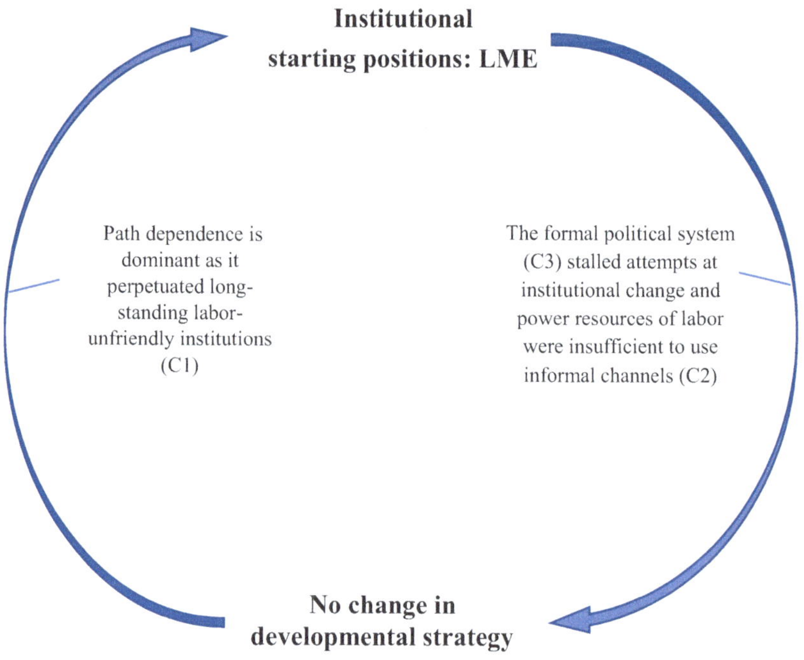

Fig. 6.10 Lack of developmental strategy shifts in USA since 1980

6.4 Social Effects of Labor Institutions in USA

One of the most common arguments in favor of flexible labor markets is the ostensibly lower unemployment rate caused by the fact that employing is easy and filled with less uncertainty. If a labor market is more heavily regulated, then dismissals are more complicated. Therefore, less regulation should cause the employers to more readily employ, as little cost is connected with a dismissal should the situation change. However, it also causes them to more easily terminate employment when demand is low (e.g. in a crisis). Figure 6.11 shows these links in the case of the USA since 1980.

Unemployment seems to closely respond to GDP growth in the case of the USA. There are four pronounced slowdowns or downturns of growth on the chart: 1982; 1991; 2001; and 2008/2009. All four were accompanied by quick and sharp increases in unemployment, which is in accordance with the VofC theory as outlined in Chapter 3 and with state of labor institutions as identified in this chapter. The data for 2020 will not be available for several months at the time of writing, but the most recent IMF estimates place real growth at –4.3% and the unemployment

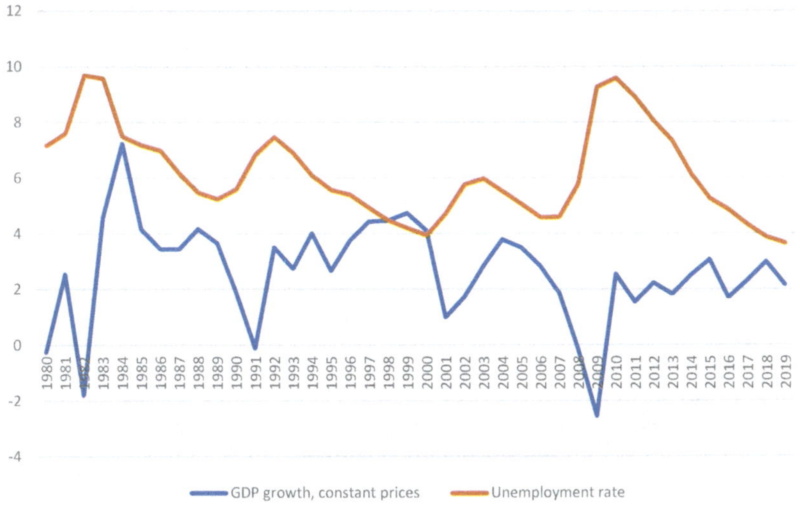

Fig. 6.11 The interaction of real GDP growth and unemployment in USA (*Source of data* IMF 2020)

rate at 8.9% (IMF 2020). Regardless of the distinct issues of the developing 2020 recession, it seems that the rapid increases of unemployment in response to downturns are to continue.

Labor institutions can also have a pronounced impact on income inequality, as strong unions can exert pressure toward a more egalitarian distribution of production income or even a more progressive tax system. An absence of strong unions can easily translate into an insufficiently progressive taxation or lower labor compensation. In terms of the developmental strategies, an intensive strategy would suggest a more egalitarian income structure as the Marginal Propensity to Consume tends to be higher in lower income earners and therefore a higher ratio of additional income will be spent in the lower income groups, contributing to GDP growth. A higher ratio of additional income will be saved rather than consumed in higher income groups contributing to capital accumulation but not directly to GDP growth. An extensive strategy can afford to accept this outcome as it is export oriented. This is one of the reasons why an extensive strategy would involve higher inequality levels. The current US strategy is, however, not oriented on the material expansion (and therefore exports) as it occurs late in the systemic cycle, during a financial expansion. As we have seen, that locks the USA in a growth model which is consumption-led in the face of trade deficits. The rising inequality is here a consequence of the increasing importance of impatient capital and shareholder value orientation (displacement), unmitigated as it remains as deliberate reform remains out of reach (drift).

The most commonly used measurement of income inequality is the GINI index which measures the inequality on an interval of 0 (perfect equality—every person earns exactly the same amount) to 1 (perfect inequality, only one person in a society has any income). Alternatively, GINI indices can be expressed on an interval of 0–100. According to World Bank (2020) data, the GINI index in the USA was at 34.5 in 1979, 37.4 in 1986, 38 in 1991, 40 in 1994, 40.5 in 1997, 40.1 in 2000, 40.3 in 2004, 40.8 in 2007, 40 in 2010, 40.7 in 2013, and 41.1 in 2016. In other words, an unmistakable trend of increasing inequality which increased the levels from moderate to pronounced income inequality.[8] The SWIID database (Solt 2020) assembles various GINI measures to

[8] Although the GINI indices suggest a slightly reduced income inequality as a result of the Great Recession, this aggregate measure may hide more complex effects. Visser (2018) finds evidence of greater wage polarization and downgrading job quality for male workers

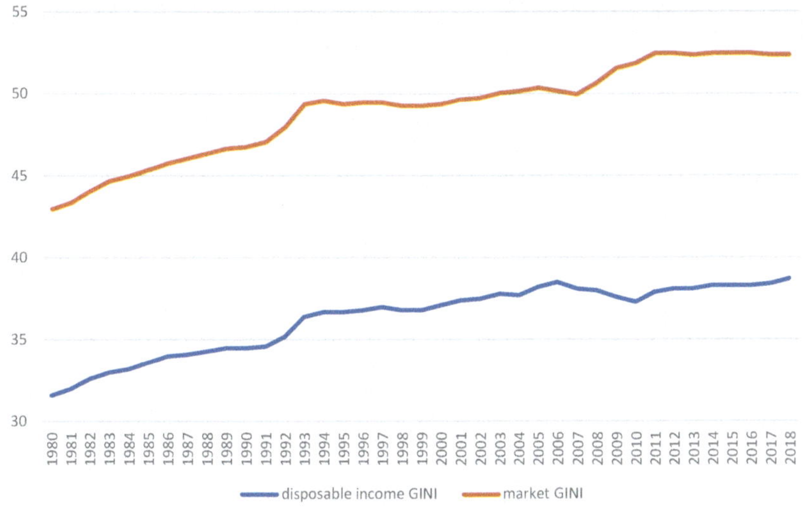

Fig. 6.12 Income inequality in USA—GINI (*Source of data* SWIID 9.0 [Solt 2020])

produce a continuous time series ensuring greater comparative capabilities among countries. It is an unusual database in that it uses imputation methods, meaning it extrapolates the missing values from existing ones.[9] While this enables unusually continuous coverage, it also may diminish the reliability of any given data point (particularly in countries with scarce coverage). It works well in those intervals and countries which are otherwise well covered and can be safely used for those in discerning general trends of inequality shifts. This makes it well suited for the purposes of these three illustrative chapters as they focus on comparative data and general patterns of change.

Figure 6.12 shows the SWIID central measures of market GINI (inequality of income before taxes and transfers) and disposable income GINI (after taxes and transfers). Both measures were on the rise since 1980, with the market index climbing from 43 in 1980 to 52.4 in 2018,

while Nau and Soener (2019) find that income precarity has increased predominantly in working families.

[9] For a comparison of available inequality databases see Ferreira et al. (2015).

and the disposable income index climbing from 31.6 in 1980 to 38.7 in 2018. While these figures seem to be lower than the World Bank estimates, the general trend of steadily rising inequality is even more recognizable. It is also interesting to note that the correction between the two indices (i.e. the effect of taxes and transfers) remains substantially the same since 1980 when the correction in index was −11.4, passing through −12.3 in 2000 and ending at −13.7 in 2017.

GINI indices are, however, not enough to meaningfully show the differences between specific groups, as they remain imprecise. For that, we will need to compare pre- and post-tax income inequality between the richest and the lower strata. Figure 6.13 shows the available data for national income shares of top 1% and the bottom 50% 1970–2019.

The benefit of observing the trends in pre-tax income is the ability to point out the distribution that occurs before the specific solutions in the tax system are activated. Direct comparisons should be careful as the methodology in the two sets of data is not identical. Pre-tax data is for income equally split among adults at the household level (presumably ameliorating the situation somewhat), while post-tax data is individual. However, we can clearly compare the trends. We can see that the pre-tax

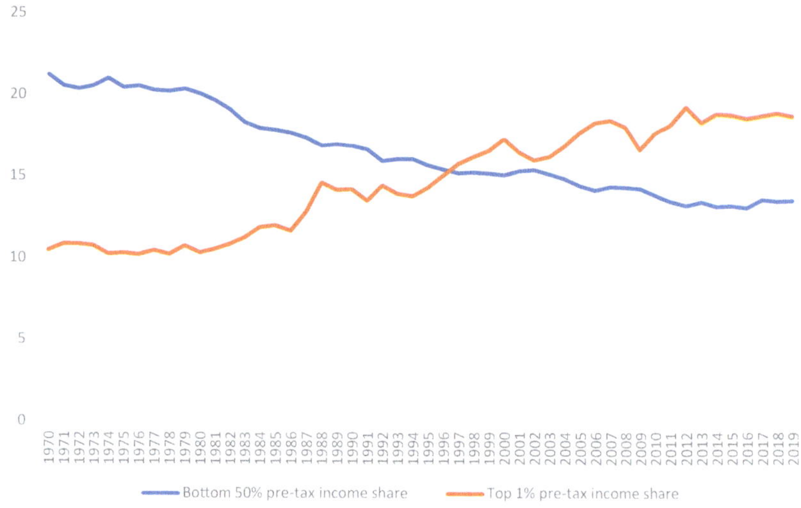

Fig. 6.13 Pre-tax income shares in USA (*Source of data* WID [2020])

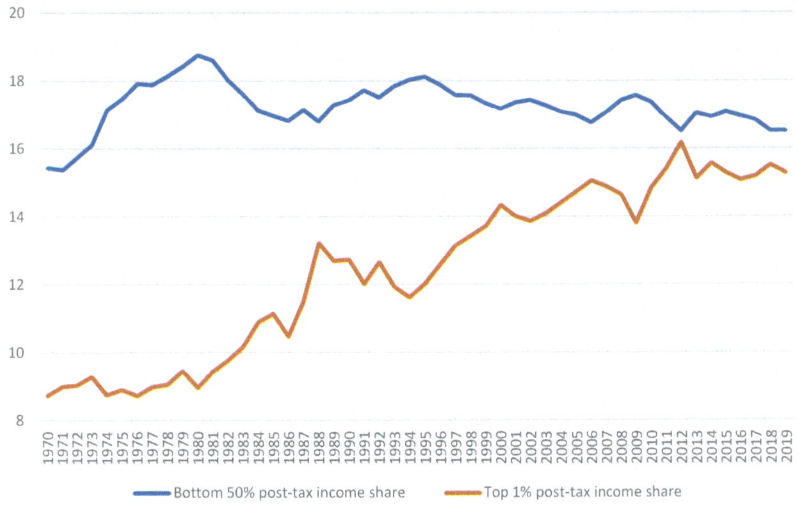

Fig. 6.14 Post-tax income inequality in USA (*Source of data* WID [2020])

income share of the bottom 50% steadily declined since 1970 (not shown on the graph is the increasing trend until 1970). The pre-tax income share of the top 1% was steady until 1980 and then began a sharp climb. The latest available data shows that the pre-tax income of the top 1% is almost 40% larger than the income of the bottom 50%. However, the USA has a progressive taxation system which tends to somewhat ameliorate the income differences (as we have seen comparing the pre-tax and post-tax GINI indices). The tax system has become riddled with various loopholes (see Steinmo 2010) and its progressive capacities have been significantly reduced in importance when compared to the 1950s,[10] but it is nevertheless a progressive system. To point at its effects, Fig. 6.14 shows the post-tax income shares of top 1% and the bottom 50% in the 1970–2019 period.

Here we can see a sharp increase of the share of the bottom 50% until 1980 to almost 19% of total income followed by a slow decrease to 16.5% in 2019. The top 1% has likewise remained stable until 1980 (again, not

[10] In 1958 the marginal tax rate for top earners was 91% (Baneman and Nunns 2012), whereas the top marginal rate today is at 37%.

apparent from the graph is the pronounced overall decreasing trend in the preceding decades) followed by a sharp increase of share to the high point of 16.2% in 2012 (and most recently at 15.3% in 2019). In other words, the net incomes of bottom 50% have grown through the 1960s and 1970s and the net income of top 1% has grown in the 1980s and 1990s and 2000s to almost meet at a higher level in the 2010s, effectively contributing to a diminishing middle class.[11] In income shares we can also roughly observe the extent of redistribution as the pre-tax ratio for the top 1% increased by 8.4% since 1980 and the post-tax ratio increased by 6.3%, while the pre-tax ratio of the bottom 50% decreased by 6.6% and the post-tax ratio decreased by 2.3%. An additional way to frame these distributional issues is the comparison of wage and profits ratios, which have essentially followed the same patterns. The ratio of corporate profits to GDP has risen from 7.4% in Q2 1980 to 11.2% in Q3 2018, while the ratio of worker compensation has decreased from 57.1 to 52.8% in the same period (FRED 2019). This data points to the structural distribution effects of the shifts in power resources discussed above as the continuous decrease in structural and associational power is consistent with a decreased capability of labor to influence income inequality.

6.5 Conclusion

American labor institutions have entered the 1980s as fairly flexible with a limited scope for labor organization. They have only continued this trend in the four decades since—and we have traced their movements firstly through the three Northian aspects of institutions. There were no major legislative innovations (formal institutions) to overturn this trend since 1980 and the power of labor to organize and bargain continued to drop

[11] These chapters do not focus on inequality causality beyond the illustration of the framework expounded in this book. However, it is worthwhile to note that Huber et al. (2019) analyze the data on 18 OECD members in the 1960–2012 period and find that the rising income share of the top 1% is related largely with union density, alongside union concentration, type of government, top marginal tax rates, and investment in public tertiary education. Kristal and Cohen (2017) analyze 43 US industries in the 1968–2012 period and find that roughly half of rising inequality can be explained by union disempowerment and a fall in the real value of the minimum wage, compared to roughly a quarter that can be attributed to computerization. Dosi et al. (2018) find that structural labor market reforms aimed at flexibilization are connected with higher unemployment and rising inequality.

(informal institutions). This has created an unfortunate situation in which marginal workers are left exposed to rampant wage theft and other forms of unlawful conduct (avoidable institutions).

We have used these aspects to explain this pattern of change through the framework developed in the previous chapter. The three channels of institutional change intertwined in the case of the USA to produce a labor hostile institutional environment. The three channels are often at odds with one another as path dependence pushes in a different direction than politically induced reforms or changes in power resources. This was not the case in American labor institutions since 1980 as the primary role was played by a virtually unopposed path dependence—pushing institutions in the direction of flexible and market-oriented labor. This continuation of labor deregulation was made possible by the formal political institutions which do not favor large and rapid reforms (disabling a countercurrent via the formal political channel) and by the inability of labor to defend its interests. This was a consequence of a diminishing associational and structural power of labor caused by the shift into post-industrial society, the financial expansion, and trade deficits. In terms of modes of change, this chapter has offered a logic overcoming the discrepancies between the Thelen view (*displacement*) and Hacker/Pierson view (*drift*). The framework we utilize develops a process timeframe hierarchy in which it becomes apparent that both descriptions are plausible in their own timeframes, with *displacement* a long-term interpretation of the general pattern of change in US labor institutions and *drift* a short-term prerequisite for its development.

From the viewpoint of systemic cycle theory, this continued path dependence, even a decade after the terminal crisis, suggests a prolonged period of systemic chaos with uncertain end-results in terms of paradigmatic organizations and strategies. The post-2008 legitimacy crisis did not produce a new social pact, and the electoral quests for change and renewed greatness are yet to manifest in a fundamentally different developmental strategy that could mitigate the adverse social effects. Our approach to institutions helped us discern the reasons for the prevalence of such path dependence. However, decades of continued growth of other large economies and a restructuring of global economy may construct fundamentally different political realities for USA as well. We now turn to two possible rivals for the central position in the world-economy.

Literature

Acemoglu, D., & Restrepo, P. (2017). *Robots and Jobs: Evidence from US Labor Markets* (NBER Working Paper Series). Available at https://www.nber.org/papers/w23285.pdf.

Baneman, D., & Nunns, J. (2012). *Income Tax Paid at Each Tax Rate, 1958–2009.* Urban-Brookings Tax Policy Center. Available at https://www.taxpolicycenter.org/sites/default/files/publication/103946/901456-Income-Tax-Paid-at-Each-Tax-Rate—Updated-.PDF.

Bernhardt, A., Milkman, R., Theodore, N., Heckathorn, D., Auer, M., DeFilippis, J., et al. (2009). Broken Laws, Unprotected Workers. In *National Employment Law Project*. New York: NELP.

Bjorklund, E. (2019). Out of Many, One? US Sub-National Political-Economies in the Post-welfare Reform Era. *Socio-Economic Review, 17*(4), 851–873.

Brudney, J. (2005). Contractual Approaches to Labor Organizing: Supplanting the Election Paradigm? In *Labor and Employment Relations Association Series, Proceedings of the 57th Annual Meeting* (pp. 106–113).

Compa, L. (2014). An Overview of Collective Bargaining in the United States. In J. G. Hernández (Ed.), *El derecho a la negociación colectiva: Monografías de temas laborales* (pp. 91–98). Seville: Consejo Andaluz de Relaciones Laborales.

Crouch, C. (2009). Privatised Keynesianism: An Unacknowledged Policy Regime. *The British Journal of Politics & International Relations, 11*(3), 382–399.

Dosi, G., Pereira, M. C., Roventini, A., & Virgillito, M. E. (2018). The Effects of Labour Market Reforms Upon Unemployment and Income Inequalities: An Agent-Based Model. *Socio-Economic Review, 16*(4), 687–720.

Doyle, A. (2017). *The Balance.* List of U.S. Employment Laws What the Law Says About Wages, Work Safety, Discrimination, and More. https://www.thebalance.com/list-of-employment-laws-2062282.

Early, S. (2013). *Save Our Unions: Dispatches from a Movement in Distress.* New York: Monthly Review Press.

Ferreira, F. H., Lustig, N., & Teles, D. (2015). *Appraising Cross-National Income Inequality Databases: An Introduction* (World Bank Policy Research Working Paper 7489). http://documents.worldbank.org/curated/en/590731467992508711/pdf/WPS7489.pdf.

FRED. (2017). *Households and Nonprofit Organizations; Credit Market Instruments; Liability, Level (CMDEBT).* https://fred.stlouisfed.org/series/CMDEBT.

FRED. (2018). *Household Debt to GDP for United States* (HDTGPDUSQ163N). https://fred.stlouisfed.org/series/HDTGPDUSQ163N.

FRED. (2019). *FRED Graph.* https://fred.stlouisfed.org/graph/?g=niHr.

FRED. (2020). *Compensation of Employees: Wages and Salary Accruals/Gross Domestic Product* (A4002E1A156NBEA). https://fred.stlouisfed.org/graph/?g=2Xa.

Frey, C. B., & Osborne, M. A. (2013). *The Future of Employment: How Susceptible are Jobs to Computerisation?* https://www.fhi.ox.ac.uk/wp-content/uploads/The-Future-of-Employment-How-Susceptible-Are-Jobs-to-Computerization.pdf.

Gilens, M. (2012). *Affluence and Influence: Economic Inequality and Political Power in America*. Princeton: Princeton University Press.

Gilens, M., & Page, B. I. (2014). Testing Theories of American Politics: Elites, Interest Groups, and Average Citizens. *Perspectives on Politics, 12*(3), 564–581.

Godard, J. (2009). The Exceptional Decline of the American Labor Movement. *ILR Review, 63*(1), 82–108.

Hacker, J. S., & Pierson, P. (2010). *Winner-Take-All Politics: How Washington Made the Rich Richer—And Turned Its Back on the Middle Class*. New York: Simon and Schuster.

Hall, P., & Soskice, D. (Eds.). (2001). *Varieties of Capitalism: The Institutional Foundations of Comparative Advantage*. Oxford: Oxford University Press.

Heritage. (2020a). *Labor Freedom*. http://www.heritage.org/index/labor-freedom.

Heritage. (2020b). *Explore the Data*. http://www.heritage.org/index/explore.

Heritage. (2020c). *Graph the Data*. http://www.heritage.org/index/visualize.

Huber, E., Huo, J., & Stephens, J. D. (2019). Power, Policy, and Top Income Shares. *Socio-Economic Review, 17*(2), 231–253.

ILO. (2017a). *The US: A Leading Role in the ILO*. Available at http://www.ilo.org/washington/ilo-and-the-united-states/the-usa-leading-role-in-the-ilo/lang–en/index.htm.

ILO. (2017b). *Ratifications by Country*. Available at http://www.ilo.org/dyn/normlex/en/f?p=1000:11200:0::NO:11200:P11200_COUNTRY_ID:102871.

IMF. (2020). *World Economic Outlook Database October 2020*. Available at http://www.imf.org/external/pubs/ft/weo/2020/02/weodata/index.aspx.

Jung, J. (2017). A Struggle on Two Fronts: Labour Resistance to Changing Layoff Policies at Large US Companies. *Socio-Economic Review, 15*(1), 213–239.

Keynes, J. M. (1930/2009). Economic Possibilities for Our Grandchildren. In *Essays in Persuasion* (pp. 192–202). Classic House Books.

Krippner, G. R. (2005). The Financialization of the American Economy. *Socio-Economic Review, 3*(2), 173–208.

Krippner, G. R. (2011). *Capitalizing on Crisis*. Cambridge: Harvard University Press.

Kristal, T., & Cohen, Y. (2017). The Causes of Rising Wage Inequality: The Race Between Institutions and Technology. *Socio-Economic Review, 15*(1), 187–212.

Nau, M., & Soener, M. (2019). Income Precarity and the Financial Crisis. *Socio-Economic Review, 17*(3), 523–544.

OECD. (2020). *OECD Data* [online]. Available at https://data.oecd.org/.

Page, B. I., & Gilens, M. (2020). *Democracy in America? What Has Gone Wrong and What We Can Do About It*. Chicago: University of Chicago Press.

Pierson, P. (2015). Power and Path Dependence. In J. Mahoney & K. Thelen (Eds.), *Advances in Comparative-Historical Analysis* (pp. 123–147). Cambridge: Cambridge University Press.

Solt, F. (2020). *The Standardized World Income Inequality Database*. SWIID Version 9.0. https://fsolt.org/swiid/.

Steinmo, S. (2010). *The Evolution of Modern States: Sweden, Japan, and the United States*. Cambridge University Press.

Tang, A. (2019). Life After Janus. *Columbia Law Review, 119*(3), 677–762.

Thelen, K. (2014). *Varieties of Liberalization and the New Politics of Social Solidarity*. New York: Cambridge University Press.

Trading Economics. (2018). *United States Households Debt to Gdp 1952–2018*. https://tradingeconomics.com/united-states/households-debt-to-gdp.

Visser, J. (2019, June). *ICTWSS Data Base: Version 6.0*. Amsterdam: Amsterdam Institute for Advanced Labour Studies (AIAS), University of Amsterdam. Open Access Database at: https://www.ictwss.org/downloads.

Visser, M. A. (2018). Restructuring Opportunity: Employment Change and Job Quality in the United States During the Great Recession. *Socio-Economic Review, 17*(3), 545–572.

WEF. (2016a). *Measuring the Global Gender Gap*. Available at http://reports.weforum.org/global-gender-gap-report-2016/measuring-the-global-gender-gap/.

WEF. (2016b). *United States*. Available at http://reports.weforum.org/feature-demonstration/files/2016/10/USA.pdf.

WID. (2020). *World Inequality Database*. Available at http://wid.world/.

World Bank. (2020). *World Bank Open Data*. http://data.worldbank.org.

CHAPTER 7

Labor Market in Germany

7.1 Introduction

This chapter will apply the framework of institutional change from Chapter 5 on the labor institutions in Germany. As already mentioned, Germany was the paradigmatic CME case, in which institutional complementarities strategically coordinate the activities of unions, organized employers and even the companies themselves. This chapter will argue for an understanding of this older conception of Germany as a CME as a side product of various drivers of change, but primarily of a developmental strategy of intensive capitalism. This strategy has been seriously challenged by the past decades of experience in labor market dualism and also through the astounding organizational innovation of the European Union in its monetary and fiscal integrations. This chapter will offer an interpretation of this innovation and this version of liberalization as a turn to an extensive developmental strategy.

The first section will survey the labor institutions in Germany and their changes through the Northian prism of institutions as formal, informal, and avoidable structures. The second section will apply the framework to the German labor institutions and explain the drivers and the three channels of institutional change since 1980. The third section will explore the social effects of these changes.

J. Lučev, *Systemic Cycle and Institutional Change*,
https://doi.org/10.1007/978-3-030-66053-6_7

7.2 Changes in Labor Institutions in Germany

German labor institutions have started as a prototype for the CME ideal-type structure which suggests high protection for well-organized and highly skilled labor. The changes in labor institutions since 1980 point to a dualized labor market, with the core industrial workers protected by formal institutions (laws and contracts) and informal institutions (relatively centralized collective bargaining), but there is also an increasingly large low-wage sector with workers without much formal or informal protection. This underprotected sector evolved through the use of new or increasingly employed legal means of fixed-term employment contracts or temp-agency work, while the original core remained protected and regulated via the open-ended employment contracts and strong union presence.

7.2.1 Formal Labor Institutions in Germany

The first aspect of institutions explains the formal, codified one, where structures may be discerned by surveying laws and statutes. Table 7.1 shows some landmark legal moments of German labor history which have created the German model of industrial relations.

The formal institutions developing after World War II gave us the legal aspect of what VofC have identified as the CME economy. The "German model" that emerged hinges on the legally sanctioned organization of labor on many levels: on the level of the shop-floor by worker councils (1952), on the level of the larger company by supervisory board cooperation according to the co-determination principle (1976) and on the level of the industry by unions and their collective bargaining (1949). All of these create the channels for strategic coordination of employers with organized labor. Co-determination law (*Mitbestimmung*) awards workers half the seats in the supervisory board of large companies, works councils protect employees on the shop-floor, and the employment legal structure as a whole awards generous protection for workers (e.g. terminations must in principle have a cause and notice periods extend to more than 7 months, depending on the years of service; see Kirchner et al. 2018).

Table 7.1 Landmark reforms of labor regulation in Germany[1]

Year	*Germany labor laws*	*Explanation*
1949	*Tarifvertragsgesetz*	Guarantees the right to collective bargaining
1952	*Betriebsverfassungs-gesetz*	Work Councils installed, giving the workers representation on the shop-floor (plant) level
1969	*Kundigundgschutz-gesetz*	Additional protection from dismissals
1976	*Mitbestimmungsgesetz*	Companies with more than 2000 employees must staff half of their supervisory board (*Aufsichtsrat*) with workers
1985	*Beschäftigungs-förderungsgesetz*	Fixed-term contracts for newly hired employees can be used without specified reasons (up to 18 months), maximum duration of agency work increased from 3 to 6 months (increased to 9 months in 1993 and 12 in 1997)
1996	Changes to *Beschäftigungs-förderungsgesetz*	Maximum duration of fixed-term contracts is increased to 24 months
2001	*Job-AQTIV*	Maximum duration of temporary work agencies is increased to 24 months
2003	*Hartz I*	Established PSA (*Personal Service Agenturen* or Personal Service Agencies), which were supposed to streamline the employment of those with low skill levels and fund their training; it also eliminated the maximum duration of temporary agency work
2003	*Hartz II*	Instituted variants of low-wage temporary employment and self-employment (*Minijob, Midijob, Ich-AG*)
2004	*Hartz III*	Job-center reform
2005	*Hartz IV*	Lowered the unemployment benefits (*Arbeitslosenhilfe*) and equated them with the levels of social security benefits (*Sozialhilfe*) and shortened the timespan in which they could be used
2015	*Mindestlohngesetz*	First national minimum wage in Germany (8.5€ per hour; increased to 8.89€ for 2016 and 8.84€ for 2017 and 2018)

Sources Kemmerling and Bruttel (2005), Emmenegger (2014), Eichhorst and Marx (2011), Deutsche Welle (2016), Thelen (2014), Bosch (2018), Kirchner et al. (2018)

[1]A more encompassing historical review would need to start at least in Bismarck's regulatory innovations in the 1880s. However, the regulatory discontinuity in the German case (particularly in the 1933–1945 period) substantially diminishes the usefulness of such a review. This overview therefore limits itself to the post-war era.

The period since 1980 brought a crucial departure from this model and enabled a secondary, less protected labor market alongside the traditional core labor market which operated in a world of open-ended contracts with substantial dismissal protection. This secondary labor market used and gradually expanded fixed-term contracts and agency work as two tools of marginalized labor. The expansion of the first category began in 1985 when the possibility to issue fixed-term contracts for up to 18 months was first legalized. This limit increased in 1996 to 24 months and in 2003 to 48 months for newly established companies (Emmenegger 2014; Eichhorst and Marx 2011). The second category also gradually expanded, with the maximum limit for temporary agency work slowly increasing from 3 months to 6 (1985 reform), 9 (1993 reform), 12 (1997 reform), and finally to 24 months (2001 reform). The ultimate normalization of marginal labor came with the Hartz reforms of the early 2000s which have eliminated the limits to temporary agency work, incentivized various forms of self-employment and part-time work and prohibited discrimination against temporary work (Thelen 2014; Eichhorst and Marx 2011). These reforms enabled a substantial deepening of the marginal position of non-core workers and made low-wage temporary employment more usual in Germany. Hartz II incentivized part-time work and it substantially grew as a percentage of total employment (it gradually grew from 12.2% in 1983 to 19.1% in 2000 before the Hartz reforms, to be found at 25.2% in 2006 and a very high 27.2% in 2019; Eurostat 2020). Hartz IV redesigned the unemployment benefits by effectively reducing the income available to the unemployed and the cost of the unemployment system as a whole[2] (Kemmerling and Bruttel 2005; Thelen 2014). At the same time, the core employment of open-ended contracts largely

[2]The older unemployment system in Germany was very generous, with dismissed employees receiving 67% (provided they had dependent children, 60% if they did not) of their last-earned salary for up to 32 months (this was known as unemployment benefit and was financed from contributions), after which they were eligible for 57% of their last wages (53% with no children) for an unlimited duration (unemployment assistance, financed from taxes). If the unemployed did not qualify (did not meet the criteria for a lack of sufficient contributions), they would receive the municipally financed social assistance. After Hartz IV, the first part of the program remained means tested and is now limited to a maximum of 12 months (18 for people over 55). After this period, the unemployed are limited to the lower (and fixed) levels of social assistance (Kemmerling and Bruttel 2005: 5–7). The levels of *Arbeitslosengeld II* as this part of the program is now called are adjusted yearly and were set at 432€ for a single person for 2020 (Die Bundesregierung 2019).

remained protected at the same standards that were prevalent in the previous decades. The notice periods may be very long for ordinary terminations, and these terminations must meet lists of social justification to be legal (for conduct, person and operational reasons), while special notifications are necessary to federal agencies prior to cases of mass dismissals (Kirchner et al. 2018). The most important changes to this primary labor market came in the form of the threshold of company size at which wrongful dismissal protection kicks in and the length of the list of social justifications for legal ordinary termination. In 1996 the threshold was increased from 6 to 11 employees, and the list of justifications for collective dismissals was introduced. Both stipulations were revoked in late 1998 and reintroduced in late 2003 (Emmenegger 2014). Nevertheless, the protection awarded to open-ended contracts remains substantial when compared to most other developed countries.

The increasingly difficult position of marginal workers eventually prompted the need for a minimum national wage law in 2015. This is significant as the established traditional collective bargaining system (which we cover under informal institutions) used to be strong enough to guarantee relatively high levels of wages making a national minimum wage superfluous. We should also note that provisions for minimum wages on the level of specific industries existed since the late 1990s, when concerns over the wages paid by foreign firms to their own nationals for work in Germany prompted this additional level of protection (Fulton 2020).

Analyzing the OECD EPL data (as explained in the previous chapter), one can observe that the individual protection of regular contract employees has slightly increased in the early 1990s. The indicator remains at 2.5 in the 1985–1994 and then at 2.6 until 2019 (time series begins in 1985 and ends in 2019). The temporary Employment Protection Legislation index has, on the other hand, had a pronounced slide from the unusually high 5 in 1985, ranging in the 3.13–3.25 in the 1986–1996 period, dropping further to 2 in the 1998–2002 period and with the Hartz reforms in place dropping down to 1 until 2013 when it began slightly improving, first to 1.13 and in 2018 once more to 1.38 (OECD 2020). This means that the maximally protected labor market for temporary and fixed-term workers has, through a series of regulatory reforms, become a very flexible market. In fact, the Hartz reforms enabled and incentivized an explosion of the self-employed and low-paying mini-job working arrangements. Alongside this severely deregulated fixed-term and temporary labor market, the more mainstream regular contracts remained virtually unchanged. This rift between traditional mainstream (open-ended) and the marginal (part-time or temporary) contracts is essentially the formal institutional face of the German labor market dualism. The continued high protection of traditional mainstream employment is the reason that Heritage index of labor freedom ranks Germany 123rd of 186 states at 53 for 2020, interpreting it as "mostly unfree" in its terminology (Heritage 2020). The index started at 48.7 in 1995 (when the series began to be calculated) and spent its first decade mostly in the "repressed" range below the value of 50.

7.2.2 Informal Labor Institutions in Germany

The formal institutions award a high level of protection to core workers and an increasingly flexible market for marginal workers. However, wherever the formal institutions leave room for uncertainty, there is a need for informal practices to assure efficiency. A relevant example is the determination of severance packages in Germany. While there is a heavily codified procedure for ordinary termination, the justifiably terminated do not generally have the guaranteed right to a severance package. However, the laid off workers have recourse to litigation and if they can prove they were wrongfully dismissed, they have the right to be reinstated with back-pay. This creates an uncertainty for both the terminated employee and the employer, and in 80% of terminations, they mutually agree to termination instead (Magotsch and Kremp 2018: 171) and agree to a severance package usually at the level of 0.5 monthly payments per year of service (ibid.: 185). This wide-spread practice can be thought of as an informal institution which enables terminations to avoid potentially costly and time-consuming litigation while enabling a financial cushion for the terminated worker.

A higher-level informal institution is the system of collective bargaining, which we have already covered as such in the chapter on the US labor market. The level of collective bargaining is a matter of willing cooperation of organized labor and organized employers. This makes any stable expectations of the level of such coordination an informal institution. As we have seen in the previous chapter, the USA has a very decentralized collective bargaining in line with its free market orientation.

In Germany, collective bargaining is mostly conducted on the level of the industry (i.e. lower than the fully coordinated national cross-industrial level and higher than the US norm of the enterprise level

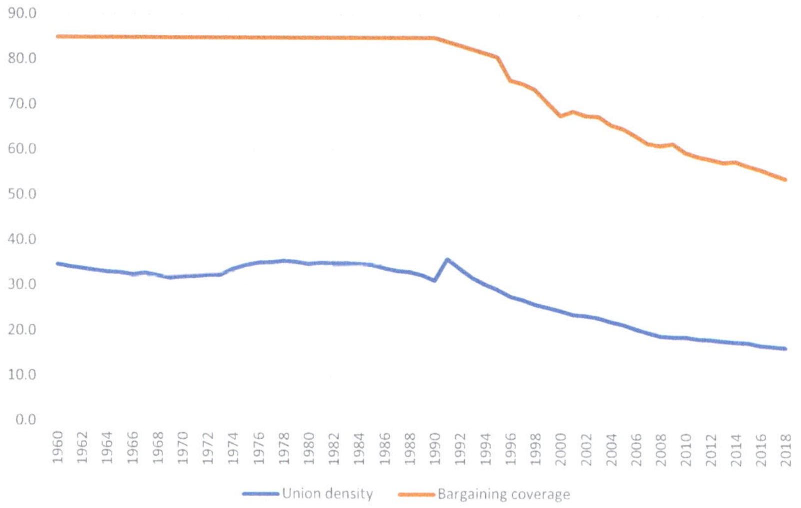

Fig. 7.1 Union density and bargaining coverage in Germany (*Source of data* ICTWSS database 6.0 [Visser 2019])

bargaining). According to the ICTWSS database, the predominance of this level remains unchanged at least since 1960 (Visser 2019). This is relevant as a more highly centralized collective bargaining suggests that a far wider sweeping coverage can be assured. However, it seems that this level of coordination is threatened by the increasingly low participation of employers in organized structures which are a prerequisite of such coordination (Fulton 2020).

Figure 7.1 shows the relationship between union density[3] and bargaining coverage in Germany.

The graph is plotted only from 1995 for bargaining coverage as the data was both unremarkable and not continuous prior to this year (it seems it was estimated at 85% in five-year intervals from 1960 to 1990),

[3] In 2020, the estimate of total labor union members in Germany derived from the addition of most recent union data stood at 7.7 million. The largest labor unions in Germany are the industrial IG Metall with 2.3 million, and transport and services oriented Ver.di with 2 million. Both belong to the DGB trade union confederation with some 6 million members overall in 2018. The most important non-DGB player is the dbb confederation, which catered to 1.3 million members (in 2018) located in the public sector and formerly public-owned companies (Fulton 2020).

while the union density was available for the full time series 1960–2018. Union density has slowly fluctuated in the 31–35.5 range in the 1960–1990 period. At this time the unification of Germany and the statistical inclusion of the more heavily unionized DDR to the data of BRD caused a rapid increase of 4.8%. After 1991 the overall union membership has been in a slow and steady decline eventually reaching the overall rate of 16.5% for 2018. Unlike the situation in the USA, however, these two curves are quite far apart as a result of a more centralized bargaining process in which the results of negotiation are applied to entire industries rather than individual enterprises, spanning a far more wide-reaching number of beneficiaries. Consequently, there tends to be a large proportion of the over-all labor force which is covered by the collective agreements even though they do not belong to any trade union (more than 40% in most years covered). This makes the legitimacy of unions disproportionately larger that which could be inferred from the relatively low overall rate of union density.

However, while German collective bargaining is strong and centralized when compared to the USA, developments in recent years have substantially weakened its erstwhile principles. Firstly, as Fig. 7.1 shows, the coverage has dropped by more than 20% since the mid-1990s. Secondly, the central contracts have an increasing tendency of delegating issues to firm-level bargaining (Palier and Thelen 2010: 120). Thirdly and most importantly, the described changes in the formal institutions have helped create a very large low-wage sector of the economy, and the trade unions are beginning to recognize that their power to negotiate with employers in the low-wage sector has become void (Bosch 2018: 19). Although the average real wage has increased by 7% in Germany in the 2006–2015 (ILO 2016), the low-wage sector (measured as percentage of workers earning less than two-thirds of median wages) expanded from 13.6% in 1995 to 17.5% in 2005 and 19.4% in 2015. It has since dropped back to 17.8% in 2018 (OECD 2020). This data illustrates the effect of the shift into an extensive strategy of material expansion with a need for a low-wage regime.

7.2.3 Avoidable Labor Institutions in Germany

Unlike the USA, wage theft is unlikely in Germany, as there are numerous channels through which organized labor can exert influence (co-determination principle, works councils, and a relatively centralized practice of collective bargaining expands the leverage of unions in industry). The rule of law is also quite strong, and the regulation is generally not circumvented, once in place. The World Justice Rule of Law index places Germany 6th globally and 8th in regulatory enforcement (WJP 2018).

However, there is a particular issue in avoiding a declarative part of employment laws, as Germany has significant issues with gender discrimination. In the 2016 World Economic Forum "Global Gender Gap Index" Germany had some of the best but also some very bad results (ranking 1st in literacy but 100th in tertiary enrollment). Contrary to VofC expectations, the German survey rate of wage gender equality was even poorer than in the USA and China and it ranked 95th with the index value of 0.591 (WEF 2016). Eurostat data is in accordance with a relatively poor gender position in Germany (Eurostat measures the gender gap as a "difference between average gross hourly earnings of male and female employees as % of male gross earnings" and shows that the German gender gap is one of the highest in EU and follows only Estonia and Czech Republic at 22.3% (Eurostat 2017). Taking overall earnings into account paints and even grimmer picture at 45% and Germany in 2014 better off only when compared with the Netherlands at 47.5% and Malta at 45.5% (Eurostat 2016). According to a 2009 report by the German Federal Ministry for Family Affairs, Senior Citizens, Women and Youth, the gender gap was far lower in former DDR than in the West (in 2008 the gap was 6% in the East and 24% in the West; BMFSFJ 2009: 10). "Women are missing in certain professions, sectors and on the upper end of the career ladder; The horizontal and vertical segregation of the labour market along gender lines continues to be a reality; Women interrupt their careers and reduce their working time for family reasons more frequently and for longer periods than men; Individual and collective pay negotiations have not yet succeeded in effectively overcoming the traditionally low evaluation of female dominated professions" (ibid.: 11).

This particular issue notwithstanding, Germany does not have substantial issues with avoidable institutions. Unlike the USA and China, the formal and informal aspects of labor institutions dominate, and they point to pronounced dualism. Formal institutional changes have increased competitiveness and lowered unemployment but provided ample room for a large low-wage sector to develop. Informal institutional changes point to a retreat of unions from the low-wage, largely service-based sector.

7.3 Explaining Institutional Change in Germany

Figure 7.2 adapts the framework from Chapter 5 to the specific national context of Germany since 1980. This section explains each institutional change driver in turn and explores their mutual interactions and effects on the institutional result through the prism of our theory.

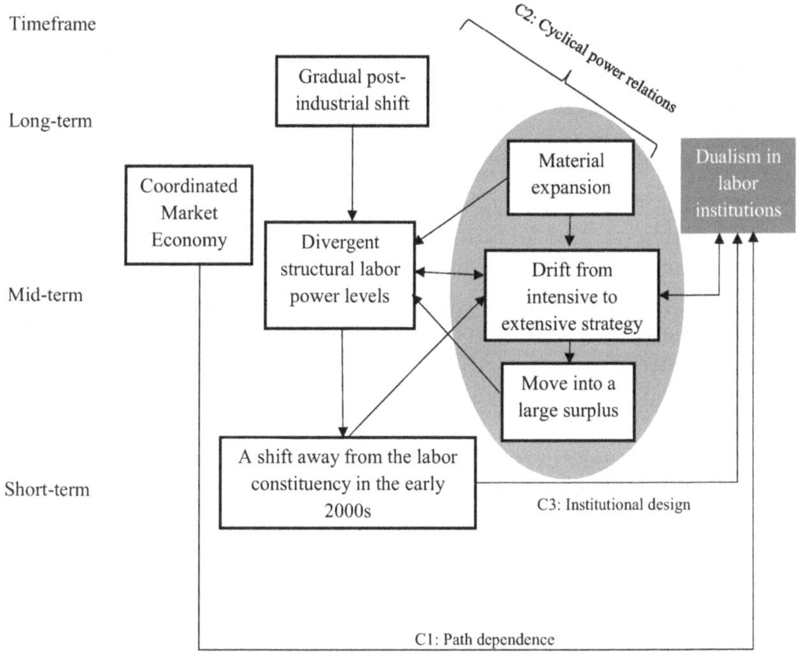

Fig. 7.2 A framework of labor-institutional change in Germany since 1980

7.3.1 *Channel 1: Path Dependence—Institutional Starting Positions of Germany*

The first channel of institutional change is path dependence, which suggests the result of change is dependent on the initial institutional conditions. In 2001 Germany was described as a paradigmatic case of a CME with its patient capital working together with strong unions and a vast network of coordination networks linking a well-developed vocational education system with firms which include workers in their management system through the legally mandated co-determination principle (Hall and Soskice 2001). At first glance, such a network may be difficult to change to the detriment of labor as the structures representing labor are quite strong. Nevertheless, as we have seen, the labor institutions have changed and moved away from labor protection.

The specific areas in which labor was made flexible is the non-manufacturing non-traditional employment, while the old labor institutions remained strong in the manufacturing traditional core, which is why many authors identify a process of dualization of labor markets in Germany (e.g. Palier and Thelen 2010; Hassel 2011; Thelen 2014; Häusermann and Schwander 2012; Eichhorst and Marx 2011; Eichhorst 2015; Pulignano et al. 2017). While German industrial relations appear to remain typical of a CME invested in high skills, a strong social partnership in the manufacturing core of the economy with high unionization rates conceals low union coverage for the growing service sector. It is worth noting that some authors view dualization as merely an intermediate step toward greater precarity, rather than a stable result (Baccaro and Howell 2017: 120). Germany also witnessed a substantial growth of a low-wage sector and substantial deregulation of agency work, fixed-term and mini jobs even as the well-protected blue-collar core was preserved. This led Thelen (2014) to explain this specific modus of this change as *drift*—a tendency to retain old institutional solutions even as they cover a decreasing segment of the labor market, which has, in the German case meant a continued protection of insiders coupled with a disregard for new social risks on the periphery.

This context is crucial for understanding the data provided in the description of labor institutions. While the EPL index for regular employment remains high (describing the well-protected regular employment market), the EPL index for temporary employment has decreased from one of the highest levels measured (in 1985) to one of the lower levels in the time series. While the bargaining coverage remains high, it has been subjected to decline compared to even higher levels in the 1980s, union density has, however, declined from moderate to relatively low levels. Investment in active labor market policies is at 0.68% of GDP in 2018, which is far higher than that in the USA (0.1%). It is, however, surpassed by levels found in Denmark (1.89%), Sweden (1.1%), and Finland (0.94%) (OECD 2020).

The path-dependent channel of institutional change perpetuates itself in part via its effect on power. As we have seen in the previous chapter, it was the relatively weak and unprotected initial position of US labor that enabled the continued liberalization (as *displacement*) of the labor market. On the other hand, the continued strength of German industrial labor created a constricted set of possible policy choices. Specifically, the institutions that emerged around manufacturing labor conditions (unions themselves, works councils, co-determination, mainstream employment arrangements, industry-level bargaining practices) were protected by the relatively high power of labor in industry. If liberalization of the labor market was to take place, it needed to circumvent this sector and orient itself onto the activities which were left underprotected by the old set of labor institutions. This need for circumvention of a labor power bastion prevented wide-sweeping *displacement* and enabled *drift*.

Interactions with other drivers and the result

(a) Power relations: initial structure is often path dependent though pronounced effects on power relations. In Germany, initial structure awarded a great importance to labor and was dependent on its high associational and structural power. As German competitiveness became an issue which prompted a top-down political reform with the goal of labor commodification, the power resources of labor guided the reform onto the under-organized outsiders. In other words, the concentrated power of industrial, core labor helped produce the dualistic labor system by protecting its own base.

(b) Phase of the systemic cycle: as we will see below, Germany has significantly developed its financial sector since 1980. However, the relative importance of patient capital is not in question and Germany remains embedded in its material expansion. The initial institutional comparative advantage of Germany focusing on production and manufacturing certainly helped steer the development options and keep Germany away from speculative predominance of the USA.

(c) The result of institutional change: path dependence of initial structures provided sufficient power to protect the core workers, but the end-result was dependent on the two other channels.

7.3.2 *Channel 2: Cyclical Power Relations in Germany*

Figure 7.3 shows the details of the second channel of institutional change we identified. The five constitutive drivers are technological change (treated as an exogenous factor—providing a long-term context), the three drivers constituting the systemic cycle—the phase of the systemic cycle, developmental strategies and trade relations—and the power relations as the balance of power resources.

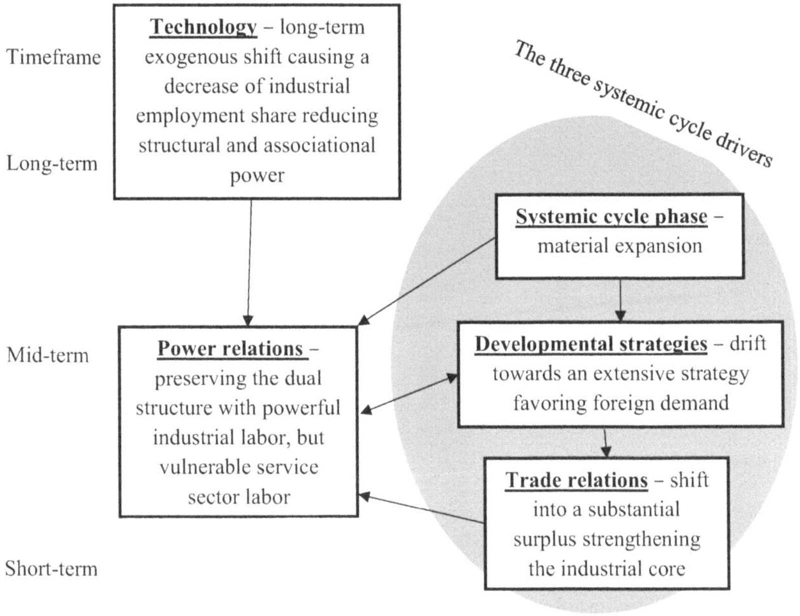

Fig. 7.3 Cyclical power relations in Germany

This segment will explain in greater detail the interactions of these five drivers among each other and with the rest of the framework.

7.3.2.1 *Technology and Sectoral Labor Market Structure in Germany*

The second channel of institutional change is a nexus of drivers which link into the power relations and help formulate the developmental strategy. The most long-term driver in this nexus is technological change.

In the Western world technological progress and implementation in production generally meant the continuous implementation of labor saving and/or capital deepening technology, gradually reducing the need to employ large numbers of workers in industry. In the late twentieth century, the trend of an overall decrease in industrial employment and increase in service employment became pronounced giving rise to the popularity of the post-industrial society thesis. Figure 7.4 shows the changing employment structure in Germany. The modern employment shares seem to be comparable with US levels in the early 1980s, pointing to the differences in developments, with the financial expansion and trade

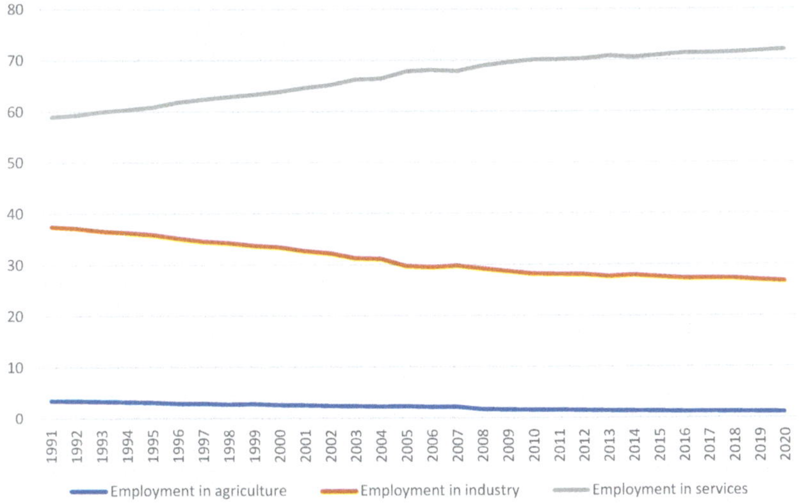

Fig. 7.4 Germany employment structure (*Source of data* World Bank [2020])

deficits in the US diminishing industrial workers, and the material expansion and trade surpluses enabling Germany to observe only a gradual decline in its sectoral share of industry.

Nevertheless, the general trend in the 1991–2020 period was typical of a developed economy and consisted of a low share of agricultural employment, as well as continually rising service and decreasing industry shares. Service share is estimated at 72.1% in 2020 (compared to 58.9% in 1991), industry is at 26.8% (compared to 37.6% in 1991), and agriculture is at a low 1.2% (compared to 3.5% in 1991). These figures are substantially different compared to the situation in the USA today as the share of the workforce in industry is 7.1% larger in Germany (at 26.8% compared to 19.7%).

Interactions with other drivers and the result

(a) Power relations: as technology changes, new methods of production are applied, and these may change the employment structure in the long run. This is significant, as the associational and structural power of labor are concentrated in industrial occupations and dispersed in service occupations. The prevalent trend was therefore the overall weakening of labor, but to a far lesser degree than in the USA—and with the remaining bastion of labor power in industry.
(b) Developmental strategy: this process created the contours of a future development strategy which needed to take the different degrees of power into account and formulate a low-wage regime around the industrial workers.

7.3.2.2 *Phase of the Systemic Cycle in Germany*

The systemic cycle is a global process with very different national/local consequences. The previous chapter has shown that in the USA, the relative importance of finance has risen, and the relative importance of manufacture has decreased. To illustrate this, we have chosen an indicator from the three levels of financialization (household/state/company). Compared to the US levels of household debt, German consumers have tapped the credit markets to a considerably lesser degree. The trend has been an increase of household debt levels through the 1990s (at 50.9% GDP at the start of the time series in 1991 and rising to the highpoint of 69.9% in 2000) and then a continuous decline (gradually dropping back to 51.7% in mid-2018), and was at 59.5% in 2008 (Deutsche Bundesbank 2018a), when this indicator for USA peaked at 97%.

Clearly, while financialization as a process may have involved every developed economy of the planet, its impact was certainly not as pronounced in Germany as it has been in the USA. The financial markets in Germany certainly gradually developed and were helped along by regulatory changes since the mid-1990s intended to produce a more market-oriented financial system (Detzer et al. 2017: 5). Impatient capital grew in importance and the non-financial companies increased their financial activities in accordance with the Arrighi-Krippner approach to financialization (ibid.: 42–49). However, this rise was not nearly as precipitous as in the USA, and the structural role of impatient capital remained relatively subdued despite all of the changes. It is perhaps sufficient to point at the relative sizes of the two types of financing. Figure 7.5 shows the sizes of the two prevalent sources of raising capital in Germany: the bank credits, which are in VofC associated with the patient capital of

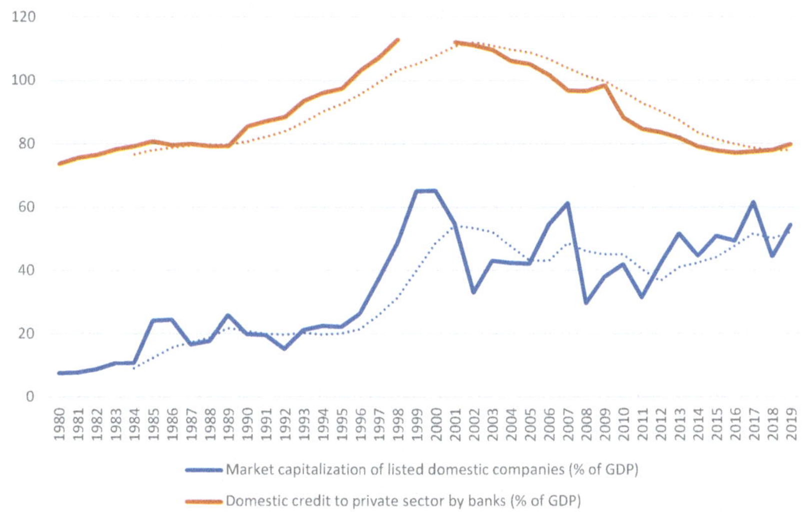

Fig. 7.5 Financing sources in Germany (*Source of data* World Bank [2017] for Domestic credit 1980–1998; World Bank [2020] for Domestic credit 2001–2019 and Market capitalization [trend-lines are 5-year moving averages])

CMEs and the market capitalization associated with the impatient capital of the LMEs—both are shown as a GDP percentage.

Unquestionably, the role of finance in general has increased, with the cumulative ratios reaching 100% of GDP in the late 1980s and rising to 130% in the early 2010s (at 134.6 in 2019). In terms of their relative shares, Germany shows characteristics in accordance with VofC theory with the role of the banks surpassing that of the stock markets by a factor of 4.8 in 1987 and by a factor of 2.5 in the early 2010.[4] The trend was certainly tending toward convergence and in 2019 the domestic credit of banks is only at 1.5 the size of market capitalization. The relative role of the stock-market finance or impatient capital has therefore increased, but the relative roles of banks and stock markets are still essentially reversed when compared to the situation in the USA. Trading activity is also far lower than in the USA, as the value of stocks traded as a percentage of GDP was in the low single digits in early 1980s, steadily grew to achieve the record 112.3% in 2008 (still only roughly a third of the US indicator that year) only to equally steadily deflate to 35.1% in 2019 (World Bank 2020). If we take this data in the context of the starting institutional positions of Germany (i.e. the manufacturing core supported by the patient capital of large banks), we can see that the impatient finance most associated with the finance expansion did not take over the economy as it did in the case of the USA. This is also in accordance with Arrighi's theory which stipulates the financialization as a process originating in the old center (USA). All of this suggests that the manufacturing labor in Germany at the very least did not lose its importance to the economy at large as a result of the systemic cycle. Nevertheless, the absolute effects of financial sector development in Germany are not to be taken lightly as major banks have shifted toward shorter-term investment banking and mergers and acquisitions have substantially increased compared to the more stagnant period of 1980s and 1990s (Lehndorff et al. 2009: 115–118; Mager and Meyer-Fackler 2017). At the same time, family firms as epitomes of patient capital in Germany have continued to thrive alongside these developments (Lehrer and Celo 2016). In other words, the short-termist, impatient financial sector expanded and became more vibrant,

[4] Bank credit indicator is also not very volatile (mostly in the 100–120% range in the past 15 years), but it is much higher than the market capitalization ratios. These are quite volatile (continually oscillating between 30 and 70%).

but the relative preponderance of long-term institutions points to a far more strategically coordinated market economy than that found in the USA. Data on manufacturing value-added as a percentage of GDP also suggests a continued structural importance of industry. The remarkable stability of this indicator shows that the value-added in manufacturing grows at the same pace as the German economy and the ratio oscillated only very slightly year-on-year (+/− less than 1% with the exception of 2009) since 1994, when it was at 20.8, only to find itself at 19.4 in 2019 (World Bank 2020). Taken together with data on sectoral employment and trade, this data suggests a continued material expansion for Germany.

Interactions with other drivers and the result

(a) Trade relations: material expansion is logically connected to a trade surplus provided the developmental strategy is extensive (i.e. foreign market oriented).
(b) Power relations: material expansion tends to orient toward an increase in manufacturing, which awards a higher level of both associational and structural power for labor in the economy. In this sense, German industrial labor should have structural power needed to defend their interests.
(c) Developmental strategies: material expansions can strategically be oriented toward foreign markets (extensive strategies) or domestic markets (intensive strategies) with different economic and political effects as discussed in Chapter 4. An extensive strategy banks on low wages and low labor power, while an intensive strategy depends on domestic demand which can be achieved with sufficient wage incomes.

7.3.2.3 Trade Relations of Germany

Chapter 5 has shown the empirical side of the German increase of a favorable trade position. This success is certainly attributable to the gradually deeper European integrations which have removed many trade policy tools from the arsenal of European peripheral states and have cemented the initial German advantage in productivity (for discussions of the role of a single currency in causing imbalances see Krugman 2012, 2013; De Grauwe and Mongelli 2005; Campos and Macchiarelli 2016). In particular, the common currency has provided Germany with a real exchange rate which is very sensitive to the effects of German wage moderation,

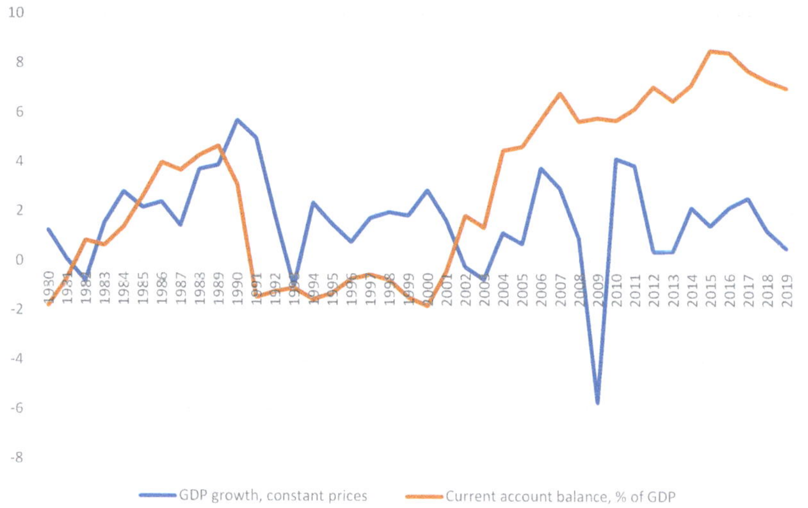

Fig. 7.6 Current accounts and real GDP growth in Germany (*Source of data* IMF [2020])

contributing to a stable and sustained surplus (Baccaro and Howell 2017: 103; Baccaro and Benassi 2017). Figure 7.6 shows the relationship of GDP growth rates and current accounts.[5]

The current account of Germany has had consistent deficits from the unification until the introduction of the euro. This has severely constricted any direct trade rebalancing (through exchange rate policy or trade restrictions) and enabled only the slow type of structural reforms intended to make labor more competitive through reduced wages.

Figure 7.7 shows trade in current USD, disaggregated on imports and exports of goods and services.

We can observe a slow and relatively balanced growth of trade in the 1980–1995 period, a stagnation until 2001 and a rapid expansion after 2001, led by a growing trade surplus. The trade contraction of 2009 was followed by a relative recovery with the levels remaining in the neighborhood of those achieved prior to the crisis.

[5] Current account balances measure the net export positions on goods and services, net income from abroad and net transfers. They are used as a rough measure of trade balances.

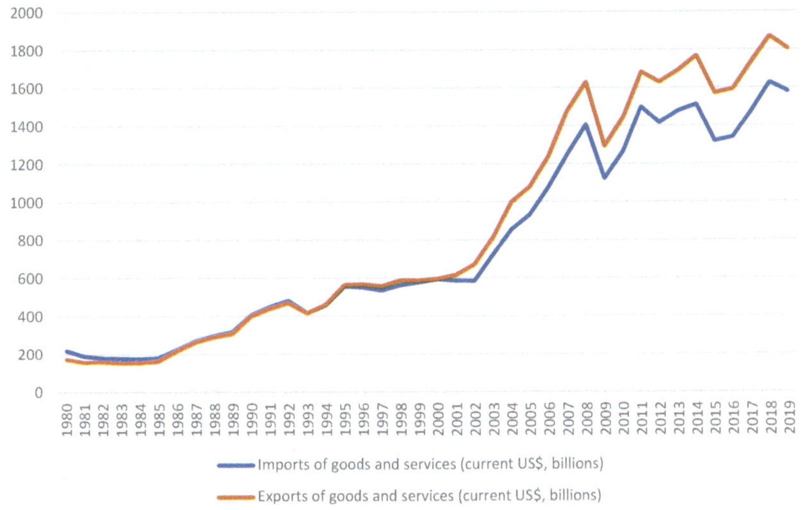

Fig. 7.7 Trade in goods and services—Germany (*Source of data* World Bank [2020])

A trade deficit reduces the relative importance of the organized workforce for the economy and vice versa. Germany had trade deficits in the years leading up to the introduction of the euro and the Hartz reforms, and a mounting trade surplus in the years since. Today, the current account surplus stands at a formidable 7.1% (IMF 2020). The labor reforms in Germany have continued to protect the manufacturing core workers but offer decreasing legal and union protection to the marginal types of employment arrangements.

Interactions with other drivers and the result

(a) Power relations: an increase in the trade surplus since 2001 suggests an increasing role of manufacturing in the economy and therefore greater structural (bargaining) power of labor.
(b) Transnational conditionality: a large trade surplus in a developed economy is generally indicative of a sufficient political pull that tends to enable avoiding transnational conditionality. However, as we will see below, in German case, there is a significant EU

dimension, embedding the international trade in a broader political context.

(c) Systemic cycle phase: trade trend of a continuing large trade surplus points to a continuation of material expansion.

(d) Developmental strategies: the 1980s were a period of slowly growing trade with a reasonable trade surplus and the 1990s brought stagnant trade without a significant surplus at any time, while the period after 2001 brought an explosion of both trade and surplus. As we have shown, this explosion occurred in the context of changing labor institutions, bringing a large and flexible low-wage sector into play. These two developments point to a successful switch from an intensive developmental strategy to an extensive one.

7.3.2.4 *Developmental Strategies of Germany*

The turn toward the dualization of German labor in combination with the new export-oriented material expansion indicates the changes in the developmental strategy this chapter is attempting to establish. The labor reforms in the context of conservative fiscal and monetary policy during a crisis have made labor more flexible and internationally competitive, and the international orientation of the material expansion increased. These are essentially the contours of the German export-led success.

In the context preceding the euro[6] and Hartz reforms, Germany was a corporatist welfare state with rigid labor markets which the institutional literature interpreted as a Coordinated Market Economy. Following Arrighi, we interpret this stage as an intensive developmental strategy, dependent as it is on the domestic markets for growth. The early 2000s brought a critical juncture in the form of a common currency and the punctuated equilibrium that developed suggests an extensive developmental strategy, primarily orientated to the EU.

Figure 7.8 portrays the changes in household consumption as a percentage of GDP.

High rates of household consumption would indicate an intensive developmental strategy during a material expansion, and low rates of household consumption (but a large export surplus) would suggest an extensive developmental strategy during a material expansion. Graph

[6] For a discussion on the effects of the euro on inequality see Ochsenfeld (2018).

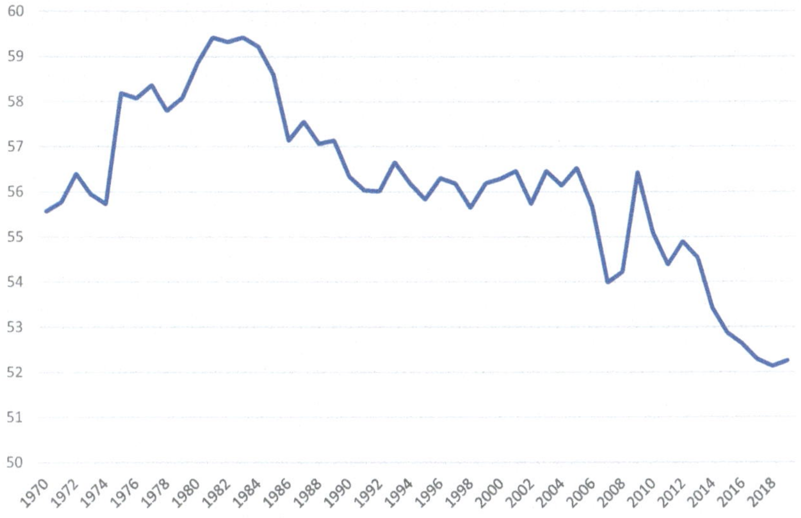

Fig. 7.8 Household expenditure in Germany (*Source of data* World Bank [2020])

shows the trend of household consumption rising in Germany until the early 1980s, falling until early 1990s and then stabilizing and stagnating until 2005 when it begins a trend of reduced domestic expenditure. We interpret this as a manifestation of the switch in developmental strategies from an intensive to an extensive one, with full implications only beginning to manifest. Figure 7.9 shows the evolution of the developmental strategy in Germany by showing the relative GDP shares of household consumption, investment, and trade in goods and services. Figure 7.8 could illustrate the household data in detail, while Fig. 7.9 shows the three relevant sources of demand in relation to each other, flattening their developments somewhat.

Household consumption in Germany has historically mostly remained in the range of 56–57% GDP but has diminished in recent years, falling from 56.4 in 2009 to 52.3 in 2019. Investment has followed a general slowly falling trend dropping from 24.5% in 2000 to 20% in 2015, but has slightly recovered to 21.6% by 2019. Net trade has notably increased since the adoption of the euro climbing from 0.2% in 2000 to 7.6% in 2015, but has somewhat dropped off to 5.8% in 2019. In all, domestic

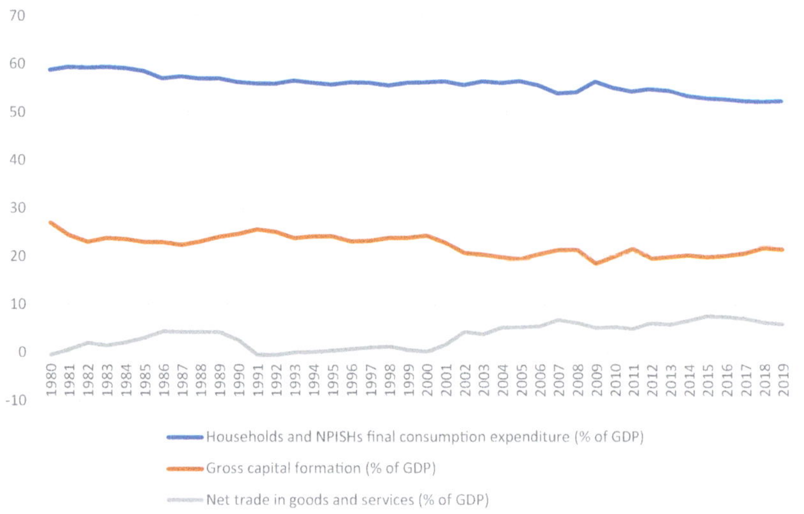

Fig. 7.9 Demand composition of Germany (*Source of data* World Bank 2020 [Household final consumption, Gross capital formation], own calculation according to data for current US GDP and net trade in goods and services in World Bank [2020] [Net trade % GDP])

demand has been reduced in recent years while the importance of foreign markets has increased, compatible with the shift into extensive strategies, as we have defined them in Chapter 4.

Once more, prepared to interpret critical junctures as either exogenously or endogenously induced periods, we can see that this shift was a result if a complex interplay of drivers. The developmental strategy is an intersection of power relations and the systemic cycle, while its successfulness merits a definition of a critical juncture. If successful, a developmental strategy is institutionalized, meaning that it incorporates a growth model which involves high or low wages with high or low equality. This makes a successful development strategy a part of the institutional result, providing the environment for future economic processes and institutional changes.

Interaction with other drivers and the result

(a) Phase of the systemic cycle: the successful extensive strategy itself is only made possible in the material expansion phase of the systemic cycle, in which manufacturing can be profitable. The manufacturing in Germany has certainly remained profitable, and as we have seen above, Germany finds itself in a material expansion.

(b) Power relations: in principle, a shift into an extensive strategy is complementary to diminished structural power in the short term, but a successful extensive material expansion would create a greater importance of labor to the economy—and therefore have a feedback effect of an increase in structural power. In Germany, the sharp divergence of power resources proved to be crucial as labor preserved associational and structural capacities in the core and sacrificed the growing and underprotected low-wage sector to the necessities of an extensive strategy.

(c) The result of institutional change: developmental strategies are a crucial aspect of institutionalization of economic developments. While the shifts in formal institutions may represent deliberate reforms intended to increase competitiveness, its successfulness (as witnessed by the increase of the relative importance of net trade to the aggregate demand) creates an institutional solution of its own—as extensive and intensive strategies hinge on low- and high-wage regimes and therefore on the short run low- and high-labor power.

7.3.2.5 Power Relations in Germany

The second channel of institutional change culminates in the relationship of power and developmental strategies. In terms of power relations, the interactions of organized labor and employers have traditionally been conducted through an essentially corporatist structure of trilateral negotiations (i.e. mediated by the state). Somewhat counterintuitively, the structural and associational power of industrial labor manifests itself in a relative lack of strikes, as collective agreements often prohibit a strike for its duration. The two recent notable spikes in strike activity (with 50 or more days per 1000 workers lost, while averages revolve around 15) were in 2006 and in 2015 (ETUI 2018). In both occurrences, it was the public and service sector workers striking, rather than the more easily organized industrial workers.

While this thesis focuses on labor power resources, as they can more easily be tracked and seem to be more susceptible to change due to various drivers, one of the valid VofC insights is that strategic coordination structures depend on the ability of both labor and employers to organize. Both labor and employer organization have faced drops in membership, but maintain their ability to bargain in the industrial core as discussed above. Union density has fallen from 35% in the early 1990s to 16.5% in 2018. Employer organization density data is only scarcely available, but according to the ICTWSS database, density has fallen from 68.8% in 2002 to 60% in 2014[7] (Visser 2019).

Power relations in Germany became a matter of a conflicting dynamics where the path dependence of initial institutional structure assumed structurally powerful labor and enabled it to act (i.e. enabled high levels of associational power), but the combination of technological and trade-related factors constricted the structural power of labor. Notably, the Hartz reforms circumvented the traditional tripartite consultations that would have involved labor, with Schröder appointing a separate commission to devise a plan and then achieving a compromise with CDU/CSU for its implementation (Kemmerling and Bruttel 2005). While labor was circumvented, the end-result was the preservation of (both structurally and associationally) strong labor in the manufacturing core but its diminishing in the periphery (including an incentivization of contracts which have a tendency to diminish the peripheral wages), spelling out the power dynamics of German dualism.

Interactions with other drivers and the result

(a) Phase of the systemic cycle: the preservation of a powerful industrial bastion is complementary to the continuation of the material expansion.
(b) Developmental strategy: the preserved structural and associational power in the industrial core have modified the extensive developmental strategy by shifting the downwards wage pressure into the marginally employed and largely into the service sector.
(c) Result of institutional change: power relations may well determine the effectiveness of deliberate institutional design and the protection of powerful "insiders" assured their acquiescence. However, this did not translate into a political success of the reforms as the

[7] While no data is available for the USA or China, the German employer organization density figures are mid- to high. They are substantially higher than levels found in UK, somewhat higher than most post-transition countries and substantially lower than figures found in Finland, the Netherlands, Belgium, Norway, Sweden, and France (Visser 2019).

> very unpopular Hartz IV remains a serious issue for the legitimacy of SPD as the party that enacted it.

The second channel of institutional change has grouped five drivers: technology (drive toward the service sector reduced associational power of labor), phase of the systemic cycle (a combination of the continued domestic material expansion in the context of global financial expansion—suggesting the continued importance of manufacturing labor in terms of structural power), trade relations (increasingly positive since the introduction of the euro, also suggestive of a high structural labor power in industry), the developmental strategy (a shift into extensive strategy suggesting diminished power in the short term to enable the strategy, but with long-term positive prospects via trade relations), and finally the power relations (crucially bifurcated between the high-power industrial labor and low-power service labor enabling the contradictions to resolve themselves through a dualistic arrangement). In terms of modes of change, the first channel described the constricted policy options due to the historically strong position of German industrial labor. This channel provides us with an explanation of the mechanisms leading to the asymmetry of power within the German labor and explains the context of institutional *drift* identified in the first channel. The developmental strategy that developed was a result of the need to reclaim market efficiency and the necessity of circumventing the labor bastion in industry, therefore leading to the dualization and the rise of flexibility in marginal types of employment on the periphery.

7.3.3 Channel 3: Institutional Design—Domestic Politics and Transnational Conditionality in Germany

Finally, the third channel of institutional change is the intentional institutional design through formal political channels. In the present case, this channel was crucial in the shift toward a dualistic labor market and an extensive developmental strategy.

The first possible aspect of this channel is domestic politics. In Germany, formal party politics are more fluid than those found in the USA. Not unlike the USA, there is also a bi-cameral system in Germany with the Bundestag (lower House) and the Bundesrat (upper House intended to defend the interests of the federal Länder). The Bundesrat has some powers which sometimes enable it to obstruct the legislative process in the Bundestag. The Bundesrat may object to a bill, meaning that (dependant on the case) it must pass the Bundestag vote again with an absolute or qualified majority. The Bundesrat also has the right to an absolute veto, but only in matters which significantly affect the interests of the Länder. Despite the rights of the Bundesrat, it seems that the formal process is in practice simpler in Germany when compared to the USA—with more power vested in the lower house. The two most important parties are the Christian-conservative CDU/CSU[8] (*Christlich Demokratische Union Deutschlands/ Christlich-Soziale Union in Bayern*) and the Social-democratic SPD (*Sozialdemokratische Partei Deutschlands*). As the Germany electoral system is representative, more parties play a role than in the USA. These two "large" parties have had use of smaller partners in forming coalitions, most importantly the economically liberal FDP (*Freie Demokratische Partei*) which is a traditional partner to CDU/CSU and the more recent Greens (*Bündnis 90/Die Grünen*) which partnered with SPD on two occasions. The sessions of Bundestag that interest us here are the 9th (1980–1983) through 19th (2017–). SPD was at the helm of coalitions in 1980–1983 (with FDP) and 1998–2005 (with the Greens). CDU/CSU was in power 1983–1998 and 2009–2013 (both intervals with FDP), and there were also two grand coalitions with CDU/CSU and SPD in power simultaneously in the period that interests us—2005–2009 and 2013–. Unlike the party divisions in the US system, the economic positions in Europe tend to be more fluid. While the CDU/CSU in the Kohl era (1982–2002) began the liberalizing reforms that started German dualism off, and the first Schröder government (1998–2002) saw the repeal of Kohl's labor reforms, it was in the SPD government that expanded and cemented the liberalizing tendencies (in the second Schröder government 2002–2005). This is counter-intuitive, considering their traditional pro-labor ideological positions, but it Schröder led the business-friendly fraction of SPD and was fond of the *Third Way* reorientation of social democratic parties to market-based agenda. The Hartz reforms themselves were successful despite protests of labor unions and the traditionalist wing of SPD. These objections were diffused through a combination of specific circumstances. Firstly, the reforms did not really threaten the core workers and therefore

[8] Formally two parties, but with a stable cooperation regime enabling a traditional joint stance on the federal electoral level.

were not overly dangerous to union insiders, which could opt to pick their fights (Palier and Thelen 2010). Secondly, Schröder was able to use a scandal concerning spurious job-placement records as a justification for an overhaul of the labor market. He instituted the Hartz Commission (named after its chairman Peter Hartz, who was a Volkswagen executive) a few months prior to the 2002 elections and campaigned on the promise to implement its suggestions, whatever they may eventually prove to be (Emmenegger 2014: 234). This choice of a post-scandal moment of uncertainty to win the public and the pre-election period to prevent reactions within his party and allies was a successful strategy on Schröder's part. Even though these reforms would eventually prove to be vastly unpopular and controversial, he succeeded in implementing a deep-cutting liberalizing reform of the German labor market.

The macroeconomic point of these reforms was not lost on analysts. Eichhorst and Marx (2011) see such reforms as proof that party ideologies play a diminishing role in determining policy and that governments respond incrementally and slowly to economic downturns (which Germany was experiencing prior to Hartz). On the other hand, Beramendi et al. (2015) interpret this move as a politically failed attempt to reorient demand from consumption to investment via competitiveness-oriented reforms (liberalization, retrenchment, tax-cuts). It has politically failed as it banked on the support of sociocultural and business professionals, while ignoring the labor constituency as a crucial coalitional subject for such a program (ibid.: 40–42). In any event, with the exclusion of labor from these reforms, a split between SPD and its traditional electoral body has been created, and SPD has failed to be reelected as the strongest party and has had its success limited to being the junior partner of CDU/CSU for 3 out of 4 governments following the Hartz reforms.

Transnational conditionality may be an enormous incentive for institutional change in specific conditions, but it seems that Germany did not truly need an external pressure to drive the specific changes that occurred. Firstly, the ILO may exert pressures (as ineffective as they are) toward some basic elements of labor protection and it enjoys a better formal relationship with Germany that it does with the USA as Germany has ratified 85 out of 189 Conventions (of which all 8 fundamental conventions, all 4 governance conventions and 73 of 177 technical conventions; ILO 2017). However, Germany has traditionally had a far stronger labor protection than that these could provide.

Secondly, there are various international pressures that may prevent a country to take the protectionist route. But the membership in the WTO is not crucial the German point of view when there is a far deeper economic integration in the form of the EU which pressures a country toward an export-oriented economy—and no country benefited from this integration as much as Germany has. Finally, the EU may, in its modern form exert pressures toward conservative macroeconomic policies (and Germany has, in fact found itself in an Excessive Deficit Procedure in the 2009–2012 period, conditioning a lower deficit; European Commission, n.d.). These may have an impact on the labor market as they may prevent active labor market policies or fiscal stimuli which could increase the income of workers. However, these are a quintessentially German way of conducting macroeconomic policy (Carlin and Soskice 2009), which suggests that Germany is remaking the EU and its rules in its own image rather than the other way around. Employment law is likewise embedded in the European law and there have been instances of adjustment to EU directives and regulations (e.g. the implementation of the European Employment Equality directive in 2006—see Kirchner et al. 2018). However, there is nothing to suggest conditional or coercive institutional change pressure in the context that interests us here—i.e. a shift toward an extensive developmental strategy.[9]

Interactions with other drivers and the result

(a) Developmental strategy: the deliberate institutional design of the Hartz reforms directly framed the shift into the extensive developmental strategy through the incentivization of a large low-wage sector.

(b) Result of institutional change: the final result was an interplay of these deliberate reforms, path dependence (awarding a continued presence of labor associational power) and power-related issues, which enabled a structurally strong industrial core of organized

[9] EU may have a significant influence over some states in some instances. However, employment law was traditionally understood as a contentious area in which there was always a widespread fear of losing national-level regulations due to external pressures. While there are several EU-level formal channels for employment law change (the Community method/directives, CJEU rulings, collective agreements, and the voluntaristic European Employment Strategy), the results have been underwhelming, as only lowest common denominator standards can be set, generally requiring only small adjustments from only a small number of states (Rhodes 2015).

> labor. This result was a compromise shifting the costs of higher competitiveness onto the margins of employment and incentivizing the unemployed to join this margin.

Unlike the first two channels, deliberate institutional design was able to change a portion of labor institutions outright. On a macro-level, Thelen is justified to describe the labor-institutional changes in Germany as *drift*. However, once we zoom in to the short-term political frame of channel 3, it becomes clear that the formal labor institutions on the periphery of the labor market were subject to a deliberate *displacement*. It was not merely a matter of the changing conditions eating away the nominally unchanged labor institutions (suggestive of *drift*). Instead, path dependence (C1) and power relations (C2) prevented a change of a part of the labor institutions as the economic landscape shifted around them (*drift*), while another part of the labor institutions was actively liberalized (C3) to promote efficiency, competitiveness, and flexibility (*displacement*). In fact, the three channels of institutional change in the German case provided a complex interplay of drivers which resulted in a pronounced dualism of labor markets, particularly deepening in the Schröder government reforms in the early 2000s. Figure 7.10 summarizes this process.

This interplay was a combination of continued union strength (associational power) in the industrial core and its weakness in the (primarily service sector margins), which we've discussed under the heading of channel 2. Schröder's government was able to work around labor power in the core by liberalizing the margins through a promotion of part-time, fixed-term, and agency employment. This created a large and growing low-wage sector, which increased the international competitiveness of Germany. In coordination with the introduction of euro and a continued capacity in high value-added manufacturing, German trade surplus vastly expanded in the intervening years. This is why we can treat it as a critical juncture scenario, which successfully institutionalized an extensive developmental strategy in the early 2000s.

7.4 Social Effects of Labor Institutions in Germany

Labor institutions have a pronounced effect on the relationship of GDP growth and unemployment. In Fig. 6.11, we could see an intimate

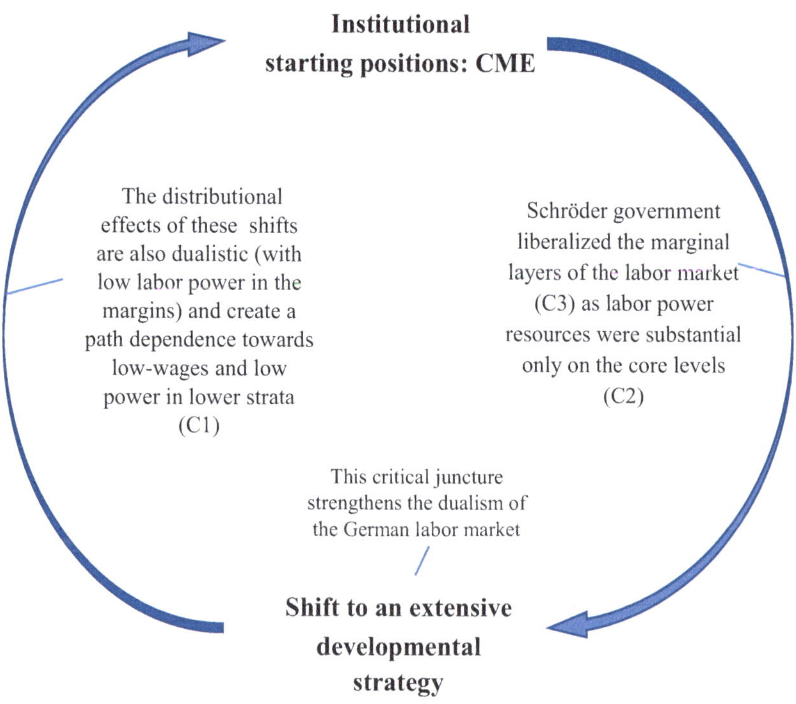

Fig. 7.10 The institutionalization of a shift to extensive strategy in Germany in the early 2000s

connection of these two curves for the USA as flexible labor markets enable an easy employment termination process when made necessary by falling demand during growth downturns. Figure 7.11 shows the same for Germany.

While unemployment rates do respond to changes in growth, they do so far more unpredictably and slowly than in the case of the USA. Particularly so in the years following the global crisis of 2009 when the unemployment rose only slightly and only for a single year and then continued its trend of falling in the context of a solidifying European project and extensive strategy.

The data for individual GINI in Germany is only available since 1991 in the World Bank database, and was at 29.2 in 1991, 28.9 in 1995, 28.8 in 2000, 31.3 in 2006, 30.5 in 2011 and rose to 31.9 by 2016 (World

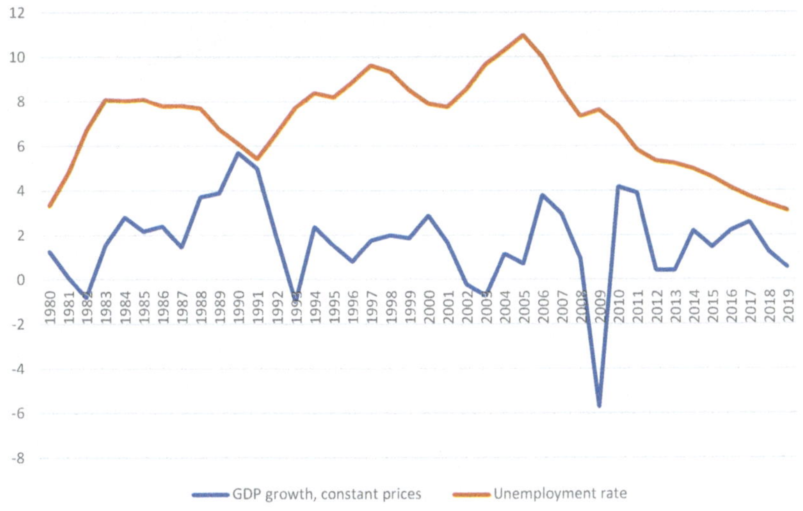

Fig. 7.11 Interaction of unemployment and real GDP growth in Germany (*Source of data* IMF [2020])

Bank 2020). This puts the income inequality at far lower levels to those found in the USA, which is to be expected from the paradigmatic CME case. The SWIID database once more provides a more encompassing data coverage. Figure 7.12 shows the disposable income and market (before taxes and transfers) GINI indices since 1980 for Germany.

Once more, the SWIID GINI indices seem somewhat lower than those found in the World Bank database. Both GINI trends show a steady increase, but while the disposable income GINI has increased from 25.9 to 29.4 in the 1980–2018 period (remaining a fairly equal final distribution), the market GINI increased more markedly from 41.4 to 52.5, which is slightly higher than the comparable value in the USA. In the first assessment, this may suggest that the processes leading to income disparity are alike in these two countries. However, the wage setting processes and/or negotiations are never naïve in terms of the difference between gross and net wages. Workers are not necessarily always paid exactly in accordance with their marginal productivity (as neoclassical economics would have us believe), but are rather also a product of various labor institutions as discussed above. Therefore, the most important lesson of Fig. 7.12 is the substantial extent of correction caused by

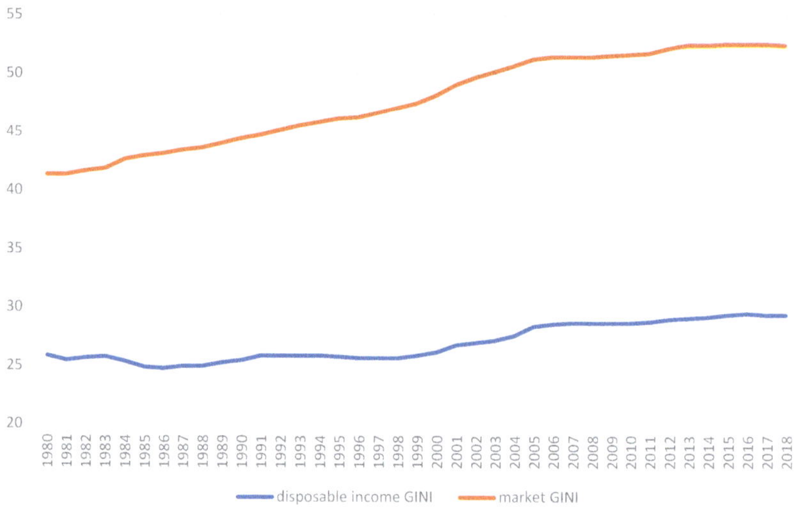

Fig. 7.12 Income inequality in Germany—GINI (*Source of data* SWIID 9.0 [Solt 2020])

taxes and transfers in Germany (all of which must be taken into account when negotiating wages). In the USA, the difference between these two curves remained relatively stable, even though it showed a slight expansion of the effect of redistribution since 1980. This expansion is more pronounced in Germany, as the difference between two indices was at 15.5 in 1980 and 23.1 in 2018. The latest data point shows an incredible correction from 52.5 before taxes and transfers to 29.4 once redistributive mechanisms performed their function.

Figures 7.13 and 7.14 show these effects by comparing the income shares of the top 1% and bottom 50% of income distribution before and after taxes. The data in these two figures can be more directly compared than was the case with USA as the data for equal-split adults is available for both. This suggests that income data is aggregated at household, rather than individual level, but equally split among adults in the household.

The pre-tax income share of the top 1% has increased from 9.8% in 1980 to 13% in 2019 (primarily in the 2003–2007 period). In the same period, the pre-tax income share of the bottom 50% decreased from 24.3% to 19.1%. Once more the general trend may be similar to that found in

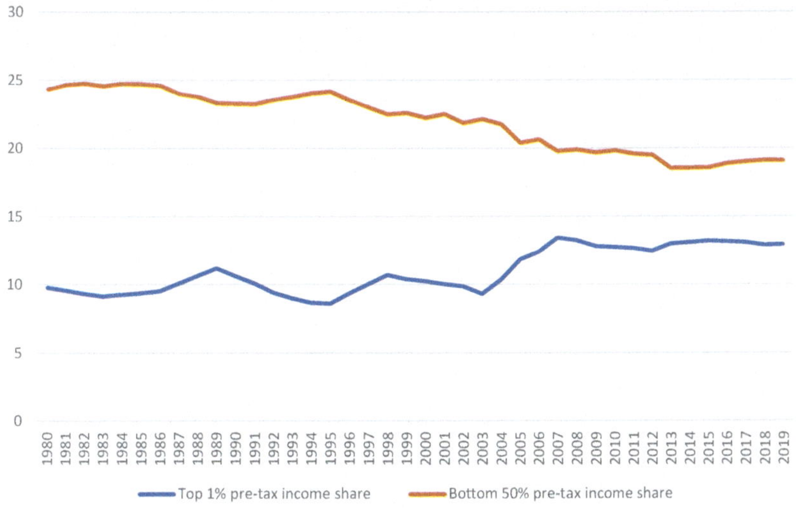

Fig. 7.13 Pre-tax income shares in Germany (*Source of data* WID [2020])

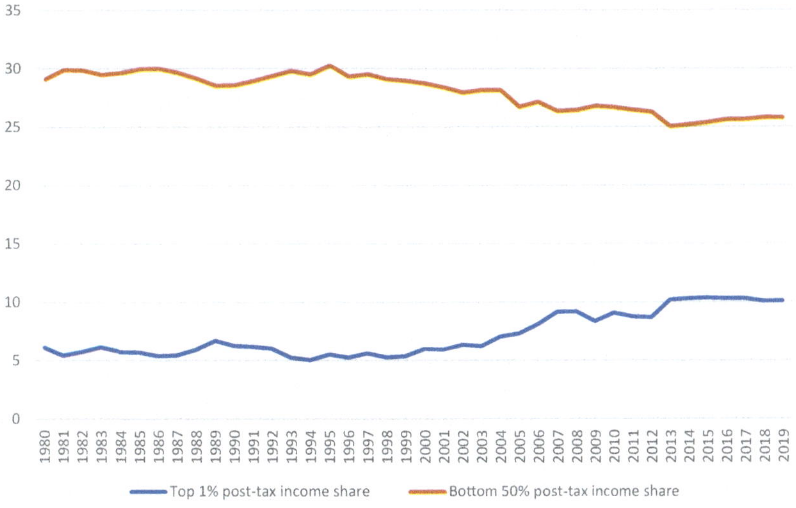

Fig. 7.14 Post-tax income shares in Germany (*Source of data* WID [2020])

USA (greater inequality), but to a far less polarized degree, mediated as it is through a substantially different set of institutions.

Figure 7.14 also points to the degree of progressiveness, but with different results. Interestingly, while the pre-tax income share of the top 1% increased by 3.16% since 1980, the post-tax income share increased by a slightly larger 4%. The pre-tax share of the bottom 50% decreased by 5.6%, and (more expectedly) its post-tax income share decreased by 3.3%.

Finally, a comparison of profit (data on total enterprise profits – Deutsche Bundesbank 2018b) and wage (worker compensation—Eurostat 2019) ratios in GDP (current prices GDP—IMF 2018, ratios are calculated by the author) is also telling. Wage shares were at respectable levels in mid- and late-1990s: at 52.2% in 1997 and at 52.9% in 2000 (at which time the effects of the euro begin being felt as well as the effects of the new German growth model), after which they rapidly contracted until 2007 (at 47.6%) when the crisis and post-crisis recovery somewhat recovered the wage share to 50.6% in 2016. The profit ratio climbed from 3.5% in 1997 (beginning of time series) to 4.3% in 2000 and 6.8% in 2007, collapsed to 3.9% in 2009 and then stabilized at 5.2% in 2015 and estimated 6.3% in 2016. The overall pattern shows a substantial shift in the 2000s before 2008 (+2.5% GDP share for profits and −5.3% GDP for wages) and a slight softening of this trend after the crisis. The 2000–2016 period brought an overall structural change of −2.5% for wages and +2% for profits. These trends are consistent with our interpretation of a German shift into an extensive developmental strategy and the accompanying partial liberalization of labor institutions.

7.5 Conclusion

This chapter has sought to apply the framework from Chapter 5 to the specific national context of labor-institutional changes in Germany since 1980. All three channels of institutional change played important roles in determining the institutional result.

Path dependence of initial structures created a crucial context in which a great role for both organized labor and organized employers was envisioned, with the state acting primarily as a mediator. However, this traditional tripartite way of conducting reforms with significant veto-players was a consequence of an older stage in the development of power relations in which levels of associational and structural labor power were higher. The second channel of institutional change describes the changes in power relations that created a bastion of labor power in industry but never built it in the growing marginal sector of the economy (largely in tertiary sector). This created a dualism of power which enabled the type of institutional reforms that took place. The third channel refers to these reforms as a result of a formal political process in which the Schröder government attempted to restore competitiveness by liberalizing the labor model and therefore reducing private consumption in its growth model. The result was the institutionalization of an extensive developmental strategy through labor dualism. It was molded by all three channels with path dependency and strong industrial labor protecting the working core and a deliberate reform and weak marginal labor producing a liberalization of marginal labor with a growing low-wage sector. In terms of modes of change, this chapter offered an interpretation along the lines of confirming Thelen's view of German labor-institutional change as *drift*, but only for the two longer-term channels—and argued for the interpretation of the deliberate institutional design as *displacement*.

In observing institutional change in the USA in the selected period, a systemic cycle perspective should expect to see organizational/institutional changes which are the equivalent of the mode of the capital accumulation shifting from material to financial expansion—i.e. changes consistent with financialization. Institutional change in China and Germany are also subject to pressures from the very center of the world-systemic core—i.e. the global trade and development needs stemming from the fact that the primary political and military power of the world (USA) is financializing. In this sense, formal political reforms and power-related developmental strategies as well as their social effects take place in the context of the systemic cycle, the phase of which evidently provides different playing grounds for Germany and the USA, as explored by our use of institutional drivers. We must now turn to China to explore a third national and developmental context.

Literature

Baccaro, L., & Benassi, C. (2017). Throwing Out the Ballast: Growth Models and the Liberalization of German Industrial Relations. *Socio-Economic Review, 15*(1), 85–115.

Baccaro, L., & Howell, C. (2017). *Trajectories of Neoliberal Transformation: European Industrial Relations Since the 1970s*. Cambridge: Cambridge University Press.

BMFSFJ. (2009). *Pay Inequality Between Women and Men in Germany: A Dossier*. Available at https://www.bmfsfj.de/blob/94442/efbd528467e3618 82848c23486fcc8d8/pay-inequality-data.pdf.

Bosch, G. (2018). The Making of the German Minimum Wage: A Case Study of Institutional Change. *Industrial Relations Journal, 49*(1), 19–33.

Beramendi, P., Häusermann, S., Kitschelt, H., & Kriesi, H. (Eds.). (2015). *The Politics of Advanced Capitalism*. New York: Cambridge University Press.

Campos, N. F., & Macchiarelli, C. (2016). Core and periphery in the European Monetary Union: Bayoumi and Eichengreen 25 Years Later. *Economics Letters, 147*, 127–130.

Carlin, W., & Soskice, D. (2009). German Economic Performance: Disentangling the Role of Supply-Side Reforms, Macroeconomic Policy and Coordinated Economy Institutions. *Socio-Economic Review, 7*(1), 67–99.

De Grauwe, P., & Mongelli, F. (2005). *Endogeneities of Optimum Currency Areas: What Brings Countries Sharing a Single Currency Closer Together?* (ECB Working Paper No. 468).

Detzer, D., Dodig, N., Evans, T., Hein, E., Herr, H., & Prante, F. J. (2017). *The German Financial System and the Financial and Economic Crisis*. Berlin: Springer.

Deutsche Bundesbank. (2018a). *Debt of Households in Germany*. https://www.bundesbank.de/dynamic/action/en/statistics/time-series-databases/time-series-databases/759784/759784?listId=www_s300_iswi_finanzw4.

Deutsche Bundesbank. (2018b). *Special Statistical Publication 5*. Available at https://www.bundesbank.de/resource/blob/651156/7b4e0871cf12eb2618b7975a83ac2806/mL/statso5-1997-2016-en-data.xlsx.

Deutsche Welle. (2016). *German Minimum Hourly Wage Bumped Up for 2017*. http://www.dw.com/en/german-minimum-hourly-wage-bumped-up-for-2017/a-19362540.

Die Bundesregierung. (2019). *Höhere Regelsätze ab 2020*. https://www.bundesregierung.de/breg-de/aktuelles/regelsaetze-1666914.

Eichhorst, W. (2015). The Unexpected Appearance of a New German Model. *British Journal of Industrial Relations, 53*(1), 49–69.

Eichhorst, W., & Marx, P. (2011). Reforming German Labour Market Institutions: A Dual Path to Flexibility. *Journal of European Social Policy, 21*(1), 73–87.

Emmenegger, P. (2014). *The Power to Dismiss: Trade Unions and the Regulation of Job Security in Western Europe*. Oxford: Oxford University Press.

ETUI. (2018). *Strikes Map Germany*. https://www.etui.org/strikes-map/germany.

European Commission. (n.d.). *Germany*. Available at https://ec.europa.eu/info/business-economy-euro/economic-and-fiscal-policy-coordination/eu-economic-governance-monitoring-prevention-correction/stability-and-gro wth-pact/corrective-arm-excessive-deficit-procedure/closed-excessive-deficit-procedures/germany_en.

Eurostat. (2016). *Gender Overall Earnings Gap*. Available at http://ec.europa.eu/eurostat/tgm/table.do?tab=table&init=1&language=en&pcode=teqges01&plugin=1.

Eurostat. (2017). *File: Unadjusted Gender Pay Gap, 2015*. Available at http://ec.europa.eu/eurostat/statistics-explained/index.php/File:Unadjusted_gender_pay_gap,_2015_(difference_between_average_gross_hourly_earnings_of_male_and_female_employees_as_%25_of_male_gross_earnings)-F1.png.

Eurostat. (2019). *Compensation of Employees—Annual Data, Million Units of National Currency*. Available at https://ec.europa.eu/eurostat/web/products-datasets/product?code=tipslm13.

Eurostat. (2020). *Part-Time Employment as Percentage of the Total Employment, by Sex and Age (%) [lfsa_eppga]*. Available at http://appsso.eurostat.ec.europa.eu/nui/submitViewTableAction.do.

Fulton, L. (2020). *National Industrial Relations, an Update*. Labour Research Department and ETUI. Online publication available at http://www.worker-participation.eu/National-Industrial-Relations.

Hall, P., & Soskice, D. (Eds.). (2001). *Varieties of Capitalism: The Institutional Foundations of Comparative Advantage*. Oxford: Oxford University Press.

Hassel, A. (2011). The Paradox of Liberalization: Understanding Dualism and the Recovery of the German Political Economy. *LEQS Paper*, 42.

Häusermann, S., & Schwander, H. (2012). Varieties of Dualization? Labor Market Segmentation and Insider-Outsider Divides Across Regimes. In P. Emmenegger, S. Häusermann, & B. Palier (Eds.), *The Age of Dualization: The Changing Face of Inequality in Deindustrializing Societies* (pp. 27–51). Oxford: Oxford University Press.

Heritage. (2020). *Graph the Data*. http://www.heritage.org/index/visualize.

ILO. (2016). *Global Wage Report 2016/17: Wage Inequality in the Workplace*. Available at https://www.ilo.org/wcmsp5/groups/public/—dgreports/—dcomm/—publ/documents/publication/wcms_537846.pdf.

ILO. (2017). *Ratifications by Country*. Available at http://www.ilo.org/dyn/normlex/en/f?p=1000:11200:0::NO:11200:P11200_COUNTRY_ID:102871.

IMF. (2020). *World Economic Outlook Database October 2020*. Available at http://www.imf.org/external/pubs/ft/weo/2020/02/weodata/index.aspx.

Kemmerling, A., & Bruttel, O. (2005). *New Politics in German Labour Market Policy? The Implications of the Recent Hartz Reforms for the German Welfare State* (WZB discussion paper). https://www.econstor.eu/bitstream/10419/44018/1/490072151.pdf.

Kirchner, J., Kremp, P. R., & Magotsch, M. (Eds.). (2018). *Key Aspects of German Employment and Labour Law*. Berlin and Heidelberg: Springer.

Krugman, P. (2012). *End This Depression Now!* New York: W. W. Norton.

Krugman, P. (2013). Revenge of the Optimum Currency Area. *NBER Macroeconomics Annual, 27*(1), 439–448.

Lehndorff, S., Bosch, G., Haipeter, T., & Latniak, E. (2009). From the 'Sick Man' to the 'Overhauled Engine' of Europe? Upheaval in the German Model. In G. Bosch, S. Lehndorff, & J. Rubery (Eds.), *European Employment Models in Flux* (pp. 105–130). Basingstoke: Palgrave Macmillan.

Lehrer, M., & Celo, S. (2016). German Family Capitalism in the 21st Century: Patient Capital Between Bifurcation and Symbiosis. *Socio-Economic Review, 14*(4), 729–750.

Mager, F., & Meyer-Fackler, M. (2017). Mergers and Acquisitions in Germany: 1981–2010. *Global Finance Journal, 34,* 32–42.

Magotsch, M., & Kremp, P. R. (2018). Termination of Employment. In J. Kirchner, P. R. Kremp, & M. Magotsch (Eds.), *Key Aspects of German Employment and Labour Law* (pp. 171–192). Heidelberg: Springer.

OECD. (2020). *OECD Data* [online]. Available at https://data.oecd.org/.

Ochsenfeld, F. (2018). Mercantilist Dualization: The Introduction of the Euro, Redistribution of Industry Rents, and Wage Inequality in Germany, 1993–2008. *Socio-Economic Review, 16*(3), 499–522.

Palier, B., & Thelen, K. (2010). Institutionalizing Dualism: Complementarities and Change in France and Germany. *Politics & Society, 38*(1), 119–148.

Pulignano, V., Doerflinger, N., & Keune, M. (2017). Re-Introducing the Company in the Analysis of Labour Market Dualisation: Variety of Patterns and Diversity of Outcomes Between Standard and Non-Standard Workers in Multinational Subsidiaries in Belgium, Germany and Britain. *Economic and Industrial Democracy, 41*(3), 586–609.

Rhodes, M. (2015). Employment Policy. In H. Wallace, M. Pollack, & A. Young (Eds.), *Policy-Making in the European Union* (pp. 293–318). Oxford: Oxford University Press.

Solt, F. (2020). *The Standardized World Income Inequality Database.* SWIID Version 9.0. https://fsolt.org/swiid/.

Thelen, K. (2014). *Varieties of Liberalization and the New Politics of Social Solidarity.* Cambridge: Cambridge University Press.

Visser, J. (2019, June). *ICTWSS Data Base.* Version 6.0. Amsterdam: Amsterdam Institute for Advanced Labour Studies (AIAS), University of Amsterdam. Open access database at https://www.ictwss.org/downloads.

WEF. (2016). *Germany.* Available at http://reports.weforum.org/feature-demonstration/files/2016/10/DEU.pdf.

WID. (2020). *World Inequality Database.* Available at http://wid.world/.

WJP. (2018). *World Justice Project.* Available at https://worldjusticeproject.org/.

World Bank. (2017). *World Bank Open Data.* http://data.worldbank.org.

World Bank. (2020). *World Bank Open Data.* http://data.worldbank.org.

CHAPTER 8

Labor Market in PR China

8.1 Introduction

This book has set out to achieve a framework of endogenous institutional change by reconciling conceptions of global capitalism (the world-system and the systemic cycle) and national capitalism (new institutionalism). One could well wonder why a people's republic would be a pertinent case study in capitalism. However, China has combined the communist heritage, symbolical legitimation, and rhetoric with several waves of marketization and privatization with the result of a party-led, development-oriented state capitalism. In the previous two chapters, we could use the VofC typology as a starting point. While the analysis of institutional change clearly demonstrated the limits of ideal-typical approaches, they were nevertheless useful as a simplified model of market functioning in the two national contexts. However, unlike the USA and Germany, China does not, nor did it ever, clearly conform to the VofC typological matrix. Instead, it is presented by its own unique set of dilemmas, closer perhaps to the transitional experiences in Eastern Europe than to those of old democracies with developed markets. Moreover, the historical, political, and economic background of Chinese political economy obviously creates substantial rifts compared to the developed countries. More than a quarter-century of the Mao era certainly provided its fair share of such rifts through the dubious developmental ideas of the Great Leap Forward (1958–1962) and the Cultural Revolution

J. Lučev, *Systemic Cycle and Institutional Change*,
https://doi.org/10.1007/978-3-030-66053-6_8

(1966–1976). Nevertheless, it was the Mao era that provided the context for the reforms and explosive growth that was to follow.

In the context of labor institutions, explicit regulation was in many ways non-existent, but the party rhetoric insisted on the workers' position as masters of the state and the enterprises in which they worked. The benefits, such as they were, were reserved for urban workers, while agricultural laborers in rural areas were treated as outsiders. The institutional form of this urban worker "mastery" was the *danwei* system under which the enterprise was responsible for organizing housing, health system, schooling, entertainment and the provision of meals for the benefit of the employees, who themselves could neither quit or be fired (Estlund 2017: 28–29). At the same time, rural workers were provided with far fewer amenities including only minimal health services (Lin 2017: 65). This division was held in place by the household registration (*hukou*) system, which limited the rural-urban migration with rural workers only finding urban employment on temporary contract basis at a smaller pay and lesser social status compared to the urban non-contract worker (Gallagher 2005: 106). In this phase, the labor contract would carry a type of stigma and symbolize the outsider status.

After Mao Zedong's death in 1976 and the collapse of the Cultural Revolution, the time was ripe for an alternative route into modernization. The latter manifested as a pronounced turn toward the free markets in the Deng Xiaoping era starting in late 1978. This eventually propelled the Chinese system to global prominence with stable and very high and export-led growth rates and low unemployment. However, this Chinese approach to capitalism is still conducted in a de facto one-party system[1] and the consequences of this far transcend the political system in the narrow sense. This combination may, in fact, suggest that the aggregate data concerning the Chinese economy presents significant challenges in comparison with western developed countries in its typological scope.

[1] The Communist Party of China considers the party-system of China to be a "multi-party cooperation system under the leadership of the Communist party" (Liu et al. 2016: 22). Apart from the CPC, there are eight more recognized political parties: China Revolutionary Committee of the Kuomintang, China Democratic League, China Democratic National Construction Association, China Association for the Promotion of Democracy, Chinese Peasants and Workers' Democratic Party, China Zhi Gong Dang, Jiusan Society and Taiwan Democratic Self-government League (China Internet Information Center, n.d.).

This chapter will apply the framework of institutional change from Chapter 5 to the change in labor institutions in China. Chapter 6 interpreted the developmental strategy in the USA as one which turned from an intensive one in the 1970s and now continues as an extensive strategy. The previous chapter interpreted the economy in Germany as an economy which has turned from an intensive to an extensive strategy 15 years ago. This chapter will offer an interpretation of the Chinese growth model as one currently changing from an extensive to an intensive developmental strategy. The space for collective bargaining and coordination is growing in recognition of the increase in structural labor power (importance of manufacturing to the economy as a whole and possible damage incurred by strikes). However, it is also constricted by the obstacles presented to labor organization (associational power), with independent organization being viewed as a competitor to the Party monopoly of political power. This chapter will firstly survey the labor institutions in China and their changes through the Northian triangle of formal, informal, and avoidable institutions and point to their changes. Secondly, it will analyze the seven drivers of change identified above through their three channels of change (path dependence, cyclical power relations and institutional design). Thirdly, it will offer a view of social consequences of these shifts.

8.2 Changes in Labor Institutions in China Since 1980

The previous two chapters showed that labor institutions of the USA and Germany could not be understood by observing only formal institutions. In the case of China, the distinction of active institutions as more than merely formal is even more important. The rule of law in general is comparatively low in China,[2] and the reasons for this are multifold. They can be economic in nature as China has rapidly moved through its phases of market development, which means that the needs stemming from underdeveloped markets are sometimes still active or at least very recent. The reliance on informal institutions is one such need, as the contracting on such markets often takes the form of an interlinked relational contract (Wang 2014: 2–3), where many types of relations are

[2] The World Justice Project ranks China as 75th of 113th surveyed countries for 2017/18, scoring particularly low in the categories of *constraints on government powers, fundamental rights* and *open government* (WJP 2018).

taken into account (social, political, economic), which is preferred to an impersonal contract more appropriate to a developed market. Pronounced formal institutional constriction may therefore not be fully compatible with underdeveloped markets. The reasons for the greater importance of informal institutions can also be political in nature. China is a one-party state, which means its political power is monopolized to the extent that the restrictions of formal regulation could be seen as an unnecessary hindrance to its functioning. The top managerial, official, and political positions intertwine, which means that the motivations which structure the activity of a person in any elite capacity are themselves a result of other positions as well (Hersh 2014). To put it bluntly, a trade union official and a top-level manager in an enterprise may be incentivized to negotiate according to their career positions in the Communist party rather than according to their respective positions in industrial relations *or* according to the law followed to the letter. Furthermore, the Chinese history of five-year planning in the midst of political upheavals of the Mao era has left a legacy in which formal regulation has tended to be conflicting, confusing, and therefore understood as guidelines rather than something to be literally followed. All of this spells out the *China paradox* consisting of a "sustained economic growth without a formal institutional infrastructure" (Wang 2014: 92). In the case of labor institutions, this is specifically reflected in a substantial *enforcement gap* (Estlund 2017), where the formally proclaimed standards are seldom met in practice.

8.2.1 Formal Labor Institutions in China

Nevertheless, formal standards provide the grounding for the practice and a rallying call for labor-related activism and protests. Even when they are imperfectly enforced, they reflect the tendencies of political intentions and provide legitimacy to the Party as well as to the negotiating processes. This is why they are far from irrelevant and must be taken seriously and studied carefully.

Table 8.1 briefly surveys the development of the Chinese legal structure concerning labor.

We can discern two crucial points in regulatory history through which the formal labor institutions developed: the first bundle of laws in the early-to-mid-1990s and the second one in 2008. We should, however, note that the regulatory history briefly shown here occurred in the

Table 8.1 Landmark reforms of labor regulation in China

Year	*Regulation*	*Explanation*
1954, 1975, 1978, 1982	*Constitution of PRC*	The original Constitution from 1954 did not explicitly recognize the right to strike, while the 1975 and 1978 versions did so. Finally, the 1982 Constitution (4th and current iteration) removed the right to strike
1992	*Trade Union Law*	Guarantees the functioning of trade unions.
1993	*Regulation on the Handling of Enterprise Labor Disputes*	Guarantees the employees of all enterprises the right to raise complaints regarding labor disputes to local Labor dispute arbitration committees
1995	*Labor Law of the People's Republic of China*	First modern labor law which caused a move from a rule by administrative decisions at the level of the workplace and instituted the labor contract
2001	*Labor Union Law of the People's Republic of China*	Not mentioning strikes explicitly, this law recognizes that a stoppage of work at a factory should be followed by the mediation of unions between employers and employees (Article 27)
2008	*Employment Contract Law*	Intended to increase the number of workers covered by labor contracts by penalizing the abstainee. It also expanded the legal protection to agency workers; amended with effect from July 1, 2013 in order to restrict the use of subcontracted and temporary labor

(continued)

Table 8.1 (continued)

Year	*Regulation*	*Explanation*
2008	*Law of the People's Republic of China on the Mediation and Arbitration of Employment Disputes*	Makes the labor dispute process less difficult to maneuver
2011	*Social Insurance Law*	Establishes the first national social insurance framework
2013	*Law of the People's Republic of China on Entry and Exit Control*	Immigration Law

Sources Gallagher (2016), Chang and Cooke (2015), Chan and Selden (2017), Estlund (2017)

context of several waves of marketization/liberalization in China. The initial 1980s era brought a gradual recognition of the private sector and an opening to foreign capital, but this process was interrupted by the aftermath of the Tiananmen Square protests in 1989—or as they are known in China—the June Fourth Incident (Lin 2017: 75–76).

The economic reforms were stalled for three years, after which, in early 1992, Deng Xiaoping delivered the vastly important "southern tour speech" which reaffirmed the states' commitment to market-based development (Ling 2016: 3). Following Deng's tour, the Communist Party held its 14th Congress in the fall of 1992. At the congress, the Chinese economy was redefined as a "socialist-market economy" (Lin 2017: 33–34). In the wake of these proclamations, the regulatory channels for a new, market-based economic reality needed to be instituted. In 1992, the law on trade unions was passed, and in 1993 the labor disputes of all enterprises could be arbitrated, which provided a rudimentary form of dispute resolution. Most importantly for the condition of formal labor institutions, the 1995 Labor Law signified the ending of the virtually guaranteed life-long rights of the old socialist worker or the breaking of the "iron rice bowl." It instituted a number of important legal stipulations including the need for a labor contract. This was a groundbreaking moment, as it brought the establishment of a single labor regime intended to replace the varied and complex network of laws, regulation and directives that structured the labor markets of China (Estlund 2017: 104). However, while contracts were necessary for the functioning of market relations, they essentially caused a reduction of rights of the average worker rather than their increase (Gallagher 2016: 240–241). In reality, this Law was virtually unenforced (Ling 2016: 4), and the high number of labor disputes and unrests were attempted to be remedied in 2008 by the National Labor Contract Law which disincentivized abstaining from formal contracts and a law on mediation of disputes intended to make the dispute process easier to maneuver (Gallagher 2016: 241–243). The contract law also restricted the use of fixed-term contracts, with the effect of a dramatically increasing use of agency workers (in order to circumvent the stipulations of the labor laws) amounting to a fifth of urban employment by 2011 (Estlund 2017: 106–108).

These renewed initiatives attempted to strengthen the labor law and occurred in the context of several moves toward more coherent and modern social assistance and medical insurance schemes. While these are not labor regulations in the narrow sense, they are complementary institutions which may fundamentally change the position of workers and even their work-related expectations. The medical insurance reforms were intended to increase coverage of health insurance and evolved through stages, with the rural scheme introduced in 2003, the urban scheme fully implemented in 2007 (having been more modestly initiated in 1998) and an ambitious and well-financed reform in 2009 forwarded the idea of government financing in the provision of health services (World Bank 2016: 1). Another important example is the *dibao*, a social assistance program that is intended to alleviate poverty. It was first piloted in Shanghai in 1993, covered all urban areas in 1999 and (crucially) became national in 2007 by fully covering the rural areas (Li and Walker 2018).

Formally, the workers in China are very highly protected. The Employment Protection Legislation index has been calculated by the OECD for China only in the 2008–2012 period. The regular employment index was at 3.26 and the temporary/fixed-term employment index was at 1.75 (OECD 2020). This makes the labor markets far more protected by the laws governing them than those of Germany. However, Heritage index for labor freedom awards a much more "free" rating to China, estimating it as "moderately free" at 64.4% for 2020 (an end result of a start at 65% in 2005, a slip into the "mostly unfree" category in the 2009–2012 period with the low point at 53.2% and a gradual return) (Heritage 2020). The OECD measure would make the regular employment market one of the most legally protected ones in the world. This reflects the ambitious nature of the 2008 laws. However, in terms of estimating actual active institutions, it seems that the Heritage foundation may be more realistic

To understand how the labor institutions in China actively function, we must turn to the informal and avoidable labor institutions.

8.2.2 *Informal Labor Institutions in China*

In keeping with the logic of informal institutions as non-codified stable activity-structuring elements, we have defined the collective bargaining practices as informal institutions. However, in the Chinese case, we must also explain the special position of the right to strike. As Table 8.1. shows, the right to strike was constitutionally guaranteed only in the 1978–1982 period. However, strikes are not explicitly illegal today, and some laws implicitly recognize them (like the Labor Union Law of 2001), even though they do not protect or advocate them (Chang and Cooke 2015: 445). Therefore, the legal stipulation that the failure to follow the employer's rules is grounds for dismissal can be used against strikers (Estlund 2017: 142). In other words, the workers can be (and often are) legally fired as a punishment for participating in strikes, provided their employers have a rule prohibiting striking. The possibility of a strike should be a tool in the hands of organized labor—a final recourse if all other approaches should fail. However, trade unions in China do not initiate strikes. These are, rather, spontaneous affairs in which the workers organize themselves in an ad hoc fashion, while unions mediate between the workers and managers (Friedman 2014; Gallagher 2016; Liu and Shi 2016; Estlund 2017). This mediating role of unions suggests that unions in China occupy a very different role compared to those in Germany and the USA. The political power embodied in the western unions stems from the position of workers (scarce, necessary, abundant, superfluous), whereas this type of political power is an attribute of ad hoc organization in China, and the Party stands behind and constricts the activities of the unions.

The legal framework for tripartite collective consultation has existed since the early 1990s (Trade Union Law of 1992 and Labor Law of 1995). These remain a formality in practice, or a "result of top-down requirements from the government or higher-level trade unions," as the unions regularly accept or approve initiatives rather than negotiate labor conditions (Chan and Hui 2013: 6–7). The result is that the tripartite "negotiations" seldom differ from the minimum legal standards (ibid.).

Therefore, while steps have been taken to institutionalize the consultation process, the worker representatives have a dual allegiance: to the management and to the party, but not necessarily to the workers as well.

It is not surprising that actual collective bargaining is not centralized and effectively takes place at the enterprise level (Visser 2019). In other words, while there exists a formal structure of national-level negotiations (the most centralized possible), the actual collective bargaining is conducted on the least centralized level. In other words, the prevailing approach to collective bargaining in China is "top-down, quota-driven, bureaucratic, and enterprise based" (Estlund 2017: 136). However, there are local exceptions. The collective bargaining on a sectoral level in Zhejiang province was seemingly a response to a rising power of the workers due to a great demand for labor—although such sectoral negotiation is also far removed from the collective bargaining in western countries as, again, both employer organizations and trade unions are Party-controlled (ibid.: 138, 139). In Guangdong province, the 2014 regulation (granted, a formal institution) was intended to promote a more substantial process of collective bargaining, but fell short of its intentions (Gallagher 2017: 76).

The result of this situation is that the ratio of workers covered by bargaining is, in fact, lower than union density. While the data is scarce and not continuous and therefore pointless to graph, the ICTWSS database shows union density at 58.6% in 1980, rose to 76.8 in 1989 and began to decline, reaching 62.3 in 1997. The time-series also covers the 2008–2013 period and shows a now rising trend, climbing from 30.4 to 42.6%. The bargaining coverage rate in the 2008–2012 period grew rapidly from 22.3 to 39.3% and in each specific year the bargaining rate was lower than union density (Visser 2019). This is in significant contrast with Germany where we found 40–50% more covered by bargaining than union density (due to a functional and relatively centralized practice of negotiations), and even the USA where bargaining coverage was only marginally higher than union density (due to unions losing power through retreating wherever they lose their function).

In China, unions formally organize labor and bargain at a formidable level (as measured by union density rates), but they actually contribute little apart from another level of party-led mediation between workers and management. The slack in organization is taken over by ad hoc organization, NGOs, and legal activists which attempt to protect and promote the workers' rights. However, this type of activity has been targeted in a 2015 law enforcement crackdown (Liu and Shi 2016: 5)[3]. Unlike unions, such activity creates a potential to politically organize outside the party and this makes such organization a potential adversary to the Party's monopoly of power. In a politically monopolistic country, labor can become co-opted via unions, pacified via mediations or targeted as it was in 2015.

8.2.3 Avoidable Labor Institutions in China

Explaining the avoidable aspect of institutions in China is crucial to understanding the Chinese political economy in general as well as labor institutions specifically. The arbitrariness in the application of laws is crucial for the political maneuvering space of the ruling bureaucracy (Milanovic 2019: 93–95). The mid-1990s have seen improvements in a more universal and less complex type of labor legislature. However, the consistent enforcement gap suggests that one type of complexity and confusion was exchanged for another. This type of institutional structure allows for substantially different effects on different groups. Most importantly, the position of old, socialist insiders, and the increasingly important migrant workers was divergent. Growth model in the Deng era needed to attract foreign capital in order to start massive production for export, which itself needed inexpensive inputs. This meant the dismantling of the old *danwei* system and a restructuring of the old state-owned industry amassed in the northeast of the country. Also, it meant the expansion of production particularly in the southern coastal regions through a loosening of the *hukou* system in order to attract migrant workers. The first became the Chinese *rustbelt* and the second became the Chinese *sunbelt* (Lee 2007). The grievances of workers from the *rustbelt* were tied to the loss of insider status through contract law and the possibility of being laid off, while the grievances of workers of the sunbelt concerned the alarmingly inappropriate working conditions in a widening enforcement gap (Estlund 2017: 31–36). If the state strived to establish a regulatory presence in the *rustbelt*, it retreated before the pressing requirements of market efficiency in the *sunbelt*.

Effectively, the conditions of workers in both areas deteriorated. In the *rustbelt*, the room for avoidable institutions slowly shrank (although, as we saw, this was a very gradual process) and slowly opened the old

[3] Likewise, 2015 saw a change in rhetoric at the top of the Party, with the promotion of sectoral collective bargaining now portrayed as a threat (Estlund 2017: 147).

protected insider relations to the market through attempts at universally applied regulation. The most visible consequence of this was the massive privatization drive in the 1998–2001 period through which 30 million workers were laid off (Gallagher 2014: 4). In the *sunbelt,* the room for avoidable institutions grew. Labor rights were habitually ignored in order to achieve a capital-friendly environment, particularly in the case of migrant workers from rural areas. These breaches include forced overtime work, hazardous working conditions and non-payment of wages (Lee 2009: 4). In the period following the southern tour speech, the coastal areas were in the process of being turned into the factory of the world with the cheap migrant labor becoming a crucial input. Such a growth model was compatible with working conditions that included industrial injuries, occupational diseases, and massive accidents such as fires, as well as low and late wages and extensive overtime (Ling 2016: 3–4). By the mid-2000s, the situation has improved somewhat with labor intensity declining and the overtime, injuries and diseases all becoming comparatively a smaller problem (ibid.: 9). The strikes, organized through informal channels as shown, started to focus on the economic and distributional issues, i.e. wage labor shares in increasingly profitable firms. This is a fundamental change and it influences the wage regime. Wherever labor is able to push for larger wages, the profitability within the existing growth model may be called into question. This was certainly the case with China where the average real wage grew by 125% in the 2006–2015 period (ILO 2016: 12). Additionally, the growing structural power of labor and the growing salience of their demands could also be felt in the noticeably larger yearly number of strikes compared to the early 2010s.[4]

While structural labor power is high, associational power remains low as there are no independent unions to protect the workers. There is only a state-controlled all covering ACFTU. It is understandable that the post-corporatist functions and arrangements of unions expected in the west simply do not apply. Worker rights are traditionally conceived as individual rights and independent worker organization is seen as political, and not necessarily compatible with the one-party socialist system of China

[4]There are no officially reported strike statistics and the best available methodology seems to be the monitoring of the media by the China Labor Bulletin, which reported 203 strikes for 2011 (first available data), 384 for 2012, 647 for 2013, 1358 for 2014, 2775 for 2015, 2670 for 2016, 1258 for 2017 and 1708 for 2018, 1385 for 2019 and 591 for 2020 as of late October (CLB 2020).

today. Where we would expect the role of the unions to be that of organizing labor from the western point of view, ACTFU mediates between ad hoc labor organization and management, which is clearly a fundamentally different role.

Chinese labor markets show a dynamic of high formal protection with a large enforcement gap all tying into a dualistic labor market with low possibilities of labor organization and independent protection. Such a structure tends to rely on informal channels of power (within the party or within the society). This means that those otherwise most vulnerable will also become the most vulnerable in the poorly enforced area of labor rights. It should not be surprising that in terms of gender inequality, the situation seems convincingly patriarchal. The World Economic Forum "Global Gender Gap Index" ranks China 99th globally (compared to German 13th and US 45th rank) with women faring badly in economic participation and opportunity receiving the index score of 0.649 (ranking 70th) in the survey rate of wage equality (quite similar to the result in the USA; WEF 2016d). It seems that the most active free market extensive years contributed to an unequitable trend. Chen uses the Chinese Health and Nutrition Survey to show the dropping trend of gender inequality in the 1989–2000 period, but a significant rise from 2000 onward (Chen 2011: 16).

8.3 Explaining the Labor Institutional Changes in China

As in the previous two chapters, we start with applying the framework of institutional change to the specific national context, in this case to the Chinese institutional context in Fig. 8.1.

We then explain the logic of each driver and their mutual interactions.

8.3.1 Channel 1: Path Dependence—Institutional Starting Positions of China

The first channel of institutional change that we identified is the channel of path dependence. To function, this mechanism requires feedback loops which can relate to the distributional/power effects (historical institutionalism) or complementarity effects (VofC). In the case of China, power-related effects are substantial as the institutional framework hinges on the power monopoly of the Communist Party of China, which cuts

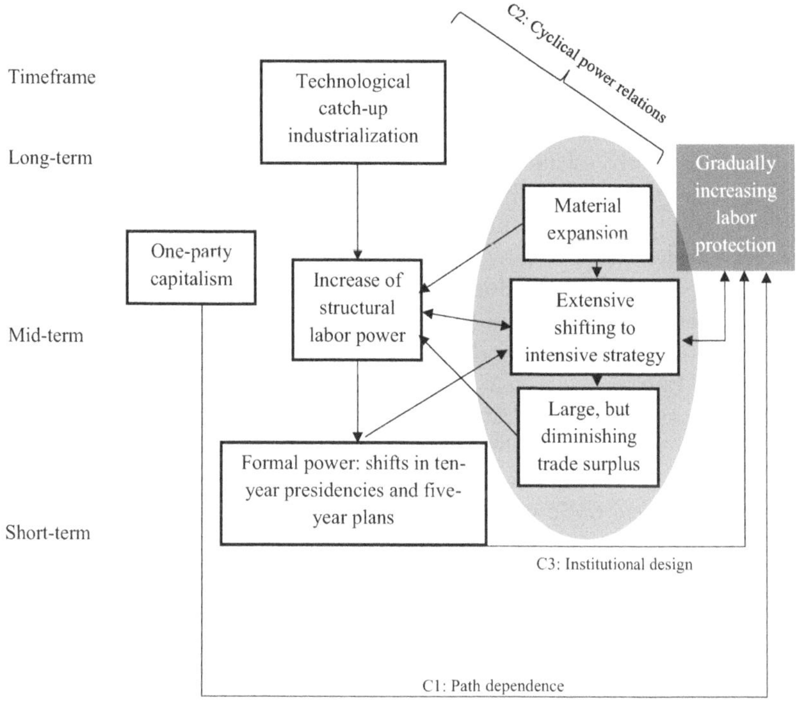

Fig. 8.1 Framework of labor institutional change in China

across labor relations, organized business, investment priorities, etc. A result of this specific overarching institutional arrangement is that the institutional complementarities have a decidedly different nature than those that can be found in LME or CME structures. The elementary concepts of the *Varieties of Capitalism* approach have been formulated with stable and developed democracies in mind. In years since its inception, the field has been expanded to a number of new countries and has been successfully adapted to a number of post-transitional countries. Slovenia and Estonia were recognized as both developmentally successful and at the same time relatively institutionally complementary countries (Buchen 2007; Feldmann 2006), with Slovenia belonging to the CME and Estonia belonging to the LME varieties of capitalism. It has also been argued that Croatian institutional arrangements bear more than a passing resemblance to CME, even though Croatia failed to capitalize in terms of sustained economic growth (Bartlett 2007; Lučev and Babić 2013). As already mentioned, Nölke and Vliegenhart (2009) suggested a new variety—DME—to explain institutional complementarity in Hungary, Poland, Czechia, and Slovakia. China has, however, presented researchers with a considerable challenge. In Central and Eastern Europe, countries underwent political transition (political liberalization, democratization) simultaneously with economic transition (economic liberalization, private market development, privatization). The institutional results were somewhat comparable with developed and stable democracies as described by Hall and Soskice, even if some post-transitional countries had left much to be desired. On the other hand, the transition in China was not multifold as it was in Europe. Markets were greatly deregulated, and private markets were developed, but political power was never shared. The Communist Party of China remained the de facto political monopolist of the political sphere, and this includes the domination over the labor markets with de facto only one trade union allowed[5]—All-China Federation of Trade Unions (ACTFU). A balance of power at the base of VofC approach is therefore not something we can expect in China—we cannot expect to see compromise between organized labor, organized capital and the state as all of the above are dominated by the Communist Party of China. Nevertheless, VofC has inspired attempts to analyze Chinese specific institutional complementarities, as the economic results are remarkable and it is worthwhile to explore possible institutional foundations.

It is certainly insufficient to merely point to state capitalism as a label, as China has developed subtle and sophisticated arrangements that ensure its State-Owned Enterprises are oriented toward profitability and internationalization (Mussachio and Lazzarini 2016: 404). In terms of

[5]ACTFU is formally a federation of 10 unions: All-China Federation of Railway Workers' Unions, National Committee of the Chinese Agricultural, Forestry and Water Conservancy Workers' Union, National Committee of the Chinese Aviation Workers' Union, National Committee of the Chinese Banking Workers' Union, National Committee of the Chinese Defense Industry, Postal and Telecommunications Workers' Union, National Committee of the Chinese Educational, Scientific, Cultural, Medical and Sports Workers' Union, National Committee of the Chinese Energy and Chemical Workers' Union, National Committee of the Chinese Financial, Commercial, Light Industry, Textile and Tobacco Workers' Union, National Committee of the Chinese Machinery, Metallurgical and Building Material Workers' Union and National Committee of the Chinese Seamen and Construction Workers' Union.

the VofC typology, Jeanne Wilson points to a “distinctive, and arguably dysfunctional, dualism” of simultaneous movement toward LME-type free market policies and state-promotion of key industrial areas (Wilson 2007: 240) as a characteristic of Chinese development. Witt (2010) agrees that China does not fit neatly into either the CME or LME type, although it “looks much more like an LME than a CME” in many respects (Witt 2010: 3). Considerable challenges to institutional analysis of China are presented by several circumstances. Firstly, formal and informal practices considerably diverge in China, and secondly, private and public firms in China play by different rules, which suggests that the institutional complementarities are diverged within the same country (Witt and Redding 2014: 16–17). The coordination of state-owned firms is certainly one of the distinguishing features of the party-led capitalism in China. A complex pyramidal structure is expected in most studies with minority and majority models of government ownership being intertwined with the party dominated state apparatus at the top (Mussachio and Lazzarini 2016: 403). An attempt at VofC inspired institutional analysis concluded that China combines elements of predatory state (with leaders and their families enriching themselves), with elements of the Japan-like Asian development state (Witt and Redding 2013). In fact, Witt and Redding (2013) conclude, that, apart from Japan, the *Varieties of Capitalism* framework cannot be neatly applied to Asian countries, and China is best described as an authoritarian capitalism within the cluster of post-transitional Asian countries. Peck and Zhang argue for a model of “variegated, polymorphic capitalism” (Peck and Zhang 2013: 385) and suggest a third, Chinese model of capitalism alongside LME and CME varieties. This model would recognize among other aspects the party control of unions, segmented labor markets, tightly knit *guanxi* relational networks and state control dominating inter-firm relations, a generous financial support of state control firms and a lacking one for private ones (ibid.: 363–364). In a similar vein, Nölke and his coauthors argue for yet another variety of capitalism describing the state-permeated capitalisms (SME—State-permeated Market Economy) of China, India, and Brazil entailing the large-scale involvement of national capital and preserving low-wage regimes in highly segregated work-forces and large domestic markets (Nölke et al. 2015: 539–545).

In all, overarching party control (rather than state control) does not create the type of complementarity that formed the basis of VofC, where all relevant institutional arrangements were cyclically embedded in each other forming a path-dependent structure. In China, particular institutional arrangements form elements which can be changed with relative ease from the top, because power is not vested in a political system dependent on elections or on various veto players functioning through structured interactions. It is vested in the power monopoly of the party, and this is the elementary fact informing path dependence in China. In other words, strategies, growth models, and institutional arrangements may change, but not in a direction overly dangerous to the power monopoly.

Interactions with other drivers and the result

(a) Power resources: As we have seen, the CCP is not willing to allow the labor to independently organize, with the only legal representatives being grouped in the party-led ACTFU. This suggests that the associational power of labor in China is necessarily very low, which diminishes the power resources available to labor due to the need to preserve the political dominance of the Communist Party.
(b) Phase of the systemic cycle: the investment cycles in China are also under direct influence of the Party and have enabled significant overcapacity. This suggests that the material expansion of China could be prolonged beyond profitable levels. In other words, the elementary process of capital flight from material to financial expansion may function with a significant delay in China, as the development strategies catch on to the changing market circumstances.
(c) Developmental strategy: initial institutional positions do not offer a strong channel for a strong labor to influence the developmental strategies in a labor-friendly direction. However, top-down Party-led strategies can be formed as a response to external shocks or in recognition of a growing structural power of labor (to preserve legitimacy and prevent wild-cat strikes harming the production). This occurred in the past decade as a labor-friendly developmental strategy was formulated by the CCP, encompassing poverty reduction, supply-side reforms focusing on higher value-added production and the labor protection gaining important traction in the legal system. These reforms were increasingly significant with the shock felt in 2009 in the Chinese export markets and Chinese real growth slowed somewhat to the "new normal" of 6–7%. At the same time, the growing structural power of Chinese labor was

felt in increasingly large illegal strikes (Honda in 2010, Yue Yuen in 2014).

(d) The result of institutional change: path dependence of initial structures provides pressures in the direction of existing institutional development, but in China the power-players are primarily located in the Party, and the business and labor elites are equally intertwined with the Party. In the specific case of China, path dependence is reliant primarily on party monopoly of power, meaning large shifts are possible as long as they do not threaten this monopoly. In other words, the growing structural power of labor can be recognized through a new and more labor-friendly developmental strategy, but its associational power must be (and is) curbed as it represents an alternative to Party organization.

As was the case in Germany, the path dependence channel builds upon a strong veto player and constricts the set of institutional change possibilities. In China, the ingrained asymmetry of power suggests that a change which does not favor the continued political monopoly of power of the Communist Party is not a plausible scenario. The next segment will discuss channel 2 and the power shifts in labor which sometimes put it at cross-ends with the path-dependent channel. In terms of modes of change, this contradiction was resolved primarily through the process of *layering*, characterized by both localized market experiments and general uncertainty caused by the domination of avoidable institutions (enforcement gaps).

8.3.2 Channel 2: Cyclical Power Relations in China

Figure 8.2 shows the details of the second channel of institutional change identified here. The five constitutive drivers are technological change (treated as an exogenous factor—providing a long-term context), the three drivers constituting the systemic cycle—the phase of the systemic cycle, developmental strategies and trade relations—and power relations as the balance of power resources.

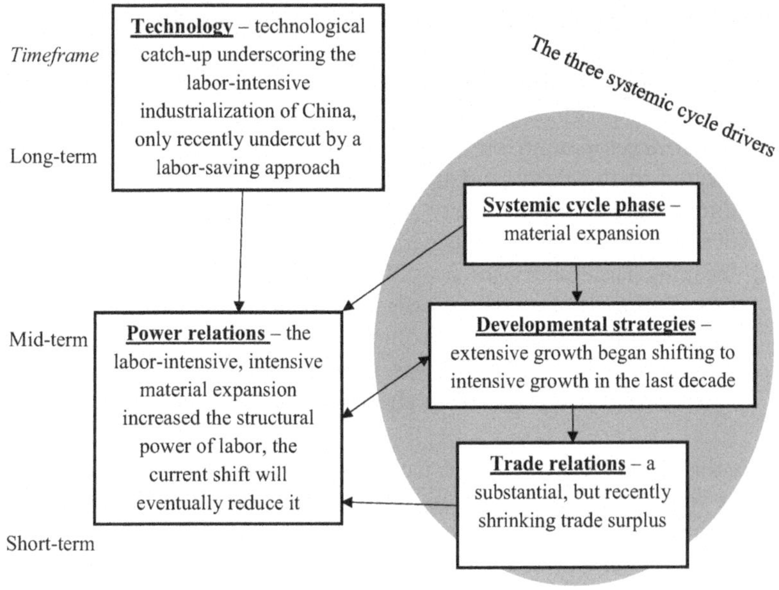

Fig. 8.2 Cyclical power relations in China

8.3.2.1 *Technology and Sectoral Labor Market Structure in China*

The second channel of institutional change is a complex nexus of technological changes, systemic cycle phases, trade relations, power relations, and developmental strategies. The longest-term process is that of technological change. Figure 8.3 shows the relative shares of overall employment for agriculture (dominates in underdeveloped countries and some emerging markets), industry and services (dominates in developed countries).

In China, the occupational shares are slightly more dramatic than those found in developed economies. Agricultural share has had a notable decline since 2002, when it was at 50%, even though it is still at a comparably high level of 24.7%. Service share has gradually increased and surpassed the industrial share in 1994 and the agricultural share as recently as 2011, to now be found at the level of 47.1%. Industry share has reached a high-point in 2012 at 30.3% and has dropped off to 28.2% by 2020. This dynamic is quite different than that in Germany and the USA. Service sector overtook the industry in the mid-1990s and has only recently surpassed the agricultural sector. This would suggest

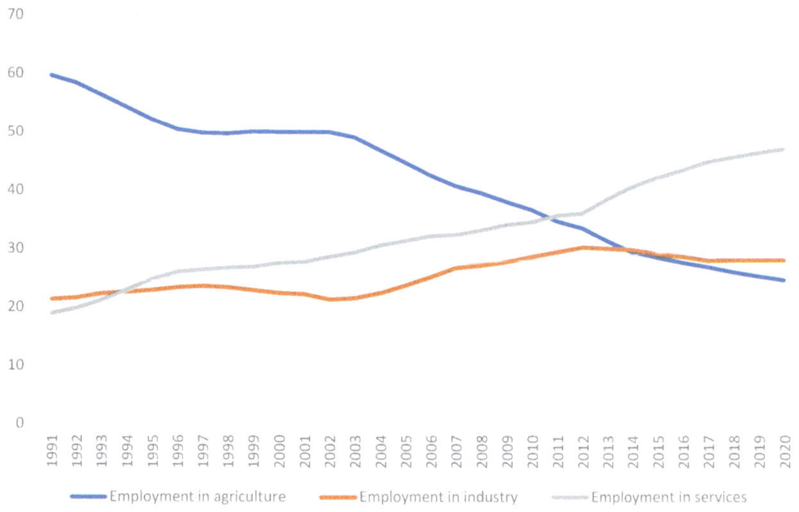

Fig. 8.3 China employment structure (*Source of data* World Bank [2020])

that (according to general trends) there was still room for the growth of urban population in the forms of industry and service employment. However, the main motor behind these shifts was cheap rural labor being used as a factor in the growing of export-oriented industry on the coast. This is a common pattern of development, but at some point, in each country cheap rural labor dries up causing a rise in both rural and urban wages. This is known as the Lewis point and some authors have argued it has been reached (Zhang et al. 2011; Das and N'Diaye 2013). This is significant as it suggests a different array of available inputs with labor gaining more structural power through its scarcity and therefore through the diminishing ability of the employers to readily replace workers.

Interactions with other drivers and the result

(a) Power resources: in sharp contrast to the effects of technology in western countries, industrial and service sectors only recently caught up with agriculture in terms of employment, which is indicative of the vast possibilities of technological catch-up in China. Such catch-up enabled Chinese material expansion and, crucially, the increase of labor structural power.

(b) Developmental strategy: supply-side reforms utilize the available expansion of IT and robotics to slowly emulate the trends prevalent in Japan, Europe and the USA—i.e. circumventing the increase of labor workplace structural power—itself contingent on the broader shift toward an intensive developmental strategy.

8.3.2.2 *Phase of the Systemic Cycle in China*

In the period of interest here, the systemic cycle of the US accumulation regime brought a financial expansion in the USA, accompanied by decreasing importance of national industry. It also resulted in mounting trade deficits which meant that the consumption on US markets incentivized production abroad. Therefore, while the effects on the Chinese economy may have been a stimulation of financial markets to some degree (e.g. as a need to accommodate FDI and manage production), they were fundamentally more likely to increase the efforts of the real economy. We can illustrate the effect by focusing on the same three levels as in the previous two chapters (household/state/company). In terms of household debt, the recent years brought a dramatic increase with household debt at 10.7% GDP in 2006, but at 49.2% in 2017 (IMF 2019). These levels are far lower than those found in the USA and still slightly lower than those found in Germany, but the rapid trend is indicative of the Chinese "new normal" world. At the level of the state or entire economy, we can compare the standard sources of capital.[6] Figure 8.4 compares two types of financing: the domestic bank credits associated with the patient capital of developed CMEs and the market capitalization rates, high rates of which are associated with the impatient stock-market capital of developed LMEs.

[6] The very existence of a well-ordered and credit-based financial system is a significant difference between capitalism and socialism, with capitalism requiring risk-taking investors who can bet with loaned funds. However, what makes this mechanism efficient is the existence of hard budget constraints in the form of a threat of liquidation should such a bet prove ill advised. The socialist alternative is a centrally allocated resource allocation, enabling soft budget constraints in order to remain focused on plan fulfillment rather than operational efficiency (Pistor et al. 2016: 353–354). In this sense, China keeps a certain soft-budget tendency in its banking sector, but has created a stock-market system providing a combination typical of its long-term market reforms. Mainland China has two stock markets—Shanghai (began operating in its current form in 1990) and Shenzhen (began operating in 1991). Their operations initially catered almost exclusively to state-owned enterprises, as the State Planning Commission selected the firms allowed to be listed. This stipulation was removed in 2000 and the privately owned enterprises steadily began to take over, becoming the majority by 2010 (Lardy 2014: 112–113).

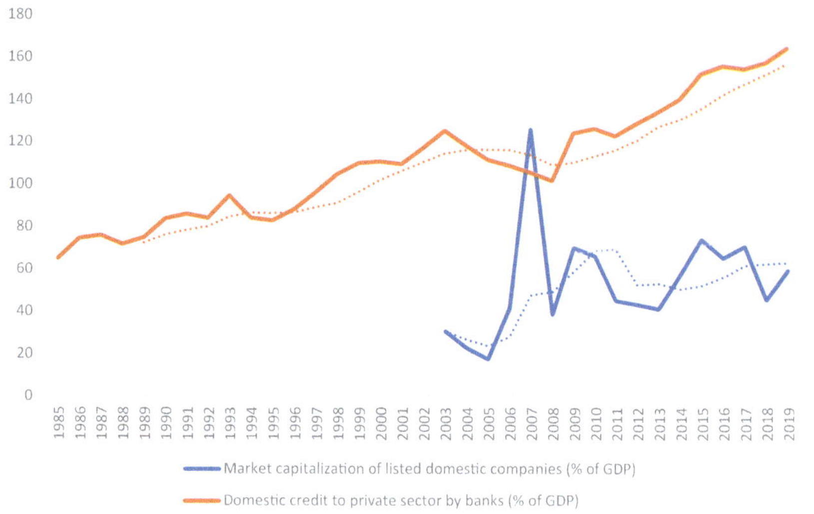

Fig. 8.4 Financing sources in People's Republic of China (*Source of data* World Bank [2020] [trend-lines are 5-year moving averages])

China exhibits consistently higher bank credit levels (similar to Germany, although more volatile), although in 2007 the market capitalization made a remarkable one-year jump exceeding the bank levels. In all, the cumulative level of these two sources was at 156% in 2003 (no data was available for market capitalizations before this date) and at 224% in 2019. Market capitalization spikes logically correspond to periods of more active trading. In terms of the ratio of traded shares to GDP, 2007 marked the high-point of 177.6%, a slowdown in 2008 was partially recovered with the ratio of 153.5% in 2009, and these were surpassed only in the dangerous year of 2015 at a remarkable 355.5% (almost two-thirds above the corresponding indicator for the USA) and the most recent available data shows 132.8% in 2019—roughly a third above the US indicator (World Bank 2020). These measures are perhaps sufficient to validate the central point: in China, the impatient stock-market may have its bubbles and crises (and apexes of trading in specific years may rise above those found even in the USA), but its averaged relative size to GDP remains far below the US levels.

This is an important distinction, as financializations/finance expansions can logically be operationalized as absolute or relative indicators. If the term was taken to be absolute, i.e. manifested in any increase in financial activity and/or the importance of various financial subjects, then any trend showing such an absolute increase could be construed as evidence of financialization. However, we approach financializations/finance expansions through the prism of the systemic cycle theory, using a relative meaning of the term. Here, a financialization/finance expansion is understood as a dominant phase of capital accumulation in relation to material expansions. The prevalence of stock-markets *over banks* would be a strong indicator of the domination of the speculative capital as envisioned by Arrighi, while a domination of banks *over stock-markets* is compatible with material expansions. In explicitly keeping with an Arrighian concept of financialization as a process in which real investments make way to financial ones, Liu and Lee (2018) use recent data on listed non-financial corporations and find evidence of an upward trend of Arrighi-Krippner financialization process in China (i.e. more financial investment for non-financial corporations). However, this is an absolute finding on the company level, and its expected relative systemic-cycle effects in terms of crowding-out manufacturing did not manifest themselves as of yet. Data on value-added in manufacturing expressed as a percentage of GDP shows a continued importance of manufacturing with 32% in 2004 (at time-series start), still at 32.1% in 2011, and dropping to 27.2% by 2019 (World Bank 2020). While this measure will presumably continue to drop in the decades to come (as China's economy matures), the current level is far above the levels found in the USA and even Germany, showing a larger structural importance of the real sector.

In other words, China is undergoing a financialization in absolute terms (rapidly rising household debt/GDP levels, a rising average level of market capitalization/GDP levels and Chinese non-financial corporations turning to financial profits) but does not display signs of a financialization in relative terms, as manufacturing remains very important. In terms of the systemic cycle theory, this state is understood as a part of a broader phase of material expansion.

Interactions with other drivers and the result

(a) Trade relations: material expansion through extensive developmental strategies suggests a trade surplus. China has had a notably export-led growth model as a basis of its development, and its material expansion was crucially supported by large net-exports.
(b) Power resources: material expansion tends to promote manufacturing employment, suggesting more structural labor power. China has had a material expansion led by exports, and the structural power of its labor made itself felt through highly damaging (and successful) illegal strikes. The high levels of structural power made evident in strikes must, however, work against the low levels of associational power.
(c) Developmental strategies: the phase of the systemic cycle does not have a direct effect on the choice of extensive or intensive strategies. However, the exhaustion of the systemic cycle in the core creates a world-systemic chaos in the sense of a growing multipolarity in which strategies can be formulated. The period after 1980 was a period of a financial expansion in the USA to which China responded with an export-led (extensive) strategy. The post-2009 world is the chaotic world in which China seems to be switching to an intensive strategy.

8.3.2.3 Trade Relations of China

Chapter 5 has shown the development of the Chinese goods surpluses. Figure 8.5 demonstrates a rougher measure of net exports (current account balance) and its interaction with the real GDP growth rate.

Two clear trends dominate the chart: an increase of both measures in the 2001–2008 period and a decrease of both measures since 2009. The current account surplus the size of 10% of Chinese GDP certainly greatly contributed to its GDP growth at 14% in 2007, and a decrease of the current account surplus to less than 2% by 2011 certainly contributed to the reduced growth rates of the *new normal*. The further reduction in the surplus in 2018 occurred in the context of the economic conflict with USA starting in that year. Figure 8.6 compares separate data for exports and imports.

Unlike the previous figure, which showed current accounts as a rough measure of trade relative to GDP levels, this one shows exports and

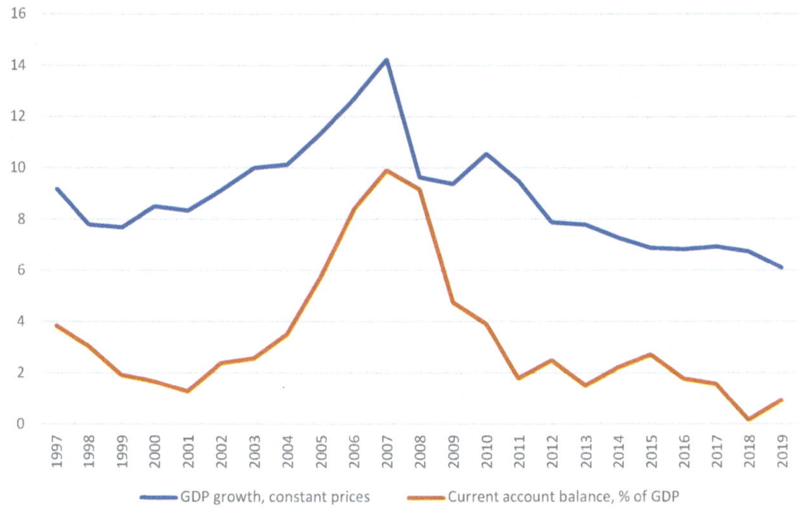

Fig. 8.5 Current accounts and real GDP growth in China (*Source of data* IMF [2020])

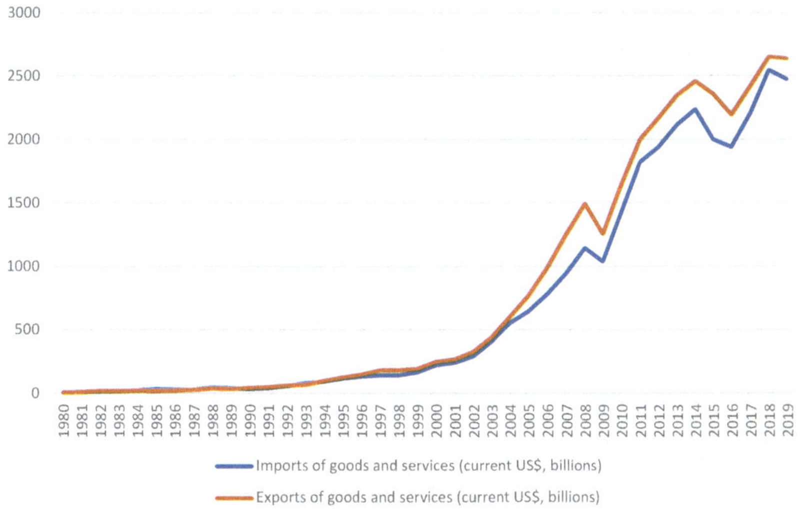

Fig. 8.6 Trade in goods and services—China (*Source of data* World Bank [2020])

imports in absolute terms of current USD. We can see that both imports and exports grew aggressively after 2001, with the growth of exports outpacing that of imports. Once more, we can see the shock of 2009 with both exports and imports shrinking and the surplus being reduced until 2011, as imports grew at greater speeds than exports, thus narrowing the gap. International trade nevertheless handsomely recovered until 2015, when we can notice another fall in both exports and imports. Recovering in 2017 and 2018, trade started slowing down once more in 2019.

These trends also point us to the incentives and disincentives for labor institutions. The 2001–2008 period was the period of export-oriented material expansion, which benefits from a flexible and low-cost labor, much like the one provided with the lax enforcement of the ambitious formal labor legal structure of China. The period since 2009 is one in which a domestic market has been developed in order to place the material expansion on sure footing.

Interactions with other drivers and the result

(a) Power resources: an increase in trade surplus suggests an expansion of manufactured goods production and greater structural labor power, as the importance of manufacturing labor grows. The interval until 2008 in China was a period of an increasingly large trade surplus suggesting an increase in structural power of labor. Growth of trade has henceforth shown signs of a focus on domestic demand with imports approaching the levels of exports (but always maintaining a surplus), and recent years show a greater contraction of imports compared to exports once producing a substantial surplus.

(b) Transnational conditionality: a large trade surplus may have an indirect effect on the ability to withstand transnational pressures toward reform. China has had a very successful export-led (i.e. extensive) growth model which has resulted in it becoming one of the most important economic powers in the world, and therefore in not being overly vulnerable to outside pressures.

(c) Systemic cycle phase: notwithstanding a recent contraction shown by data, a steady expansion of trade alongside the continued trade surplus remains consistent with the continued material expansion. Next segment will, however, show that the relative importance of this continued surplus to the Chinese GDP has shrunk.

(d) Developmental strategies: an extensive strategy in our interpretation oriented to the export markets in its growth model, while an intensive strategy is oriented toward domestic markets. A strong surplus in trade would itself suggest either the extensive path or a presence of a strong export niche, while a deficit during continued growth of production suggests an intensive path. China has used the last decade to start its switch from extensive to intensive growth.

8.3.2.4 Developmental Strategies of China

The period after the Deng Xiaoping's reforms banked on the low wage, low labor protection growth model, which increasingly catered to the foreign markets. Its resulting success as an extensive developmental strategy propelled the remarkable growth rates of China. However, in the mid-2000s the formal institutions began to take labor into greater account and the global 2008/09 crisis solidified this shift. The post-2009 period brought the need for fiscal stimuli in order to prevent a GDP downturn. These stimuli can be seen in the gradual increase of the government expenditure of China from 18% GDP in 2007 to 32% in 2016 (IMF 2018). Taken alongside various other programs, it seems to suggest the new developmental strategy, which no longer depended on the low-wage regime. These programs are the poverty reduction programs including the *dibao* scheme and reducing income inequality (both recognized as explicit goals in the still current five-year plan; "The 13th Five-Year Plan," 2016: 154–161; 180–182), an explicit focus on consumption-led growth (at least since the 12th five-year plan starting in 2011; see CIPG/CATL 2016: 127), as well as supply-side reforms of the production chains intended to remove overcapacity in obsolete manufacturing and introduce high-tech industrialization (a part of the Made In China 2025 industrial policy; see Wübbeke et al. 2016). All of this suggests a shift from an extensive strategy banking on low-cost labor to an intensive strategy dependent on a strong domestic demand (and therefore a strong domestic overall income)—but no longer able to bank on permanently low labor costs, necessitating a shift into high-tech, high added value industries.

We can discern these movements in the changing composition of the demand structure as well. Figure 8.7 shows the Chinese demand composition by comparing the relative levels of household

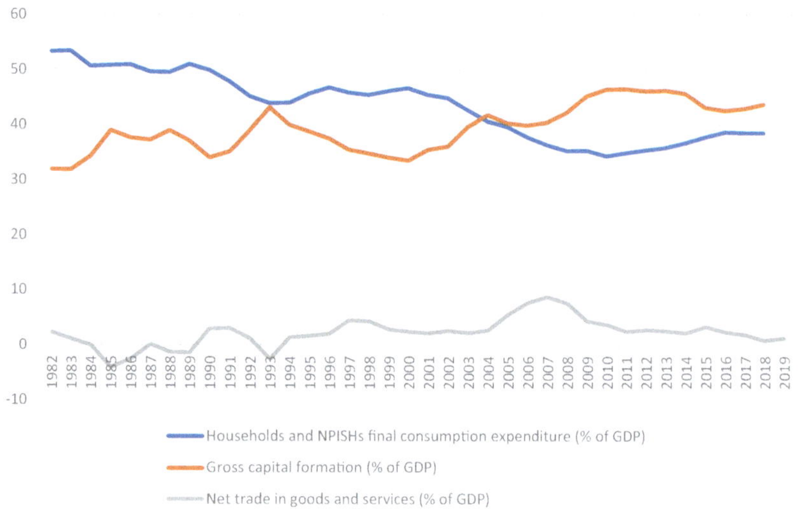

Fig. 8.7 Demand composition in China (*Source of data* World Bank [2020] [Household final consumption, Gross capital formation], own calculation according to data for current USD GDP and net trade in goods and services in World Bank [2020] [Net trade % GDP])

consumption, investment (i.e. gross capital formation) and net trade. The general historical trend was one of a falling share of household demand in GDP (more than 50% in the early 1980s, 44–47% through most of the 1990s, dropping to 34.3 by 2010) but then leveling off and growing to 38.5% in 2018. At the same time, investment in China historically mostly remained in the 30–40% range until the early 2000s, when it began to grow, reaching the high-point in 2011 at 46.7% of GDP. This has prompted comments on overinvestment in China with infrastructure projects bringing growth only during construction itself due to poor efficiency and hidden costs spreading throughout the economy (Lee et al. 2012; Ding et al. 2019; Ansar et al. 2016). Recently, the GDP share of investment has begun to shrink, reaching 42.6% in 2016, and slightly correcting to 43.8% by 2018. Finally, pre-2008 Chinese GDP growth rates were dependent on the extensive trade surplus, which substantially decreased with the collapse of Chinese export markets. Net trade constituted 8.7% of GDP in 2007 and rapidly fell by several points, mostly remaining below 2.5% since 2011, with the latest available data showing

1.1% for 2019. The tendencies in recent years seem to point toward the initial stages of a new growth model with overinvestment and poverty being recognized as problems alongside in the context of a deteriorated situation in international trade. The result is the fall in the shares of both net trade (−7.6% since 2007) and investment (−2.9% since 2011) and an increase in household spending (+4.2% since 2010). This trend is consistent with an extensive strategy and if China's signalled move toward an intensive strategy of development is successful, this measure will substantially increase through the years to come. This will certainly suggest a different type of labor markets, as higher consumption levels suggest higher wages, which are compatible with a higher tier in the global supply chain (i.e. higher quality goods). This in turn suggests a higher structural power of workers. As the development of this model continues, this will be increasingly difficult to subdue through the channels currently employed by the Party.

Once more, if we interpret critical junctures as we have above (either endogenous or exogenous events, and periods of developmental strategy institutionalization), we can see that Chinese labor markets have experienced a critical juncture through the Deng Xiaoping reforms which institutionalized an extensive developmental strategy. The last decade brought a shift toward an intensive developmental strategy. If successful, this shift will have provided the second critical juncture for the Chinese labor markets in the selected timeframe.

Interaction with other drivers and the result

(a) Power resources: we are most likely witnessing the beginnings of a more labor-friendly developmental strategy in China. It is at least a partial response to the growing structural power of labor, which was increasingly able to spontaneously organize (in spite of obstacles to associational power) and fight for higher wages.
(b) Trade relations: a long-standing extensive strategy focused on external markets, while the seeming shift into intensive strategy in necessitated by the development of domestic markets (enabling growth even when foreign demand diminishes).
(c) The result of institutional change: the intensive strategy can be interpreted as the moment in which the compromises of power relations are institutionalized—which would put the greatest emphasis on the structural power of labor. In China, this process certainly takes labor into account, but is by its nature a top-down

decision. Its continued enforcement and institutionalization will also be a product of path dependence on a lower level, as an increase in wages will lock in a consumption-driven growth model.

8.3.2.5 *Power Relations in China*

Power resources of labor in China follow two major tendencies. Firstly, the level of associational power is very low as the Party has a monopoly on legal labor organization and it does not tend to use it to truly represent labor. Secondly, the structural power of labor has increased until the mid-2000s as a result of a successful growth model building on an export-oriented material expansion—a nexus which has been called into question as net-exports drop and a new growth model emerges.

Power resources also function according to channels different than those in western countries as the true nature of resources of interest groups do not manifest through structured interactions between employers and labor but are largely held within the confines of the Communist Party. As already explained, the union density numbers do not necessarily suggest leverage of the unions nor their ability to exert pressure in the name of labor—which has produced spontaneous outbursts of labor anger. Again, this suggests the very low level of associational power of unions.

Even as strikes are not recognized in China, they have seen "explosive growth since the 1990s" (Lee 2009: 1), reaching high-points in the 2010 Honda riots and the 2014 Yue Yuen strike (Estlund 2017: 10–16; Gallagher 2017: 199–200; Ling 2016). In assessing the prospects for the future Chan and Hui conclude that the consultations have progressed from "collective consultation as a formality, through a stage of collective bargaining by riot, and towards a new party state-led form of collective bargaining," unlikely to reach a western-type stage of worker-led collective bargaining in the near future (Chan and Hui 2013: 19). Cynthia Estlund's 2017 book *A New Deal for China's Workers?* also sought to compare the position of Chinese workers to those found in the West, and primarily the USA. She answers her titular question negatively, as the ideal of "collective bargaining through autonomous, freely chosen and reasonably democratic trade unions" (Estlund 2017: 207) is not shared by the Party leadership, which sees to forestall any political opposition. In Estlund's interpretation, the improvement in labor institutions (through better minimum labor standards and access to legal remedies) should be seen as an attempt at suppressing demand for independent organization. At the same time, Party leadership is attempting to suppress the supply of independent labor organization through legally targeting activists (ibid.: 207–208). The ad hoc organization manifest most visibly in strikes is always a possibility, but the main difference between the USA of 1920s and 1930s and modern China is the difference in the scope of strikes. While the strikes may be very large in absolute numbers, the relative numbers (percent of strikers in working age population) show that China is far behind the situation of working power concentration in (pre-)New Deal America with the US percentage reaching more than 2% in 1920, 1922 and 1937 and the Chinese percentage reaching its high in 2015 (according to available data) with around 0.1% (ibid.: 211). This underlines the central labor power issue—the role of labor in the overall economy (structural power) may rise to considerable levels through material expansion, but the capacity to organize (associational power) necessary to translate it into a continuous pressure toward a pro-labor regime is subdued for political reasons. Instead, the potential of labor power is recognized through a series of top-down reforms, which provide a network of pressure valves (dispute resolution, labor laws, anti-poverty measures) to accommodate disgruntled workers.[7]

Interactions with other drivers and the result

(a) Phase of the systemic cycle: high levels of structural power of labor will prolong the shift to financial expansion. However, a long-term effect of a high-wage labor regime may prove to be lower structural power of labor as low-complexity, low-wage, labor-intensive manufacture moves to less developed countries. Shift into the financial expansion will presumably occur after structural power of labor sufficiently diminishes in the long run.

[7]The emergent reforms in China do not resemble the New Deal-era USA as they are not driven by manifest labor power and union activities. The more pertinent comparison would be to Bismarck-era Germany, in which the vastly influential German model of welfare state was established. The vast reforms of the 1880s (sickness insurance, accident insurance, old age and disability insurance) were passed in the context of Bismarck's anti-socialist efforts which effectively banned trade unions and obstructed the functioning of social-democratic political forces. This was a matter of establishing pro-labor solutions and therefore taking the growing structural power of labor in Europe into account (fearing a German version of the 1871 Paris Commune), while still preventing the manifestation of structural power through association. In this sense, modern China and late nineteenth-century German Empire have more in common in terms of labor reforms than modern China and the 1930s USA.

(b) Developmental strategy: as explained below, developmental strategies are determined in a top-down fashion in the one-party dynamics of Chinese politics. However, in its quest for legitimacy and efficiency, the Party must acknowledge both the high structural power of labor and the growing need to rely on the internal market to ensure adequate growth rates. In this sense, the Party must also act as though labor had legal means to have its high structural power felt politically.

This channel has combined five drivers of change: technology (a long catch-up period in combination with Lewisian development, which has reduced the structural labor power due to the availability of migrant labor), phase of the systemic cycle (material expansion, which increased structural labor power), trade relations (a large surplus, most notable before 2008, suggestive of rising labor structural power), developmental strategy (an ongoing shift into an intensive growth model is itself a recognition of high structural power of labor) and power relations (high structural power curbed in two crucial ways—extremely low associational power due to the inability of independent labor organization and the continuous flow of migrant labor undercutting the manifestations of structural power until recently).

In terms of modes of change, these dynamics remain complementary to the layering tendencies that were already identified. Firstly, there are different interests of old insiders and migrant labor (visible also in terms of economic geography with clusters of older and newer industries, but also in terms of localized special economic zones)—and the historical importance of migrant labor flows undercut the structural labor power that could have been manifested during the material expansion. Secondly, the pronounced discrepancy between structural and associational power stands in direct contrast to both previous cases (in the USA both types of labor power are low, and in Germany the industrial sector retains high levels of both types of labor power). All of this suggests a patchwork of uncertainties which helps to produce the localized and variegated institutional solutions typical of layering. These discrepancies are also the reason for the very important role of channel 3 in the Chinese case.

8.3.2.6 *Channel 3: Institutional Design—Transnational Conditionality and Domestic Politics in China*

The third channel of institutional change is the deliberate design via formal politics. The visible political channels are distinct in the case of China, as it has become relatively impervious to transnational pressures while maintaining a stable internal political situation, not dependent on elections or public opinion to formulate policies. This makes the timeframe for the domestic formal politics substantially longer than those found in liberal democracies (10 years with the tendency to become substantially longer in the future).

In terms of international standing, China has become a substantial economy and a substantial global power player. It is no easier to imagine a transnational organization forcing China to take reforms its government does not wish to take, than it would be for the USA or Germany. In fact, it has created a number of alternatives to the organizations of the American-led twentieth century,[8] which is a move Wallerstein and Arrighi would interpret as a bid for global hegemony. However, in 1980, at the beginning of the timeframe of interest here, China was underdeveloped and still vulnerable to external pressure. Firstly, China has been a member of the IMF since 1980 and has used loans twice: in 1981 and 1986 (IMF 2004). These are the early years of the free market Xiaoping reforms, which coincide with the years of notoriously conditioned and free market-oriented IMF loans. However, as this was before the Fund reformed its transparency policies, we can only infer any connection between these two facts, although, according to some interpretations, China has maneuvered to reduce conditionality (Jacobson and Oksenberg 1990: 124). Secondly, the cooperation with the ILO as the relevant labor-oriented organization seems only slightly better than is the case with the USA as China ratified 26 out of 189 ILO conventions (4 of 8 Fundamental; 2 of 4 Governance and 20 of 177 Technical Conventions)—all of which either until 1936 or since 1988 (ILO 2017). Finally, the WTO accession in 2001 was conditioned on various trade-related issues like tariffs, anti-dumping measures or non-discrimination (Bhattasali et al. 2004: 1–13), which would have

[8] The Asian Infrastructure Investment Bank was established in 2014 and has been interpreted by the Economist as the Chinese version of the World Bank (Why China is creating a new "World Bank" 2014). The BRICS Contingent Reserve Arrangement (CRA), established also in 2014 is interpreted as an alternative to the IMF (An acronym with capital 2014), with China as the leading partner with largest voting rights.

had an enormous effect on what we interpret as an extensive strategy of Chinese export orientation, but only an indirect effect on labor. In all, while China was vulnerable to outside pressures in the period we analyze, the transnational conditionality as a driver of institutional change in the sphere of labor in China was either non-existent, inconclusive or indirect.

In terms of open domestic political struggle, the conflicting agendas are not as easy to identify as in the case of the USA and Germany. China is formally a semi-presidential system and a de facto one-party state. Any opposition to reform in the actual political system primarily takes form internally in the Party or among the administrative levels, and not in the highly visible and codified ways we can observe in the USA or Germany. While China does have formal institutions (President, Peoples' Congress, Premier…) it is difficult to disentangle them from Party institutions. The National Congress of the CCP (more than 2200 members) is the highest organ in the Communist Party and meets every five years to discuss ideological principles and developmental strategies and also to name the Central Committee of the CCP (more than 200 voting members) which is the central Party administrative body, meets once or twice yearly and handles various policy and strategic decisions It also elects the Politburo of the CCP with (generally) 25 members, which is the highest decision-making body and the Politburo standing committee, with currently 7 members meeting in weekly intervals (Heilmann 2017: 64–68). This onion-like structure is mirrored on the state level. The highest authority is vested in the National People's Congress, which is the legislature dominated by CCP delegates. It meets every five years and has almost 3000 members. Between its meetings, the legislative power is vested in the Standing Committee of the National People's Congress (170 members). The executive power is vested in the State Council of the People's Republic of China (roughly 35 members—headed by the premier), which has a Standing Committee (10 members). However, the politics of China tends to revolve around the Presidency, which is becoming increasingly centralized in terms of functions and the length of terms it implies. Arguably, the most important political position is the General Secretary of the Communist Party of China (held by Hu Yaobang 1981–1987, Zhao Ziyang 1987–1989, Jiang Zemin 1989–2002, Hu Jintao 2002–2012 and Xi Jinping since 2012). The modern position of the President of PRC was instituted in the 1982 Constitution in order to separate state and party power (apart from the Secretary and President, the other main leaders envisioned were the Premier and the

Chairman of the Central Military Commission). Only Li Xiannian (1983–1988) and Yang Shangkun (1988–1993) held such a separate presidential position. In 1982, the post of the Chairman of the Central Military Commission of PRC was instituted alongside the Chairman of the Central Military Commission of the CPC—another example of state post alongside a party post, although it was always held by the same person. Deng Xiaoping held the very important party position from 1981 to 1989, and the state position from 1983 to 1990. Jiang Zemin took over both positions and in 1993 consolidated these with the aforementioned positions of President and Party Secretary. After Jiang, both Hu and Xi hold all of these positions simultaneously effectively centralizing the political power in China far beyond levels found in the presidential system in the USA. Additionally, the 2018 constitutional change centralized this power further by removing the two-term limit of the presidential tenure (Berger 2018).

In such a system, comparisons to electoral politics in western countries are very problematic. The closest analogy would be the intra-party faction rivalry, but these processes are necessarily opaque in nature and therefore difficult to analyze. A more attractive option is to observe the programs of the ruling cadre. Here we can notice some shifts toward greater protection of labor in the Hu and Xi presidencies. In this, the concepts used in speeches or plenary session reports seem to have a far more consistent and symbolical nature than in the west. Hu accentuated the concepts of a *harmonious society* and a *moderately prosperous society*. Xi has signaled similar intentions and argued in favor of supply-side reforms and targeted poverty alleviation (Zhao 2016).

The formal political institutions are obviously vastly different from those found in Germany and the USA with a concentrated one-party political-structure intent to preserve its power monopoly—and the improvement of labor rights may be the means to that goal. In other words, while there is a serious problem with a lack of autonomous and independent representation of workers, the party leadership reacts to the possibility of strikes and labor activism by working to improve the position of labor, producing a situation which may in some respects even emulate the existence of independent unions.

Interactions with other drivers and the result

(a) Developmental strategy: in the Chinese case, transnational conditionality did not play a role in labor institutional changes, but the direct, formal political channel (of the single party intertwined with state) plays a dominant role in determining developmental strategies including the latest shift.
(b) Result of institutional change: all of this makes formal political channels one of the three channels of institutional change. The end result is dependent on all three: developmental strategies will be truly institutionalized if the power relations (which can be felt on the informal level) support it and if the path-dependent mechanisms are aligned with these two channels or weaker than them.

In terms of modes of change, deliberate institutional design has been able to gradually replace the iron rice-bowl *danwei* labor institutions with firstly a market-based system and secondly some semblance of modern labor protection. As we have seen, the primary backlash to reforms came from the specific interests of old insiders and new outsiders. However, it was not manifested through formal channels, nor could it have been, as the political monopoly of CCP was preserved through the insistence on only Party-led unions. This led to the already discussed dissociation of associational and structural labor power in China, which has in turn created the need to take labor interests into account regardless of the labor capacity to independently organize or even articulate these interests. Formal labor reforms were therefore implemented by the only real veto-player (CCP), which has needed to take a strong, if invisible, player (labor) into account. Unlike the US and German cases, all three channels in China point to a single mode of change, which is a specific form of layering.

In all, the three institutional change channels combined a one-party power monopoly path dependence (channel 1), a rising structural power of labor (channel 2) and the power of the formal political governance to institute large scale reforms (channel 3). Figure 8.8 summarizes the three processes.

Labor institutions in China have developed in the context of a stubbornly preserved one-party power monopoly, providing a principal

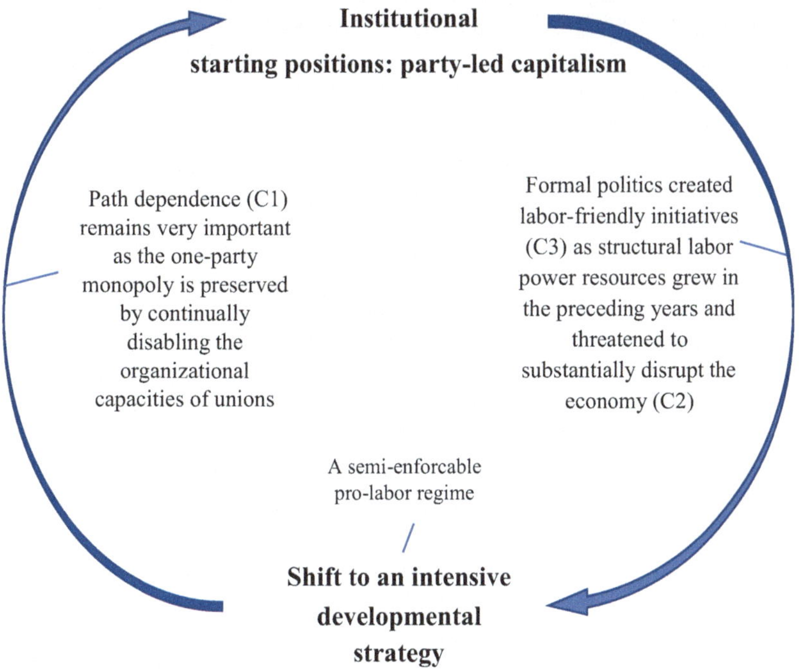

Fig. 8.8 The institutionalization of a shift to intensive strategy in China since the late 2000s

driving-force of path dependence (channel 1). For this monopoly to be preserved, the organizational or associational power of labor needed to be curbed and kept under Party control, making independent unions impossible. However, the structural power of labor grew along with the expansion of industry and trade surplus in goods that were the hallmarks of the extensive strategy of the period between 1980 and the late 2000s (channel 2). Since the late 2000s, the Party has instituted reforms (channel 3) toward an intensive strategy, increasing incomes, decreasing poverty, improving the formal regulation of labor and meandering on the possibility of collective bargaining.

8.4 Social Effects of Labor Institutions in China

In the previous two chapters, we started our brief surveys of social effects of labor institutions by showing the interrelation of GDP growth and unemployment. Figure 8.9 shows the real GDP growth and the unemployment rate in China since 1980. The high formal protection might lead us to expect slow and aberrant reactions of unemployment to changes in GDP (similar to the ones in Germany) and the low actual protections may lead us to suspect very sharp and quick reactions (similar to the ones in the USA).

What we see instead is a very slowly changing statistic of very low unemployment. If this official statistic were taken at face value, the conclusion might be that the full socialist employment only makes sense in the context of Fig. 8.3 (showing the shifts from agriculture into the secondary and tertiary sector). Here, the army of potential employees in industry and service comes not from the unemployed, but rather from the less developed rural areas of China. This is presumably why the unemployment rate remained stable even in the face of large migrant labor

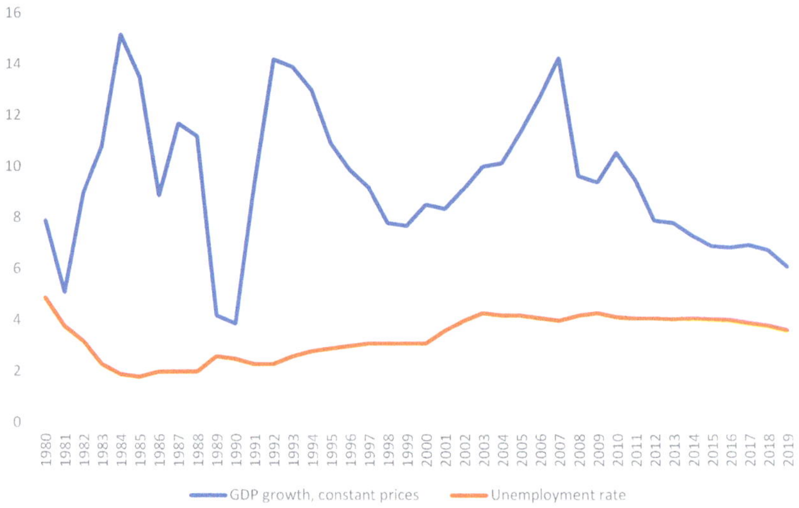

Fig. 8.9 Real GDP growth rate and unemployment in China. Data point for unemployment in 2019 is an IMF staff estimate (*Source of data* IMF [2020])

waves and changes in the speed of economic growth. However, the officially reported statistics of unemployment is often viewed with suspicion. A recent study used a representative sample of urban population to derive unemployment rate movement in China and assess significantly higher rates than those reported. The authors suggest that the actual rate of unemployment rose rapidly in the 1995–2002 period, in which state-owned enterprises shed a vast number of employees (with the SOEs employing 60% of total in 1995 and only 30% in 2002) and would reach the averages of 10.9% in the 2002–2009 period (Feng et al. 2015: 14–34). This uncertainty of official statistics makes it impossible for us to follow the relationship between GDP and unemployment as closely as we did in the previous two chapters.

Regardless of actual unemployment, a very positive trend in China's recent history has been the continued reduction of poverty. Measured in terms of the ubiquitous poverty level of $1.9 per capita per day consumption in 2011 PPP prices, the poverty in China has dramatically dropped from 40.3% as late as 1999 to a very low 0.5% in 2016 (World Bank 2020). This indicator's drop by 86% in the 1980–2013 period constitutes the sharpest decline of poverty in history (Jain-Chandra et al. 2018: 6). This trend has developed in the context of the vastly successful growth model described above, as sufficiently consistent high rates of economic growth enable such development.

However, the extensive developmental strategy in China before the mid-2000s has not been oriented toward egalitarian incomes, and the impressive absolute poverty reduction was accompanied by significant increases in income inequality. Individual income GINI as measured by the World Bank (2020) shows scarce data and estimates it at 32.2 in 1990, 35.2 in 1996, 38.7 in 1999, 42 in 2002, 43 in 2008, 43.7 in 2010, 42.2 in 2012 and 38.5 in 2016. These were very high inequality levels, surpassing even those found in the USA in the late 2000s, but showing a decreasing trend since 2010. The household GINI levels were even higher. As assembled for the World Bank in Sicular (2013), GINI levels were below 30 until 1986 and rose steadily (with a brief correction in the mid-1990s notwithstanding), reaching almost 50 by the global crisis of 2009 and showing some signs of a slight decrease afterward. The SWIID database also enables a continuous tracking of individual GINI (as it did in the previous two chapters). Figure 8.10 shows the disposable income (before taxes and transfers) and market GINI indices.

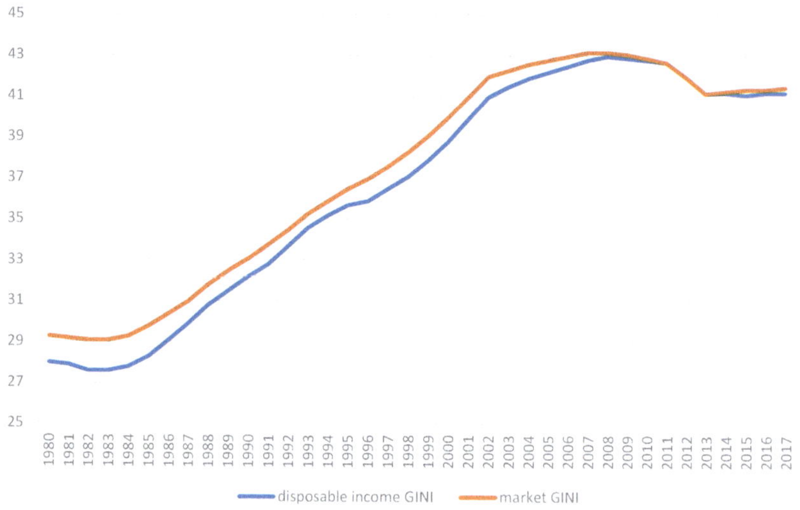

Fig. 8.10 Income inequality in China—GINI (*Source of data* SWIID 9.0 [Solt 2020])

Figure 8.10 enables us to discern two clear trends. Firstly, there is a general trend of steadily rising inequality far beyond the levels found in the USA and Germany. Secondly, the redistributive capacity of taxes and transfers is very weak compared to the previous two cases. The disposable income GINI has had a significant decline since 2008 (when it was at the highest point at 43), dropping to 41.2 in 2017. The market GINI index has followed the same trend, dropping from a high point of 43.2 in 2008 to 41.5 in 2017. If this data was taken at face value, it would suggest that redistribution in China is increasing, compared to the 2011–2013 period, when it was non-existent.

The deliberate reforms in line with the shift toward an intensive developmental strategy certainly played important roles in the reversal of the disposable income inequality trend. These include income tax reforms increasing the thresholds for its applicability, minimum wage hikes, the *dibao* social assistance system and other poverty-alleviation measures (Jain-Chandra et al. 2018: 10–11). More active redistribution, however, is not the only factor in play in the trend toward reducing inequality. The GINI indices in China have generally been greatly influenced by the urban-rural gap in incomes (Kotarski 2015), and the decline in inequality may also be influenced by the catch-up between regions. Spatial inequality explained 50% of overall income inequality in China in 2007, but its effects have been declining since (Zhuang and Li 2016: 9). Another important cause of income inequality is the education premium, which explains 25% of the urban-rural gap, but the effects of the skill premium are also declining as the low-skill sector wage growth has outperformed growth in high-skill sectors since 2009 (ibid.: 6). To survey the market effects, Fig. 8.11 shows the data on the pre-tax income shares of top 1% and bottom 50% adults available in the World Inequality Database.

These two income shares started in a relatively egalitarian structure with the top 1% earning 6.4% of total pre-tax income and the bottom 50% earning 26.7% of pre-tax income. The two curves have gradually moved closer. The share of the top 1% has slightly surpassed the share of the bottom 50% prior to the crisis of 2009 with the situation turned today showing a slight trend toward greater equality.

While the post-tax data is not available for China, it is indicative that the relative positions of the top 1% and the bottom 50% are at the same level in the USA only after the progressive taxation system has done its work, while this is the situation in China with gross income. In other

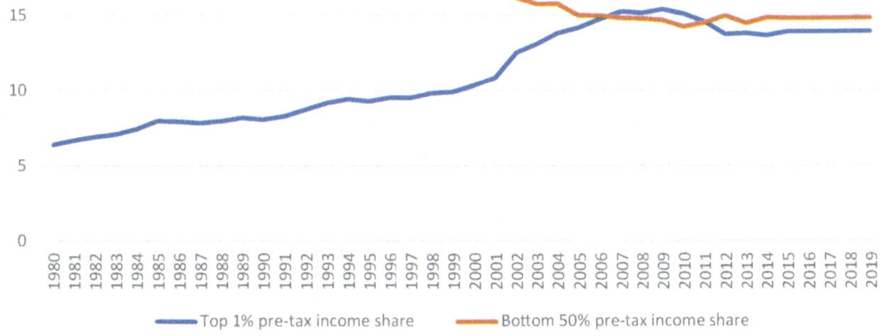

Fig. 8.11 Pre-tax income shares in China (*Source of data* WID [2020])

words, even though some of the GINI measurements have pointed to a greater income inequality in China than that found in the USA, the super-rich in the 1% are not as dominantly the ones that have been skewing the income.

In terms of functional distribution of income, the labor share of income remained in the 52–54% range in the 1994–2003 period, only to rapidly drop to 47% in the 2003–2011 period and recover to 51% by 2013 (ILO 2016: 18). Molero-Simarro uses the official data of the National Statistical Yearbooks to calculate somewhat different figures. The labor share of income is placed at 50% in 1992, with a slight improving tendency until the late 1990s, when it began a steady decline to some 43% in 2007 and recovered to approximately 46% in 2014. The capital share dropped from 39% in 1993 to 35% in 1999 and then steadily recovered to more than 40% by 2007 and returned in later years to approximately 38% in 2014 (Molero-Simarro 2016: 10). While these two measures point to slightly different ratios and periodizations, the same general trend can be discerned. The late 1990s to mid-/late 2000s was a period of diminishing labor share and growing capital share of income, with the situation somewhat reversing in recent years. These trends are consistent with the disposable income GINI markedly declining since 2008 and the top 1%/bottom 50% income shares reversing their polarizing tendencies since 2010. All of these trends demonstrate the effects to the significant change in the past decade, to which we have pointed throughout this chapter, as the labor institutions became increasingly pro-labor. Granted, labor itself played a side-role in these changes and the present analysis shows the importance of institutional design and path dependence in China. As argued above, this is the case as the effective manifestation of structural labor power throughout the Chinese material expansion has been curbed through the limits placed on labor organizations and therefore its associational power.

8.5 Conclusion

This chapter has sought to illustrate the framework from Chapter 5 by surveying labor-related institutional change with Chinese characteristics. To do so, we followed the three hypothesized channels (path dependence, institutional design and power relations) and their seven institutional change drivers. These have followed distinct patterns in accordance with conditions not found in liberal democracies. The channel of path dependence is largely tied into the basic power-related feedback loop in the

Chinese institutional framework. This is the political monopoly of the CCP, which will work to prevent any modes of development that could be perceived as a direct threat to the Party monopoly. It has curbed the associational power of labor by enabling only the Party-dependent trade unions and more recently by prosecuting labor rights activists. The preponderant channel in China is the deliberate design of institutions through formal political channels and it is increasingly shifted toward ideas of a middle-class creation, poverty alleviation, high-tech industries and other programs which are compatible with an intensive model of aggregate demand, focusing on domestic consumption.

The historical functioning of the power relations channel in China is a result of the dynamics between structural labor power (which has substantially grown over the years, driven by export-driven material expansion and technological catch-up) and the requirements of the extensive export-led model complementary with a low-wage regime. As the structural labor power grew and as the increasingly loud worker demands shifted toward distributional issues, an important piece of the extensive puzzle went missing as real wages significantly increased. This was compatible with an intensive developmental strategy which focused on developing domestic markets.

If these movements continue, the intensive developmental strategy of China will become institutionalized as a labor-friendly regime. In the long run of several decades, this may well spell out the conditions of a high-wage growth with an additionally diminished export competitiveness. In this context, the material expansion will certainly give way to a profit squeeze leading to both the financial expansion phase of the systemic cycle and the diminished structural labor power.

Literature

An acronym with capital. (2014, July 19). *The Economist*. Available at https://www.economist.com/finance-and-economics/2014/07/19/an-acronym-with-capital.

Ansar, A., Flyvbjerg, B., Budzier, A., & Lunn, D. (2016). Does Infrastructure Investment Lead to Economic Growth or Economic Fragility? Evidence from China. *Oxford Review of Economic Policy, 32*(3), 360–390.

Bartlett, W. (2007). The Western Balkans. In D. Lane & M. Myant (Eds.), *Varieties of Capitalism in Post-Communist Countries* (pp. 201–218). London: Palgrave Macmillan.

Berger, B. (2018). All That Xi Wants: China's Communist Party Is Trying to Reform the Country from the Top Down. *DGAP-Standpunkt*, 5. https://nbnresolving.org/urn:nbn:de:0168-ssoar-56259-4.

Bhattasali, D., Li, S., & Martin, W. J. (Eds.). (2004). *China and the WTO: Accession, Policy Reform, and Poverty Reduction Strategies*. World Bank Publications.

Buchen, C. (2007). Estonia and Slovenia as Antipodes. In D. Lane & M. Myant (Eds.), *Varieties of Capitalism in Post-Communist Countries* (pp. 65–89). London: Palgrave Macmillan.

Chan, C. K. C., & Hui, E. S. I. (2013). The Development of Collective Bargaining in China: From "Collective Bargaining By Riot" To "Party State-Led Wage Bargaining". *The China Quarterly, 217*, 221–242.

Chan, C. K. C., & Hui, E. S. I. (2014). The Dynamics and Dilemma of Workplace Trade Union Reform in China: The Case of Honda Workers' Strike. In X. Richet, V. Delteil, & P. Dieuaide (Eds.), *Strategies of Multinational Corporations and Social Regulations: European and Asian Perspectives* (pp. 203–217). Berlin: Springer.

Chan, J., & Selden, M. (2017). The Labour Politics of China's Rural Migrant Workers. *Globalizations, 14*(2), 259–271.

Chang, K., & Cooke, F. L. (2015). Legislating the Right to Strike in China: Historical Development and Prospects. *Journal of Industrial Relations, 57*(3), 440–455.

Chen, X. (2011). *Gender Wage Gap in China from 1989–2009*. Available at https://ir.vanderbilt.edu/handle/1803/10296.

China Internet Information Center. (n.d.). *The Non-Communist Parties*. Available at http://www.china.org.cn/english/features/38466.htm.

CIPG, CATL. (2016). *Keywords to Understand China*. Beijing: New World Press.

CLB. (2020). *Strike Map*. Available at https://maps.clb.org.hk/strikes/en.

Das, M., & N'Diaye, M. P. M. (2013). *Chronicle of a Decline Foretold: Has China Reached the Lewis Turning Point?* (No. 13-26). International Monetary Fund.

Ding, S., Knight, J., & Zhang, X. (2019). Does China Overinvest? Evidence from a Panel of Chinese Firms. *The European Journal of Finance, 25*(6), 489–507.

Estlund, C. (2017). *A New Deal for China's Workers?* Harvard University Press.

Feldmann, M. (2006). Emerging Varieties of Capitalism in Transition Countries: Industrial Relations and Wage Bargaining in Estonia and Slovenia. *Comparative Political Studies, 39*(7), 829–854.

Feng, S., Hu, Y., & Moffitt, R. (2015). *Long Run Trends in Unemployment and Labor Force Participation in China* (No. w21460). National Bureau of Economic Research.

Friedman, E. (2014). *Insurgency Trap: Labor Politics In Postsocialist China*. Cornell University Press.

Gallagher, M. E. (2005). *Contagious Capitalism: Globalization and the Politics of Labor in China*. Princeton University Press.

Gallagher, M. E. (2014). China's Workers Movement & the End of the Rapid-Growth Era. *Daedalus, 143*(2), 81–95.

Gallagher, M. E. (2016). The Social Relations of Chinese State Capitalism. In B. L. Liebman & C. J. Milhaupt (Eds.) *Regulating the Visible Hand? The Institutional Implications of Chinese State Capitalism* (pp. 225–250). Oxford University Press.

Gallagher, M. E. (2017). *Authoritarian Legality in China: Law, Workers, and the State*. Cambridge University Press.

Heilmann, S. (Ed.). (2017). *China's Political System*. Rowman & Littlefield.

Heritage (2020). *Graph the Data*. http://www.heritage.org/index/visualize.

Hersh, A. S. (2014). *China's State-Owned Enterprises and Nonmarket Economics. Testimony before the U.S.-China Economic and Security Review Commission*. Available at https://cdn.americanprogress.org/wp-content/uploads/2014/03/Hersh-testimony.pdf.

ILO. (2016). *Global Wage Report 2016/17: Wage Inequality in the Workplace*. Available at https://www.ilo.org/wcmsp5/groups/public/—dgreports/—dcomm/—publ/documents/publication/wcms_537846.pdf.

ILO. (2017). *Ratifications by Country*. Available at http://www.ilo.org/dyn/normlex/en/f?p=1000:11200:0::NO:11200:P11200_COUNTRY_ID:102871.

IMF. (2004, September 1). *At a Glance—China and the IMF*. https://www.imf.org/external/country/chn/rr/glance.htm.

IMF. (2018). *World Economic Outlook Database April 2018*. Available at http://www.imf.org/external/pubs/ft/weo/2018/01/weodata/index.aspx.

IMF. (2019). *Household Debt, Loans and Debt Securities*. Available at https://www.imf.org/external/datamapper/HH_LS@GDD/CHN.

IMF. (2020). *World Economic Outlook Database October 2020*. Available at http://www.imf.org/external/pubs/ft/weo/2020/02/weodata/index.aspx.

Jacobson, H. K., & Oksenberg, M. (1990). *China's Participation in the IMF, the World Bank, and GATT: Toward a Global Economic Order*. University of Michigan Press.

Jain-Chandra, M. S., Khor, N., Mano, R., Schauer, J., Wingender, M. P., & Zhuang, J. (2018). *Inequality in China—Trends, Drivers and Policy Remedies*. WP/18/127. International Monetary Fund.

Kotarski, K. (2015). Financial Deepening and Income Inequality: Is There Any Financial Kuznets Curve in China? The Political Economy Analysis. *China Economic Journal, 8*(1), 18–39.

Lardy, N. R. (2014). *Markets Over Mao: The Rise of Private Business in China*. Columbia University Press.

Lee, C. H. (2009). *Industrial Relations and Collective Bargaining in China*. Geneva: ILO. Available at http://ilo.ch/wcmsp5/groups/public/—ed_dialogue/—dialogue/documents/publication/wcms_158350.pdf.

Lee, C. K. (2007). *Against the Law: Labor Protests in China's Rustbelt and Sunbelt*. University of California Press.

Lee, M. I. H., Syed, M. M. H., & Xueyan, M. L. (2012). *Is China Over-investing and Does It Matter?* (No. 12–277). International Monetary Fund.

Li, M., & Walker, R. (2018). Targeting Social Assistance: Dibao and Institutional Alienation in Rural China. *Social Policy & Administration, 52*(3), 771–789.

Lin, Y. M. (2017). *Dancing with the Devil: The Political Economy of Privatization in China*. Oxford University Press.

Ling, Q. (2016). Introduction: The Survival and Collective Struggles of Workers in China's Coastal Private Enterprises since the 1990s. In H. Ren, Z. Li, & E. Friedman (Eds.). *China on Strike* (pp. 1–26). Haymarket Books.

Liu, S. D., & Shi, W. (2016). Worker Struggles and Factory Occupation in China During the Current Economic Crisis. *Social Movement Studies, 16*(3), https://doi.org/10.1080/14742837.2016.1259106.

Liu, J. et al. (2016). *The Communist Party of China: The Past, Present and Future of Party Building*. People's Publishing House.

Liu, G., & Lee, C. C. (2018). Financialization and Stagnant Capital Accumulation in China. *Bulletin of Monetary Economics and Banking, 21*(1), 23–32.

Lučev, J., & Babić, Z. (2013). Tipovi kapitalizma, ekspanzija neoliberalizma i socijalni učinci u baltičkim zemljama, Sloveniji i Hrvatskoj: komparativni pristup. *Revija Za Socijalnu Politiku, 20*(1), 1–19.

Milanovic, B. (2019). *Capitalism, Alone: The Future of the System That Rules the World*. Harvard University Press.

Molero-Simarro, R. (2016). Inequality in China Revisited: The Effect of Functional Distribution of Income on Urban Top Incomes, The Urban-Rural Gap and The Gini Index, 1978–2015. *China Economic Review*, 42.

Mussachio, A., & Lazzarini, S. (2016). Chinese Exceptionalism or New Global Varieties of State Capitalism. In B. L. Liebman & C. J. Milhaupt (Eds.), *Regulating the Visible Hand? The Institutional Implications of Chinese State Capitalism* (pp. 403–431). Oxford University Press.

Nölke, A., ten Brink, T., Claar, S., & May, C. (2015). Domestic Structures, Foreign Economic Policies and Global Economic Order: Implications from the Rise of Large Emerging Economies. *European Journal of International Relations, 21*(3), 538–567.

Nölke, A., & Vliegenthart, A. (2009). Enlarging the Varieties of Capitalism: The Emergence of Dependent Market Economies in East Central Europe. *World Politics, 61*(4), 670–702.

OECD (2020). *OECD data* [online]. Available at https://data.oecd.org/.

Peck, J., & Zhang, J. (2013). A Variety of Capitalism… With Chinese Characteristics? *Journal of Economic Geography, 13*(3), 357–396.
Pistor, K., Li, G., & Chun Z. (2016). The Hybridization of China's Financial System. In B. L. Liebman & C. J. Milhaupt (Eds.), *Regulating the Visible Hand? The Institutional Implications of Chinese State Capitalism* (pp. 353–376). Oxford University Press.
Sicular, T. (2013). The Challenge of High Inequality in China. *Inequality in Focus, 2*(2), 1–5.
Solt, F. (2020). *The Standardized World Income Inequality Database*. SWIID Version 9.0. https://fsolt.org/swiid/.
"The 13th Five-Year Plan". (2016). http://en.ndrc.gov.cn/newsrelease/201612/P020161207645765233498.pdf.
Visser, J. (2019). *ICTWSS Data Base*. version 6.0. Amsterdam: Amsterdam Institute for Advanced Labour Studies (AIAS), University of Amsterdam. June 2019. Open access database at https://www.ictwss.org/downloads.
Wang, Y. (2014). *Demystifying the Chinese Miracle: The Rise and Future of Relational Capitalism*. Routledge.
WEF. (2016d). *China*. Available at http://reports.weforum.org/feature-demonstration/files/2016/10/CHN.pdf.
Why China is creating a new "World Bank" (2014, November 11), *The Economist*. Retrieved from https://www.economist.com/the-economist-explains/2014/11/11/why-china-is-creating-a-new-world-bank-for-asia.
WID. (2020). *World Inequality Database*. Available at http://wid.world/.
Wilson, J. (2007). China's Transformation Towards Capitalism. In D. Lane & M. Myant (Eds.), *Varieties of Capitalism in Post-Communist Countries* (pp. 239–257). Hampshire: Palgrave Macmillan.
Witt, M. A. (2010). *China: What Variety of Capitalism?* (INSEAD Working Paper No. 2010/88/EPS). https://papers.ssrn.com/sol3/papers.cfm?abstract_id=1695940.
Witt, M. A., & Redding, G. (2013). Asian Business Systems: Institutional Comparison, Clusters and Implications for Varieties of Capitalism and Business Systems Theory. *Socio-Economic Review, 11*(2), 265–300.
Witt, M. A., & Redding, G. (2014). China: Authoritarian Capitalism. In M. A. Witt & G. Redding (Eds.), *The Oxford Handbook of Asian Business Systems* (pp. 11–32). Oxford: Oxford University Press.
WJP. (2018). *World Justice Project*. Available at https://worldjusticeproject.org/.
World Bank. (2016). *Deepening Health Reform in China: Building High-Quality and Value-Based Service Delivery—Policy Summary*. Washington, DC: World Bank Group. http://documents.worldbank.org/curated/en/800911469159433307/Deepening-health-reform-in-China-building-high-quality-and-value-based-service-delivery-policy-summary.
World Bank. (2020). *World Bank Open Data*. http://data.worldbank.org.

Wübbeke, J., Meissner, M., Zenglein, M. J., Ives, J., & Conrad, B. (2016). *Made in China 2025*. Mercator Institute for China Studies. Papers on China (2), 74.

Zhang, X., Yang, J., & Wang, S. (2011). China Has Reached the Lewis Turning Point. *China Economic Review, 22*(4), 542–554.

Zhao, L. (2016). China's 13th Five-Year Plan: Road Map for Social Development. *East Asian Policy, 8*(03), 19–32.

Zhuang, J., & Li, S. (2016). *Understanding Recent Trends in Income Inequality in the People's Republic of China* (Asian Development Bank Economics Working Paper Series (489)).

CHAPTER 9

The Three Cases and Their Patterns

Chapter 3 has identified five ways to discuss endogenous institutional change and the three predictive channels of path dependence, cyclical power relations and deliberate institutional design. These three channels were taken up by Chapters 4 and 5 to formulate a framework of institutional change and by Chapters 6, 7 and 8 to illustrate the framework through the analysis of labor institutional changes in the USA, Germany and China. The two descriptive tools of modes of change and evolutionary narratives will be utilized in this chapter to sum up and compare the three illustrative chapters.

In the first section, we will compare the labor institutions of the three cases, the three specific patterns of change they exhibited, and the roles played in these patterns by the three channels we identified. We will also use Thelen's notion of the modes of change to attempt to compare the three patterns across her criteria. The second section will interpret the institutional changes on the national level as portions of the world-system, compare their successfulness and use these changes to show the limitations of evolutionary narratives in the case of national-level institutions.

J. Lučev, *Systemic Cycle and Institutional Change*,
https://doi.org/10.1007/978-3-030-66053-6_9

9.1 Shapes of Labor Institutions; Patterns of Change

Having explored the national labor institutions of the USA, Germany, and China in the previous three chapters, we can now take stock and adopt a comparative stance. The simplest way to do so is by observing the relevant data as equilibria and compares the three cases in the two static points of 1980 and today via the most recent data. Table 9.1. does so in order to compare income inequality, the role played by labor expressed in bargaining coverage and union density, the role of household consumption in GDP and labor market regulation expressed by EPL indices.

Table 9.1 Changes in institutions and social effects

	USA 1980 or closest year	*USA most recent year*	*Germany 1980 or closest year*	*Germany most recent year*	*PRC 1980 or closest year*	*PRC most recent year*
Household final consumption % GDP	61.3%	68.2% (2018)	58.9%	52.3% (2019)	50.9%	38.5% (2018)
GINI	31.6	38.7 (2018)	25.9	29.4 (2018)	28	41.2 (2017)
Bargaining coverage	25%	11.2% (2018)	85%	54% (2018)	15% (1990, adjusted)	39.3% (2012, unadjusted)
Union density	22.3%	10.1% (2018)	34.9%	16.5 (2018)	58.6%	42.6 (2013)
Employment Protection Legislation for regular employment	0.09 (1985)	0.09 (2019)	2.5 (1985)	2.6 (2019)	–	3.26 (2012)
Employment Protection Legislation for temporary employment	0.25 (1985)	0.25 (2019)	5 (1985)	1.38 (2019)	–	1.75 (2012)

Sources World Bank (2020) (Household final consumption); OECD (2020) (Employment Protection indices); Visser (2019) (Bargaining coverage, adjusted; Union density); Solt (2020) (GINI, disposable income)

We can observe that the USA began the period of interest to us with the most consumption-led growth model at 61.3% GDP, with (West) Germany fairly close at 58.9% and China at a lower position of 50.9% and that their relative demand foci have substantially diverged with the USA even more consumption oriented today at 68.2%, but Germany and China considerably less so at 52.3 and 38.5%, respectively. Inequality data is not as readily available and continuous as we would like, and we have used the SWIID database to compensate. China and the USA stand out today as representative of very high-income inequality with Germany remaining relatively more equal (although gradually moving toward greater inequality). Labor organization in terms of union density data is formally highest in China,[1] mid-level in Germany and very low in the USA, with bargaining coverage starting high in Germany and relatively low in the USA and China and ending moderately high in Germany, somewhat lower (although more than doubled in 12 years) in China and very low in the USA. In terms of regulatory protection, the USA has had unchangingly very flexible employment laws, Germany has moved from high protection for regular and very high for temporary workers to a dualistic structure of high protection for regular and low for temporary workers, while China, having enacted modern labor laws in the interim, has formally high protection for regular and intermediate protection for temporary workers. Even in such cursory comparison, we could surmise that the labor markets showed clear tendencies toward liberalization in all three cases, but that this turn to free markets did not happen in a uniform manner. While such a static comparison of two equilibria states can be useful, it clearly misses the comparison of the processes which lead from one to the other equilibrium.

This thesis has argued for an in-depth analysis of institutional change, which went far beyond such limitations of static comparisons. We have firstly observed specific constellations of institutions through the Northian prism which encompasses institutions in their formal, informal, and avoidable aspects. In the USA, the avoidable aspect is particularly strong, as the unions are generally too underpowered to protect the low-wage workers even at the level of securing the enforcement of their employment contracts. The collective bargaining practices (treated here as informal

[1] As we have seen in the previous chapter, this data shows membership in the party-led ACTFU, which does not organize labor in the same sense as the unions in liberal democracies do.

institutions) are decentralized and slanted in favor of the employers, while regulations (formal institutions) are very flexible and free market oriented. In Germany, the avoidable aspect is not overly relevant as the formal institutions preserve the high protection at least for mainstream employment, while informal institutions (practices of collective bargaining) remain relatively centralized with outcomes dependent on the unions, which remain strong in manufacture. In China, the avoidable aspect is even more relevant than is the case with American labor institutions, as formal institutions are often treated as guidelines rather than rules and the collective bargaining practices are only slowly formed due to a lack of independent worker representation.

The changes in these institutions since the 1980s also followed distinct patterns—which we tracked through the three channels of path dependence, formal political pressures and systemic cycle-driven power resources. In the USA, the predominant channel was path dependence. The labor institutions were free market oriented to begin with and changes in the post-1980 period only exacerbated these tendencies. The power resources and systemic cycle driven channel could not overcome path dependence and orient the formal and informal institutions toward a labor-friendly regime as labor had low structural and associational power throughout the period of interest to us. The financial expansion only exacerbated this, resulting in a dysfunctional developmental strategy that favored the paradoxical combination of a domestic consumption-led growth model and a diminishing wage ratio of GDP. Finally, the formal political channel is designed to help political minorities resist reforms and the labor legislation was kept in a state which provided for a flexible regulation of labor and severely constricted the ability of unions to organize labor. The process of labor liberalization in the USA can be broken down into the seven separate drivers of change we identified and was under the influence of: initial institutional conditions of free market-oriented coordination; a long-term cumulative technological change favoring labor-saving techniques in industrial production (diminishing labor structural power); the systemic cycle which has: (a) driven the US economy into a financial expansion, (b) substantially expanded the US trade deficit as production for its market moved off-shore and has therefore (c) created the conditions for a growing superfluity of manufacturing labor and an accompanying decrease of labor union density; an extensive developmental strategy which is essentially a supply-side-oriented free market policy paradigm and finally, an absence of effective transnational conditionality or mechanisms of domestic politics geared toward large reforms.

In Germany, all three channels intertwined to produce the pronounced modern dualism of labor institutions. Path dependence worked in favor of labor veto power and the systemic cycle-power resources channel bifurcated power on the strong presence of unions (high associational power) in the industrial core and weak presence (low associational power) in the service sector. This set the stage for the third channel of deliberate institutional design through formal politics, which was used by the Schröder government to try to restore market efficiency by making labor institutions more flexible. This reform contributed to a move toward an extensive developmental strategy and was itself a compromise taking into account the strong position of core labor due to the first two channels and the less structurally and associationally strong labor on the margins. Breaking it down into seven drivers, the German labor liberalization through dualization is a result of: initial institutional conditions of a coordinated market economy (including high associational power of labor); long-term cumulative technological change favoring labor-saving techniques (diminishing labor structural power); the systemic cycle which put Germany in a phase of material expansion (increasing labor structural power) and in the context of which a developmental strategy could be chosen. This enabled a move from an intensive to an extensive developmental strategy coinciding with the introduction of the euro and the intensifying of the eurozone economy interaction with Germany—which in turn expanded the trade surplus (increasing labor structural power). These changes worked to increase the structural labor power in manufacturing, which remained a latent veto player necessitating a design (made possible by a political system which enables reforms) of an extensive strategy which circumvented the core labor and focused on the marginal labor as a target for flexibilization.

Finally, the two channels of path dependence and deliberate institutional design have proven crucial in institutional change in China. The channel defining the interactions of the systemic cycle and power describes the changes in structural power in labor, and as structural labor power has a consistent history of rising in China, the interests of labor were increasingly likely to be taken into account. However, as associational power is low due to a Party-led labor organization monopoly, labor has very little capacity to directly influence institutional change. Path dependence is important in keeping this capacity low as it provides the major neutralizer for the rising structural power of labor. The key element of path dependence in China in this respect is the position occupied by the Communist Party which strives to preserve its de facto political monopoly of power, including the prevention of independent labor organization. This allows the third channel to fully articulate, largely as developmental strategies, which remain the top-down led preserves of the formal political process led by the Party. The institutional changes have been directed toward an extensive developmental strategy in most of the post-1980 period but show pronounced tendencies toward an intensive shift in recent years. To break down this increase in labor protection into drivers: the specific type of a search for higher labor standards is a result of initial structures which favor the one-party monopoly of power (virtually disabling associational power of labor), long-term cumulative technological change favoring labor-saving techniques but a recent history of catch-up favoring a continued increase of labor use; the systemic cycle which enabled China to undergo a material expansion (increasing labor structural power), an increase in trade surplus as a result of labor low cost (increasing labor structural power) and an ongoing move from an extensive to an intensive developmental strategy (i.e. opposite to the German move) in order to provide an internal market as an alternative.

Comparing these patterns with modes of change (as discussed in Chapter 3), we can see that these two approaches may be somewhat compatible as this strand of literature primarily describes how rather than why institutional change takes place. Thelen's description of the change in American labor institutions is displacement, which evokes a clear break with old rules—or a deregulation pure and simple—enabled by low veto power of the defenders of old institutional arrangements and low discretion in institutional interpretation. The change in German labor institutions is discussed as an example of drift or preserving of the old form of institutions while also deliberately neglecting the old functions of institutions as the environment changes and renders the old form inefficient, while this change is enabled by the high veto power of the defenders of the old arrangements and high levels of discretion in institutional interpretation (Mahoney and Thelen 2010; Thelen 2012, 2014). One could argue against these descriptions on several points. Firstly, we could claim that all national-level institutional frameworks surely exhibit some signs of several modes of change—conforming not to a simple matrix or agent description, but to many overlapping levels of agent interactions. In this sense, it is entirely logical that Hacker and Pierson (2010) describe US labor institutional change as drift, as they observe the change as taking place at the level of formal politics. Secondly, and more specifically, American institutions changed through a very long process where a relatively deregulated labor was further deregulated, which in itself hardly evokes a clear break. If we accept the view of labor institutions as interconnected and ultimately intended to provide the rules for employment and work conditions, then we may also have some difficulties in using the simple matrix of agents, political contexts and institutional characteristics. The level of discretion in interpreting institutions on the operative level in the USA must be high rather than low as showed by the high importance of the avoidable aspect of labor institutions. Thirdly, German labor institutions exhibit a number of new measures intended to help the most vulnerable, which hardly constitutes deliberate neglect which supposedly accompanies institutional drift. However, such arguments could easily overshoot. Thelen provides us with a low-resolution cognitive map for comparing modes of change on a national level, and in this sense, she succeeded admirably. US labor institutions did undergo a clear (although slow and path dependent) pattern of deregulation, which enables her to group it under displacement. German labor institutions likewise did undergo the dualistic bifurcation of labor institutions, enabling her to focus on the continuation of the function of old rules in the industrial core and the lack thereof on the margins—and therefore to describe it as drift. While these patterns should not be taken literally and should be used with caution, they can help us understand and describe specific, national-level institutional change.

We have tried to increase the useful resolution offered by the modes of change by integrating the modes of change with the three channels of change. Table 9.2 summarizes this integration.

Table 9.2 Integrating modes and channels of change

	USA	*Germany*	*China*
Path dependence (C1)	Displacement	Drift	Layering
Cyclical power relations (C2)	Displacement	Drift	Layering
Institutional design (C3)	Drift	Displacement	Layering

In the US case, we have interpreted the two longer-term channels (path dependence and cyclical power relations) as examples of displacement and the shorter-term channel of deliberate institutional design as drift. In other words, both the diagnosis of Kathleen Thelen (displacement) and Hacker and Pierson (drift) are correct, once placed in their appropriate contexts in terms of timeframe and unit of analysis. In the German case the relationship of the path-dependent channel and the cyclical power-relations channel spelled out drift (with an all-out liberalization prevented by industrial labor power-bastions enforced both through material expansion and path dependence), but the crucial reforms also having been designed and enacted (suggesting active displacement and not passive drift at least in the fixed-term portion of the labor market). In each chapter, our second channel of institutional change has served to illustrate the shifts in power underlining episodes of change in labor markets. Here, the systemic cycle has helped us to offer an interpretation of the relationship between structure (institutional stability) and agency (institutional entrepreneurship) in the context of changing economic flows. With the channels of path dependence and deliberate institutional design often providing conflicting tendencies (as we can see in the Thelen-Hacker/Pierson dilemma), an important part is played by the political power of interested parties.

We were left only with the need to interpret the mode of change for labor institutions in China. It seems that Thelen's description of layering best describes the initial period of changes we analyzed in Chapter 8. The period of the early 1980s to mid-2000s saw China move to an extensive developmental strategy with increasingly lax labor regulation and incrementally reduced labor rights. The old iron rice bowl was broken, but the system still supported the coexistence of insiders (old industrial concentrations) and outsiders (particularly migrant labor). The turn to free markets in China in general started through a type of localized experimentation typical of layering in the Special Economic Zones. More specific to the labor institutions, the fledgling universal legal order (introduction of a unified labor law in 1995) was in many ways seen as a legalization of the lower order of outsider workers, as the labor contracts were a step down from the position of the *danwei* system. This layered, dualistic structure of the Chinese labor market persisted and evolved. With the outsider migrant labor increasing in importance (and structural power) through a vastly effective developmental strategy, it attempted to secure better conditions via collective organization and strikes. However, China continues to exhibit an old unchanging layer of institutions in which labor representation is a monopoly of the Communist Party (suggesting very low levels of associational power). The Party prefers to endow labor with rights in its own time and without independent pressures and it has been introducing various new measures enabling some basis for labor rights, collective bargaining and dispute settlement since the mid-2000s.

This has created exactly the type of conflict described by Thelen ideal-typically, as the increased knowledge of legal basis and use of existing mechanisms strengthened the ability of workers to self-organize and enabled a growth of pro-labor legal activists. However, the CCP remains a veto player *par excellence* and it has dealt with the conflict with a crack-down on the activists. The fundamental issue remains the question of the continued development of the structural power of labor without enabling an independent associational power structure to act as an ordered valve. This is essentially the layering conflict in labor institutions with Chinese characteristics. If the reforms prove successful and fully turn the Chinese growth model to intensive development and combine it with functional collective bargaining, we may in the future be in the position to analyze the period after the mid-2000s as a case in institutional conversion (as the solutions are devised in a top-down manner and institutions are redefined as well as replaced). However, at this juncture, we can still observe the conflict which is a long-term companion of layering.

It is also useful to note the differences between the approach in this book and the approach of the excellent Baccaro and Howell (2017). They are similar to this approach in their focus on labor institutions as central to capitalism, in choice of time period to observe change and the inclination to include power and growth models in the analysis of institutions. It is dissimilar in the chosen cases with only Germany being the common case, and in the authors' approach to capitalist processes. Baccaro and Howell take a page from the regulationist book and primarily argue the common trajectory of political economies in Western Europe, which they call the neoliberal convergence. They recognize that such convergence does not result in common institutional forms (ibid.: 15), and only seem to use the term convergence to describe the various tendencies toward increasing employer discretion. By the end of the book, the authors argue for an inherent instability of growth models (export-led and debt-led) that have developed on such basis. In contrast, the view of capitalism inspired by the systemic cycle theory enables a more historically informed approach. While Baccaro and Howell are entirely correct in assessing the growth models in the developed world as unstable, the theory developed here allows us to see all historic growth models as inherently unstable. The focus of systemic cycle theory could be interpreted as the identification of alterations in development strategies. What makes these alterations otherwise unobvious are the perpetual changes in circumstances, technology, predominant organizational forms and supranational economic relations. As expounded in Chapter 2, the systemic cycle theory focuses on the common elements across the various historical episodes and lands on material and financial expansions conducted in the context of extensive and intensive capitalism (Arrighi) and the four fixes alternating between crises of legitimacy and profitability (Silver). While the historicity of this theory may make it somewhat vague, the present book has reinterpreted its crucial categories in order to adapt it for the use of institutional change analysis. We can use it to operationalize the common trajectory but also to focus on systemic differences within it.

9.2 Interactions of the Systemic Cycle and Darwinistic Narratives

This section will first deal with the uses and limits of Darwinistic analogies in connecting global and national capitalisms in segment 9.2.1. It will then turn to interpreting our findings from the previous three chapters through a systemic cycle perspective in segment 9.2.2.

9.2.1 Using Darwinistic Analogies in Interpreting National-Level Changes

As we have seen in Chapter 3, evolutionary analogies are one of five common ways to conceptualize institutional change. To function, these analogies need to identify three phases: variation, selection and inheritance. The applicability of these three phases in connecting national and global capitalism is limited in the modern world, although they have certainly existed for most of modernity. We could claim that the historical periods of hegemonic transitions offered such examples. Different growth models provide a phase of variation (e.g. early entrepreneurship in Britain, nation-state-oriented capitalism in the Netherlands or late absolutism in Eastern Europe). A great power war until the end of World War II could be considered a definite selection phase of institutions. Here, growth models provide the tax and debt basis of financing a war machine (to simplify matters somewhat: Habsburgian v. Dutch, French and Swedish in the seventeenth century; British v. French in the late eighteenth century and early nineteenth century and German/Austro-Hungarian v. British, Russian, French and American in the first half of the twentieth century). Wars tended to drag on until the fiscal and organizational capabilities of one side is exhausted and the other side assumes the leading position in Europe, extracts war reparations, adds more territory or appropriates more colonies. Finally, we could argue for a phase of inheritance if a defeated side adopted some institutional elements of the winning side. A most recent example would be the defeat of Germany, Italy, and Japan in World War II, after which all three adopted (or were mandated to adopt) more democratic and more liberal-economic institutional frameworks. However, the advent of nuclear weapons pushed the world in a technological direction which would suggest a great power war would result in mutual annihilation. This prevents the crucial aspect of direct Darwinism in institutions. There is no direct destruction of inefficient institutional forms and this provides one of the possible causes for the preservation of socially damaging institutions (e.g. rampant corruption, clientelism or predatory politics) as long as they provide net-increases of power resources of those who are best positioned to change or stabilize them. As we have seen in Chapters 2 and 4, this also influences the shifts in capital accumulation cycles as it results in our modern and historically unprecedented state of radical divergence between economic and military power, which is a state favoring the continued global predominance of the US military capacity. This creates a notably different picture than could be discerned from the ideal-typical systemic cycle in Fig. 4.1, which is notably evolutionary in terms of winning institutional solutions and developmental strategies (intensive-extensive). In place of sharp distinctions of winners and losers in the competition for hegemonic (or central) position, the modern world produces a slow crawl where the lost edge in productivity is punished in the political or military sense only with a substantial and increasing delay. It seems that Wallerstein's understanding of hegemonies as brief moments is increasingly relevant with a prolonged following phase of losing various elements of dominance. Currently, the US military is still by far the largest, but its ability to finance large overseas missions or gather large alliances is diminished, suggesting a limited use for military capacity.

However, there are indirect ways in which the phases of variation, selection, and inheritance may play a role in national capitalisms. As we have seen in Chapter 3, Steinmo sees ideas as a type of variation producing mutations. This falls outside of the scope of the present thesis which opted to focus on power, systemic cycle, path dependence and deliberate institutional design. If we had focused on ideas, we would likely attempt to explain the genesis of the Hartz Commission plan as an attempt to copy the existing flexicurity solutions and the obstinance of US and Chinese reforms to outside ideas.[2] Research based on such an analogy could explore the flow of ideas within the epistemic communities and international organizations. In the context of policy promoters like the EU, OECD, IMF and the World Bank, it would certainly prove relevant in analyzing more vulnerable and smaller states, but our research did not point to an important role of transnational conditionality in the three selected cases. The evolutionary analogy is more likely to resonate with the present thesis through a more subtle and systemic-cycle-oriented interpretation of relative successfulness of specific institutional sets and changes, to which we now turn.

9.2.2 Interpreting National Changes as Elements of the Systemic Cycle

World-systemic analysis interprets the world-system as a world-wide division of labor which has a developed, industrialized core (exporting manufactured products high in the supply chain) and an underdeveloped periphery (exporting primary products). If we are looking for indicators of relative world-systemic successfulness, we could do worse than to analyze the mutual trade relations of the three economies in question. There are six possible directions of trade (US exports into China and Germany, German exports into China and the USA and Chinese exports into the USA and Germany), and the latest available data from Harvard Economic Complexity Atlas (all for 2018) can help us track their value and composition. The USA runs trade deficits against both Germany (exports are valued at $58 billion and imports at $134 billion) and China (exports

[2] With Barack Obama being denigrated as a European Socialist by his opponents during the drive for the Affordable Care Act, and the infamous Chinese Document no. 9 from 2013 which was a CCP internal document warning against the dangers of the spread of Western values like universal rights, independent judiciary, free press, constitutional democracy, etc Buckley (2013).

at $120 billion and imports at $455 billion[3]). Germany and China are relatively balanced, with a more moderate advantage of China (German exports into China were at $87.3 billion and imports at $110 billion). The composition of these exports is consistent with traditional conceptions of patterns of trade between developed economies, as all six routes are dominated by exports of machinery and transports—most notably in German exports to China (67.9%), to the USA (57%) and Chinese exports to Germany (52.2%) and the USA (51.6%), but less pronounced in US exports to Germany (37.7%) and China (36.2%). In principle, all other significant categories are also manufactured goods or chemicals. The only exception is US exports to China which have a substantial primary goods proportion as 24.8% are either agricultural products, minerals, stone or metals (CID 2020). Taking their mutual trade as representative of competitiveness and capacity, it would seem that between the three national capitalism cases, the highest position on the global supply chain is occupied by Germany, and the lowest by the USA.

During the Trump administration, there was a notable trade confrontation, particularly toward China, and particularly in 2018/2019. It could be argued that this has been a response to the strategic improvements in China's economy and trade. Made in China 2025 aimed to increase the technological complexity of manufacturing while Belt and Road actively develops closer economic ties with strategic partners. These strategies may have caused some hegemonic apprehension in the USA (Kim 2019; Kwan 2020). However, while the results of this shock are not yet entirely visible, they have certainly hurt both parties (Itakura 2020). Likewise, the COVID-19 pandemic of 2020 has caused another shock to global economy and trade. As of October 2020, it seems that Chinese exports are recovering far more quickly than those of USA (WTO 2020). Therefore, it seems that the established hierarchy of complexity is likely to be maintained. It may be a counter-intuitive conclusion from the point of view of traditional Wallersteinian approach to world-systems, which saw the relative positions within the world-system as relatively fixed. The original positions of the core-type economic development in the USA and the periphery-type in China would be expected to replicate themselves longitudinally. However, these conclusions are consistent with the systemic cycle theory of this thesis, which built upon Arrighi and

[3]This suggests that the US deficit was dominated by its deficit with China in 2018 (almost a half of the value).

Silver. Firstly, the systemic cycle theory conceptualizes the world-system as dynamic and dependent on various national-level strategies. In this conceptualization, a successful strategy produces a shift in the relative positions of economies. Secondly, the major predictor is the phase of the systemic cycle. The economy that was the global leader in production and trade (USA) is predicted to eventually exhaust the profitable options in such activities and enter the phase of the financial expansion, which brings a form of deindustrialization and conceivably, a slide back down the global supply chain. Eventually, the weakening economic position leads to political results including a more multipolar world and possibly, internal destabilization. Silver and Payne (2020) have recently pointed to the controversial response to COVID-19 and the wave of US protests of 2019/2020 as indicators of a deepening hegemonic crisis. In all of this, large economies undergoing a material expansion face a more interesting situation in which vastly different institutional pathways are possible. China and Germany are two cases which were analyzed in this thesis. Their economies encompass complex solutions which spell out their unique positions. We first briefly describe the general puzzles of these two economies and then describe the ways in which our approach (i.e. three channels, seven drivers) made their institutions comparable to each other and the US framework.

The Chinese development combined strict control in areas of interest such as capital flows with rapid liberalizations in labor markets. This selective, but massive turn to a novel form of capitalism was conducted in the context of a completely and persistently closed political environment providing us with an oddity in transitional studies. Post-socialist countries in Central and Eastern Europe (much of former Soviet space notwithstanding) have for the most part constructed functional democracies. Many former Soviet republics are formally democracies, but often sport political elites which dabble in autocratic governing style. However, both of these variants accept at least the normative ideal of a liberal democracy, which has in Fukuyamesque manner accompanied the economic transition in the vast majority of countries undergoing transition in the post-1989 period. China has on the other hand kept its de facto one-party system even as the sequential and managed economic liberalization attracted capital. Its exports sky-rocketed under a favorable political climate, in which political success is connected to the personal involvement with an export increase. An independent labor organization is prohibited through a single party-controlled trade union umbrella—ACTFU (Clarke et al. 2004; Chan and Hui 2014). Its society has grown more unequal, with a period in which it overtook even the US levels. Following the occidental normative perspective, one could expect this structure of asymmetrical freedoms (economic freedom/political repression) to collapse either way: either for the prolonged economic growth to spill into a growing demand for democracy or for a stifling political regime to slowly suffocate the free economic growth.[4] The relevant scenario from our point of view is the maturation of Chinese economy. This phase of its development has occurred in the context of what Arrighi would interpret as a terminal crisis of the US-led finance expansion. The reforms in China entail several processes: reducing the role of exports in its economy, more expensive labor which translates into larger household demand, supply-side reforms which must cut excess production capacity created under the old extensive development strategy which consisted of export-led growth benefiting

[4] Acemoglu and Robinson think that the closed political top-heavy economic system (extractive institutions) must eventually push China into a stifling growth regime Acemoglu and Robinson (2013: 442 and passim). With the standard economic growth models (Solow-Swan), this is not inconceivable. Continuous technological breakthroughs are necessary for continued high growth rates. However, there are at least two reasons why this prognosis seems inapplicable, at least as it concerns innovations. Firstly, Chinese research and development is not stagnant in the least. The number of patents applied for each year is growing, and now dwarfs the numbers found elsewhere. In 2015, the number of patent applications was almost as high as the combined numbers of the USA, Japan and Korea WIPO (2016: 12). This suggests that the technological innovation atmosphere may have moved substantially away from the catch-up model. Secondly, the standard growth models via Acemoglu and Robinson assume a closed economy, with no new technological innovations being developed outside it. This is obviously not true, as the global system allows for a free flow of patents. In short, economic growth may be measured nationally, but the technological innovations that support it are global, and will presumably continue to be global. Therefore, China will not necessarily suffer from a growth slump caused by non-existent technological innovations. Even if it would cease to produce worthwhile inventions (which it will most probably not), it would still be able to utilize innovations from abroad, except in the event of global wars (which are also not likely to occur—see Lučev 2014). China may be facing a challenging situation in the Schumpeterian sense of innovation, i.e. in creative destruction that Acemoglu and Robinson (2013: 445 and passim) also take issue with. The issue is the continued functioning of capitalism if the government persists in choosing winners and losers rather than allowing the market to level the playing field. Here, the faith in the continued growth potential of unfettered markets (i.e. of Schumpeterian creative destruction) seems normative and hinges on an idealized view of free markets. Remarkable Chinese growth and an institutional mix which seems aberrant from the Western point of view (as the Acemoglu and Robinson approach shows) must be viewed on its own merits.

from very abundant labor and low costs, eventually more open capital markets, but a continued closed political system.

The German way seems to point to organizing the economy through the European Union led by Germany itself as the productivity motor. Here we have a vast experiment in levels of economic regulation through which the traditional welfare state is deconstructed, and many relevant macroeconomic decisions removed from the agenda of individual states. Namely, most aspects of social, health, labor, and military policies are left to the discretion of the individual states. However, the ways in which crisis response is constricted decisively influences these areas as most individual responses are prevented or severely restricted (tariff protectionism, individual monetary response within the eurozone and active anti-cyclical fiscal policy). These constrictions leave only the slow and arduous process of improving competitiveness through falling real wages as a crisis response, while the fiscal responsibilities of states in all of the recounted "untouched policies" are often cut. The member states are encouraged to increase the competitiveness (e.g. through the Euro + pact) which can under these conditions only mean a liberalization of the labor market (or flexicurity, as one form of this process is affectionately named). This is a very roundabout way to indirectly ensure the wide-spread pressures toward the German labor solution—i.e. extensive developmental strategy. In particular, the German led EU can be interpreted as a formation of a new, tighter economic nexus, which indirectly exerts the downward pressure on the real wages of its immediate periphery—increasing the competitiveness of European exports. This pressure is issued through a form of macroeconomic agenda setting where all crisis responses are eliminated, save for the ones pertaining to real wages. The VofC agenda enables the location of institutional complementarities, which turn a nominally relatively modest institutional influence of the EU into a substantial force of institutional change in crisis circumstances.

We have used the framework from Chapter 5 to open the three cases to analysis, rather than to forgo them to the fog of ostensible exceptionalism. The framework sought to establish the theoretical basis for the connection between the systemic cycle and institutional change. To do so, it identified three channels of institutional change. The first channel of path dependence is a tendency for the initial institutional positions to perpetuate, suggesting that types of change are constricted with the institutions already in place. In terms of institutional starting positions, Germany is historically a paradigmatic case of the Coordinated Market Economy which is a position justified by its traditional welfare state, corporatist institutions, protected labor markets and strong unions. However, Germany has more recently undergone changes which have resulted in a dualized economy more open to free markets. Here, the entire apparatus of the CME is used to protect the core industry workers while the more vulnerable groups are left to the market. The USA is a paradigmatic case of an LME and its tendency toward liberalization has only been exacerbated in the recent years as no strong labor organization exists which could prevent it. Finally, China is an unclear variety of capitalism as the VofC framework was intended only to describe developed countries, but its institutional tradition points primarily to the strong party at the core with party insiders networked across management and union structures. The issue there is the slow and arduous process of the associationally weak and structurally strong labor making its influence felt in policymaking. Another channel is the deliberate design of institutions under the influence of formal political mechanism of transnational conditionality and domestic politics, with the latter being able to provide crucial pressure in Germany (compromising with the other two) and China (benefiting from path dependence), and often being conspicuously absent in labor issues in the USA.

The crucial interplay occurs in the systemic cycle inspired channel, between the phase of the systemic cycle, power relations and developmental strategies. In terms of power resources, we have utilized the distinction of associational and structural power of labor. Associational power refers to the ability of unions to organize labor. The union density has been falling in all the three cases and is the highest in China, significantly lower in Germany and the lowest in the USA. However, as the analysis of informal institutions has shown, the highest leverage of unions would certainly be found in Germany (even though the power is bifurcated) as the collective bargaining practices are centralized. China, on the other hand, treats its unions as a part of the Communist Party and they do not yet have the functions we would expect in the West. The structural power refers to bargaining power of labor (and in practice, primarily industrial labor), which is primarily derived from its importance to the economy. Structural power is influenced by a number of factors and we focused on the phase of the systemic cycle, developmental strategy, technological shifts and trade relations. The systemic cycle increased structural labor power in China and Germany (as they underwent material expansions) and reduced structural labor power in the USA (financial expansion). In this context, the developmental strategies and trade relations were developed with the successful post-2001 extensive strategy of Germany providing a trade surplus and therefore an additional increase in structural labor power in industry, and a long-standing extensive strategy doing the same for China until challenged in the last decade. An intensive material expansion which is currently developing will produce a balanced trade position, if successful, and a trade deficit if unsuccessful. Currently, China is still running a comfortable trade surplus, which is helping create a divergence of low associational and high structural power.

Literature

Acemoglu, D., & Robinson, J. A. (2013). *Why Nations Fail: The Origins of Power, Prosperity and Poverty*. New York, NY: Crown Business.

Baccaro, L., & Howell, C. (2017). *Trajectories of Neoliberal Transformation: European Industrial Relations Since the 1970s*. Cambridge: Cambridge University Press.

Buckley, C. (2013, August 19). China Takes Aim at Western Ideas. *New York Times*. https://www.nytimes.com/2013/08/20/world/asia/chinas-new-leadership-takes-hard-line-in-secret-memo.html.

Chan, C. K. C., & Hui, E. S. I. (2014). The Dynamics and Dilemma of Workplace Trade Union Reform in China: The Case of Honda Workers' Strike. In X. Richet, V. Delteil, & P. Dieuaide (Eds.), *Strategies of Multinational Corporations and Social Regulations: European and Asian Perspectives* (pp. 203–217). Heidelberg: Springer.

CID (2020). *The Atlas of Economic Complexity*. Available at https://atlas.cid.harvard.edu/explore.

Clarke, S., Lee, C. H., & Li, Q. (2004). Collective Consultation and Industrial Relations in China. *British Journal of Industrial Relations, 42*(2), 235–254.

Hacker, J. S., & Pierson, P. (2010). *Winner-Take-All Politics: How Washington Made the Rich Richer–And Turned its Back on the Middle Class*. New York, NY: Simon and Schuster.

Itakura, K. (2020). Evaluating the impact of the US–China trade war. *Asian Economic Policy Review, 15*(1), 77–93.

Kim, M. (2019). A Real Driver of US–China Trade Conflict: The Sino–US Competition for Global Hegemony and its Implications for the Future. *International Trade, Politics and Development, 3*(1), 30–40.

Kwan, C. H. (2020). The China–US Trade War: Deep-Rooted Causes, Shifting Focus and Uncertain Prospects. *Asian Economic Policy Review, 15*(1), 55–72.

Lučev, J. (2014). How Long Before NATO Aircraft Carrier Force Projection Capabilities are Successfully Countered? Some Effects of the Fiscal Crises. *Croatian International Relations Review, 20*(71), 121–151.

Mahoney, J., & Thelen, K. (Eds.). (2010). *Explaining Institutional Change: Ambiguity, Agency, and Power*. Cambridge: Cambridge University Press.

OECD. (2020). *OECD Data* [Online]. Available at: https://data.oecd.org/.

Silver, B. J., & Payne, C. R. (2020). Crises of World Hegemony and the Speeding up of Social History. In P. Dutkiewicz, T. Casier, & J. A. Scholte (Eds.), *Hegemony and World Order: Reimagining Power in Global Politics* (pp. 17–31). London: Routledge.

Solt, F. (2020). *The Standardized World Income Inequality Database*. SWIID Version 9.0. https://fsolt.org/swiid/.

Thelen, K. (2012). Varieties of Capitalism: Trajectories of Liberalization and the New Politics of Social Solidarity. *Annual Review of Political Science, 15*, 137–159.

Thelen, K. (2014). *Varieties of Liberalization and the New Politics of Social Solidarity*. Cambridge: Cambridge University Press.

Visser, J. (2019, June). *ICTWSS Data Base*. Version 6.0. Amsterdam: Amsterdam Institute for Advanced Labour Studies (AIAS), University of Amsterdam. Open access database at: https://www.ictwss.org/downloads.

WIPO. (2016). *WIPO IP Facts and Figures 2016*. http://www.wipo.int/edocs/pubdocs/en/wipo_pub_943_2016.pdf.

World Bank. (2020). *World Bank Open Data*. http://data.worldbank.org.

WTO. (2020). *Monthly Trade Trends: July 2020—August 2020*. Updated on 23 October 2020. https://www.wto.org/english/res_e/statis_e/daily_update_e/month_latest.pdf.

CHAPTER 10

Conclusions

This book set out to provide a theoretical solution to the problem of endogenous institutional change by bridging the gap between national and global capitalism. We have argued that the systemic cycle theory can be fruitfully used in a multi-theoretical framework which encompasses power resource theory, path dependence, and formal political channels. The conceptual gap this thesis is attempting to resolve is the issue faced by the dominant comparative capitalism schemes, which focus on the microeconomic, ideal-typical, and national and can therefore not explain the relevant change drivers as endogenous. These theories rely on exogenous events instead. The central methodological maneuver of this thesis was to elevate the unit of analysis to the transnational level in order to capture the many drivers of change that occur beyond the limits of a nation-state.

To do so, we needed to reconstruct a theory which could handle two distinct levels: a global-level theory of economic change and a national-level theory of institutions. The first element needed to be able to explain the variegation of pressures on different geographic locations and at different historical points. This in itself is an ambitious task and we found a theory which could manage it in the systemic cycle. Chapter 2 has analyzed the systemic cycle and its central dilemmas including the overly supply-sided approach and an inability to handle notions of institutional variety. Chapter 3 has surveyed institutional thought and pointed out the

J. Lučev, *Systemic Cycle and Institutional Change*,
https://doi.org/10.1007/978-3-030-66053-6_10

general tendencies, strengths, and shortcomings in new institutionalism, including the central issue of an under-conceptualized endogenous institutional change. Chapter 4 has argued that the deficiencies and strong points of Arrighi and new institutionalism could plausibly be compatible and mutually beneficial if they were adequately developed. It proceeded to develop the two central regime types in Arrighi through Keynesian notions of aggregate demand structures to provide useful categories. In particular, the intensive and extensive capitalism is interpreted in terms of developmental strategies in which aggregate demand management is focused on exports (extensive) or the generation of internal demand (intensive).

Chapter 5 has offered a framework of institutional change which integrated technological change, path dependence, power resources, phases of the systemic cycle, developmental strategies, trade relations, and deliberate institutional design. These were organized according to the timeframe necessary for the development of processes they entail and ultimately grouped into three channels of institutional change: channel 1—path dependence; channel 2—cyclical power relations; and channel 3—institutional design. Channel 3 pertains to explicit reforms dependent on both domestic political processes and international conditionality—mechanisms which are themselves well researched in mainstream political science and sociology. Channel 1 refers to a more specific concept of path dependence, itself also well explored within the confines of historical institutionalism. However, channel 2 provides an original concept as it combines the reinterpreted systemic cycle categories (reinterpreted in Chapter 4) with power resources and technological changes. This framework has enabled us to conceptually transcend three important rifts and therefore supply an improvement in the theory of institutional change—firstly, we surpassed the national fetters of institutional analysis by embedding developmental strategies and trade relations into a framework dealing with national-level institutional change; secondly, we encompassed growth models and demand management into a traditionally supply-side oriented analysis and thirdly, we focused on power and its many possible manifestations. Specifically, the three channels of change all deal with different aspects of power in institutional change: path dependence depends on power feed-back mechanisms and manifests as a pressure to perpetuate the existent institutional development; cyclical power relations describe the interactions of the organizational capacity and structural power resources (i.e. leverage); and institutional design designates the most observable aspect of power as decision making.

Chapters 6, 7, and 8 have applied this framework to the illustrative cases of labor institutions in the USA, Germany, and China since 1980. While all three institutional sets were subject to liberalizations, each displayed a specific dynamic of institutional change and the three channels interacted to produce idiosyncratic institutional results. In the USA, all three mechanisms reinforce each other gradually pushing toward lower labor power and less labor-friendly institutions. In Germany, path dependence was exacting pressures toward a continued high labor power and a labor-friendly institutional set, while power relations produced a dualist formation in which labor power was concentrated in industry. This was exploited by the third channel, and a dualist regulatory structure was deliberately constructed to achieve greater competitiveness—with liberalization of the labor market largely relegated to the low labor power sectors. In China, path dependence primarily preempted the ability of labor to organize (very low associational power), while the continued material expansion created substantial hypothetical leverage for labor (increasing structural power). This dilemma was resolved through the third channel with a succession of labor-friendly reforms.

Finally, Chapter 9 has taken stock of the three illustrative chapters in order to compare their patterns of change. In terms of modes of change, the existing literature is not uniform in their diagnosis as Thelen interpreted the labor liberalization in the USA as *displacement*, while Hacker and Pierson argue for *drift*. The framework developed here helped us to produce a more nuanced and systematic approach to modes of change by using the timeframe hierarchy and specific mechanisms of the three channels of change. Both versions of descriptions of the mode of change in US labor institutions were found to be sound, but at different levels of analysis—with *displacement* at the level of channels 1 (path dependence) and 2 (cyclical power relations) and *drift* at the level of channel 3 (institutional design). Likewise, we found German institutional changes to be a combination of *drift* (channel 1 and 2) and *displacement* (institutions) (channel 3), while *layering* dominates in all three levels in Chinese institutional changes, with a possibility of a future development into *conversion*.

The end-result is a study which focuses on shifts in power and the connections between power, global economic flows, and developmental strategies, alongside more familiar themes of path dependence and formal politics. Further research might fruitfully expand into ideational change or analyze the effects on smaller labor markets, which have necessarily eluded us as we focused on three major international economy players. In any event, this book is an attempt to add to the studies dealing with endogenous institutional change, as one of the most obstinate issues in contemporary social sciences. The fundamental maneuver of applying systemic cycle theory to institutional change may seem bold. However, if we are even to attempt to tackle the obstinate problems, we must surely look for bold solutions.

Appendix: Curriculum Vitae

Josip Lučev was born in 1986 in Novo Mesto, Slovenia. Following the completion of primary and secondary education in Slovenia, he enrolled at the Faculty of Political Science in Zagreb to study political science in 2005. There, he attained his B.A. degree in Political Science in 2009, his M.A. degree in Political Science in 2010. He earned another M.A. degree in Social Policy at the Faculty of Law in Zagreb in 2013 and his Ph.D. in 2020 at the Faculty of Political Science. His work experience is primarily in higher education teaching. He worked as an external associate at the Faculty of Political Science from 2010 to 2014; he was employed at the Dag Hammarskjöld University College of International Relations and Diplomacy from 2015 to 2019, and at Libertas International University in 2019/20. He is currently employed at the Faculty of Political Science at the University of Zagreb. His teaching activities have centered on political economy, management and institutional change across more than 20 courses. He has authored and co-authored dozens of papers, including peer-reviewed scientific papers, chapters, book reviews and conference papers. He also has substantial experience in academic editing and review, having served as one of the editors in *little Leviathan* (*mali Levijatan*), executive editor in *International Studies* (*Međunarodne studije*), as peer reviewer for *Croatian Political Science Review* (*Politička misao*), *Croatian International Relations Review* and *International Studies,* and a contributing editor for *Algoritam* and *Jesenski i Turk*. He also has research

J. Lučev, *Systemic Cycle and Institutional Change*,
https://doi.org/10.1007/978-3-030-66053-6

experience in an international context, having cooperated with universities in Budapest, Wrocław and Salzburg. Josip Lučev is a member of Croatian Mensa and Rotary Club Zagreb Metropolitan. He is a husband and father.

Literature

Acemoglu, D., & Restrepo, P. (2017). *Robots and Jobs: Evidence from US Labor Markets* (NBER Working Paper Series). Available at https://www.nber.org/papers/w23285.pdf.

Acemoglu, D., & Robinson, J. A. (2005). *Economic Origins of Dictatorship and Democracy*. Cambridge: Cambridge University Press.

Acemoglu, D., & Robinson, J. A. (2013). *Why Nations Fail: The Origins of Power, Prosperity and Poverty*. New York: Crown Business.

Adams, J. (2011). The Political Economies of Slovenia and Croatia: Does EU and Eurozone Membership Play a Role at All? In *EUSA 2011 Conference*. Boston.

Aglietta, M. (1979/2015). *A Theory of Capitalist Regulation: The US Experience*. London: Verso Books.

Aglietta, M., & Rebérioux, A. (2005). *Corporate Governance Adrift: A Critique of Shareholder Value*. Cheltenham: Edward Elgar Publishing.

Akamatsu, K. (1962). A Historical Pattern of Economic Growth in Developing Countries. *The Developing Economies, 1*(s1), 3–25.

Aldrich, J. (2004). The Discovery of Comparative Advantage. *Journal of the History of Economic Thought, 26*(3), 379–399.

Amable, B. (2003). *The Diversity of Modern Capitalism*. Oxford: Oxford University Press.

An acronym with capital. (2014, July 19). *The Economist*. Available at https://www.economist.com/finance-and-economics/2014/07/19/an-acronym-with-capital.

J. Lučev, *Systemic Cycle and Institutional Change*,
https://doi.org/10.1007/978-3-030-66053-6

Ansar, A., Flyvbjerg, B., Budzier, A., & Lunn, D. (2016). Does Infrastructure Investment Lead to Economic Growth or Economic Fragility? Evidence from China. *Oxford Review of Economic Policy, 32*(3), 360–390.

Arrighi, G. (1994/2010). *The Long Twentieth Century: Money, Power, and the Origins of Our Times*. London: Verso Books.

Arrighi, G. (2007). *Adam Smith in Beijing*. London: Verso.

Arrighi, G., Hamashita, T., & Selden, M. (Eds.). (2003). *The Resurgence of East Asia: 500, 150 and 50 Year Perspectives*. London: Routledge.

Arrighi, G., & Moore, J. W. (2001). Capitalist Development in World Historical Perspective. In R. Albritton, M. Itoh, R. Westra, & A. Zuege (Eds.), *Phases of Capitalist Development* (pp. 56–75). Basingstoke: Palgrave.

Arrighi, G., & Silver, B. J. (1984). Labor Movements and Capital Migration: The United States and Western Europe in World-Historical Perspective. In C. Bergquist (Ed.), *Labor in the Capitalist World-Economy* (pp. 183–216). Beverly Hills: Sage.

Arrighi, G., & Silver, B. (Eds.). (1999). *Chaos and Governance in the Modern World System*. Minneapolis: University of Minnesota Press.

Arrighi, G., & Silver, B. J. (2001). Capitalism and World (Dis)Order. *Review of International Studies, 27*(5), 257–279.

Baccaro, L., & Benassi, C. (2017). Throwing Out the Ballast: Growth Models and the Liberalization of German Industrial Relations. *Socio-Economic Review, 15*(1), 85–115.

Baccaro, L., & Howell, C. (2017). *Trajectories of Neoliberal Transformation: European Industrial Relations Since the 1970s*. Cambridge: Cambridge University Press.

Baccaro, L., & Pontusson, J. (2016). Rethinking Comparative Political Economy: The Growth Model Perspective. *Politics and Society, 44*(2), 175–207.

Baneman, D., & Nunns, J. (2012). *Income Tax Paid at Each Tax Rate, 1958–2009*. Urban-Brookings Tax Policy Center. Available at https://www.taxpolicycenter.org/sites/default/files/publication/103946/901456-Income-Tax-Paid-at-Each-Tax-Rate—Updated.pdf.

Bartlett, W. (2007). The Western Balkans. In D. Lane & M. Myant (Eds.), *Varieties of Capitalism in Post-Communist Countries* (pp. 201–218). Basingstoke: Palgrave Macmillan.

Becker, U. (2007). Open Systemness and Contested Reference Frames and Change: A Reformulation of the Varieties of Capitalism Theory. *Socio-Economic Review*, *5*(2), 261–286.

Becker, U. (2009). *Open Varieties of Capitalism: Continuity, Change and Performances*. Basingstoke: Palgrave Macmillan.

Beckert, J. (2010). How Do Fields Change? The Interrelations of Institutions, Networks, and Cognition in the Dynamics of Markets. *Organization Studies, 31*(5), 605–627.

Bell, D. (1976/1999). *The Coming of Post-Industrial Society: A Venture in Social Forecasting*. New York: Basic Books.

Beramendi, P., Häusermann, S., Kitschelt, H., & Kriesi, H. (Eds.). (2015). *The Politics of Advanced Capitalism*. New York: Cambridge University Press.

Berger, B. (2018). All That Xi Wants: China's Communist Party Is Trying to Reform the Country from the Top Down. *DGAP-Standpunkt*, 5. https://nbnresolving.org/urn:nbn:de:0168-ssoar-56259-4.

Bernhardt, A., Milkman, R., Theodore, N., Heckathorn, D., Auer, M., DeFilippis, J., et al. (2009). Broken Laws, Unprotected Workers. *National Employment Law Project*. New York: NELP.

Bhattasali, D., Li, S., & Martin, W. J. (Eds.). (2004). *China and the WTO: Accession, Policy Reform, and Poverty Reduction Strategies*. Washington, DC: World Bank Publications.

Bjorklund, E. (2019). Out of Many, One? US Sub-National Political-Economies in the Post-Welfare Reform Era. *Socio-Economic Review, 17*(4), 851–873.

Blyth, M. (2003). Same as It Never Was: Temporality and Typology in the Varieties of Capitalism. *Comparative European Politics, 1*(2), 215.

Blyth, M., Hodgson, G. M., Lewis, O., & Steinmo, S. (2011). Introduction to the Special Issue on the Evolution of Institutions. *Journal of Institutional Economics, 7*(3), 299–315.

BMFSFJ. (2009). *Pay Inequality Between Women and Men in Germany: A Dossier*. Available at: https://www.bmfsfj.de/blob/94442/efbd528467e361882848c23486fcc8d8/pay-inequality-data.pdf.

Bohle, D., & Greskovits, B. (2007). Neoliberalism, Embedded Neoliberalism and Neocorporatism: Towards Transnational Capitalism in Central-Eastern Europe. *West European Politics, 30*(3), 443–466.

Bosch, G. (2018). The Making of the German Minimum Wage: A Case Study of Institutional Change. *Industrial Relations Journal, 49*(1), 19–33.

Boyer, R. (2005). How and Why Capitalisms Differ. *Economy and Society, 34*(4), 509–557.

Braudel, F. (1992a). *Strukture svakidašnjice*. Zagreb: August Cesarec.

Braudel, F. (1992b). *Igra razmjene*. Zagreb: August Cesarec.

Braudel, F. (1992c). *Vrijeme svijeta*. Zagreb: August Cesarec.

Brudney, J. (2005). Contractual Approaches to Labor Organizing: Supplanting the Election Paradigm? In *Labor and Employment Relations Association Series, Proceedings of the 57th Annual Meeting* (pp. 106–113).

Buchen, C. (2007). Estonia and Slovenia as Antipodes. In D. Lane & M. Myant (Eds.), *Varieties of Capitalism in Post-Communist Countries* (pp. 65–89). Basingstoke: Palgrave Macmillan.

Buckley, C. (2013, August 19). China Takes Aim at Western Ideas. *New York Times*. https://www.nytimes.com/2013/08/20/world/asia/chinas-new-leadership-takes-hard-line-in-secret-memo.html.

Bukharin, N. (1917/1972). *Imperialism and World Economy*. London: Martin Lawrence.

Campbell, J. L. (2010). Institutional Reproduction and Change. In G. Morgan, J. Campbell, C. Crouch, O. K. Pedersen, & R. Whitley (Eds.), *The Oxford Handbook of Comparative Institutional Analysis* (pp. 87–116). Oxford: Oxford University Press.

Campos, N. F., & Macchiarelli, C. (2016). Core and Periphery in the European Monetary Union: Bayoumi and Eichengreen 25 Years Later. *Economics Letters, 147*, 127–130.

Carlin, W., & Soskice, D. (2009). German Economic Performance: Disentangling the Role of Supply-side Reforms, Macroeconomic Policy and Coordinated Economy Institutions. *Socio-Economic Review, 7*(1), 67–99.

Castells, M. (1989). *The Informational City: Information Technology, Economic Restructuring, and the Urban-Regional Process* (pp. 234–235). Oxford: Blackwell.

Castells, M. (2000). Toward a Sociology of the Network Society. *Contemporary Sociology, 29*(5), 693–699.

Chamberlin, E. (1933/1962). *Theory of Monopolistic Competition*. New York: Oxford University Press.

Chan, C. K. C., & Hui, E. S. I. (2013). The Development of Collective Bargaining in China: From "Collective Bargaining by Riot" to "Party State-Led Wage Bargaining". *The China Quarterly, 217*, 221–242.

Chan, C. K. C., & Hui, E. S. I. (2014). The Dynamics and Dilemma of Workplace Trade Union Reform in China: The Case of Honda Workers' Strike. In X. Richet, V. Delteil, & P. Dieuaide (Eds.), *Strategies of Multinational Corporations and Social Regulations: European and Asian Perspectives* (pp. 203–217). New York: Springer.

Chan, J., & Selden, M. (2017). The Labour Politics of China's Rural Migrant Workers. *Globalizations, 14*(2), 259–271.

Chang, K., & Cooke, F. L. (2015). Legislating the Right to Strike in China: Historical Development and Prospects. *Journal of Industrial Relations, 57*(3), 440–455.

Chase-Dunn, C., & Podobnik, B. (1999). The Next World War: World-System Cycles and Trends. In V. Bornschier & C. Chase-Dunn (Eds.), *The Future of Global Conflict*. London: Sage.

Chen, X. (2011). *Gender Wage Gap in China from 1989–2009*. Available at https://ir.vanderbilt.edu/handle/1803/10296.

China Internet Information Center. (n.d.). *The Non-communist Parties*. Available at http://www.china.org.cn/english/features/38466.htm.

CID. (2020). *The Atlas of Economic Complexity*. Available at https://atlas.cid.harvard.edu/explore.

CIPG/CATL. (2016). *Keywords to Understand China*. Beijing: New World Press.

Clarke, S., Lee, C. H., & Li, Q. (2004). Collective Consultation and Industrial Relations in China. *British Journal of Industrial Relations, 42*(2), 235–254.

CLB. (2020). *Strike Map*. Available at https://maps.clb.org.hk/strikes/en.

Coase, R. H. (1937). The Nature of the Firm. *Economica, 4*(16), 386–405.

Coase, R. H. (1960). The Problem of Social Cost. *Journal of Law and Economics, 3*, 1.

Commons, J. (1934/1959). *Institutional Economics: Its Place in Political Economy*. Madison: University of Wisconsin Press.

Compa, L. (2014). An Overview of Collective Bargaining in the United States. In J. G. Hernández (Ed.), *El derecho a la negociación colectiva: Monografías de temas laborales* (pp. 91–98). Seville: Consejo Andaluz de Relaciones Laborales.

Crawford, S. E., & Ostrom, E. (1995). A Grammar of Institutions. *American Political Science Review, 89*(3), 582–600.

Crouch, C., & Streeck, W. (Eds.). (1997). *Political Economy of Modern Capitalism: Mapping Convergence and Diversity*. London: Sage.

Crouch, C. (2009). Privatised Keynesianism: An Unacknowledged Policy Regime. *The British Journal of Politics and International Relations, 11*(3), 382–399.

Crouch, C. (2010). Complementarity. In G. Morgan, J. Campbell, C. Crouch, O. K. Pedersen, & R. Whitley (Eds.), *The Oxford Handbook of Comparative Institutional Analysis* (pp. 117–137). Oxford: Oxford University Press.

Das, M., & N'Diaye, M. P. M. (2013). *Chronicle of a Decline Foretold: Has China Reached the Lewis Turning Point?* (No. 13–26). International Monetary Fund.

De Grauwe, P., & Mongelli, F. (2005). *Endogeneities of Optimum Currency Areas: What Brings Countries Sharing a Single Currency Closer Together?* (ECB Working Paper No. 468).

Detzer, D., Dodig, N., Evans, T., Hein, E., Herr, H., & Prante, F. J. (2017). *The German Financial System and the Financial and Economic Crisis*. Cham: Springer.

Deutsche Bundesbank. (2018a). *Debt of Households in Germany*. https://www.bundesbank.de/dynamic/action/en/statistics/time-series-databases/time-series-databases/759784/759784?listId=www_s300_iswi_finanzw4.

Deutsche Bundesbank. (2018b). *Special Statistical Publication 5*. Available at https://www.bundesbank.de/resource/blob/651156/7b4e0871cf12eb2618b7975a83ac2806/mL/statso5-1997-2016-en-data.xlsx.

Deutsche Welle. (2016). German Minimum Hourly Wage Bumped Up for 2017. http://www.dw.com/en/german-minimum-hourly-wage-bumped-up-for-2017/a-19362540.

Die Bundesregierung. (2019). *Höhere Regelsätze ab 2020*. https://www.bundesregierung.de/breg-de/aktuelles/regelsaetze-1666914.

Ding, S., Knight, J., & Zhang, X. (2019). Does China Overinvest? Evidence from a Panel of Chinese Firms. *The European Journal of Finance, 25*(6), 489–507.

Dixit, A. K., & Stiglitz, J. E. (1977). Monopolistic Competition and Optimum Product Diversity. *The American Economic Review, 67*(3), 297–308.

Djelic, M. L. (2010). Institutional Perspectives—Working Towards Coherence or Irreconcilable Diversity? In G. Morgan, J. Campbell, C. Crouch, O. K. Pedersen, & R. Whitley (Eds.), *The Oxford Handbook of Comparative Institutional Analysis* (pp. 15–40). Oxford: Oxford University Press.

Dosi, G., Pereira, M. C., Roventini, A., & Virgillito, M. E. (2018). The Effects of Labour Market Reforms Upon Unemployment and Income Inequalities: An Agent-Based Model. *Socio-Economic Review, 16*(4), 687–720.

Doyle, A. (2017). *The Balance*. List of U.S. Employment Laws What the Law Says About Wages, Work Safety, Discrimination, and More. https://www.thebalance.com/list-of-employment-laws-2062282.

Early, S. (2013). *Save Our Unions: Dispatches from a Movement in Distress*. New York: Monthly Review Press.

Eichhorst, W. (2015). The Unexpected Appearance of a New German Model. *British Journal of Industrial Relations, 53*(1), 49–69.

Eichhorst, W., & Marx, P. (2011). Reforming German Labour Market Institutions: A Dual Path to Flexibility. *Journal of European Social Policy, 21*(1), 73–87.

Elsner, W. (1989). Adam Smith's Model of the Origins and Emergence of Institutions: The Modern Findings of the Classical Approach. *Journal of Economic Issues, 23*(1), 189–213.

Emmenegger, P. (2014). *The Power to Dismiss: Trade Unions and the Regulation of Job Security in Western Europe*. Oxford: Oxford University Press.

Epstein, G. A. (Ed.). (2005). *Financialization and the World Economy*. Cheltenham: Edward Elgar Publishing.

Esping-Andersen, G. (1990). *The Three Worlds of Welfare Capitalism*. Cambridge: Polity Press.

Estlund, C. (2017). *A New Deal for China's Workers?* Cambridge: Harvard University Press.

ETUI. (2018). *Strikes Map Germany*. https://www.etui.org/strikes-map/germany.

European Commission. (n.d.). *Germany*. Available at https://ec.europa.eu/info/business-economy-euro/economic-and-fiscal-policy-coordination/eu-economic-governance-monitoring-prevention-correction/stability-and-growth-pact/corrective-arm-excessive-deficit-procedure/closed-excessive-deficit-procedures/germany_en.

Eurostat. (2016). *Gender Overall Earnings Gap*. Available at http://ec.europa.eu/eurostat/tgm/table.do?tab=table&init=1&language=en&pcode=teqges01&plugin=1.

Eurostat. (2017). *File:Unadjusted Gender Pay Gap, 2015*. Available at http://ec.europa.eu/eurostat/statistics-explained/index.php/File:Unadjusted_g

ender_pay_gap,_2015_(difference_between_average_gross_hourly_earnings_of_male_and_female_employees_as_%25_of_male_gross_earnings)-F1.png.

Eurostat. (2019). *Compensation of Employees—Annual Data, Million Units of National Currency*. Available at https://ec.europa.eu/eurostat/web/products-datasets/product?code=tipslm13.

Eurostat. (2020). *Part-Time Employment as Percentage of the Total Employment, by Sex and Age (%)* [lfsa_eppga]. Available at http://appsso.eurostat.ec.europa.eu/nui/submitViewTableAction.do.

Feldmann, M. (2006). Emerging Varieties of Capitalism in Transition Countries: Industrial Relations and Wage Bargaining in Estonia and Slovenia. *Comparative Political Studies, 39*(7), 829–854.

Feng, S., Hu, Y., & Moffitt, R. (2015). *Long Run Trends in Unemployment and Labor Force Participation in China* (No. w21460). National Bureau of Economic Research.

Ferreira, F. H., Lustig, N., & Teles, D. (2015). *Appraising Cross-National Income Inequality Databases: An Introduction* (World Bank Policy Research Working Paper 7489). http://documents.worldbank.org/curated/en/590731467992508711/pdf/WPS7489.pdf.

FRED. (2017). Households and Nonprofit Organizations; Credit Market Instruments; Liability, Level (CMDEBT). https://fred.stlouisfed.org/series/CMDEBT.

FRED. (2018). *Household Debt to GDP for United States* (HDTGPDUSQ163N). https://fred.stlouisfed.org/series/HDTGPDUSQ163N.

FRED. (2019). *FRED Graph*. https://fred.stlouisfed.org/graph/?g=niHr.

FRED. (2020). *Compensation of Employees: Wages and Salary Accruals/Gross Domestic Product* (A4002E1A156NBEA). https://fred.stlouisfed.org/graph/?g=2Xa.

Frey, C. B., & Osborne, M. A. (2013). *The Future of Employment: How Susceptible Are Jobs to Computerisation?* https://www.fhi.ox.ac.uk/wp-content/uploads/The-Future-of-Employment-How-Susceptible-Are-Jobs-to-Computerization.pdf.

Friedman, E. (2014). *Insurgency Trap: Labor Politics in Postsocialist China*. Ithaca: Cornell University Press.

Fulton, L. (2020). *National Industrial Relations, an Update*. Labour Research Department and ETUI. Online publication available at http://www.worker-participation.eu/National-Industrial-Relations.

Gallagher, M. E. (2005). *Contagious Capitalism: Globalization and the Politics of Labor in China*. Princeton: Princeton University Press.

Gallagher, M. E. (2014). China's Workers Movement and the End of the Rapid-Growth Era. *Daedalus, 143*(2), 81–95.

Gallagher, M. E. (2016). The Social Relations of Chinese State Capitalism. In B. L. Liebman, & C. J. Milhaupt (Eds.), *Regulating the Visible Hand? The*

Institutional Implications of Chinese State Capitalism (pp. 225–250). Oxford: Oxford University Press.

Gallagher, M. E. (2017). *Authoritarian Legality in China: Law, Workers, and the State*. Cambridge: Cambridge University Press.

Gilens, M. (2012). *Affluence and Influence: Economic Inequality and Political Power in America*. Princeton: Princeton University Press.

Gilens, M., & Page, B. I. (2014). Testing Theories of American Politics: Elites, Interest Groups, and Average Citizens. *Perspectives on Politics, 12*(3), 564–581.

Godard, J. (2009). The Exceptional Decline of the American Labor Movement. *ILR Review, 63*(1), 82–108.

Goldstein, J. S. (1985). Kondratieff Waves as War Cycles. *International Studies Quarterly, 29*(4), 411–444.

Goldstein, J. S. (1988). *Long Cycles: Prosperity and War in the Modern Age*. New Haven, CT: Yale University Press.

Goldstein, J. S. (2006). The Predictive Power of Long Wave Theory, 1989–2004. In T. C. Devezas (Ed.), *Kondratieff Waves, Warfare and World Security*. Berlin: IOS Press.

Greif, A., & Kingston, C. (2011). Institutions: Rules or Equilibria? In *Political Economy of Institutions, Democracy and Voting* (pp. 13–43). Berlin, Heidelberg: Springer.

Greif, A., & Laitin, D. D. (2004). A Theory of Endogenous Institutional Change. *American Political Science Review, 98*(4), 633–652.

Hacker, J. S., & Pierson, P. (2010). *Winner-Take-All Politics: How Washington Made the Rich Richer—And Turned Its Back on the Middle Class*. New York: Simon and Schuster.

Hall, P. (1999). The Political Economy of Europe in an Era of Interdependence. In H. Kitchelt, P. Lange, G. Marks, & J. Stephens (Eds.), *Continuity and Change in Contemporary Capitalism* (pp. 135–163). Cambridge: Cambridge University Press.

Hall, P. (2010). Historical Institutionalism in Rationalist and Sociological Perspective. In J. Mahoney & K. Thelen (Eds.), *Explaining Institutional Change: Ambiguity, Agency, and Power*. Cambridge: Cambridge University Press.

Hall, P. (2017). Varieties of Capitalism in Light of the Euro Crisis. *Journal of European Public Policy, 25*(1), 7–30.

Hall, P. (2018). *The Electoral Politics of Growth Regimes* (Working Paper). Available at https://scholar.harvard.edu/files/hall/files/hall2018_growth_regimes.pdf.

Hall, P., & Gingerich, D. (2004). *Varieties of Capitalism and Institutional Complementarities in the Macroeconomy: An Empirical Analysis* (Max- Planck-Institut für Gesellschaftsforschung Discussion Paper, 4/5). http://www.mpi-fg-koeln.mpg.de/pu/mpifg_dp/dp04-5.pdf.

Hall, P., & Gingerich, D. (2009). Varieties of Capitalism and Institutional Complementarities in the Political Economy: An Empirical Analysis. *British Journal of Political Science, 39*(3), 449–482.

Hall, P., & Soskice, D. (Eds.). (2001). *Varieties of Capitalism: The Institutional Foundations of Comparative Advantage*. Oxford: Oxford University Press.

Hall, P., & Soskice, D. (2003). Varieties of Capitalism and Institutional Change: A Response to Three Critics. *Comparative European Politics, 1*(2), 241–250.

Hall, P., & Taylor, R. C. (1996). Political Science and the Three New Institutionalisms. *Political Studies, 44*(5), 936–957.

Hall, P., & Thelen, K. (2009). Institutional Change in Varieties of Capitalism. *Socio-Economic Review, 7*(1), 7–34.

Hancké, B. (2013). *Unions, Central Banks, and EMU: Labour Market Institutions and Monetary Integration in Europe*. Oxford: Oxford University Press.

Hancké, B., Rhodes, M., & Thatcher, M. (2007). *Beyond Varieties of Capitalism: Conflict, Contradictions, and Complementarities in the European Economy*. Oxford: Oxford University Press.

Hardin, R. (1982). *Collective Action*. London/Baltimore: John Hopkins University Press.

Harvey, D. (1989). *The Condition of Postmodernity: An Enquiry into the Origins of Cultural Change*. Oxford: Blackwell.

Harvey, D. (1999). *The Limits to Capital*. London: Verso.

Harvey, D. (2001). Globalization and the "Spatial Fix". *Geographische Revue, 3*(2), 23–30.

Harvey, D. (2005). *A Brief History of Neoliberalism*. Oxford: Oxford University Press.

Harvey, D. I., Kellard, N. M., Madsen, J. B., & Wohar, M. E. (2010). The Prebisch-Singer Hypothesis: Four Centuries of Evidence. *The Review of Economics and Statistics, 92*(2), 367–377.

Hassel, A. (2011). *The Paradox of Liberalization: Understanding Dualism and the Recovery of the German Political Economy* (LEQS Paper, 42).

Hassel, A. (2015). Trade Unions and the Future of Democratic Capitalism. In P. Beramendi, S. Häusermann, H. Kitschelt, & H. Kriesi (Eds.), *The Politics of Advanced Capitalism* (pp. 231–258). New York: Cambridge University Press.

Häusermann, S., & Schwander, H. (2012). Varieties of Dualization? Labor Market Segmentation and Insider-Outsider Divides Across Regimes. In P. Emmenegger, S. Häusermann, & B. Palier (Eds.), *The Age of Dualization:*

The Changing Face of Inequality in Deindustrializing Societies (pp. 27–51). Oxford: Oxford University Press.

Hayek, F. A. (1945). The Use of Knowledge in Society. *American Economic Review, 35*(4), 519–530.

Hayek, F. A. (1990). *The Fatal Con.* Chicago: University of Chicago Press Economics Books.

Heilmann, S. (Ed.). (2017). *China's Political System.* Lanham: Rowman & Littlefield.

Helpman, E., & Krugman, P. R. (1985). *Market Structure and Foreign Trade: Increasing Returns, Imperfect Competition, and the International Economy.* Cambridge: MIT Press.

Helpman, E., & Krugman, P. R. (1989). *Trade Policy and Market Structure.* Cambridge: MIT press.

Heritage. (2020a). *Labor Freedom.* http://www.heritage.org/index/labor-fre edom.

Heritage. (2020b). *Explore the Data.* http://www.heritage.org/index/explore.

Heritage. (2020c). *Graph the Data.* http://www.heritage.org/index/visualize.

Hersh, A. S. (2014). *China's State-Owned Enterprises and Nonmarket Economics. Testimony Before the U.S.-China Economic and Security Review Commission.* Available at https://cdn.americanprogress.org/wp-content/uploads/2014/03/Hersh-testimony.pdf.

Hilferding, R. (1910/1981). *Finance Capital: A Study of the Latest Phase of Capitalist Development.* London: Routledge.

Hope, D., & Soskice, D. (2016). Growth Models, Varieties of Capitalism, and Macroeconomics. *Politics and Society, 44*(2), 209–226.

Huber, E., Huo, J., & Stephens, J. D. (2019). Power, Policy, and Top Income Shares. *Socio-Economic Review, 17*(2), 231–253.

Ietto-Gillies, G. (2005). *Transnational Corporations and International Production: Concepts, Theories and Effects.* Cheltenham: Edward Elgar Publishing.

Illich, I. (1973). *Tools for Conviviality.* New York: Harper & Row.

ILO. (2016). *Global Wage Report 2016/17: Wage Inequality in the Workplace.* Available at https://www.ilo.org/wcmsp5/groups/public/—dgrepo rts/—dcomm/—publ/documents/publication/wcms_537846.pdf.

ILO. (2017a). *The US: A Leading Role in the ILO.* Available at http://www.ilo.org/washington/ilo-and-the-united-states/the-usa-leading-role-in-the-ilo/lang—en/index.htm.

ILO. (2017b). *Ratifications by Country.* Available at http://www.ilo.org/dyn/normlex/en/f?p=1000:11200:0::NO:11200:P11200_COUNTRY_ID:102871.

IMF. (2004, September 1). *A a Glance—China and the IMF.* https://www.imf.org/external/country/chn/rr/glance.htm.

IMF. (2018). *World Economic Outlook Database April 2018*. Available at http://www.imf.org/external/pubs/ft/weo/2018/01/weodata/index.aspx.

IMF. (2019). *Household Debt, Loans and Debt Securities*. Available at https://www.imf.org/external/datamapper/HH_LS@GDD/CHN.

IMF. (2020). *World Economic Outlook Database October 2020*. Available at http://www.imf.org/external/pubs/ft/weo/2020/02/weodata/index.aspx.

Itakura, K. (2020). Evaluating the Impact of the US–China Trade War. *Asian Economic Policy Review, 15*(1), 77–93.

Iversen, T., & Soskice, D. (2015). Democratic Limits to Redistribution: Inclusionary Versus Exclusionary Coalitions in the Knowledge Economy. *World Politics, 67*(2), 185–225.

Iversen, T., Soskice, D., & Hope, D. (2016). The Eurozone and Political Economic Institutions. *Annual Review of Political Science, 19*, 163–185.

Jacobson, H. K., & Oksenberg, M. (1990). *China's Participation in the IMF, the World Bank, and GATT: Toward a Global Economic Order*. Ann Arbor: University of Michigan Press.

Jain-Chandra, M. S., Khor, N., Mano, R., Schauer, J., Wingender, M. P., & Zhuang, J. (2018). *Inequality in China–Trends, Drivers and Policy Remedies*. WP/18/127. International Monetary Fund.

Jessop, B. (1990). *State Theory: Putting the Capitalist State in Its Place*. Pennsylvania: Penn State Press.

Jessop, B. (2012). The World Market, Variegated Capitalism, and the Crisis of European Integration. *Globalisation and European Integration: Critical Approaches to Regional Order and International Relations, 25*, 91.

Jung, J. (2017). A Struggle on Two Fronts: Labour Resistance to Changing Layoff Policies at Large US Companies. *Socio-Economic Review, 15*(1), 213–239.

Kalinowski, T. (2013). Regulating International Finance and the Diversity of Capitalism. *Socio-Economic Review, 11*(3), 471–496.

Kandori, M. (1992). Social Norms and Community Enforcement. *The Review of Economic Studies, 59*(1), 63–80.

Kemmerling, A., & Bruttel, O. (2005). *New Politics in German Labour Market Policy? The Implications of the Recent Hartz Reforms for the German Welfare State* (WZB Discussion Paper). https://www.econstor.eu/bitstream/10419/44018/1/490072151.pdf.

Keynes, J. M. (1924). *A Tract on Monetary Reform*. London: Macmillan. http://delong.typepad.com/keynes-1923-a-tract-on-monetary-reform.pdf.

Keynes, J. M. (1930/2009). Economic Possibilities for Our Grandchildren. In *Essays in Persuasion* (pp. 192–202). Classic House Books.

Keynes, J. M. (1936/2013). *General Theory of Employment, Interest and Money*. Cambridge: Cambridge University Press.

Kim, M. (2019). A Real Driver of US–China Trade Conflict: The Sino–US Competition for Global Hegemony and Its Implications for the Future. *International Trade, Politics and Development, 3*(1), 30–40.

Kirchner, J., Kremp, P. R., & Magotsch, M. (Eds.). (2018). *Key Aspects of German Employment and Labour Law*. Berlin: Springer.

Kitschelt, H., Lange, P., Marks, G., & Stephens, J. D. (Eds.). (1999). *Continuity and Change in Contemporary Capitalism*. Cambridge: Cambridge University Press.

Knell, M., & Srholec, M. (2007). Diverging Pathways in Central and Eastern Europe. In D. Lane & M. Myant (Eds.), *Varieties of Capitalism in Post-Communist Countries*. Hampshire: Palgrave Macmillan.

Korpi, W. (1985). Power Resources Approach vs. Action and Conflict: On Causal and Intentional Explanations in the Study of Power. *Sociological Theory*, *3*(2), 31–45.

Korpi, W. (2001). Contentious Institutions: An Augmented Rational-Action Analysis of the Origins and Path Dependency of Welfare State Institutions in Western Countries. *Rationality and Society, 13*(2), 235–283.

Korpi, W. (2006). Power Resources and Employer-Centered Approaches in Explanations of Welfare States and Varieties of Capitalism: Protagonists, Consenters, and Antagonists. *World Politics, 58*(2), 167–206.

Kotarski, K. (2015). Financial Deepening and Income Inequality: Is There Any Financial Kuznets Curve in China? The Political Economy Analysis. *China Economic Journal, 8*(1), 18–39.

Krippner, G. R. (2005). The Financialization of the American Economy. *Socio-Economic Review, 3*(2), 173–208.

Krippner, G. R. (2011). *Capitalizing on Crisis*. Cambridge: Harvard University Press.

Kristal, T., & Cohen, Y. (2017). The Causes of Rising Wage Inequality: The Race Between Institutions and Technology. *Socio-Economic Review, 15*(1), 187–212.

Krugman, P. (1998). What's New About the New Economic Geography? *Oxford Review of Economic Policy*, *14*(2), 7–17.

Krugman, P. (2012). *End This Depression Now!* New York: W. W. Norton.

Krugman, P. (2013). Revenge of the Optimum Currency Area. *NBER Macroeconomics Annual, 27*(1), 439–448.

Kwan, C. H. (2020). The China–US Trade War: Deep-Rooted Causes, Shifting Focus and Uncertain Prospects. *Asian Economic Policy Review, 15*(1), 55–72.

Lapavitsas, C., & Powell, J. (2013). Financialisation Varied: A Comparative Analysis of Advanced Economies. *Cambridge Journal of Regions, Economy and Society,* *6*(3), 359–379.

Lardy, N. R. (2014). *Markets Over Mao: The Rise of Private Business in China*. New York: Columbia University Press.

Lee, C. K. (2007). *Against the Law: Labor Protests in China's Rustbelt and Sunbelt*. Berkeley: University of California Press.

Lee, C. H. (2009). *Industrial Relations and Collective Bargaining in China*. Geneva: ILO. Available at http://ilo.ch/wcmsp5/groups/public/—ed_dialogue/—dialogue/documents/publication/wcms_158350.pdf.

Lee, M. I. H., Syed, M. M. H., & Xueyan, M. L. (2012). *Is China Over-Investing and Does It Matter?* (No. 12–277). International Monetary Fund.

Lefkofridi, Z., & Michel, E. (2017). The Electoral Politics of Solidarity. In K. Banting & W. Kymlicka (Eds.), *The Strains of Commitment: The Political Sources of Solidarity in Diverse Societies* (pp. 233–267). Oxford: Oxford University Press.

Lehndorff, S., Bosch, G., Haipeter, T., & Latniak, E. (2009). From the 'Sick Man' to the 'Overhauled Engine' of Europe? Upheaval in the German Model. In G. Bosch, S. Lehndorff, & J. Rubery (Eds.), *European Employment Models in Flux* (pp. 105–130). Basingstoke: Palgrave Macmillan.

Lehrer, M., & Celo, S. (2016). German Family Capitalism in the 21st Century: Patient Capital Between Bifurcation and Symbiosis. *Socio-Economic Review, 14*(4), 729–750.

Lenin, V. I. (1917/1999). *Imperialism: The Highest Stage of Capitalism*. Online Version: Lenin Internet Archive (marxists.org).

Li, M., & Walker, R. (2018). Targeting Social Assistance: Dibao and Institutional Alienation in Rural China. *Social Policy and Administration, 52*(3), 771–789.

Lin, Y. M. (2017). *Dancing with the Devil: The Political Economy of Privatization in China*. New York: Oxford University Press.

Ling, Q. (2016). Introduction: The Survival and Collective Struggles of Workers in China's Coastal Private Enterprises Since the 1990s. In H. Ren, Z. Li, & E. Friedman (Eds.), *China on Strike* (pp. 1–26). Chicago: Haymarket Books.

Liu, J., et al. (2016). *The Communist Party of China: The Past, Present and Future of Party Building*. People's Publishing House.

Liu, G., & Lee, C. C. (2018). Financialization and Stagnant Capital Accumulation in China. *Bulletin of Monetary Economics and Banking, 21*(1), 23–32.

Liu, S. D., & Shi, W. (2016). Worker Struggles and Factory Occupation in China During the Current Economic Crisis. *Social Movement Studies, 16*(3). https://doi.org/10.1080/14742837.2016.1259106.

Lowndes, V. (2005). Institucionalizam. In D. Marsh & G. Stoker (Eds.), *Teorije i metode političke znanosti* (pp. 86–104). Zagreb: Politička misao.

Lučev, J. (2014a). How Long Before NATO Aircraft Carrier Force Projection Capabilities Are Successfully Countered? Some Effects of the Fiscal Crises. *Croatian International Relations Review, 20*(71), 121–151.

Lučev, J. (2014b). Duhovi kapitalizma i mjere štednje. *Politička misao, 51*(4), 26–40.

Lučev, J., & Babić, Z. (2013). Tipovi kapitalizma, ekspanzija neoliberalizma i socijalni učinci u baltičkim zemljama, Sloveniji i Hrvatskoj: komparativni pristup. *Revija za socijalnu politiku, 20*(1), 1–19.

Mager, F., & Meyer-Fackler, M. (2017). Mergers and Acquisitions in Germany: 1981–2010. *Global Finance Journal, 34,* 32–42.

Magotsch, M., & Kremp, P. R. (2018). Termination of Employment. In J. Kirchner, P. R. Kremp, & M. Magotsch (Eds.), *Key Aspects of German Employment and Labour Law* (pp. 171–192). Berlin: Springer.

Mahoney, J., & Thelen, K. (Eds.). (2010). *Explaining Institutional Change: Ambiguity, Agency, and Power.* Cambridge: Cambridge University Press.

March, J. G., & Olsen, J. P. (1983). The New Institutionalism: Organizational Factors in Political Life. *American Political Science Review, 78*(3), 734–749.

Marx, K. (1867/1894/1979). *Kapital: Kritika političke ekonomije I-III.* Beograd: Prosveta.

Milanovic, B. (2019). *Capitalism, Alone: The Future of the System That Rules the World.* Cambridge: Harvard University Press.

Mill, J. (1844). *Elements of Political Economy* (3rd ed.). London: Henry Bohn.

Mises, L. V. (1949). *Human Action.* Ludwig von Mises Institute.

Mjøset, L. (2007). An Early Approach to the Varieties of World Capitalism: Methodological and Substantive Lessons from the Senghaas/Menzel-Project. In L. Mjøset & T. H. Clausen (Eds.), *Capitalisms Compared* (pp. 123–176). Amsterdam: Elsevier.

Modelski, G. (1978). The Long Cycle of Global Politics and the Nation-State. *Comparative Studies in Society and History, 20*(2), 214–235.

Molero-Simarro, R. (2016). Inequality in China Revisited: The Effect of Functional Distribution of Income on Urban Top Incomes, the Urban-Rural Gap and the Gini Index, 1978–2015. *China Economic Review, 42,* 101–117.

Mussachio, A., & Lazzarini, S. (2016). Chinese Exceptionalism or New Global Varieties of State Capitalism. In B. L. Liebman & C. J. Milhaupt (Eds.), *Regulating the Visible Hand? The Institutional Implications of Chinese State Capitalism* (pp. 403–431). Oxford: Oxford University Press.

Nash, J. F. (1950). Equilibrium Points in N-Person Games. *Proceedings of the National Academy of Sciences, USA, 36*(1), 48–49.

Nau, M., & Soener, M. (2019). Income Precarity and the Financial Crisis. *Socio-Economic Review, 17*(3), 523–544.

Neumann, J., & Morgenstern, O. (1944). *Theory of Games and Economic Behavior.* Princeton: Princeton University Press.

Nölke, A. (2016). Economic Causes of the Eurozone Crisis: The Analytical Contribution of Comparative Capitalism. *Socio-Economic Review, 14*(1), 141–161.

Nölke, A., & May, C. (2013). Vergleichende Kapitalismusforschung im Zeitalter der Krise der Finanzialisierung: Vom inter-nationalen zum inter-temporalen

Studium ökonomischer Institutionen. *Zeitschrift für Außen-und Sicherheitspolitik, 6*(1), 51–70.

Nölke, A., ten Brink, T., Claar, S., & May, C. (2015). Domestic Structures, Foreign Economic Policies and Global Economic Order: Implications from the Rise of Large Emerging Economies. *European Journal of International Relations, 21*(3), 538–567.

Nölke, A., & Vliegenthart, A. (2009). Enlarging the Varieties of Capitalism: The Emergence of Dependent Market Economies in East Central Europe. *World Politics, 61*(4), 670–702.

North, D. C. (1990). *Institutions, Institutional Change and Economic Performance*. Cambridge: Cambridge University Press.

North, D. C. (1991). Institutions. *Journal of Economic Perspectives., 5*(1), 97–112.

North, D. C. (1994). Economic Performance Through Time. *The American Economic Review, 84,* 359–368.

Ochsenfeld, F. (2018). Mercantilist Dualization: The Introduction of the Euro, Redistribution of Industry Rents, and Wage Inequality in Germany, 1993–2008. *Socio-Economic Review, 16*(3), 499–522.

OECD. (2017). *OECD Data* [online] Available at https://data.oecd.org/.

OECD. (2020). *OECD Data* [online]. Available at https://data.oecd.org/.

Ohlin, B. (1933/1935). *Interregional and International Trade*. Cambridge: Harvard University Press.

Orhangazi, Ö. (2008). *Financialization and the US Economy*. Cheltenham: Edward Elgar Publishing.

Orrell, D., & Chlupatý, R. (2016). *The Evolution of Money*. New York: Columbia University Press.

Ostrom, E. (2005). *Understanding Institutional Diversity*. Princeton: Princeton University Press.

Ostrom, E., & Basurto, X. (2011). Crafting Analytical Tools to Study Institutional Change. *Journal of Institutional Economics, 7*(3), 317–343.

Page, B. I., & Gilens, M. (2020). *Democracy in America? What Has Gone Wrong and What We Can Do About It*. Chicago: University of Chicago Press.

Palier, B., & Thelen, K. (2010). Institutionalizing Dualism: Complementarities and Change in France and Germany. *Politics and Society, 38*(1), 119–148.

Peck, J., & Zhang, J. (2013). A Variety of Capitalism… with Chinese Characteristics? *Journal of Economic Geography, 13*(3), 357–396.

Peters, B. G. (1999). *Institutional Theory in Political Science: The New Institutionalism*. New York: Pinter.

Pierson, P. (2000). Increasing Returns, Path Dependence, and the Study of Politics. *American Political Science Review, 94*(2), 251–267.

Pierson, P. (2015). Power and Path Dependence. In J. Mahoney & K. Thelen (Eds.), *Advances in Comparative-Historical Analysis* (pp. 123–147). Cambridge: Cambridge University Press.

Piketty, T. (2017). *Capital in the Twenty-First Century*. Cambridge: Harvard University Press.

Pistor, K., Li, G., & Chun Z. (2016). The Hybridization of China's Financial System. In B. L. Liebman & C. J. Milhaupt (Eds.), *Regulating the Visible Hand? The Institutional Implications of Chinese State Capitalism* (pp. 353–376). Oxford: Oxford University Press.

Polanyi, K. (1957/1999). *Velika preobrazba: Politički i ekonomski izvori našeg vremena*. Zagreb: Jesenski i Turk.

Pulignano, V., Doerflinger, N., & Keune, M. (2017). Re-introducing the Company in the Analysis of Labour Market Dualisation: Variety of Patterns and Diversity of Outcomes Between Standard and Non-standard Workers in Multinational Subsidiaries in Belgium, Germany and Britain. *Economic and Industrial Democracy, 41*(3), 586–609.

Raffer, K., & Singer, H. W. (2001). *The Economic North-South Divide: Six Decades of Unequal Development*. Cheltenham: Edward Elgar Publishing.

Rhodes, M. (2015). Employment Policy. In H. Wallace, M. Pollack, & A. Young (Eds.), *Policy-Making in the European Union* (pp. 293–318). Oxford: Oxford University Press.

Ricardo, D. (1817/2016). *Principles of Political Economy and Taxation*. London: Dover Publications.

Robinson, J. (1933/1969). *The Economics of Imperfect Competition*. London: Macmillan.

Robinson, W. I. (2011). Giovanni Arrighi: Systemic Cycles of Accumulation, Hegemonic Transitions, and the Rise of China. *New Political Economy, 16*(2), 267–280.

Rovny, A. E., & Rovny, J. (2017). Outsiders at the Ballot Box: Operationalizations and Political Consequences of the Insider-Outsider Dualism. *Socio-Economic Review, 15*(1), 161–185.

Rueda, D., Wibbels, E., & Altamirano, M. (2015). The Origins of Dualism. In P. Beramendi, S. Häusermann, H. Kitschelt, & H. Kriesi (Eds.), *The Politics of Advanced Capitalism* (pp. 89–111). New York: Cambridge University Press.

Ruffin, R. (2003). David Ricardo's Discovery of Comparative Advantage. *History of Political Economy, 34*(4), 727–748.

Ruggie, J. G. (1993). Territoriality and Beyond: Problematizing Modernity in International Relations. *International Organization, 47*(1), 139–174.

Sapsford, D., Sarkar, P., & Singer, H. W. (1992). The Prebisch-Singer Terms of Trade Controversy Revisited. *Journal of International Development, 4*(3), 315–332.

Schmidt, V. (2003). French Capitalism Transformed, Yet Still a Third Variety of Capitalism. *Economy and Society, 32*(4), 526–554.

Schmidt, V. (2010). Taking Ideas and Discourse Seriously: Explaining Change Through Discursive Institutionalism as the Fourth 'New Institutionalism'. *European Political Science Review, 2*(1), 1–25.

Schumpeter, J. A. (2013). *Capitalism, Socialism and Democracy.* Routledge.

Shepsle, K. A. (2006). Rational Choice Institutionalism. In *The Oxford Handbook of Political Institutions* (pp. 23–38). Oxford: Oxford University Press.

Shonfield, A. (1965). *Modern Capitalism.* Oxford: Oxford University Press.

Sicular, T. (2013). The Challenge of High Inequality in China. *Inequality in Focus, 2*(2), 1–5.

Silver, B. (2003). *Forces of Labor: Workers' Movements and Globalization Since 1870.* Cambridge: Cambridge University Press.

Silver, B. (2014). Theorising the Working Class in Twenty-First-Century Global Capitalism. In M. Atzeni, *Workers and Labour in a Globalised Capitalism* (pp. 46–69). Basingstoke: Palgrave Macmillan.

Silver, B. (2019). "Plunges into Utter Destruction" and the Limits of Historical Capitalism. In R. Atzmüller, B. Aulenbacher, U. Brand, F. Décieux, K. Fischer, & B. Sauer (Eds.), *Capitalism in Transformation.* Cheltenham: Edward Elgar Publishing.

Silver, B. J., & Arrighi, G. (2003). Polanyi's "Double Movement": The Belle Époques of British and US Hegemony Compared. *Politics and Society, 31*(2), 325–355.

Silver, B. J., & Payne, C. R. (2020). Crises of World Hegemony and the Speeding Up of Social History. In P. Dutkiewicz, T. Casier, & J. A. Scholte (Eds.), *Hegemony and World Order: Reimagining Power in Global Politics* (pp. 17–31). Abingdon: Routledge.

Smith, A. (1776/2003). *The Wealth of Nations.* New York: Bantam Dell.

Solt, F. (2020). *The Standardized World Income Inequality Database.* SWIID Version 9.0. https://fsolt.org/swiid/.

Soskice, D. (2007). Macroeconomics and Varieties of Capitalism. In B. Hancké, M. Rhodes, & M. Thatcher (Eds.), *Beyond Varieties of Capitalism: Conflict, Contradictions, and Complementarities in the European Economy* (pp. 89–121). Oxford: Oxford University Press.

Steinmo, S. (2008). Historical Institutionalism. In D. Della Porta & M. Keating (Eds.), *Approaches and Methodologies in the Social Sciences: A Pluralist Perspective* (pp. 118–138). Cambridge: Cambridge University Press.

Steinmo, S. (2010). *The Evolution of Modern States: Sweden, Japan, and the United States.* Cambridge: Cambridge University Press.

Stiglitz, J. (2002). *Globalization and Its Discontents.* London: Penguin Books.

Streeck, W. (2010). Institutions in History: Bringing Capitalism Back in. In G. Morgan, J. Campbell, C. Crouch, O. K. Pedersen, & R. Whitley (Eds.),

The Oxford Handbook of Comparative Institutional Analysis (pp. 659–686). Oxford: Oxford University Press.

Streeck, W. (2011). E Pluribus Unum? Varieties and Commonalities of Capitalism. In M. Granovetter & R. Swedberg (Eds.), *The Sociology of Economic Life* (pp. 419–455). New York: Westview Press.

Streeck, W. (2016). Varieties of Varieties: "VoC" and the Growth Models. *Politics and Society, 44*(2), 243–247.

Streeck, W., & Thelen, K. A. (Eds.). (2005). *Beyond Continuity: Institutional Change in Advanced Political Economies*. Oxford: Oxford University Press.

Strpić, D. (1998). *Promjena*. Zagreb: Politička Misao.

Strpić, D. (2010). *Karl Marx i politička ekonomija moderne*. Zagreb: Nacionalna zajednica Crnogoraca Hrvatske.

Strpić, D. (2015). *Prema novoj političkoj ekonomiji*. Zagreb: Disput.

Sugihara, K. (2003). The East Asian Path of Economic Development. In A. Arrighi, H. Takeshi, & M. Seldon (Eds.), *The Resurgence of East Asia* (pp. 78–123). London: Routledge.

Tang, A. (2019). Life After Janus. *Columbia Law Review, 119*(3), 677–762.

Tang, S. (2011). *A General Theory of Institutional Change*. London: Routledge.

Tausch, A. (2006, May 11–12). From the "Washington" Towards a "Vienna Consensus"? A Quantitative Analysis on Globalization, Development and Global Governance. In *Centro Argentino de Estudios Internacionales, EU-Latin America and Caribbean Summit 2006*. Vienna [online]. Available at http://www.forschungsnetzwerk.at/downloadpub/CAEI_Buenos_Aires_Vienna_Summit_arno_tausch.pdf.

"The 13th Five-Year Plan". (2016). http://en.ndrc.gov.cn/newsrelease/201612/P020161207645765233498.pdf.

Thelen, K. (2004). *How Institutions Evolve: The Political Economy of Skills in Germany, Britain, the United States, and Japan*. Cambridge: Cambridge University Press.

Thelen, K. (2012). Varieties of Capitalism: Trajectories of Liberalization and the New Politics of Social Solidarity. *Annual Review of Political Science, 15*, 137–159.

Thelen, K. (2014). *Varieties of Liberalization and the New Politics of Social Solidarity*. New York: Cambridge University Press.

Thelen, K., & Mahoney, J. (2015). Comparative-Historical Analysis in Contemporary Political Science. In J. Mahoney & K. Thelen (Eds.), *Advances in Comparative-Historical Analysis* (pp. 3–36). Cambridge: Cambridge University Press.

Thelen, K., & Steinmo, S. (1992). Historical Institutionalism in Comparative Politics. In S. Steinmo, K. Thelen, & F. Longstreth (Eds.), *Structuring Politics: Historical Institutionalism in Comparative Analysis* (pp. 1–32). Cambridge: Cambridge University Press.

Tilly, C. (1995). Globalization Threatens Labor's Rights. *International Labor and Working-Class History, 47*, 1–23.

Torrens, R. (1815). *An Essay on the External Corn Trade: With an Appendix on the Means of Improving the Condition of the Labouring Classes*. J. Hatchard.

Toye, R., & Toye, J. F. (2003). The Origins and Interpretation of the Prebisch-Singer Thesis. *History of Political Economy, 35*(3), 437–467.

Toynbee, A. J. (1954). *A Study of History* (Vol. 9). London: Oxford University Press.

Trading Economics. (2018). *United States Households Debt to Gdp 1952–2018*. https://tradingeconomics.com/united-states/households-debt-to-gdp.

Van Treeck, T. (2009). The Political Economy Debate on 'Financialization'—A Macroeconomic Perspective. *Review of International Political Economy, 16*(5), 907–944.

Vernon, R. (1966). International Investment and International Trade in the Product Cycle. *The Quarterly Journal of Economics, 80*, 190–207.

Visser, J. (2019, June). ICTWSS Data Base. Version 6.0. Amsterdam: Amsterdam Institute for Advanced Labour Studies (AIAS), University of Amsterdam. Open Access Database at: https://www.ictwss.org/downloads.

Visser, M. A. (2018). Restructuring Opportunity: Employment Change and Job Quality in the United States During the Great Recession. *Socio-Economic Review, 17*(3), 545–572.

Wallerstein, I. (1974a). *The Modern World-System I: Capitalist Agriculture and the Origins of the European World-Economy in the Sixteenth Century*. New York: Academic Press.

Wallerstein, I. (1974b). The Rise and Future Demise of the World Capitalist System: Concepts for Comparative Analysis. *Comparative Studies in Society and History, 16*(4), 387–415.

Wallerstein, I. (1980). *The Modern World-System II: Mercantilism and the Consolidation of the European World-Economy, 1600–1750*. New York: Academic Press.

Wallerstein, I. (1989). *The Modern World-System III: The Second Era of Great Expansion of the Capitalist World-Economy (1730–1840s)*. San Diego: Academic Press.

Wallerstein, I. M. (2000). *The Essential Wallerstein*. New York: New Press.

Wallerstein, I. M. (2001). *Unthinking Social Science: The Limits of Nineteenth-Century Paradigms*. Philadelphia: Temple University Press.

Wallerstein, I. (2011). *The Modern World-System IV: Centrist Liberalism Triumphant, 1789–1914*. Berkeley: University of California Press.

Wallis, J. J., & North, D. (1986). Measuring the Transaction Sector in the American Economy, 1870–1970. In *Long-Term Factors in American Economic Growth* (pp. 95–162). University of Chicago Press. Available at http://www.nber.org/chapters/c9679.pdf.

Wang, Y. (2014). *Demystifying the Chinese Miracle: The Rise and Future of Relational Capitalism*. London: Routledge.

WEF. (2016a). *Measuring the Global Gender Gap*. Available at http://reports.weforum.org/global-gender-gap-report-2016/measuring-the-global-gender-gap/.

WEF. (2016b). *United States*. Available at http://reports.weforum.org/feature-demonstration/files/2016/10/USA.pdf.

WEF. (2016c). *Germany*. Available at http://reports.weforum.org/feature-demonstration/files/2016/10/DEU.pdf.

WEF. (2016d). *China*. Available at http://reports.weforum.org/feature-demonstration/files/2016/10/CHN.pdf.

Weiss, L. (1998). *The Myth of the Powerless State*. Ithaca: Cornell University Press.

Why China Is Creating a New "World Bank". (2014, November 11). *The Economist*. Retrieved from https://www.economist.com/the-economist-explains/2014/11/11/why-china-is-creating-a-new-world-bank-for-asia.

WID. (2020). *World Inequality Database*. Available at http://wid.world/.

Wilensky, H. L. (2002). *Rich Democracies: Political Economy, Public Policy, and Performance*. Berkeley: University of California Press.

Williamson, O. E. (2000). The New Institutional Economics: Taking Stock, Looking Ahead. *Journal of Economic Literature, 38,* 595–613.

Wilson, J. (2007). China's Transformation Towards Capitalism. In D. Lane & M. Myant (Eds.), *Varieties of Capitalism in Post-Communist Countries* (pp. 239–257). Hampshire: Palgrave Macmillan.

WIPO. (2016). *WIPO IP Facts and Figures 2016*. http://www.wipo.int/edocs/pubdocs/en/wipo_pub_943_2016.pdf.

Witt, M. A. (2010). *China: What Variety of Capitalism?* (INSEAD Working Paper No. 2010/88/EPS). https://papers.ssrn.com/sol3/papers.cfm?abstract_id=1695940.

Witt, M. A., & Redding, G. (2013). Asian Business Systems: Institutional Comparison, Clusters and Implications for Varieties of Capitalism and Business Systems Theory. *Socio-Economic Review, 11*(2), 265–300.

Witt, M. A., & Redding, G. (2014). China: Authoritarian Capitalism. In M. A. Witt & G. Redding (Eds.), *The Oxford Handbook of Asian Business Systems* (pp. 11–32). Oxford: Oxford University Press.

WJP. (2018). *World Justice Project*. Available at https://worldjusticeproject.org/.

World Bank. (2016). *Deepening Health Reform in China: Building High-Quality and Value-Based Service Delivery—Policy Summary*. Washington, DC: World Bank Group. http://documents.worldbank.org/curated/en/800911469159433307/Deepening-health-reform-in-China-building-high-quality-and-value-based-service-delivery-policy-summary.

World Bank. (2017). *World Bank Open Data*. http://data.worldbank.org.

World Bank. (2020). *World Bank Open Data*. http://data.worldbank.org.

Wright, Q. (1942). *A Study of War*. Chicago: University of Chicago Press.

Wright, E. O. (2000). Working-Class Power, Capitalist-Class Interests, and Class Compromise. *American Journal of Sociology*, 105(4), 957–1002.

WTO. (2020). *Monthly Trade Trends: July 2020—August 2020 Updated on 23 October 2020*. https://www.wto.org/english/res_e/statis_e/daily_update_e/month_latest.pdf.

Wübbeke, J., Meissner, M., Zenglein, M. J., Ives, J., & Conrad, B. (2016). Made in China 2025. *Mercator Institute for China Studies: Papers on China, 2*, 74.

Zhang, X., Yang, J., & Wang, S. (2011). China Has Reached the Lewis Turning Point. *China Economic Review, 22*(4), 542–554.

Zhao, L. (2016). China's 13th Five-Year Plan: Road Map for Social Development. *East Asian Policy, 8*(3), 19–32.

Zhuang, J., & Li, S. (2016). *Understanding Recent Trends in Income Inequality in the People's Republic of Chin*a (Asian Development Bank Economics Working Paper Series, 489).

Index

J. Lučev, *Systemic Cycle and Institutional Change*, https://doi.org/10.1007/978-3-030-66053-6

The manufacturer's authorised representative in the EU is Springer Nature Customer Service Centre GmbH, Europaplatz 3, 69115 Heidelberg, Germany. If you have any concerns regarding our products, please contact ProductSafety@springernature.com

Printed and bound by CPI Group (UK) Ltd, Croydon, CR0 4YY

30/09/2026

02225700-0008